ONE YEAR OF LIFE

BOOKS BY CECIL ROBERTS

Novels

SCISSORS
SAILS OF SUNSET
THE LOVE RACK
LITTLE MRS. MANINGTON
SAGUSTO
DAVID AND DIANA
INDIANA JANE
PAMELA'S SPRING SONG
HAVANA BOUND
BARGAIN BASEMENT
SPEARS AGAINST US
PILGRIM COTTAGE
THE GUESTS ARRIVE
VOLCANO
VICTORIA FOUR-THIRTY
THEY WANTED TO LIVE
ONE SMALL CANDLE
SO IMMORTAL A FLOWER
EIGHT FOR ETERNITY
A TERRACE IN THE SUN

Miscellaneous

GONE RUSTIC
GONE RAMBLING
GONE AFIELD
GONE SUNWARDS
AND SO TO BATH
AND SO TO AMERICA
AND SO TO ROME
THE DIARY OF RUSSELL BERESFORD
ALFRED FRIPP : A BIOGRAPHY
HALF WAY : AN AUTOBIOGRAPHY
A MAN AROSE
ONE YEAR OF LIFE

from Gordon

December 5th: 1952

Robert Browning returns home to the Palazzo Rezzonico,
Venice, 1889

ONE YEAR OF LIFE

Some Autobiographical Pages

by

CECIL ROBERTS

" When I am buried, all my thoughts and acts
Will be reduced to lists of dates and facts,
And long before this wandering flesh is rotten
The dates which made me will be all forgotten ;
And none will know the gleam there used to be
About the feast-days freshly kept by me. . . ."

John Masefield

LONDON

HODDER & STOUGHTON

First Printed 1952

MADE AND PRINTED IN GREAT BRITAIN FOR
HODDER AND STOUGHTON LIMITED LONDON
BY C. TINLING & CO., LTD., LIVERPOOL, LONDON
AND PRESCOT

To
Mrs. J. L. Boehm
Aubrey Cartwright
Hon. Simon Stuart
Companions on the way

Itinerary

Illustrations

Foreword

IT amused me to write this diary because I am not a person of regular habits in the matter of work and I was curious to know how long I should stay the course.

I shall not apologise for such egotism as is reflected in it. How can a man keep a personal diary without projecting himself? It is, among many aspects, autobiographical. At the age of thirty-five I wrote an autobiography, *Half Way*, taking the Psalmist's span of life for my division. I have to run through another decade of life before I can complete the whole. This diary, to some extent, comprises an interim supplement.

I have not published all I wrote, for it would be too long and too personal. Things of much interest have been omitted because they might have seemed a betrayal of secrets or have given pain to living people. Though I have deleted passages, in no case have I altered anything in retrospect ; right or wrong, the record stands. I wrote it without thought of publication but not ignoring the possibility ; in short, it was an act of enjoyment in personal expression.

One morning on entering my study I interrupted a guest in the act of turning over a page of this diary, which lay open on my desk. He started guiltily and began to stammer an apology. I burst into laughter and told him that all my life I have been consumed with curiosity to read the papers on another man's desk.

I hope this diary provokes and satisfies such curiosity.

C. R.

Palazzo Vairo,
Alassio,
Italy.

Monte Carlo

January 1, 1950.

IT is a few minutes after midnight. The New Year has opened. I am lying in bed in an apartment overlooking the bay at Monte Carlo. Next door to me in the Avenue de Grande Bretagne is the English Church which has red pantiles and an illuminated cross over its portico. At the present moment some of the greatly diminished and impoverished British colony are within singing a hymn in celebration of the New Year. The familiar words take me back to the occasion of a Watch Night Service on the passing of the Nineteenth Century into the Twentieth. I was seven years old and readily agreed to go to church with my mother, not because I was interested in the service but because it was an opportunity to sit up late, always an exciting event for the very young. We sang doleful hymns, then we were very silent, and suddenly the vicar spoke, announcing the New Year and asking God's blessing upon it. Queen Victoria was on the throne, Britannia ruled the waves, the Empire was intact, and being then enlarged by a small war against some obstinate Boers in South Africa. I recall this war only because at a local music-hall I had heard a woman dressed as Britannia singing a song about " forty thousand horse and foot going to Table Bay." The last line of Kipling's jingle ended with " Pay ! Pay ! Pay ! " Britannia then put on a tin helmet and held up a shield to protect herself while the emotional audience threw pennies on the stage for a Red Cross Fund for the volunteers fighting in South Africa. Pay ! Pay ! Pay ! has been the refrain of the British people ever since, throughout fifty troubled years of a shrinking Empire and a mounting National Debt. But on January 1st, 1900, I was troubled by no thought of the future and could not foresee that I should live to see the shrinkage of the British Empire, the loss of many of our liberties, and a people taxed to death. It is the great asset of the young that they cannot make comparisons and are therefore naturally cheerful.

The singing in the church next door has ceased but across the Avenue, in the high apartment houses that climb up the precipitous cliff-face of Monte Carlo, revelry has broken out. It is a warm drizzly night, all the windows are open, the champagne is flowing, voices are raised in a discordant version of *Auld Lang Syne*. Down in the *Casino* restaurant there is a Gala Supper, as also at the *Hotel de Paris*, but there is a spectre at the board. Monte Carlo, depleted of the rich, the reckless, and its international flotsam and jetsam, is desperately carrying on. There are gaps at the gaming tables. Some hotels have been closed for several years and in others a few old ladies and gentlemen sit amid the palm pots of the empty lounges looking like derelict boats with the tide gone out. The British Colony is in a bad way. It consists mostly of those too old and too poor to go home. They came here many years ago to live on small pensions and annuities, to mitigate their rheumatism, and await a peaceful end in pleasant surroundings. Now they have had a third of their incomes cut away by devaluation of the £, and the cost of living has doubled. Most of the people they knew at home have died. The housing shortage and prohibitive rents make a retreat to England impossible. By giving up a maid and buying margarine instead of butter they contrive to exist. The English here are a quiet, proud and diminishing colony. They no longer garden in the terraced villas, give dinner parties, subscribe generously to local charities, and, courted and respected, dominate the scene. Most of the Americans have vanished. The Russian, Czech, Polish and German patrons have been eliminated. The only high gamblers at the *Casino* tables are rich Italian industrialists, *pescecani*, from Genoa and Turin.

The telephone has just rung. It is genial and indefatigable Mrs. J, who wishes me a Happy New Year. She is staying in a villa with two Serene Highnesses who are augmenting their reduced incomes by taking paying guests. An American divorcée, with thirty-five thousand dollars a year alimony, she can afford a nice suite and give her friends a good time. She purrs in a princely heaven which lacks only iced water.

Every morning a faded little old woman leaves on my threshold two pots of yoghourt. She carries them around in a small battered attaché case. She lives with a crippled husband in the basement rooms of a large villa which had its roof, the top storey, and all of its windows blown out in the 1945 bombing. Her husband was a former Ambassador of the Shah of Persia, who was a great friend, but in a revolution he lost his friend and his post. The Shah had given him this villa at Monte Carlo, and the letting of rooms in it was his only asset. Now, in dire circumstances, his old wife makes yoghourt and peddles it round the town. She is reticent and retains the quiet manners of her former status.

I have been glancing through my diaries to see where I have spent the last five New Year Eves. In 1948 I had a villa at Alassio on this coast, and at midnight I looked out from my balcony over the bay, with the promontory of Cap Mele mountainous under the moon. The acetylene flares of the fishing fleet off Laigueglia were like a cluster of diamonds on the reflective waters.

In 1947 I spent New Year's Eve in New York at a party given by the Duke and Duchess of Windsor in their suite in the Tower (44th floor) of the Waldorf-Astoria Hotel, when the Duke sang some Scotch songs, *à la* Harry Lauder, with extraordinary verisimilitude.

In 1946 I was in Palm Beach, a guest at *Estella*, Mrs. Aubrey Cartwright's villa. I breakfasted every morning on a lawn beside an azure swimming-pool with the thermometer at 80° in the shade. The sunsets from the tower in which I wrote *Eight for Eternity* looked like a conflagration of the end of the world.

In 1945 I attended a New Year's Eve party in a New York house, given by a retired circus tightrope-walker and snakecharmer of French-Russian origin, who, in these latter years, had made a fortune as a manufacturer of perfumes, and now kept basketfuls of snakes in the ornate home of a former millionaire which she had bought. I had seen her, slim, agile in her forties, taking wire-walking exercises over the roof, from a friend's adjacent apartment and felt that I must know her. She was as charming as she was amazing, with a house full of retired acrobats, equestriennes, lion-tamers, etc., who composed her court. She had published an excellent autobiography.

In 1944 I arrived at 11 p.m. on New Year's Eve, at a small apartment I was then sharing with a friend, a King's Messenger, a port of call on his South American circuit. It was on the edge of Biscayne Bay, Miami, Florida. At midnight in sub-tropical heat, I colour-photographed the moon over the palm-fringed bay, while a disturbed pelican flapped overhead ; and thus added one more Kodachrome to my collection of five thousand.

Each New Year's Eve I made a resolution to keep a diary of

my somewhat singular experiences, but I never fulfilled it. This coming year I will make a serious effort. I am curious to see how far I shall keep this up, and what experiences await me.

January 2.

I owe my comfortable lodgings to my ingenious friend G, who for the past thirty years has lived in the most delectable spots of this globe. He has contrived to travel to far away places, despite the blocking of his modest income, a war measure perpetuated in the name of " national emergency " by governments notorious for profligacy with their victims' money.

When my train drew into Monte Carlo, last November, he was there amid the palms and aloes. He has found a *pied-à-terre* with his usual genius for a bargain, and I find myself installed in a delightful apartment. Poor fellow, he did not know that he was to revert to a former role of nurse within three weeks of my arrival, when I took to my bed, felled by the old enemy. When, in 1944, I was in New York Hospital with a duodenal ulcer, caused by too much work on behalf of an ungrateful Government, he was ever at hand. To him, and to Sir Thomas and Lady Beecham who took me out of hospital and nursed me, I owe lasting gratitude.

January 3.

Three wretched days and nights. It transpires that to the old ulcer trouble I have now added fibrositis. It is not in the Oxford Dictionary. It sounds like a plant disease. I got up yesterday, crawled out into the morning sunshine along the Boulevard des Moulins, collapsed, and came back to bed. Six friends have recommended infallible doctors, one an Englishman aged eighty-two ! G suggests a French doctor. I resist strongly. He will tap me, want me X-rayed and opened up for exploratory exercises. I firmly refuse and have gone back to the milk bottle and yoghourt-diet, but nothing relieves the fibrositis in neck and shoulder. Very wretched. Such a lovely blue sky seen from my Louis-Seize prison.

January 4

A bad night. Got up for an hour but could not sustain the effort. Somerset Maugham telephoned from Cap Ferrat and in a moment of wild optimism I have accepted an invitation to lunch with him next Tuesday.

G has brought in Dr. Crimeaux. He found me rebellious and inclined to think I have cancer of the stomach, a brain tumour and arthritis instead of fibrositis. The usual black scarf bound on my arm for blood pressure (normal), the usual typewriting on my stomach (what cold fingers doctors have !), the usual verdict. Ulcer in the duodenum, congestion, wind (gas, if you please, in U.S.A.). He is very thorough, smooth, quiet. " I suppose you think I am a complete neurasthenic and would be cured if I had to work for a living ? " I asked, when he was searching for a verdict. He looked hurt at my attack. " You *are* ill," he said. The conversation proceeded in French. He said I must diet strictly. " How does a man reduced to milk through most of his existence do that ? " I asked, peevishly. We had an animated debate yet I found myself liking the young man. He was in the Dunkirk retreat, in June 1940, and got over to Dover in a small launch belonging to an heroic London solicitor who made five trips under fire. We are the salt of the earth in his eyes, and in the eyes of a Frenchman that is something.

When he had gone, after three-quarters of an hour's animated conversation, there was the usual verdict behind the patient's back. I waited, knowing that, like the report of a Cabinet meeting, it never tells the whole truth. " What did he say ? " I demanded. " He said you are *très amusant*." I banged the pillow in disgust. " But he says you have a lot of pain and you must keep in bed." G produced two sheets of prescriptions. I have become an expert in deciphering medical abracadabra. I found Dr. C had resorted to the usual formula in one prescription, with bismuth, of course. The other contained bromide. They give that to neurotics. I shall have it out with the young man when he returns to-morrow.

There are worse things than bed. When my head permits I have an orgy of reading. I am deep in *Charles V.* (Karl Brandes) and *Le Dernier Siècle de la Rome Pontificale* (Hayward) and *Letters of Cicero* (L. Wilkinson).

A glorious sunset over the bay. How beautiful this coastline is ! But why, when it grows jewelled in the dusk, do I recall H. G. Wells's caustic description—" a luminous eczema on the fringe of the sea." He meant, of course, the *de luxe* hotels and villas with their occupants getting into their *décolletage* and ' smoking ' at this dinner hour.

January 6.

I crawled out this morning, mounted innumerable steps to the
Boulevard des Moulins and found myself taking the air with
doddery old ladies and gentlemen with poodles, and halting as
often as they did. I reached the gardens in front of the *Casino*,
which always look like a basket in a florist's shop, so artificial in
their well-groomed defiance of the season. There G and I encountered the Monégasque baron whom we have dubbed the
Baron Brasserie. He seems to have walked out of Proust. He
lives in a villa that the Germans fitted up for a little private
torturing of those they interrogated. It retains all the bars and
locks of that grim period. He has crammed it with bric-à-brac
from the villas of the vanished potentates. " *Êtes-vous un
antiquaire?* " I asked him. " *Non, monsieur, je suis un connaisseur,*" he
retorted. He looks exactly like a super in an opera that calls for
cloaked conspirators. To-day he is unshaven and, apologising, he
explained that he had been very busy and was up all night—' on
a political mission.' Noticing our surprise, he explained that he
plays an important role in the forthcoming Monaco elections.
" I am working hard against the Communists. I am very alert,
messieurs ! " He left us, bound on State business. I wondered
how he got his black eye.

There are some very odd things about Monte Carlo which few
people seem to know. If in Italy you post a letter to Monaco,
the name of the Principality, it will most likely go to Munich in
Bavaria, since Monaco is the equivalent Italian for München.
Then also it must be made clear that Monaco is a town in the
principality of that name. It takes precedence of Monte Carlo,
which is larger and richer and more famous. This small domain
derives its name from a Greek temple of *Hercules Monoikos*, epithet
of Hercules in Southern Gaul, according to Strabo writing 25 B.C.
It was founded by the Phœnicians. The Prince of Monaco lives
in a palace, he has an army of eighty men from which is drawn
a personal guard of one dozen soldiers, gay with epaulettes,
aiguillettes, plumed hats and medals. In the true tradition of
a musical comedy court, the palace has battlements, cannon
(corroded), a throne room, state apartments, and part-time court
officials. The reigning Prince Rainier is a young man who has
just inherited his grandfather's throne but he has not yet had his
coronation which takes place in two months. He is not rich as is
widely believed. The revenues from the *Casino* do not belong

to him, and in any case the *Casino* is no longer profitable and is desperately hanging on hoping for better days. There is a constitutional crisis among the Monégasques, though I hope no revolution will bring about the downfall of the Grimaldis who have preserved their throne, by some ingenious interpretations of legitimacy, since it was founded in A.D. 968 by a Genoese admiral. The Grimaldi line, length considered, has few equals in Europe. The Prince of Monaco carries also the title of Duke of Valentinois which was once held by Cesare Borgia.

January 7.

For some years now my Spanish publisher has suggested that I should visit Spain. He wrote to my agent—

" The royalties due to Mr. Roberts are very elevated. Would he not be interested in spending them on a trip to Spain, as recently did Mr. Somerset Maugham and other writers ? Mr. Roberts is the most populous writer of foreign authors in Spain."

It is pleasant to learn this. What I do not understand is why my books, fifteen of which have been translated into Spanish, sell there so well. It is a country I have never visited and of which I know nothing. In our schools Spanish history is wholly neglected. This is very different from American schools where the early Spanish civilisation in America has made its history essential. You cannot live in Toledo, El Paso, or San Francisco, or travel on the Santa Fé to Albuquerque, without wondering how they got those names. Our own knowledge of Spain seems confined to the fact that Ferdinand and Isabella received Columbus on his return from discovering America, that Drake defeated the Spanish Armada, that Wellington fought in the Peninsula, and that Sir John Moore was buried by night at Corunna. Now I have an opportunity to repair a defect of my English education.

I have written to my Spanish publisher, asking for some particulars. Señor de Caralt writes from Barcelona—

" As you will have observed by the selling statements, your works have meant a great success in Spain and proved you to be one of the most admired English novelists in my country. Now would you not like to make also an acquaintance with my country ? It would mean satisfaction to you, being able to learn the great sympathy Spanish readership is feeling towards you and your works. . . . I do so beg you to accept this my suggestion as a proof—perhaps a somewhat saucy one—of my goodwill and of my desire to be of your service."

It would be churlish not to respond to such a delightful invitation so I have decided to go, although at the moment I seem destined for a nursing home rather than a tour. My movements these days are prescribed by a good milk supply. I am enquiring into Spanish cows. I have known for years that *je parle Français comme une vache espagnole.* Now I have another attachment to them.

I have fun with my doctor who finds me in a large bed surrounded by books.

DOCTOR. Your blood pressure is down to-day.

SELF. I thought it would be right up.

DOCTOR. Why?

SELF. A letter from my bank this morning informs me that the income-tax took almost two-thirds of my income last year.

DOCTOR. You must be very rich!

SELF. Not at all. No one can be rich in England to-day, unless he is one of "the bright boys," an increasing brood. All my tax was on a book that took me three years to write. I am taxed on the year of publication. If I divided my net income into three, I have earned, annually, about as much as an Inspector of Police. He gets a pension. I do not. Last year our greatest living historian paid £11,000 tax on a book that took him fifteen years to write. He told the Government, after paying tax, that it could keep the balance.

DOCTOR. In France we do not tax authors as we do businesses.

SELF. The French are an intellectual race. An author is a *maître* in France, a *maestro* in Italy, a *maestrazo* in Spain, and a freak in England. Despite the greatest literature in the world, we regard authors as abnormal. Our profession is a form of vagrancy.*

I am not sure Dr. C doesn't take the English view. On the

---

* A French author, after deduction of 33⅓ per cent expenses, pays 18 per cent on his net income. A Spanish author, and other artists, pays a *taxe intellectuelle* of 5 per cent. But El Greco, the artist, improved on this in the 17th century. When a tax-collector assessed him for work he had done at Illescas, he refused to pay and carried the case to the royal court. He won. It decreed that earnings from the three noble arts of painting, sculpture and architecture, all of which El Greco practised, should be free of tax.

staircase the other day he told G that I was *un homme tellement incroyable.* I pull my doctor's leg, a pastime no Latin can understand. When I told him today that I was thinking of going to Spain on a *wagon-lit-d'hôpital,* he said, gravely, *"Non, par couchette."* He is right. G returns with the information from Cook's that only *couchettes* run from Monte Carlo to Port Bou, the frontier station for Spain.

January 8.

Awake half the night again, in pain. As dawn came I settled down and read Stendhal's *Promenades dans Rome.* Poor fellow, how he adored Rome and hated being stationed as French Consul in Civitavecchia.

I drag myself out each day at noon, despite Dr. C, for with me to rest is to rust. We have found a little café in a corner down by the harbour where we sit in the warm sun. G has his after-lunch coffee, I drink hot milk. The palace-fortress stands silhouetted on the rock, all in deep shadow. The water of the port is azure, the few yachts have riggings that dance in the sky when a passing boat undulates them. What a passion for poodles there is ! They all sport gay little winter jackets. It seems they too have stomach trouble. A cold snap is fatal.

While we were sunning ourselves we were saluted by the Baron Brasserie. He halted briefly and gave us a little information as a Monégasque upon the local political scene, which has all the intrigues in miniature of the great world. He explained what the party of the Right stands for, and what provoked the recent crisis and general election. The agreement of 1945 between the French Government and Monaco has always irked many Monégasques with its restrictions, demands, and unfair apportioning of taxes and revenues. The Prince, it is alleged, has become something of a puppet in their hands. The elected Council passed resolutions but, the Executive power being wholly in the hands of the Prince, nothing resulted. Moreover, the Monaco Government had retained a French lawyer to handle the Principality's relations with France. They charged that, in effect, he aided the *laissez-faire* policy of the Prince, who seems to have taken his line from his grandfather who made the Treaty of 1945 and never resisted the French pressure. The Council, exasperated, denounced this complaisance of the Prince, and the lawyer resigned. The bolder spirits have run the election. They

propose to have the Treaty denounced if its onerous terms are
not revised, to appoint another lawyer and to request the Prince
to show some firmness towards France. We asked the Baron
what would happen if they denounced the Treaty, which has no
date for expiration. Could not France, all powerful, crush any
opposition ? " Not at all. Ours is a dynasty of a thousand years
of freedom. Dare France declare war on little Monaco ? The
whole world would cry shame. No, *messieurs*, she dare not risk
that ! " The Baron excused himself, he had an appointment and
rushed off.

I had a vision of the Monégasque army being mobilised—all
eighty, and the stone cannon balls on the ramparts being loaded
in the antique cannon. The Baron is right in one respect. All
the world would cry shame on France if she attempted anything
by force. It would be Goliath against David.

January 9.

I made a great effort to-day and was well rewarded. I had
daringly undertaken to go over to Cap Ferrat and lunch with
Somerset Maugham. He sent his car for me to Pont St. Jean.
A most lovely morning, the sky blue, the sea calm, the sun shining
warmly. When I got downstairs I felt so shaky that I was on the
point of cancelling the trip. I wondered what my doctor would
think, having seen me in bed yesterday, very depressed. Gradually
the gay morning raised my spirits, and all along the Middle Corniche Road the beauty of the scene, the mountainside, the indented villa-fringed bays, the pine woods, the luxurious crescent
of Beaulieu, and the thickly-wooded promontory of Cap Ferrat,
gave me intense pleasure. When I reached the Villa Mauresque
I was in good spirits. " You don't look like a sick man," said
Maugham coming into his salon, which is something of a baronial
hall. I had not seen him since we had lunched in New York
five years ago. At seventy-five he is still a well-preserved man
with no diminution of mental vigour. He has announced that he
will write no more plays or novels but his industry is continuous
and he is employed on revised editions, groups of short stories,
etc. He has now embarked on a new career. He has made
excellent personal prologues to some of his filmed stories, being
possessed of a charming speaking voice. He is also engaged to
make television appearances in U.S.A. In private, Willie, as
all his friends call him, suffers from an impediment in his speech,

which, to my mind, increases the weight of what he says by a deliberation, in his case, inevitable, and not like Winston Churchill's, effectively adopted. Whenever I have heard Maugham speak in public his diction has not only been good, with pleasing modulation, but it has lost the impediment that sometimes afflicts him in private.

He lives very quietly now and the gregarious gatherings at his table and round his swimming pool are much curtailed. The villa and its terraces high above the long bay of Villefranche have extensive gardens requiring four gardeners in this climate. Very wisely he allows no one to interfere with his siesta. After half an hour with his guests, following lunch, he vanishes, and, if tactful, they do.

We discussed before lunch a writer who had attracted us both by his odd Victorian personality. I have long collected the works of Augustus Hare whose *Walks in Rome* still holds the field and is a joy forever. I had contemplated a book on him, for he was a finicky snob with aristocratic connections and an obsession about knowing 'the right people.' Spinsterish and precise, there was in him a tough spirit. He not only walked in Rome, picking up social and historical bric-à-brac with the quick eye of a jackdaw, but he also walked in Spain, Sicily, Holland, France and Scandinavia, and, astonishing for a hot-bottle-and-mittens personality, in Russia, in the days of the troika and the knout. His books reached many editions, deservedly, for he had a unique blend of travelogue that would have won him fame in these days of the film. It was characteristic that he should have written an autobiography in six volumes and have called it *The Story of My Life*. It was full of reminiscences of bishops, the university, great ladies, and the Church and State.

A few days ago I was surprised to find in the *Cornhill* a delectable essay on Hare by Maugham who, as a young man, had known him and went to stay with him. It is a perfect portrait of a Victorian who regarded himself as one of the pillars of Society and is, to my mind, more devastating and accurate than anything from the acrid pen of Lytton Strachey. But I was dismayed to find that so formidable a rival as Maugham had discovered Hare as a subject, and I was disposed to ' lay off.' Maugham assured me that he had said all that he had to say on the subject and encouraged me to carry out my intention.

Two hours passed very pleasantly and the time of the siesta

was approaching. I announced my departure. He was appalled at my intention to walk all the way back to Monte Carlo, about ten miles, but I felt so well, released from my pain, that I would have tackled the Matterhorn at that moment. We parted after he had given me some advice on my proposed visit to Spain. The author of *Don Fernando* had much worth hearing on that little-known land. When I left I asked if he had any idea when last I had been his guest. We were neither of us quite sure. It was in the pre-war days. Often in U.S.A., during the war, we had wondered if ever he would see the villa again.*

I accomplished my walk. The afternoon was so lovely and the coast road by Beaulieu so beautiful that I did not want to miss any part of it. I was well rewarded when at last, in growing fatigue, I rounded Cap d'Ail and suddenly saw, glowing in the

---

* I have long had a habit of writing contemporaneous notes in the flyleaf of any book I happen to be reading. After the passage of years, encountered again, they are apt to be amusing or saddening. Four months after this visit I picked up my copy of Maugham's *Cakes and Ale* and found I had made the following entry, nineteen years ago.—*Wednesday, January* 14, 1931.—Lunched with Somerset Maugham at his house, the Villa Mauresque, Cap Ferrat. It is a large white villa set on the hill-side amid olive groves overlooking the harbour of Villefranche with a distinct view of fort-crowned Mont Boron which hides Nice, and of the tip of Cap d'Antibes to the west, an exquisite vista of blue sea and coloured mountains breaking down to the villa-dotted shore. The house itself, high up on the hillside and towards the end of the promontory, is a large white building originally erected by a French bishop who made a competence converting the heathen in North Africa. On the gate of the villa and over the stone portal is Maugham's sign manual, used on the cover of his books, which he told me was adopted by his father, being a Moorish device against the evil eye. He has it engraved in red on the white stone.

After passing through a high entrance hall I was shown by the French butler into a salon of splendid proportions with a large fireplace of Arles stone. It was tastefully furnished in modern style, with books in the Gothic alcoves, all the colours being cheerful. Maugham came forward to greet me and had with him Gerald Haxton, his secretary, young Rowley Leigh, the lyric writer, and a lady. Short of stature, with a rather grim expression and tight downward curving mouth, the description ' sinister ', characteristic of some of his works, is perhaps justified but the cordiality of his manner towards me dispelled this impression. He has a slight impediment in his speech which tends to disappear as he grows accustomed to his guest. His voice has beautiful tones. A man of some fifty-six years, with neat hair and a dark close-cropped moustache on a full face, his eyes are vital and his expression somewhat judicial.

After lunch, perfectly served in a charming round dining-room, with good modern paintings, he took me through the grounds, kept by four gardeners. These comprise a tennis court, a game of which he is fond, an orangery, and gardens planned in terraces on the side of the hill. At the back, in the shape of a small amphitheatre facing the sea, he has built an open marble-lined swimming pool.

On the roof of the house there is a large writing-room built over a guest annexe and garage. It has no windows to the south, thus shutting out the disturbing beauty of the view, but in the west wall there is a window of painted glass. This is of Eve, holding an apple, the work of Gaugin, bought from a native's house in the Brush, where he painted it during convalescence. As I left the house in the late afternoon the rose of sunset tinged the white walls of the villa, picking it out in a roseate glow against the cool blue sky and the dark ground of the shadow-filled olive groves.

last light of the sunset, the rock of Monaco, a wall of rose rising sheer from the purple sea. The high promontory, crowned by the palace-fort, shone like a pilgrim's vision. Then it faded into the blue dusk of evening.

By the time I reached Monte Carlo I was utterly exhausted and almost collapsed in a tea-house. It was very foolish of me to have walked that distance but the beauty of the afternoon seemed worth the effort. Why do these tea-rooms dotted along the Riviera coast always fill me with melancholy ? They are at Cannes, Nice, Monte Carlo, Mentone, etc., wherever there has been an English colony which towards five o'clock had a nostalgic yearning for buttered toast, muffins and tea. The British coat of arms is surely a teapot, with two spinsters for supporters; crest : a flowerpot, with aspidistra, wilting. The owners of these tea-shops always appear to be Scotch, judging from the pre-eminence of scones, shortbread, and the names of these establishments, usually The Wee Teashop, The Scotch Teahouse, Bide-a-Wee, etc. Their cosy lights seem to allure the lost souls of the exiled. The tattered copies of *The Tatler* and *The Illustrated London News*, the sleek cat, the waitresses in plaid aprons, the quiet-voiced elderly ladies, the sagging Colonels, make some corner of a foreign tea-shop that is forever British. If you should be in doubt a small notice on the cash desk tells you where the English Church is, and begs donations for the English Hospital.

After a rest I crawled home, chastened, and into my bed. The faithful G brought me a tray and chided me. I was quite impenitent. I slept from nine until one a.m., woke, wrote for two hours, and slept till dawn when I saw a ball of fire come up out of the dark water, pause on the rim of the world for a moment and then turn the sea into a sheet of silk.

January 10.

My young doctor is not pleased with me to-day. The pills are changed again. He thinks I have rheumatism and that I shall always have it. This coast is bad for rheumatism, he says, which greatly surprises me. I thought elderly people came here to escape the damp. He is pessimistic to-day, and I am optimistic. I do not believe I have rheumatism. We had a long conference on French and English literature, for relief. He has very little English, picked up while billeted on a family in a Kent village. We could not have a better propaganda agent for the

English way of life. " My heart is much there always," he said, simply.

Things observed

In the Paris *Herald-Tribune* to-day—

Somewhere in Europe there must be someone who can use a young American woman, attractive, intelligent, university graduate, 3 years' travel in Europe, fluent French, extensive experience journalism. Prefer decadent Europe to big paid job home.

I am glad an American has said it. I would not have dared lest I seemed ungrateful and hurt many of my friends there. But these are my sentiments after many inducements to become an American. Some prefer American cheese, some Camembert. It is a matter of taste or birth.

> Breathes there a man with soul so dead
> Who never to himself has said
> ' One's home is where one's born in bed ? '

January 11.

A little better, and up for four hours to-day. We called on a long-time resident. He lives in an eyrie with a wide terrace commanding a magnificent view of the town and the coast as far as Italy. Strange things happen here. One day his house companion put his head in the gas oven and committed suicide. " The gas is so bad here that it takes only an hour to finish you," he said, describing the tragedy. I found myself wondering as I looked out over this earthly paradise which sometimes seems on very close terms with Hell, whether gas that is good for cooking should be considered bad for suicide. I suppose, gas apart, there is no place on earth where a man can take leave of life with less fuss made about his decision. There is a minimum of enquiries and the greatest expedition is shown with the corpse. Any dependants are given a free ticket home.

January 12.

After another whole day in bed, I went out this morning for a couple of hours in the noonday sun. I walked delicately along the Boulevard des Moulins. In the secondhand bookshop I bought a copy of my autobiography *Half Way* for fifty francs, about one shilling. It was the sixpenny edition published twelve years ago. There will never again be any sixpenny editions. The tremendous rise in the cost of paper to-day would set the price at five shillings. I speculated whether the story of my life up to thirty-five would have another half as a sequel. In my present state it seems doubtful. I also pondered whether I had gone up in value from sixpence to five shillings.

At another bookshop I halted and meditated on the French obsession with *l'amour*. The titles in the window were—

> *Toutes Femmes seront à Vous*
> *Mes Amours à Vingt Ans*
> *L'Art d'Être Aimée*
> *Les Plus Belles Nuits de Casanova*
> *Corps et Ames* (2 vols.)
> *Psychologie des Rapports Sexuels*
> *Anthologie de l'Eroticism*
> *Filles et Toi*
> *La Vénus d'Île.*

It was a most respectable bookshop, which also sold expensive stationery and perfumed ink. On second thoughts I wondered whether this display was for the foreigner and not for the native.

The Condamine is not only a promenade for poodles, the youngest generation takes an airing there. To-day I saw two tots, a little boy and girl, I swear not more than four or five, solemnly driving a small motor-car along the pavement. It had a radio mast and was broadcasting music as the pair sailed along. On the back of the car was the legend *Toutelectrique*. The fond parents, obviously of the prosperous shopkeeper class, were beaming at this *de luxe* transit of their offspring. I do not know what the outfit cost but the children of Europe are starving in places and the Americans are pouring in dollars to keep Europe from anarchy.

There is still an old-fashioned form of transit here for children, preferable to anything *Toutelectrique*. It operates in the *Casino* gardens. I have two delightful little friends there, Desirée and Ninette, who are beautifully turned out, their shoes spotless, the bandeaux over their brows very gay. We have a few minutes of cheerful conversation whenever we meet by the oleanders, where they are always to be found. They are the two donkeys, well-groomed, who draw a small carriage in which children may ride

sedately for a few francs. This morning in the little fruit market
that spreads out on one of the terraces of Monte Carlo—actually
it is in Beausoleil, therefore in France and not in Monaco—I
bought a small bunch of carrots, expecting to give pleasure to
my two friends. To my surprise, after a sniff and a shaking
of ears, they refused the offering. "Monsieur, ils sont très
exigeante," commented the owner, apologetically. Crestfallen, I
walked for fifty yards wondering what I should do with a bunch of
carrots in the bright noon. I came to the cab rank and approached
a pair of horses harnessed to a landau. There was not a moment's
hesitation. The driver raised his peaked cap. "Mille mercis,
m'sieur. Ils aiment beaucoup les petites choses." What do
Desirée and Ninette like—chocolates?

January 14.

Much amused by a letter from my Spanish friends, Juan and
Lucienne de Cardenas. Juan was the Spanish Ambassador at
Washington for many years and is now retired in Madrid. We
had very happy times together in Washington, and one of the
attractions of my visit to Spain is the chance of seeing them again
—also Timmy the large white poodle, a special friend of mine.
He is among the handsomest of dogs. I wrote some verses to
him which appeared in a Washington newspaper and after this
publicity Timmy took precedence of all the dogs in the *Corps
Diplomatique.* A line in Lucienne's letter puzzles me—"All the
Bourbons are lined up for you." What this means exactly I do
not know, not being familiar with the movements of the Bourbons,
a much scattered family these days. I have a vision of the great
clan standing in line down the longest hall in the Escorial and
greeting me in turn. But which particular Bourbons? There
are the Bourbons of Spain, the Bourbon-Anjou, in three branches;
the Bourbon-Sicilies, the Bourbon-Parme, the Bourbon-Orleans;
all told, about one thousand.

January 16.

In this town there are no young people. It has a population
of the middle-aged and elderly, of those who have retired and now
await the end with such tranquillity as the times allow. The
apartment house in which I dwell has its quota of ancients, going
up and down in the lift. But the other day a young voice
piped up, and the landings sometimes echo with his gay treble.

It is the voice of a chubby little lad of about five, with merry eyes, and I suspect somewhat of a handful for his English governess. He scorns the lift. It is like encountering a spring flower in a wintry chasm.

January 18.

My doctor does not veto the Spanish trip but he thinks it is foolish. I am tired of the view from my room, of the Boulevard des Moulins, and of the habits of an invalid. My enquiries about the Spanish milk supply are not encouraging. Alas, I am compelled to travel by 'the milk route' these days. In this sense the U.S.A. is a paradise. One can obtain any quantity of good milk anywhere at any time of the day and night. I used to buy a carton of milk at the drug store near Madison Avenue and 79th Street, New York, at two a.m. in the morning on my way home. Despite Coca-cola, Americans are the greatest milk drinkers in the world.

This noon we sat on the terrace of the Casino. The band played, the sun was warm and, framed between the two tall palms at the end of the wide terrace, the snow-capped Italian mountains lay under a sky of brightest blue.

January 22.

This morning to the terrace again, a brilliant day. I was emboldened to lunch out, fortified by one of Dr. C's pills, and then went to a mediocre performance of *Faust* in the rococo *Casino Théâtre*. In between the acts I met Baron Maurice de Rothschild, elephantine and depressed. He has been coming to Monte Carlo for forty years, he says, impelled here by long habit. " Now it's a morgue ! " he complained. He looks down a very long vista of dinners at the *Café de Paris*, and the ghosts of jewelled ladies hovered in the wings. His world is dead. It was murdered at a bridge in Sarajevo on June 28th, 1914.

There is an election in England and J. B. Priestley has broadcast a pæan of praise for the Labour Party. His argument that England is eating well while the Continent is famished has filled the English colony with mingled derision and indignation. From a land of four ounces of meat a week, three ounces of butter and one egg, this diatribe is nonsense. He should see the butter, meat, eggs, confectionery and sweetmeats that cram the shops and the market-stalls all along this coast in France and Italy. The

throngs of working-class people in the markets and shops prove
who buys and eats these things.   It may be, if the report is true,
that with a large farm in the Isle of Wight, J.B.P. has lost touch
with reality.   Farmers these days appear to be well-cushioned
against food shortages, and the Government, which for generations
neglected them and reduced them to bankruptcy, now pets and
subsidises them.   A few weeks ago a Labour Under-Secretary
was shocked into protest and made an exposure of the state of
farming affairs in the House of Commons but was smothered by
the party.   The rush to farm by those who hardly know the habits
of a cow results in some singular experiments.   " I have just
bought a £50,000 farm, on mortgage, and hope to lose £3,000
a year and take it off my income-tax, as well as have all the butter,
eggs, meat, and petrol and cars I want," said a City acquaintance
one day, urging me to buy a farm.   " Everybody's doing it,"
he said.   " Another war, and your capital's still there."

January 27.

Out again after four days in bed.   A beautiful day with a brilliant sky and vivid colouring sharpened by the clear atmosphere.
We took a bus to La Turbie on the Grande Corniche, with its
Tower of Augustus, a much-repaired ruin spectacular against
the sky.   It is a relic of the trophy erected by the Roman Senate
after a decree to commemorate the victories of the Emperor
Augustus over the tribes of Southern Gaul.   It was completed in
6 B.C. and now requires much imagination to restore to it its
ancient splendour, as when it was ornamented with a colonnade
of pillars and a colossal statue of Augustus.   Even so, to con-
template it is to have a vista down the illimitable corridor of Time.
It was part of the Roman town that marked the highest point of
the Aurelian Way, a road almost eight hundred miles long, from
the Roman Forum to the Forum of Arles, begun 241 B.C.   It
reached its highest point here, and we can imagine the fatigue of
the Roman hiker, sitting down and mopping his brow in the
little hill-town, knowing the worst part of the journey was over.
La Turbie was on the route of march of the Romans, Gauls,
French, and Italians.   Napoleon III took away part of the inscription on the old Tower, later built into an archway, and sent
it to the museum of St. Germain-en-Laye.   In return for this he
gave La Turbie a copy of Raphael's " St. Michael and the
Dragon."   It hangs now in the church built of stones plundered

from the monument. Nearby, on Mont Justicier, are the stone
foundations of a grim gallows whose crossbeam carried six bodies
at a time.

January 28.

I heard a little *Casino* history from the Baron Brasserie to-day.
In the spring of 1921 a party consisting of a beautiful lady and
three gentlemen arrived in Monte Carlo. They stayed at
separate hotels and seldom played at the same table in the
Casino, wishing to avoid any suspicion of co-operation. But
shrewd observers noticed they held frequent consultations together
and seemed to be working a system. It was a season of high play
and their operations went unnoticed by many. The later history
of this ' syndicate ' was remarkable. They were four members
of the court of the ex-Emperor Charles of Austria, then living in
exile in Switzerland. When he fled from Austria he had succeeded in carrying away a part of the crown jewels, and other
property of his House, much of it having been seized. He
depended wholly on the jewellery he had escaped with for the
support of himself and his fellow exiles. A plot to regain his
throne by an armed rising being considered, it was necessary to
raise funds for the enterprise. His capital insufficient for the
purpose, he was induced by some daring spirits to stake his
resources on the tables at Monte Carlo, on a system guaranteed
to quadruple it. He succumbed to this crazy suggestion and
four inconspicuous members of his suite set off for Monte Carlo.
They lost everything at the tables. The ill-financed invasion,
attempted in October, 1921, failed. Reduced to poverty the
Royal Party, driven out of Switzerland, existed in very strait-
ened circumstances at Funchal, Madeira, where the Emperor,
all his hopes shattered, died five months later. Of all *Casino*
stories this seems to me one of the craziest and saddest. The
Baron during the telling shed a tear. " Je suis tellement
sympathique, messieurs," he said.

January 29.

Another excursion to-day, being encouraged by the beauty of
the morning. We took the autobus to Cap Martin, alighting
there to walk along the peninsula. In the bus, a tall Englishman and his wife and a son of five sat near. I do not think I have
ever seen such a splendid trio—the English breed at its finest ;

the man fair, handsome and aristocratic in bearing ; his wife, slim, *distingué* in dress and manner.   The infant son was crowned with blond hair, had pink cheeks, unfathomable blue eyes and a voice like the song of a bird.   Upper middle-class, reserved, amiable and well-mannered.   I reflected that it had taken a thousand years to produce this breed, a patterned way of life, a convention of behaviour, a slowly evolved system of education, a class neither opulent nor impoverished, assured but not arrogant—the *summum bonum* of the human race, which we are now eliminating by vindictive taxation.

The walk was depressing despite the beauty of the setting, with vistas through pine trees of a sunlit azure sea.   The ornate villas were empty and falling into decay ; gardens overgrown with a rank sub-tropical vegetation, the massive wrought iron gates all rusting, the glass *porte-cochères* shattered, shutters hanging loose from the ravages of the gales.   I liked the motto inscribed above a horse-trough outside the Torre Clementina—" A ceux qui travaillent et qui souffrent sans murmure."   The motor-car has mercifully eliminated these dumb victims through the years.

We lunched in the shadow of a vast hotel, all shuttered and empty, a sad derelict from prosperous days, and then we walked into Mentone.   On the side of the Villa Fanny a Fascist pro- clamation painted in black letters became an essay in futility— " In questa battaglia fra l'oro e il sangue l'idea giusto che vive nell anima dei giovani popoli ha scelto.   Vinceremo ! Mussolini." (In this battle between gold and blood the just idea living in the soul of the young peoples has decided.   We shall triumph !) Thousands rushed to their doom inspired by these trashy incan- tations.   On a quiet Sunday afternoon, as the bourgeois inhabi- tants of Mentone promenaded, the unheeded proclamation, shabby from exposure to the elements, took on an air of pathetic futility.   The invaded French had not even troubled to obliterate the boast.

February 3.

To-day, after three days in bed, I ventured as far as Cap Ferrat, to visit my friends the Conways who have taken the Villa Prima- vera for a sojourn in the sun, a little domain with its own rocky cove and a long garden wandering down to a promontory.   It happened that one of their guests was a professor from Guy's Hospital who gave me a free diagnosis.   I now put fibrositis back into my assortment. A pleasant lunch with the sun pouring into the loggia. Conway, like Keats' figure on a Grecian urn, is forever young in Sargent's portrait in the Tate Gallery of the Wertheimer family, of which he is a member. I envy him his fine collection of Sargent's watercolours of Venice.

February 12.

I got up to-day after a wretched week and struggled to the *Casino Théâtre* to see a very poor performance of *La Traviata*. The only pleasure I derived from it was the presence of Rimsky-Korsakoff, my name for the unknown soulful Russian whose acquaintance we have made in a small restaurant we frequent. He always looks like a depressed bloodhound but he is gentle and battered. Poor man, I suspect he lives in a back bedroom on almost nothing, left derelict here after the Russian revolution. There was once quite a large colony of ruined Russians here but they have moved on or died out. M'sieur Rimsky-Korsakoff looks like last year's billpost, weather-worn, faded, recalling long-vanished gaiety. I suspect he once drove in a troika through the snow-powdered streets of St. Petersburg. His present role is chameleonic. He has a voice, and one source of income is derived as a member of the *Casino Théâtre* opera chorus. I have seen him, gay in shirt and tails, as a diner-out in *La Dame aux Camélias*, as a Sicilian peasant in striped stockings in *Cavalleria Rusticana*, as a black bolero-clad Spaniard in *Carmen*. Sometimes, in addition to his lusty singing in the chorus he does a caper with a tambourine, or twangs a lute, or flourishes a beer jug in a German *weinstube* ; but no disguise of costume or acting ever quite hides his long lugubrious countenance. Poor fellow, in the make-believe world of the stage he remains a sad victim of Fate. He induces in me, even in his gayest roles and costumes, a deep melancholy.

This afternoon I could not sit out the performance and left early, being in too much pain. I have a *couchette* ticket for Barcelona in my pocket, for the 14th. It seems sheer folly but I shall make the attempt. I do not want to die in Monte Carlo. Its bedizened atmosphere weighs me down. It has too many Rimsky-Korsakoffs.

Spain

BARCELONA

February 16.

TWO days ago I made the jump. G saw me off, very motherly and a little concerned at my enterprise. We drew out of Monte Carlo at 6 p.m., and so good-bye to the palms and the *Casino*. I have said harsh things about it, due in part to the state of my health. It is a gem set in the Mediterranean sea, of a perfection not surpassed ; but perfection cloys and after a month Monte Carlo is like a diet of wedding-cake.

My companions in the *couchette* proved amusing. Two of them, joining the train at Nice, were business men of French and Spanish nationality, coming from Genoa and going to Perpignan and Barcelona. After dinner the Spaniard, learning I was making the journey to Barcelona, suggested I should get off at eight in the morning at Perpignan, where he had left his car, have breakfast at his French colleague's home, and then go on to Spain with him, by car. He knew all the Customs people, he said, and it would be easier and pleasanter. I accepted the offer and in the morning left the train. My French host had the singular name of Diogène. He lived in anything but a tub. Mother, two daughters, married son and daughter-in-law met the train. There was quite a demonstration, I thought M. Diogène had been away at least a year. But it was only five days. For a moment amid the embracing I was an unnoticed extra piece of baggage. Then we were whirled away to the house, whereupon mother and daughter went into the kitchen. Soon rolls and coffee appeared. While the two men transacted business I went to look at the town. Early February is no time to judge a place, but the long avenues of plane trees must make shady retreats in summer heat. The river has been canalised. The great sight is the glorious snow-crowned Canigou. It fills the horizon with its massive splendour. Kipling paid it a glowing tribute which the French have treasured ever since.

Lunch was formidable. Madame and her two daughters had been busy in the kitchen ; soup, a great sole *bonne femme*, two roast ducks, asparagus (not out of tins), young potatoes, a fruit *flan*,

22

ices, all these were accompanied by four *vins du pays*, then coffee and liqueurs in the salon. I made polite conversation with my kind hosts but the height of hospitality would have been a couch and an hour's siesta. I began to hear them talking to me down a long corridor, and also I feared that Nemesis would overtake me in the shape of an outraged ulcer denied its milk. At three o'clock we parted from these kind souls, but not before I had fathomed a mystery. In what kind of business were my two train friends engaged? I made all kinds of guesses. There came a moment when M. Diogène must have discerned my groping for the light. " Shall we tell him? " he asked his companion. The other nodded. The ladies at the table giggled. " We have a *lastic* concession for France and Italy," said my host. I looked puzzled. He pulled a small object out of his pocket. " We make *lastic* panties in Barcelona," he said, holding up a small female garment amid general mirth.

I set off with my Spanish friend. We wound in and out of narrow passes in the Pyrenees by the Col de Perthuis, on the route taken by Hannibal in his invasion of Italy. It was dark and nine o'clock when we arrived at my hotel in Barcelona. There I learned of my misdemeanour. The concierge became excited when he learned who I was. " But, señor, there has been a deputation at the railway station to meet you, and another deputation has waited for over two hours here." Alas, I had told my publisher I should arrive by train at six o'clock.

February 17.

Señor de Caralt, my publisher, and my translator called after breakfast. They have graciously accepted my apologies and are obviously delighted at my arrival. Señor de Caralt reeled off a list of engagements made for me. I was dismayed but I could not rebuff his kind heart. Last night I went without dinner, and the lunch that I failed to resist yesterday is still in revolt. But how can I tell these good souls I am on a milk diet? I must go to the banquets and nibble and then resort to Dr. C's powders.

By ten a.m. I knew I was lost. Eight pressmen arrived and interviewed me separately. The translator of my novels has been pressed into service as interpreter. I find him a very intelligent and agreeable young man. The general politeness is almost suffocating, but I am in the domain of the *hidalgo*. Even the small page boys have a superlative Ritz standard of courtesy. They

B

wear white gloves, and bow on every possible occasion. Later, six photographers appeared to deal with the most unphotogenic creature in the universe. I become a mixture of criminal and hard-boiled egg before any lens. At noon operators with a portable microphone arrived. Questions and answers ; my interpreter very quick, but perspiring, poor young man. This afternoon I was whirled round the city. All the bookshops and kiosks on the boulevards are full of my books. I do not know a word of Spanish, I do not know an inch of Spain, I have never thought of Spain, yet it seems that I have been having a very active life here for some years. Early this evening I went to a beautiful bookshop, and after cakes and sherry I autographed books for two hours. This evening at about ten there is a dinner for me. I shall juggle with the courses. I was up twice last night in much pain. Shade of Dr. C!

February 18.

This morning Señor de Caralt, who is *Delgado de Cultura* in the Provincial Government, took me to call on the Mayor, and the Governor of the Province of Catalonia, and to view their respective quarters ; very impressive, with fine stairs, ceilings and heraldic decorations. In the Mayor's office I was introduced to the Abbot of Montserrat, where I am invited to visit to-morrow. This evening I again went to a bookshop to autograph books. I signed for almost two hours. It is a tantalising task. I wanted to look at and converse with these Spaniards who read my books, but I had no time. They like their full names written in their books. Spanish names are fearsomely long, for to their own they add those of their parents. A name like Carmen Isabel Villamediana y Yanez, unfamiliar, has to be closely copied from the visiting card. Thus I miss the lovely faces that parade before me and am frustrated when we attempt a few polite words. I get alluring smiles and flashing eyes but not, as yet, Andalusian lips, à la Byron. I have attempted no addition to my signature, unlike an English predecessor who wrote in each book " Je t'adore Espagna," a mixture of French, Spanish and fulsomeness that caused surprise.

It was almost ten o'clock when I left the bookshop but as no one dreams of dining before that hour I was well in time for a dinner party which began at eleven. I have just written this at 2.30 a.m. People are talking in the next bedroom !

February 19.

My young translator and guide, Señor Julio Fernandez-Yanez Gimeno, called this morning to motor me out to the monastery of Montserrat. It is situated on a mountain ledge nearly three thousand feet high on a thirteen-mile long spine of rocks that rises abruptly from the Catalonian plain. It is said to have been created by the earthquake at the time of the Crucifixion. In the Middle Ages they believed the castle of the Holy Grail was situated here. It is a tremendously impressive pile of serrated peaks, much in the formation of the Dolomites. The monastery, apart from the beauty of its Renaissance basilica, is famous for its choir school. With singular kindness the Abbot had the ambulatory chapel, behind the high altar with its revered black wooden Madonna, allegedly carved by St. Luke, opened for me, and forty young choristers assembled there that I might hear them sing. They grouped themselves in a half-circle, and a little fellow stood in front and conducted while a benign old monk, their music master, clasped a Psalter to his paunch. Their voices were like silver trumpets and their little black heads, angel faces, white collars and long black gowns, backed by the rich stained-glass windows of this ambulatory chapel ablaze in the afternoon sun, composed a deeply moving picture.

I returned home, after an adventure on the precipitous slopes of the mountain, for we missed the last cable-car, and were led by peasants down a perilous *sentier*. I was so exhausted that I had to lie down on the roadside while our car was fetched from its rendezvous. So home, to give a talk on the Barcelona Radio at ten p.m.

February 20.

One of the hotel page boys, an animated lad, knows a little English. He has taken special charge of me. He carries up to my room books for me to autograph, and exercises his discrimination with callers for whom he interprets. He wears white gloves and when he has specially difficult passages to interpret he uses his hands ; it looks as if he were conducting an orchestra. This evening at another bookshop I signed over one hundred books. My signature has become still more illegible, I fear.

Barcelona might be a beautiful city, if its sea-front were not cluttered with wharves, sheds and decayed buildings, but the Rambla is a wide animated boulevard with trees running down to the sea and is lined on two sides with stalls and newspaper kiosks. One section, the flower market, is a blaze of colour. The squares and boulevards are very fine.

The secretary of the British Council here had asked me if I would give a talk. I was astonished to find this evening that in a couple of days he had collected an audience of about four hundred in the lecture hall of their pleasant headquarters. I began very slowly, knowing that I was addressing an audience of Spanish students of English but soon, finding they were following me quite well, I slipped into my usual pace. A better audience could not be wished for, and I believe I am a good judge after forty years of platform life. They were quick on the points, they had a sense of humour and one was soon *en rapport* with them. I spoke for over an hour and shall remember them and their warm welcome with pleasure. I went from the lecture hall to dine with Señor Pedro Block, my cicerone from Perpignan to Barcelona, in a beautiful flat high up in an apartment house on a wide avenue. It was a charming party that went on until 2 a.m. When we left the electricity had been cut off, the lift did not run, and the butler lighted us with a candelabra down six flights of stairs. Replete with food and mellow with wine, I began to laugh. " Why do you laugh ? " asked my host. " I feel like a Cardinal," I replied. " Why do you feel like a Cardinal ? " " The last time I saw a servant carrying a candelabra downstairs was in a palace in Rome where I had dined. One of the guests was a Cardinal and as is the custom there, when he came and when he departed he was preceded by a footman carrying a lighted candelabra."

MADRID

February 22.

Arrived at 9 a.m. in Madrid, and was met by my Chilean artist friend, Manuel Huidobro. He, Felix Kelly and I were in Rome together all last June, where they joined me after a long Spanish sojourn. I last saw Manuel at Felix's exhibition in the Leicester Gallery last November on the eve of my departure for Monte Carlo. Manuel is here for an exhibition of his portraits, of Spanish society beauties. He has taken for me a room with a terrace, high up, overlooking Madrid, a city on a high plateau, with a view of snowy mountain ranges. Madrid, from a first glimpse, is surprisingly modern. Its sharp atmosphere, wide avenues, and tall buildings remind me of New York more than of any other city in Europe. This evening I went with Manuel to see his exhibition. He has a very fine line and in his work these Spanish beauties lose none of their glamour.

I find all my books on the kiosks and in all the shops. This Spanish double of me seems everywhere. I am still not used to him and wonder who is masquerading under my name.

February 24.

All this morning and all this afternoon I have been in the hands of the interviewers. The Lord only knows what they will write for it has been a two-way business. Poor Manuel was asked questions in Spanish which he translated for me and then my reply was translated back to them. He worked very hard and by the evening we were quite exhausted. I lunched with Professor Starkie of the British Institute here. The author of *The Raggle-Taggle Gipsies* is a truly astonishing character and *persona grata* with all the Spaniards by reason of his great knowledge of their folk-lore and music. We lunched in a delightful native restaurant. The walls were lined with bright faience tiles, the waitresses wore Andalusian costume. The food and wines were superlative. We were a party of six. The lunch ended at four o'clock and then we adjourned to a café for cigars and coffee.

Photographs are in all the evening papers and what an object I am ! I think I have struck a low-water mark in the gallery of horrors that purport to be me.

February 25.

Having to go to the leading bookshop to autograph my books I took precautions and asked my old friend, Doña Lucienne de Cardenas, wife of the former Spanish Ambassador at Washington, to go with me. She is not old and indeed is a beautiful Roumanian who was very popular in U.S.A. But I had not prepared the bookseller for such a glamorous companion, and plainly he was puzzled. He was not enlightened and he probably jumped to the most romantic conclusion, a compliment to my taste.

It seems to be the custom in Spain to welcome visiting authors with sherry and cakes before the photographing and the signing begin. Photographically, on this occasion, I looked like Winston

Churchill, a chubby baby-look that long ago at school earned me the nickname of Winston. It was a most enjoyable excursion and when I left I again had a present of beautiful illustrated books. My rapidly expanding Spanish library is becoming a problem. What I liked most about the whole proceeding was my host's name—Afrodisio Aguardo. He is not only a bookseller but a publisher of *de luxe* books. I carried away a beautiful morocco leather-bound India paper edition of *Don Quixote*. I am ashamed to confess that I have never read it, that I did not know Cervantes' name was Saavadra, or that the book begins with a Prologue and a series of sonnets. The Prologue opens with the words *Desocupado lector*—unoccupied reader ! Could anything be more fitting as a prelude to a story a thousand pages long ? Finding literature an inadequate support, Cervantes humbly applied for one of the four posts vacant in the new American colonies. His letter was never answered but some bureaucrat wrote on the margin " Let him look for something nearer home ! " The poor man, his hopes unfulfilled, went into the country and wrote *Don Quixote*. His life was more romantic and incredible than anything he wrote. He served a Cardinal in Rome, was wounded in the Battle of Lepanto, was a prisoner and slave in Algiers, a chandler for the Armada, was in prison in Seville on a charge of fraud, and died in poverty.

I find I am beginning to recognise my own offspring. *Victoria Four-Thirty* is *Estacion Victoria a las 4.30*. That is easy, but *Los huespades llegan* (The Guests Arrive), *Una pequena llama* (One Small Candle), *Queremos vivir* (They Wanted to Live), are more difficult. *Scissors* has quite baffled the translator, so it becomes *Le vida une y separa*— Life Unites and Separates.

To-night the de Cardenases gave a dinner for me. Juan de Cardenas, a retired ambassador, is now Director of the Spanish Diplomatic School, and examines the candidates for the Diplomatic Service. He has served in Mexico, Lisbon, Berlin, Bucharest, Tokio and Paris. He descends from a line of diplomats. One of his ancestors was Don Alfonso de Cardenas who was Ambassador in London at the time of the execution of Charles I. He bought for his royal master some of the paintings in the palace at Whitehall, disposed of by Cromwell, which now hang in the Prado. When I first met Juan he was the doyen of ambassadors in Washington where for many years, with his beautiful wife, he was very popular. I was often their guest there and in New York. A man of letters, a connoisseur, he is famed as a gourmet and his dinners are much sought after. To-night fourteen guests were present, and one old friend, Timmy, the famous white poodle to whom I wrote some verses.

> Elegant gentleman, do you suppose
> He's a prince of the blood with his Bourbon nose ?

I was affectionately greeted by Timmy the moment I arrived, and by one other poodle, his living double. I then learned what Lucienne had meant when she wrote saying " All the Bourbons are lined up for you." Timmy has stunned Madrid by proving to be a lady and by producing a son, whom I now met, the image of his mother !

I can only do justice to Juan's table by quoting Flecker. It had

> " Such sweet jams meticulously jarred
> As God's own prophet eats in Paradise."

The dining-room was illuminated by vitrines filled with my host's famous collection of silver salvers. Among the guests was a lady who evoked many memories of London in the Edwardian era, the widow of the Marqués Merry del Val, once the Spanish Ambassador to the Court of St. James. He was one of the most popular figures in London society and designed, with the approval of King Alfonso, who had some claims as an amateur architect, as the Ritz Hotel here proves, the present Spanish Embassy in Belgrave Square. The old lady's memories and triumphs were all of the past, but what a gallery of Edwardian figures she evoked !

March 2.

Commander Segrave, Naval attaché at our Embassy, and Mrs. Segrave gave a very pleasant lunch for me at their home. The rooms were full of flowers and sunshine and one had the impression of being in a country house on a glorious midsummer's day. After lunch, which finished at four o'clock, Starkie motored me back to my hotel where another Press ordeal awaited me. My friend Manuel is tireless in the role of interpreter and works with great ease and fluency. How very fortunate I am to have him with me! He has been coaching me in a speech in Spanish which I have learned, parrot-like. The Madrid Radio men came with their machine to take a recording. It seems I had learned my parrot speech too well for they asked me to repeat it with a little more foreign accent.

March 5.

This morning a party of us, Lucienne de Cardenas, Mr. Armour, the U.S. attaché here, and his wife, motored to Avila to lunch with the Marqués de Santo Domingo.   The road ran over the barren snow-powdered Sierra de Guadarrama which I have seen shining from my terrace.   I had my first glimpse of the massive Escorial in a pocket of the mountains.   The sky was a beautiful pale blue of the utmost clarity, the sunshine touched everything with a crystal light, and the vast uplands, empty, treeless, stretched endlessly under the brilliant sky.   To see Avila is never to forget it.   Here is the perfectly preserved medieval walled city.   It is, I think, superior to Carcassonne, reconstructed by Viollet-le-Duc with too much thoroughness, so that the patina of Time is somewhat lost.   On a little hill, apart from the city, they have built a canopied belvedere from which one can look across the valley and get the whole plan of the crenellated walls and towers crowning the undulating plateau.   It stands 3,946 feet above sea level. There are ten gateways and eighty towers built of granite blocks twelve-feet thick.   It was begun in A.D. 1090 though the city claims to have been founded by Hercules in 1660 B.C. and named for his mother.   Even the magnificent cathedral is a half-fortress built into the walls.   Before the age of artillery it must have been impregnable.   It was the birthplace of Santa Teresa.   The dreaded Inquisitor-General of the Inquisition, Torquemada, died here in 1498.

My host has built into the tower wall a low one-storey house. His garden incorporates an inside angle of the walls, and when he wishes to take an evening stroll he can walk along the parapets high above the town.   Within this domain, in which there is a swimming-pool presided over by a friendly gander, my host is the medieval lord.   The house has been most carefully built with period oak, postern doors, embrasured windows, and it is almost impossible to detect that it was not here when Don Ramon of Burgundy conducted building operations in A.D. 1088.

Santo Domingo fulfilled his reputation as a host with a perfect Spanish lunch.   The guests included a Spanish duchess of tremendous individuality whose life is a picaresque novel in itself, including a period in gaol as an irrepressible Royalist.

After a long lunch we toured the churches. I think the most notable thing I saw was the renowned *Retablo* of the high altar, of the time of Ferdinand and Isabella ; what depressed me was the terrible poverty of the beggars about the church door. This frieze of misery winds over every scene in Spain, and nowhere does it seem more noticeable than in the shadow of the great cathedrals which express the enormous wealth of a country that once dominated the world. This human misery is not an indictment of the Franco régime, it is part of the scarcely changed tradition through which the social conscience has slept for five hundred years. Beggary is allied to sanctity and by this supposition the Madonnas may be plated with gold and jewels while the hungry poor cluster about the church doors. Once, when I remarked on this in Italy, where the extremes of wealth and poverty are not so stark, a friend observed, in extenuation, " Where there is no poverty there is no charity, how otherwise do we achieve Christian humility ? " It seemed to me a singularly perverse reasoning.

There is some effort now being made to alter this state of affairs. The Church has missions of succour, especially of the children ; a few of the wealthy landed proprietors are making some effort to change the labourers' lot but the great majority lead luxurious lives, often beyond their means, for with diminishing revenues they maintain an impressive façade. Among too many of the rich there is a shocking disregard of the misery in which the poor live. It is stupid of them. Thousands of them were massacred in the Civil War in 1936 but they do not appear to have learned anything from that murderous experience. The fires still smoulder and they are kept from bursting into flames because both sides dread equally the outbreak of another fratricidal war. Franco makes gestures and experiments but he confronts a solid block of traditionalists. The so-called democratic nations for over ten years have done their best to starve Spain into acceptance of their own ideology, and only now, because they want Spain's soldiers to contribute to their own front against Russia, are they making concessions. They have given millions of dollars to Communist Tito because he flouts Stalin, and have refused help to Franco who has always flouted him. Dictators of any creed are an abomination but we fervently embraced Stalin in our hour of need, and our kiss to the leper shows we are not so particular when self-interest is involved.

B*

March 9.

A leading Spanish publisher, Señor Aguilar, has shown me much hospitality. Despite the fact that I am with a rival house he invited me to view his extensive editorial plant. To-day, with his son, he motored me to Toledo and conducted me over this fabulous city. In the great cathedral I saw the monstrance made with the gold brought back from the Indies by Christopher Columbus, and reflected on the terrible rape, torture and massacre he let loose upon the unoffending natives of Hispaniola in his lust for gold, under the necessity of fulfilling his promises of untold wealth for the Spanish sovereigns.

How beautiful Toledo is when seen from across the deep ravine spanned by the bridge of Alcantara, high-arched above the Tagus. Against the sky stands the shattered Alcazar where the Nationalists made their epic defence. And how movingly simple is the home of that strange genius El Greco, Domenikos Theotokopoulos, who settled in Toledo, and who in May, 1582, before the local tribunal of the Inquisition, for which he acted as translator in the trial of a fellow Greek, stated that he was a native of the city of Candia. It is believed that he learned to paint in his native Crete. He tarried in Venice where he became Il Grecco—later adapted by the Spaniards to El Greco—and studied under Titian. He then migrated via Rome (what did he do in Rome one wonders? History is silent) to Toledo and there he painted, amid much other work, his masterpiece *The Burial of Count Orgaz*, for the San Tomé church. By a miracle it survived the Civil War. For me, seeing it there to-day it was all and more than all I had anticipated. Its colour, its drama, its sheer beauty paralyse one.

Who was this Count Orgaz thus immortalised? He was Gonzalos Ruiz, governor of Orgaz, who had repaired this church.* The picture is the story of a miracle. The Count had shown great devotion to St. Augustine and St. Stephen so, on his death, they descended from heaven and attended his burial. Here they are, and with them we see a row of Spanish courtiers like a frieze across the picture, with El Greco's own son, a boy of twelve, as an attendant page. What I found curious, and no one seems to have pointed it out in the books I have studied on the painter, was that although Count Orgaz was buried in 1312 all the

---

* "There is Count Orgaz, the descendant of El Greco's count," said a friend one evening, as we sat in the Café Chicote, at Madrid.

costumes and portraits are of the late 16th century, contemporaneous with the painter. It is as if Augustus John had painted the funeral of William Shakespeare and put all the attendants in to-day's costume. The witnesses, sartorially considered, at Count Orgaz's funeral might all have been present at the court of Philip II and have known Mary Tudor, whereas they had lived some three hundred years earlier.

El Greco's house has been preserved with its gallery and patio. He painted in a room that has a south window. All artists crave a north window. I was not surprised, therefore, to see that he had had large shutters placed on the window. When he died in 1614 he was buried in great pomp, all Toledo attending. So it was, for once, a success story, with fame and fortune in his lifetime. At the close of his life he inhabited twenty-four rooms of a palace, possessed a good library, was witty, generous and popular. His natural son, Georges-Manuel, became a painter, architect and sculptor. El Greco founded no school for " no one cared to follow his capricious and extravagant style which was only suitable to himself." But what a self, unique as Everest and as lonely in his eminence.

March 11.

I kept in bed all day to-day. I was physically and mentally tired. There is so much for the mind to digest, and I find that without a period of retirement one is not capable of a full and clear enjoyment. Moreover, I never go anywhere without some preparation for what I am about to see. I spend the day making notes and reading the history and background of the scenes I am to visit. I have long made a rule, but, alas, often break it, to keep to my bed for one day a week. A man goes into retreat for the good of his soul, why not for the good of his mind and body?

March 12.

This morning Mr. Johnson, an attaché at the American Embassy, and his wife called to take me out to the country place of the Marqués and Marquésa de Casa Valdes who have shown me much hospitality. We went up into the arid Sierra de Guadarramas, in the direction of Guadalajara, and found them at a long low farmhouse. Here under a great oak tree we all lunched *al fresco*, with serving maids in Spanish

costume. They carried out between them an immense flat
two-handled copper pan in which was something that looked
like a giant omelette. It was a *paella*, a renowned speciality,
made of rice, crabs, tomatoes, fish, mayonnaise, superlatively
good.

After lunch we motored over the barren plain to the disused
monastery of Lupiana, San Bartolomé, the first monastery founded
in Spain, in 1330, for the Order of St. Jerome. It is superb.
It has a large Gothic cloister, built in 1472, around a great patio.
The monastery is now adapted to a private residence. My host's
friends gave a large dance there one evening but somehow it
seemed a desecration and none of the guests felt comfortable ;
some swore they saw ghosts in the large gallery over the cloister.
No wonder the ghosts are unhappy for some former occupant
had converted the roofless ruined church into a garden with a
modern swimming-pool.

We got back for tea in front of an immense log fire and found
a large and gay company around an enormous table lit with
candles. I was lucky enough to sit next to my host's daughter,
Maria, twenty, beautiful, vivacious and, since an English governess
has always lived with the family, there was no language barrier.
I made a disconcerting discovery. At tea a lady began to talk
to me in fluent Spanish. When finally I had to confess I could
not understand a word of what she was saying she opened her
eyes wide and exclaimed—" But you speak beautiful Spanish,
and fluently ! I heard you the other evening on the radio ! "
I confessed to the parrot-trick.

March 13.

Lectured this evening at the British Institute. A crowded
hall, Starkie in the chair. So far as I could tell from the quick
responses the audience had no difficulty in following me. Like
most extempore speakers I am inclined to go fast but on the whole
I kept my resolution to speak slowly. I could not have had a
pleasanter audience which included our Chargé d'Affaires,
Hankey and his wife, with whom I am to lunch to-morrow. There
was a cocktail party afterwards—the Spanish variety is noisier
than the English but does not achieve the parrot-house of the
American. A Spanish lady, when introduced : " From your
books I thought you a little grave stout man, and you are tall,
thin, comic ! " Comic ? How, one wonders, did my books

give her that other impression, and how can one look like one's books ?

March 14.

A too full day. Recorded for Radio Madrid for the London and Foreign Service, lunched at the British Embassy, signed books at the shop of Afrodisio Aguardo, a second session with more Spanish beauties with interminable names and unfathomable eyes ; cocktails at the Duchess de Villada's (wonderful pictures), and dined with a most hospitable young American couple, Mr. and Mrs. Conrad Ulmer of the American Embassy. Home at 2 a.m. and wrote up this diary. So far the old ulcer has not made a protest—shade of Dr. C and his prescriptions ! The dining-room at the British Embassy had four beautiful water-colour landscapes which I greatly admired. On enquiry I learned that they were the work of my host's brother. My curiosity, there-fore was unpremeditatedly tactful !

Manuel Huidobro is drawing my portrait. Last year in Rome Manuel and Felix Kelly both drew me, but what a different person they made of me ! Felix designed a beautiful jacket for *And so to Rome* and put me in as the bust of a senator amid the ruins of Rome. I objected to a tilted laurel wreath that gave me a bibulous air ! Manuel, on the other hand, saw me as a late eighteenth-century squire-dilettante. I wonder what I shall emerge as in this new attempt. I have come to the conclusion that every portrait is really a projection of the artist himself. A Gainsborough subject is a Gainsborough, a Reynolds a Reynolds, an Orpen an Orpen, and, like one's own voice, we are unknown to ourselves.

March 16.

Señor Aguilar took me to-day to the Escorial. This colossal monastery-palace-pantheon-cathedral has a sinister air with its grey stone façades and slate tiles, its senseless acres of galleries, rooms, terraces. It is devoid of any graces though it achieves by sheer size a heavy majesty. It is backed by the barren moun-tain out of which its building material was quarried ; austerity is the keynote throughout. The Escorial was designed in the form of the gridiron on which St. Lawrence is reputed to have been roasted, and built as a thanksgiving to him. It roasts itself to-day in the summer heat, and in winter is icily bitten by the winds that whistle along its miles of corridors. It impresses one, as the Great Pyramid, by its gigantic futility.* It has sixteen courtyards, nine towers, fifteen cloisters, eighty-six staircases, three hundred cells, twelve hundred doors and two thousand six hundred and seventy-three windows. In all this, including the Habsburg palace esconced in it, I did not see one room I would wish to live in. This vast edifice was erected partly to make a tomb for the great Charles V who, in contradiction of this grandeur, abdicated and retreated to a small house where he died in monastic simplicity. It was a strange end after a very strange beginning for he was the son of Joana the Mad, and was born in a lavatory to which she retired at a ball in Ghent in 1500. Charles who had lived very little in Spain died breathing his last words there, in Spanish—" Yo vengo, Señor Cristo, yo vengo ! "—I come, Lord Christ, I come.

By the altar of the high domed church there are two monuments. They cover no mortal remains. The one on the left is a memorial to Charles V, the one of the right to his son Philip II. These impressive groups of sculpture in bronze depict, kneeling in devotion, the Emperor, his beloved wife Queen Isabella, his daughter the Empress Maria, and his two sisters Queen Eleanor of France and Queen Maria of Hungary. On the opposite side are the effigies of Philip II, with his son Don Carlos, and his first, third and fourth, wives. His second wife ? She is not there. She was Mary Tudor, Queen of England. An upright, self-righteous man, Philip had the grim task of committing his son Don Carlos to prison, where he died. Philip killed his administration by too much conscientious writing of minutes. He was nicknamed *El Rey Papelero*, the Royal Paperer. It is in the octagonal pantheon, built under the high altar, that we find the dead Spanish kings assembled, tier upon tier of them, Charles V and his descendants. There is only one space left in all these tiers. It is wide open, inviting a defunct king to complete the pantheon. The corpse is ready for the space, but the time is not opportune, for the last king of Spain, Alfonso XIII, destined to be buried here, lies waiting in Rome. He died in exile and his coffin now rests there in the Spanish church of Montserrat. When in Rome last year I asked the Infanta Beatrice, Princess Torlonia, daughter

---

* It ruined Spain. Architectural *folie des grandeurs* still exists. Franco to-day is building a vast War Memorial (1936) in the Valley of the Fallen. He has excavated a mountain and through a hole in its peak has erected a giant Cross. The inside of the mountain is lined with marble. It has used up 90 per cent of all Spain's cement.

of ex-king Alfonso, whether Franco had refused permission for her father's interment in the pantheon. She replied, " We did not ask him. My father will go there one day in his own right." With the coming of Alfonso XIII the pantheon will have completed its purpose. Other kings of Spain, should they follow, must lie elsewhere.

There is a second pantheon that spreads endlessly in the basement, a nineteenth-century affair mostly, devoted to the Infantes. Its Spanish name—*El Pudridero*—is macabre, it means the Putrefying Place. In its wedding-cake pomp it is hideous but I was glad to discover one tomb, that of the great Don John of Austria, Charles V's illegitimate son, whose defeat of the Turks at Lepanto has supplied a theme for the paintings and tapestries in many of Europe's art galleries and palaces.

I bring away one singular memory of this visit. In a gallery fronting the nave of the church is the white marble figure of Christ on a black marble cross. This crucifix is the work of Benvenuto Cellini. He tells us in his memoirs that when his rival Bandinelli was given the great block of marble intended for his own Neptune he turned in chagrin to work on a crucifix. When the Duchess of Florence, who had opposed him in favour of her favourite Bandinelli, asked him what he was doing he replied —" My Lady, I have taken in hand for my pleasure one of the most laborious pieces which has ever been produced. It is a Christ of the whitest marble set upon a cross of the blackest, exactly of the same size as a tall man. You must know, My Lady, I would not sell it for a thousand ducats ; it is of such difficult execution that I think no man ever attempted the like before."

Cellini was ever a boaster but here he was completely justified. Bandinelli, whose frightful work disfigures the Piazza della Signoria at Florence, got his block of marble and made his clumsy *Pietà*. Cellini offered his crucifix to the church of Santa Maria Novella, which made such conditions that the enraged sculptor declined to erect it there. The Duke and Duchess came to see the crucifix and greatly admired it. Finally the Duke bought it for fifteen hundred golden crowns and took it to the Pitti Palace, in 1565. It was given in 1576 by the Grand Duke Francesco to Philip II who placed it in the Escorial. This masterpiece is little observed being in an obscure position. It is a miracle of marble. As I lingered behind to look at it more closely a verger came up. An absurd little silk apron had been hung from the waist. " You will observe," said the verger, lifting it, " the statue is perfect in every detail."

We lunched in the delightful summer villa that Señor Aguilar has built for himself in the village of the Escorial, with windows framing the monastery seen through apple-blossom boughs. A log fire blazed in the grate, a friendly dog gave us welcome and Señor Aguilar and his wife presided over an excellent lunch, punctuated by so many various wines that I fail to recall the name of one in trying to remember all. After lunch we went by car, climbing over the high Guadarrama range to Segovia where we had a brief sight of its fairytale castle perched on a rocky prow thrust skywards above a deep ravine, sheer Hans Andersen. We paused under the high arches of the great Roman aqueduct and then went on to La Granja, the first royal seat built by a Bourbon in Spain. Philip V, French by birth and education, remembered Versailles and sought to surpass it. He gave it twenty-six giant fountains and filled wooded vistas with statuary. There he elected to lie beside his wife, not wishing to be buried with members of the House of Austria in the Escorial pantheon.

March 17.

The Duchess de Durcal, whom I had known in Venice, gave a lunch for me. I was glad to meet there Señor Sanchez Canton, the eminent art connoisseur who presides over the great treasures of the Prado Gallery. This famous gallery stands just across the road from my hotel so that I often visit it *en pantoufles* while my room is being tidied. I had particularly wished to meet Señor Canton for last week I made an astonishing discovery. Just behind the Goya room hangs a full-size portrait of a young man in a scarlet coat, braided in gold, with a white waistcoat, white neckerchief, cuffs, and tricorne hat. He leans against a classical plinth while the dome of St. Peter's in the background proclaims the scene is Rome. It was painted by Pompeo Batoni in Rome in 1778. The portrait is labelled *Un Caballero en Roma*, a Gentleman in Rome. I was astonished to recognise, from a drawing in my possession, that the Caballero is my ancestor Charles Roberts of Thorpe Langton, Leicestershire, a young lieutenant of the 56th Regiment of Foot, who went through the siege of Gibraltar, and married, in 1784, Amabel Hesilrige, the eldest daughter of Sir Arthur Hesilrige of Noseley, Leicestershire, the seventh baronet. The immediate question in my mind is how did this portrait, painted in Rome, get here ? In 1774 Charles was in Rome with his kinsman Thomas Coke, later known as Coke of Norfolk. Young Tommy Coke—the name Coke had been assumed by his father, Wenman Roberts—had set England and Italy by the ears in 1773. Bonnie Prince Charlie, fifty-two years of age, had married by proxy the Princess Louise of Stolberg, a vivacious girl of nineteen. To Tommy Coke, setting forth on the Grand Tour, fell the pleasant lot of escorting the young bride to Rome. He was nineteen years of age, tall, handsome, and the claims of youth outbid caution. Soon there was scandal abroad in Rome concerning them, the young couple being seen about together. It was intimated to young Mr. Coke that he should leave. Unfortunately the young wife of the Pretender crowned her folly by commissioning the most fashionable painter of Rome, Pompeo Batoni, to paint Tommy's portrait. He depicted him dressed as a cavalier in pearl grey satin vest and breeches, plumed hat in hand. The Princess, or Queen, as the Pretender insisted on her being styled, bore a resemblance to a recently discovered statue of Ariadne lamenting the loss of Theseus. In her folly she had this statue placed in the background of Tommy's portrait. " I hear that the young Mr. Coke has returned from abroad in love with the Pretender's Queen," wrote Horace Walpole. The young man brought back with him Batoni's portrait, which now hangs in Lord Leicester's collection at Holkham Hall. It was this same artist who, four years later, painted the portrait of Charles Roberts, who had lingered on in Italy until he was called home to join his regiment, ordered to Gibraltar.*

What is this portrait of Charles Roberts doing in Madrid ? Did the young man, recalled, depart hurriedly from Italy, leaving the portrait to be forwarded ? If so, how did it get from Rome to Madrid, and how has it got into the Prado collection ? The Prado catalogue does not help much. It says, " In 1814 it was in the apartment of the Infante Don Carlos in the Royal Palace, Madrid." How did it get there ? Had it by chance emigrated into the collection of the Bourbons at Naples, and been transported to Madrid in the collection of the Italian-born Charles IV, father of Don Carlos ? Or was it in the loot when Joseph Bonaparte went from Naples to Madrid in 1808 to become King of Spain ? All this is conjecture and I put the problem before

---

* I have told the story of the young Pretender's wife, the Countess of Albany, fully in *And So To Rome*.

Señor Canton, a cautious and authoritative art historian, and sought his help but he could not provide any clue to the mystery.*

March 18.

This evening the Marqués Santo Domingo gave a cocktail party at his apartment for Prince Nicholas of Roumania. There were about fifty present but the guest of honour, motoring to Madrid, did not arrive. About ten-thirty the company melted away to dinner. Dinner at eleven is nothing unusual and the restaurants and hotels are just getting into their swing. I lingered behind, for the departure of the guests enabled me to examine the many beautiful things Santo Domingo has collected. I was particularly struck by a 16th century painting, very small, very exquisite, of a Madonna and Child. Its authorship is uncertain (Domenico Beccafumi ?) but its merit is quite arresting. The colour, the expression of the Madonna, the intent wonder of the Child, looking at a green parrot sitting sedately before Him, fill one with that intense joy conveyed by supreme art. I coveted it dearly, and in the candlelit apartment it diffused a serene grace distilled from the centuries.

Near eleven o'clock, as I was just about to depart and our number was reduced to four, Prince Nicholas arrived, with many apologies for having been delayed on the road. Tall, good-looking, I had not seen him since, a handsome youth who turned all the American girls' heads, he had arrived in the United States on that famous visit of his mother, Queen Marie of Roumania. Now, middle-aged, he had still the air of a young man. Knowing he had been living for some years in the Abbazia San Gregorio, at the mouth of the Grand Canal in Venice, I asked him if he had ever seen the ghost it was reputed to possess. He was astonished that I should know its history. I confessed that in 1933 I had played with the idea of leasing this exquisite little palace. Splendidly situated at the end of the Grand Canal, it has a magnificent panorama of the Santa Maria della Salute, the Doges' Palace, the Campanile and the Riva degli Schiavoni as far as the Lido. The Abbazia has a fine wrought-iron grille through which the passer-by on the Grand Canal has an enticing glimpse of the galleried cloister, courtyard and well-head within.

---

* There is the famous migration of Leonardo da Vinci's drawings now at Windsor Castle. They were among the notes and drawings bequeathed by Leonardo to his pupil, Francesco Melzi, acquired after his death in 1570 by Pompeo Leoni who took them to Spain, and in due course by the Earl of Arundel who took them to England.

But the place was then in too dilapidated a state for my purse. Later it was bought by Prince Mdvani on his marriage to Barbara Hutton, the Woolworth heiress.   They spent a large sum of money on it and outraged the Venetians by cutting windows in the upper wall looking on to the fondamenta and the great flight of steps of the Salute church.   When later I went to the Abbazia I forgave them for they had opened a window on to one of the finest prospects in Europe.   The fourteenth-century Abbazia belonged to the adjacent church of San Gregorio, now a roofless ruin, in which was once kept the skin of Marcantonio Bragadin, who was flayed alive by the Turks in 1571, an event prior to the stripling Don John of Austria leading a united fleet that destroyed eighty thousand Turks at the battle of Lepanto.*

March 19.

Last night at 3 a.m. I awoke and found that my elusive Muse had twitched my blanket and commanded me to write.   She visits me now after long periods of absence, whereas in my youth she was my constant companion.   But now, as then, she is just as insistent.   I turned on the light, found a pad and pencil and wrote some lines on the painting that had delighted me at Santo Domingo's.

Madonna and Child with Parrot
God was Thy Father but the hand of Man,
Infant, hath surely made Thee twice divine :
The enamelled flowers and the green-plumed bird
Attend Thee, on the breast of Her whose shrine
Glows now before us.   Death twice finds defeat—
Since the transcendant love enfolds Thee, Child,
And the immortal brush of one long dead
Keeps Thee from Time's contagion, undefiled.

Lunched with a friend in his apartment at the back of the Prado.   With his wife and infant son he is happily established here on some mission for a British company.   He is enjoying

---

* While the Venetians, Philip II of Spain, and the Pope, collected their fleet the Turks took Cyprus, capturing its defender, Bragadin.   They emasculated, hanged and carved in shreds, four of his captains and massacred the Venetian soldiers, wives and children before his eyes.   They then hung him up by the hands in the public square and skinned him alive.   Mustapha had his skin stuffed and carried the puppet at his masthead to Constantinople.   A ransomed Veronese in Constantinople, indebted to Bragadin, broke into the Turkish arsenal, retrieved the ' trophy ' and succeeded in getting it to Venice.   It is now in the church of San Giovanni and Paolo.

Spain with youthful zest. A few days ago he gave me a terrible shock by calling me up to announce the death of a mutual friend, Francis R. Flamboyant, kind, with irrepressible spirits, Francis lived like a Renaissance prince. He had a large house in Scotland where he entertained lavishly. Two or three car-loads of his guests would set off for picnics on the moors. He was always going somewhere, by ship, boat or plane. He was so fond of the United States that he took steps to emigrate there, but always suspended final action. He visited it yearly on busi-ness, living regally at the Plaza Hotel. He once descended on me by air at Palm Beach, hired an electric bath-chair, and insisted on whisking me up and down the ocean front. He bought with-out restraint, and, having a passion for American gadgets, always came home with an enormous amount of luggage. Once, when we crossed together, on the *Queen Mary*, he had a bill of fifty pounds for excess luggage. He transported a frigidaire, an electric washing-machine, a television set, an electric fruit-masher, two complete divan bedsteads and innumerable oddments. For these he had to charter a special lorry at Southampton but the beds would not go in. They made a separate journey by rail, were lost, and arrived in Scotland two weeks later, where they were collected in triumph and made immediately ready for guests who had arrived that day. In order that no one should make the length of the London-Inverness journey an excuse for not visiting him he had scheduled sleeping reservations on the night express.

Francis suffered from a duodenal ulcer so we compared notes, but I could never take his ailment seriously as he ate and drank everything he fancied. His table was lavish. When I departed from Victoria Station for Monte Carlo last November he touched me by coming to see me off at nine in the morning. He loathed rising early and this had entailed a journey across London from his hotel. For a parting gift he gave me a black Shetland wool scarf (he owned a woollen mill) that was a blessing during my illness at Monte Carlo. He had promised to join me there, never came, but arranged a rendezvous in Madrid. Meet-ing my friend in Paris, and invited to motor to Madrid with him, he set off, but the food en route made him so ill that he flew home on arrival there, went into a nursing home, was operated on, and removed to his home in Scotland. A few days later he had a hemorrhage and died before he could be got to the hospital.

I shall always lament that I missed him here by a few days. Francis professed being a convert to the Roman Church and sometimes descended to breakfast dressed in a cardinal's robes, but at his death it was revealed that he had never ' gone over.' Oddly enough, he never liked Italy but he flew his local priest to Rome for the *Anno Santo*. He enjoyed every moment of his life, only some forty-five years, and gave a lot of pleasure to people. One can want no better epitaph.

March 21.

Santo Domingo, to whom I sent a copy of my lines on his painting, is delighted and says he will make a reproduction of the picture with the poem for his next Christmas card.

There is a small colony of young Englishmen here who have fallen in love with Spain. They make some kind of a living, variously employed, teaching, doing jobs for UNESCO, the British Institute, or broadcasting for the English service of Radio Madrid. They love the summer heat, the late hours, the pleasant café life, the boulevards and the galleries, above all the cheap living and the courtesy of the Spanish people. There is a café, the Gijón, on La Castellana Avenue, where towards eleven at night all the poets, artists, novelists and critics forgather. I find they also forgather there after lunch. I am constantly baffled by the elastic hours of this city.

Yesterday evening we were amused to discover that a young Spaniard, Ignacio Rived, who sat opposite at our table, had translated my first book into Spanish.

This afternoon one of my English companions, a tall blond young man, a Cambridge graduate with something of the scholar-gipsy attitude to life, conducted me to a little street in which is the house once occupied by the dramatist, Lope de Vega. It happens to be in a street inappropriately called the Calle Cervantes. There is a little garden behind the house with a corner table and chair at which it is said he wrote many of his plays. They ran into hundreds—" More than a hundred of my comedies have taken only twenty-four hours to pass from my brain to the boards of the theatre," said de Vega.* He dominated Spanish letters in the opening of the 17th century, much as Voltaire dominated French letters, and like him, he defied the law, was banished,

* y mas de una, en horas venticuatro,
  passeron de las musas al Teatro.

dealt with his noble patrons on an equal footing and was a power
in the land.   Papal legates called on him, Pope Urban VIII gave
him a diploma and an Order which made him both Doctor and
Frey.   He fought with the Armada in the English Channel.   He
had a streak of religious fanaticism, took priest's orders, and every
Friday scourged himself until the walls of his rooms were sprinkled
with blood.   He had a small chapel placed in his house so that
he could look upon its altar from his bed.   Sorrows visited him
at the end of his life.   His only son died and from this house his
beloved daughter, a nun, eloped with a young blood, leaving
him old, sick and alone.   The house has a long room which
contains his library and in the attic is the bedroom, with a small
terrace, in which his son slept.   The whole house has been ad-
mirably restored and even the roots of old trees were dug up in
the garden and analysed so that the same trees, as in his day,
could be planted.   One could almost hear the coach of a Grandee
arrive at his door, making a call of homage to Spain's most famous
figure.

March 28.

The Duke of Berwick and Alba asked me to lunch at his apartment near the Martires de Alcala.   Nearby is his roofless, gutted
Palacio Liria which was burnt out in the 1936 revolution, with
the loss of many great art treasures.   The Duke now occupies
a floor of an adjacent apartment house and he has turned the floor
below into a museum and gallery for the treasures that were
rescued from the ruined palace.   He maintains this gallery
for the use of the public.

The Duke is one of the most picturesque figures in Spain to-day.
A man of great wealth, handsome, cultured and of much personal
charm, he carries a list of titles that sound a fanfare through
European history.   He was an extremely popular figure when he
represented the Spanish Government in England, but showing
too much independence for the mind of a dictator, he resigned
and maintains his freedom of action and thought with considerable
courage.   The possessor of castles, palaces and great estates,
he does not apologise for filling the much-abused role of aristocrat, Grandee, landowner and art connoisseur, as well as a
princely entertainer.   An excellent conversationalist, a perfect
host, informatively aware of the treasures he possesses, and the
historic roles his ancestors have played, he has some foibles,

endearing rather than irritating. He is, for instance, not only a descendant of King James II of Great Britain but also of the dreaded Duke of Alba whose persecutions in the Netherlands sound such a dreadful note throughout Motley's *The Rise of the Dutch Republic.* The Duke, however, regards Motley as a libeller, and his history as woefully wrong in its estimate of his famous forbear. My host did not hesitate to descend upon Oxford and give a lecture there " to defend the good name of one who has not, to my mind, always been treated with justice by your historians." The great Duke, whatever the historical truth concerning his conduct in the Netherlands, had pleasant relations with England. He was present at the wedding of Philip II with Mary Tudor, and his duchess tried to rescue the doomed Lady Jane Grey who, in gratitude, left her a green parrot.

It is tantalising to be a guest in a house in which every yard of the walls holds a treasure. In one superb apartment, as we went through to lunch, I noticed a Zuloaga of the duke with his dog, and a Madrazo of his father and mother. A portrait of the first Duke of Berwick, a natural son of James II by Arabella Churchill, the Duke of Marlborough's sister, from whom the Spanish duke is descended, gives him a distant kinship with Winston Churchill.*

The history of the portrait provoked from my host the comment, " Yes, we are all bastards ! "

At lunch the Duke's only child, the young Duchess of Montoro and her husband joined us. They were married a few years ago in Seville Cathedral with a pageantry that revived the ancient splendour of Spain.

After lunch my host took me and an American guest, Otis Taylor, to the floor in which is housed his great collection. The manuscripts include the letters and maps of Christopher Columbus, to whom the Duke is related, a letter from Drake, in most courteous terms addressed to the great Duke of Alba, a letter from Titian, dated Venice, Oct. 31, 1525, a receipt from Lope de Vega to the house of Alba for his pension of 4,000 pesetas, and a letter from Bonnie Prince Charlie repudiating his father's

---

* The kinship with Marlborough is very faint for the male line of the house of Churchill is extinct. The Duke of Marlborough's daughter married Charles Spencer, Earl of Sunderland, and under a special dispensation their progeny became the Dukes of Marlborough. The present-day Churchills are Spencers, as Winston Spencer Churchill is always careful to denote. In 1807 the fifth Duke of Marlborough by Royal licence assumed the name of Churchill.

actions.* There is a wonderful collection of tapestries and
pictures too numerous to name in detail. Seeing portraits
of the Young Pretender, his brother Henry, Cardinal Duke of
York, and of the Pretender's wife, the wayward Countess of
Albany, near a bust of Alfieri, her lover, I learned with astonishment that the Countess was related to the Albas, her sister being
the mother of the fourth Duke of Berwick and Alba. Among
several Winterhalter portraits there is one of the Empress Eugénie,
sister of my host's grandmother. She died in his palace in Madrid
and extracted from him a promise that he would be married in
England, which he kept. The Duke has a fine Sèvres vase with
a painting recording the reception of a Chinese delegation by the
Emperor and Empress, with the young Prince Imperial standing
by the throne. Apropos of this occasion, the Empress told the
Duke that the chief delegate, having scrutinised her and her ladies-
in-waiting, turned to the Emperor and said, "Your first lady is
very beautiful but the rest of the harem is much too old ! "
    At lunch the talk turned on Velasquez and his works, of which
the Duke has some fine examples. The famous portrait of Pope
Innocent is now in the Doria palace in Rome. The Duke told
me that this portrait is not the actual painting made by Velasquez
from the sitting given by the Pope. The artist made originally
a small study of the head and this went eventually into the Hermitage collection at St. Petersburg. When the Bolsheviks at the
beginning of the Russian revolution wanted a dollar loan they
approached Andrew Mellon, the United States Financial Secretary of Finance and, knowing he was a wealthy art collector,
offered to sell him works out of the Royal Gallery. Among the
pictures he bought was this first study by Velasquez, now in the
Mellon Art Gallery at Washington.† The Bolsheviks did not get
their loan. My host told me that the Duke of Wellington has
another version at Apsley House.
    Speaking of Rubens the Duke of Alba said that when the artist
went as ambassador to Spain he advised Philip IV to send
Velasquez to Rome. On the death of Rubens, Philip approached

---

* " I protest against anything whatsoever my Father has done or may do against
my Interests and Personal Effect."—10th December, 1755.

† The Mellon sketch is 19½ by 16½ in. It was originally owned by Robert Walpole
and later by Catherine the Great. The Duke of Wellington believes that his *Innocent X*
is a copy made by Velasquez for Philip IV, captured after the battle of Vitoria, in
King Joseph Bonaparte's baggage, and given to the Iron Duke by Ferdinand VII of
Spain.

the artist's widow, Helen Fourment, being anxious to buy the pictures in his studio. She would not sell those in which she had posed nude but she was ultimately persuaded to sell him a picture on condition that it should not be shown in her lifetime. The picture *The Three Graces*, for which Rubens' wife was a model, now hangs in the Prado having come from the royal collection.

Before I left, my host very kindly offered me the use of his library. I shall see him again to-night when I am his guest at at a small dinner party, men only, at the Nueva Club on the eve of my departure for Seville.

March 29.

The dinner at the Nueva Club last night was a quiet affair of some elderly gentlemen of Spain, among whom I felt quite a juvenile. The Duke presided. About twenty were present, at one long table. My host apart, I knew only one of the company, my old friend Juan de Cardenas. I sat at my host's right, and had on my right Don Antonio Pastor. I am not sure who spoke the more perfect English. Señor Pastor, I learned, was at Balliol College, had been a lecturer at Oxford University and a professor at the University of London. He assisted the Prince of Wales in the preparation of his South American tour in 1931. He was at one time in charge of the Spanish Information Services in London. He is now director of Spain's leading bank. He was a fund of information.

I was somewhat overwhelmed by my host's kindness. Don Antonio remarked that it was a most interesting dinner. I agreed, for we proceeded from a delicious *boula-boula* to a memorable *truites à la gelée* (from which limpid Spanish river had this enormous trout been drawn ?) and then to a *rosbif asado à la broche*—perhaps selected because the guest of the evening does not now meet it on his native soil ! It was not the food but the company of which my neighbour was speaking, however. " Perhaps you will be interested to know that there are half a dozen Grandees at the table," he confided, and began to enumerate them. I looked at them with deep interest. They seemed most amiable and modest gentlemen. A Grandee of Spain stands, in English minds, for all that is pomp and circumstance, and sometimes arrogance. " Who does he think he is—a Grandee ? " we say, in protest.

I find the niceties of caste still entrenched here. Spanish society moves in a morass of titles, which can be appropriated from the female line by marriage. Charles V once ennobled the whole of the inhabitants of a town that pleased him by its warm welcome. It became necessary, therefore, to distinguish the more important nobles from the mass. The Order of a Grandee was an additional dignity conferred by the sovereign and included, in the time of Ferdinand and Isabella, such privileges as sitting uncovered in the royal presence, immunity from taxation and arrest, and the right even to make war on the king without being charged with treason. To this day the Dukes of Medinaceli, all powerful, recognise the King of Spain only by condescension, they having a better claim to the throne. At every coronation a messenger from the Duke appears protesting formally, in a loud voice, that the King occupies the throne with less right than the Duke, a descendant of Alonzo X. The response to the Duke's claim keeps the same form. The Court headsman calls on the Duke and by threats of decapitation induces him to sign a paper surrendering his claim. Honour is satisfied.

The rights of the Grandees were nicely defined. There were three classes : those who spoke to the king and received his reply with heads uncovered ; those who spoke to him uncovered but put on their hats to hear the answer ; those who awaited permission of the king before covering themselves. We may wonder how it ever got like that, but Spain has no monopoly of absurdity, for do not our own court officials walk backwards, contrary to nature which gave them no eyes in the back of their heads ? It is amazing, through all history, what one man has imposed upon another. King Joseph Bonaparte abolished the Grandees, then he, too, was abolished, and back they came in 1834, addressing the king as " My cousin." As a boy I had often read of Grandees. Did they not walk the poops of the Armada ? But I never dreamed of sitting at table with six of them and finding them such modest kindly gentlemen.

SEVILLE

March 30.

Yesterday morning I flew from Madrid to Seville. I confess to being terrified. We started an hour and a half late, which in Spain is nothing to remark. We took two runs to get up off the aerodrome. We were crammed with passengers, a crate of hens and boxes of fruit. The very pretty stewardess flirted with one of the passengers. We swooped and fluttered like an ecstatic butterfly over the grim grey landscape. There was one great thrill when we circumnavigated Toledo, granite-grey on its rocks, hemmed in by the deep ravine of the Tagus, spanned by the spidery Alcantara bridge. In colour and pattern it was exactly like El Greco's famous painting of the city as he saw it from a precipitous cliff. We made a perfect landing on what was really a rough field, for the aerodrome is in course of construction. Isolated, as is the fashion of airports, several miles outside the city, we waited for a bus to take us bumping over potholes into Seville. Yet the airline has an unbroken record of safety, and achieves all this with ancient machines and the greatest sangfroid and courtesy.

I arrived at the Hôtel Madrid, an old establishment, with a great patio, palms, parrots, balconies and fountain, to find my American friend Mrs. Boehm awaiting me. An inveterate traveller, she had just come up from Gibraltar having left the world cruise of the Cunard *Caronia*, which has been round by Africa. She was glad to leave the enervating *de luxe* atmosphere. It was all sumptuously arranged, including imported ' beauticians ' and orchids preserved in frigidaires. The cabins were so stuffed with millionaires and their gorgeously arrayed spouses that it was called ' the mink-and-orchid cruise.' There was an enormous plucking in every port when the dollar cavalcade landed. Socialist England is doing strange capitalistic things these days to float its Welfare State.

Tonight the Director of the British Institute here, Mr. Kearney, gave a dinner for me at the Hôtel Angleterre facing a square full of orange and rose trees in full bloom. The air is heavily scented with them. About twenty guests were present. With immense patience, someone had made a table decoration composed of flower petals in the form of a large Union Jack.

March 31.

I lectured last evening at the British Institute. A very friendly audience, quick in response although listening to a foreign language. At a buffet supper later two pretty señoritas engaged me in conversation and bowled me over with a close cross-examination on the characters in my novels. An author very rapidly forgets his old characters, especially those in books written over twenty years ago ; he is obsessed with his current creations. Readers overlook this time factor and find the author, when questioned, rather dim or stupid. We have to shed the creatures of our mind for the next blossoming. We are not *helichrysum* though we aspire to be *sempervivum* plants.

To-day I motored with my companion to Jerez de la Frontera, the centre of the sherry industry. Many of the great bodegas are in the hands of Anglo-Spanish families, settled here and inter-married but with strong filiations, for the boys are sent to English Catholic public schools, and the men order their suits in Sackville Street. We lunched with Guy Williams in his beautiful home and were conducted through the great bodegas of Humbert and Williams, the exporters of the famous Dry Sack. These bodegas, dim, immense in height, are reminiscent of cathedrals. We walked down long aisles and were given sherry from vats laid down by the Queen of Spain, the Prince of Wales and the Duke of York on their visit in 1927.

Out in the garden we found plucked fighting-cocks strutting around—a legacy of the time of Wellington's Army in the Peninsula War—a tame heron, and, high up on a chimney stack, some storks. These last provoked an astonishing story from our host. Some joker placed a goose's egg in a stork's nest. This was duly hatched. When the other storks saw the gosling they took it down to the ground and held a solemn council over it. The verdict reached, they despatched the intruder and then went off and killed the foster-mother—for infidelity !

We motored in the afternoon to Cadiz. The cathedral is the great attraction although it has no great architectural merit. At the close of the 18th century history was made there for Cadiz blossomed into a great musical centre. Haydn's chamber music was very popular and the cathedral authorities commissioned him to write some Passion Music based on *The Seven Last Words from the Cross*. When finished it was really a sequence of seven sonatas, with an introduction and an 'earthquake' finale.

After an exhortation preached by the bishop, based on each of the Seven Words, came Haydn's appropriate sonata, while the bishop prostrated himself at the high altar. Thus the composition took the form of *intermezzi* spacing a sermon. It was first performed in the cathedral on Good Friday, 1785, and was a sensational success.

I found Cadiz itself disappointing. Its name rings with so much lurid history of daring raids and Spanish treasure-galleons that one expects an exciting city. Its streets are not as picturesque as those of Jerez de la Frontera, whose floral windows are encased in ancient grilles. The town stands out on a promontory, with the famous bay and harbour on one side, the Atlantic ocean on the other. It is connected with the mainland by a long raised causeway, with white pyramids of salt taken from the salt pans dotted over the marshy landscape. It is treeless and the glare is frightful. There is little here to recall the great port founded by the Phœnician merchants from Tyre, or the scene of Drake's famous exploit of 1587, when he raided the harbour and burned all the shipping, "singeing the beard of the King of Spain." The town was sacked nine years later by the forces under the Earl of Essex. There followed the Duke of Buckingham's costly adventure, Nelson's bombardment, and Wellington's relief of the town twelve years later. It has been much plagued by the English for it was once a rich town to which the Spanish galleons brought all their treasure from the West.

Under the Romans it was famous for girls, gaiety and gastronomy. It invokes a memory of schooldays. Cornelius Balbus, Caesar's friend, came from Cadiz, that builder of the memorable wall recorded in a sentence by which we learned, in our first Latin primer, the nature of subject, verb and object. His nephew, the younger Balbus, was born here, a frightful blackguard who appears in a letter from Pollio in Cordova, Spain, to Cicero in Rome, written on January 8, 43 B.C. He was Borough Commissioner of Cadiz, decamped with the town's funds, and without paying the troops. He was ferociously cruel, as the letter informs us.

"Fadius, a soldier of Pompey, was pressed into a gladiatorial show. He was victorious over his opponent twice, but was not paid by Balbus. He therefore refused another engagement and, on pursuit, took refuge in the crowd. Balbus ordered his cavalry to charge it, and Fadius was captured. Balbus had him buried up to the waist in the gladiators' school and burnt him alive.   When the wretched man cried out 'I am a Roman citizen,' Balbus strolling about in slippers, with his tunic undone, retorted, 'Then go off, and appeal to the people !' He has also thrown Roman citizens to the wild beasts, including a deformed pedlar well known in Seville. Such is the monster I have had to deal with.   I will tell you more when we meet."

To-day the white walls of Cadiz sleep and crumble in the sun, recalling their Moorish masters for over five hundred years.

On the way back to Seville, in the falling of the sun, we saw all the colour and loveliness of the Andalusian landscape, gold, mauve and scarlet, soon to vanish in the withering heat of summer.

April 2.

Last evening I dined with a young American medievalist, Dr. Adele Kibre.   She is a remarkable character, shy, but with deep reserves of knowledge and shrewdness.   During the war she was in Stockholm on the U.S.A. Government Information Service. She is a specialist in medieval manuscripts and is living here in charge of a small staff employed, under a U.S. University and Government grant, in making copies of all the manuscripts relating to Spanish America, drawing on the great collection in the Archives of the Indies.   She lives the life of a scholar recluse in the vast Andalucia Palace Hôtel.   She resents the turmoil of the *Semana Santa* (Holy Week) and the *Feria* (Fair) because the hotel is then crammed with visitors and she cannot follow her habit of wandering about the corridors between midnight and dawn, an owl-like pastime that soothes her nerves.

At the next table to us ex-King Umberto of Italy was dining. He has come over from his place of exile in Portugal where there is a colony of ex-crowned heads, pretenders and other aspirants. I had not seen him for seventeen years.   When last I saw him, in Venice, he was young and debonair, a popular Crown Prince newly married.   To-night he seemed careworn, and the old vivacity of his manner had vanished, as had also most of his hair.   He lost his throne by a very narrow vote, but the gulf has widened since then, with revelations about his inglorious father who shared the loot with Mussolini and dismissed him in the hour of reckoning.

Yesterday morning after having ascended the great Giralda Tower I went down a narrow street to a little workshop where they make the costumes for bullfighters. It carries the tradition of over a hundred years. Joselito, Gonzalos, Manolete, all the great heroes of the arena have ordered their costumes here. I found a dozen girls patiently sewing thousands of sequins with gold thread to the silk jackets, stiff with embroidery. A costume costs some 7,000 pesetas (£160) and upwards. Friends tried to persuade me to order a waistcoat. When could I wear this parrot-sheen and what on earth should I look like ! Once upon a time, perhaps, but my fancy-dress days are over and I have grown immune to that disease of tourism, the acquisition of useless objects, which alluring in their own setting, are embarrassing and preposterous when transported to other climes.

Yesterday I learned in the Ambassador's Court of the Alcazar that the beautiful gesso, so wonderfully carved and a feature of much Moorish decoration, is not of plaster. It is composed of honey, powdered straw and chalk. Carved while soft, it hardens rock-like in the air. It has endured for seven centuries.

I have met again my three young Englishmen; Moorsom, Ley and Fitzgibbon. Two of them live in Madrid. One of them astonished me by saying that a descendant of Sir Francis Drake is living in Seville and was in prison during the Civil War. With my compatriots there was an intense young Spaniard, Jesu Pardo de Santayana, a kinsman of George Santayana. They are all rewarding company with their informed enthusiasm. Fitzgibbon has settled in Spain, married a Spanish girl, is rearing an Anglo-Spanish family and teaches at the British Institute.

Yesterday he took me to six churches to see the decorated Madonnas with whose history he is familiar.

April 4.

We are in the midst of the hysteria of Holy Week. Towards dusk the heavily-decorated Madonnas, carried aloft on great floats borne invisibly by sweating stevedores, start their long processions to the cathedral from which they return after midnight. Ablaze with candles and jewels, each Madonna is escorted by a Fraternity in monks' habits, with tall conical cowls that have slits for the eyes, suggesting the horrors of the Inquisition. They all carry long candles. It is part of the Middle Ages that have never left Spain, a blend of religious ecstasy and fanatical theatricality touched with festive pantomime. This is an opportunity for the young clerk to get off his stool, don a habit and cowl, carry a candle, walk barefoot, and make a ' date ' with a señorita at the barrier. While the procession pauses, the stevedores, drawn from Seville's docks, come out from under their Madonnas and rush into the nearest bodega for ' a quick one ' before resuming their burden.

The costumes of the Madonna are fabulously rich and beautiful. They are much admired in the churches before they set out. The great ladies and the lesser lend Her their jewels. We have been to see about a dozen Madonnas to-day, all ablaze with diamonds, emeralds and rubies. The young Duchess of Montoro has lent seventeen million pesetas' worth of jewels to the Madonna in the church of San Lorenzo. They were carefully stitched on to the Madonna's embroidered train, seven yards long. The Duchess was present in the dark church to give the signal for the start of the procession through the crowded streets.

We are wilting. The crowds, the frenzy, the packed streets and hotels, the moonlit patios, the enchanted gardens of the Moorish Alcazar, haunt of Pedro the Cruel, the long processions of jewelled Madonnas in a quivering blaze of candles, the vast dim cathedral through whose gloom the glittering effigies pass, the late hours merging into dawn before the quiet comes, the scent of orange-blossom heavy in the warm air—it is all wonderful but exhausting.

April 6.

We motored to Ronda to-day. It surpasses everything I had expected. The stupendous gorge, the multi-coloured pattern of the vast *vega* displayed below, the high-arched bridge that seems to span heaven itself, the house of the Moorish Kings above the internal passages carved out of the cliff-rock, descending six hundred feet to the river bed, from which the Christian slaves had to carry up water, the streets climbing the mountain side, with the flower-like iron grilles of garden walls framing lovely vistas, all this and more we saw in the vivid golden light of an Andalusian spring.

April 7.

I went with young Moorsom and Pardo de Santayana five miles out to Italica to see the Roman arena. How very ruined

THE AUTHOR

as seen in Rome by Felix Kelly

THE AUTHOR
as seen in Rome by Manuel Huidobro

and dead it all is ! Yet once this was a thriving Roman city, founded in 133 B.C. by Scipio Africanus as a settlement for his veterans. It gave birth to three Roman emperors, Trajan, Hadrian and Theodosius. Now there are only a few hovels, scratching hens, pestilent gypsy beggars. Did a mob once roar for blood as the wild beasts came out of the dens we can still see ? Such silence, such utter desolation to-day.

Last night I wrote, on coming in, from 2 a.m. until 5 a.m. and then went out into the golden dawn. The Giralda Tower rose like a lily in a saffron and emerald sky. In the marble-paved Plaza Neuva the scent of roses and orange blossom in the fresh dawn was overpowering, the perfumes of Araby haunting the old Moorish city. A flock of doves settled in the date palms. This Plaza once held the cloisters of a convent, and the patio contained a statue of the Comendador, a Roman in his toga. It was the statue of the supper scene in Mozart's *Don Giovanni*, a son of Seville. I walked on until I came to the long grille before the Royal Tobacco Factory, actually a vast rectangular baroque palace. Carmen was one of the two thousand *cigarreras* once employed here. Bizet, composer of the opera, was never in Spain, yet gave us what purports to be its most characteristic music. To-day the factory stands empty and is to become the new seat of the University. From there I went on through the Park, in whose dense foliage myriad birds were fluting in the dawn, and thence to the delightfully named *Paseo de las Delicias* beside the Guadalquivir River, until I came to the Tower of Gold. I watched a boat come up river and wondered how long it was since the last galleon freighted with American gold berthed there in the shadow of the tower built by the Moors in the thirteenth century. What a city of fragrance, of long memories, of great names, for down its streets went Columbus, Velasquez and our own Black Prince.

April 8.

The Duke of Alba had suggested I should visit his Palacio de las Dueñas here, and gave me a card to his secretary. When I called this morning his young son-in-law, the Duke of Montoro, greeted me and showed me over the house. It was built in the fifteenth century, and was formerly a Moorish palace that once had eleven patios, nine fountains and one hundred marble pillars. It is still a fairy-tale palace rising behind a courtyard where a

c

bright fountain splashes in a setting of palm, myrtle and orange trees. There is a great outside staircase up which twenty men could walk abreast, leading to a long upper gallery, arcaded and open. The palace contains beautiful pictures, tapestries and singular trophies such as the mounted head of the bull killed by Joselite the great toreador.

This afternoon we had tea with the Kearneys. An English girl of singular beauty was a fellow guest. It transpired she was the wife of a young Englishman, who was buried deep in some remote Andalusian village during research on Spanish dialects. We are an astonishing race. We get everywhere. I recall an English spinster, complete with paintbox and easel, who was sitting in the middle of the ruins of Agamemnon's bathroom, scene of a classic murder, on the very pinnacle of a hill in remote Mycenae, twenty punishing donkey-miles across the Grecian plains. The Kearneys' windows overlooked the old belfry of San Isidoro, embellished with coloured tiles. At six o'clock a tiny boy in a scarlet and white *cotta* took a rope from the belfry wall and began to toll the great bell that swung in and out of its Gothic arch. He went up and down with the rope like a little monkey and once or twice I thought he would never come to earth again for the bell hesitated at the top of its swing, undecided whether to go the whole way round. The church into which we went later had a masterpiece by Roelas, depicting the death of the titular saint, which Murillo once studied.

April 9.

I have been to the great bullfight in the Arena. Everyone seemed to be going there this Sunday afternoon. The vast arena was familiar to me from David Roberts' famous studies. The crowd rose tier on tier above the great sanded arena. The expensive seats at bullfights are in the shade, on the side of the President's box. The pageantry of the opening, with the procession of toreadors in their gaudy costumes, was superb. Six bulls were on the programme, six bulls that would never leave that sanded death-pit alive, no matter how bravely they fought.

The Englishman will never understand the vogue of the bull-fight. He finds it cruel, unsporting—and dull. Every bull meets the same fate, it is dead within twenty minutes of entering the arena. On the death of the third bull, stabbed to death in the neck after it had fallen to its knees from loss of blood, I left. I entirely agree with a Mr. Finck, who recorded his impression over fifty years ago. " Six bulls were killed. I left after the third had been butchered and his carcase dragged out by mules, equally disgusted and bored. . . . No man who has a sense of true sport would engage with a dozen other men against a brute that is so stupid as to expend its fury a hundred times in succession on a piece of red cloth, ignoring the man who holds it." I made the surprising discovery that the bulls die of shortness of breath and from slow bleeding. The provoked bull rushes around the ring, and never having had the functions of a racehorse, or having violently exercised itself, it is soon winded. It is induced to gore a stationary blindfolded horse while a man on the poor animal's back sticks a pike with a six-inch prong into the bull's shoulder muscles. The bull exhausts itself by trying to lift the horse with its horns, sometimes getting under the padded coverlet, in any case breaking the horse's ribs if not goring its belly. The bull, now bled and winded, the matador walks into the arena and sometimes has the utmost trouble in getting the bewildered brute to charge. Our third bull, dazed and exhausted, suffered its head to be lifted by the horns to enable the matador to insert his sword in the vital spot ! He failed three times to give it the *coup-de-grâce*, and finally the poor beast was stabbed to death as it lay twitching on the ground. I came away while the crowd hooted its displeasure at this clumsy finale. Like bridge-players *aficionados* are often more exasperated than entertained.

They tell me football is making such strides in public favour that they have come to an agreement not to have a match on the day of a bullfight. But so much romance and tradition about bullfighting is bred into the Spaniard from childhood, and it offers such a chance for the peasant lad to spring from poverty to wealth and fame, that it will be a long time before the sport dies out. We have cruel sports ; we hunt the fox, the otter, the stag, but five thousand people do not pay for ringside seats to see and cheer the spectacle of prolonged slaughter. I have no objection to the prize fight. If two men like to pummel one another into a wobbling jelly, they are masters of their own fate, and well rewarded if they find a crowd depraved enough to pay for such a spectacle. If from the start the matadors went into the ring with the bull, and not when it is worn down, that would be a sporting contest with no inevitable end. Sometimes the matador is killed by the bull, for there are moments of great

daring, allied with skill, but the long odds are against the bull.
It never comes out of the arena alive. Why should it? ask the
Spaniards. They tell a heart-rending story of a bull so brave
that it was reprieved and taken back to the ranch to enjoy an
honourable old age, but a few days later it was killed in battle
with another bull ; which demonstrates the folly of kindness to
bulls !

GRANADA

April 11.

We left Seville yesterday and arrived at Granada. We are
actually living within the grounds of the Alhambra, for the Spanish Government has made one of its excellent tourist hotels out
of the old convent of San Francisco. What an enchanting setting
it has ! From a terrace gay with pink peach-blossom we look
across a valley to the high gardens of the Generalife. Beyond a
ravine rises the Albaicín, the hillside honeycombed with gypsy
earth-dwellings whose whitewashed façades gleam in the evening
light. A murmur of voices and music drifts faintly across to
us from this human anthill.

April 12.

The Mayor kindly arranged for us to see the gypsies dance.
We went to a cave on the Albaicín, by night. It was crammed
with gypsies in bright costumes, old, fat, young and slim. Three
young men strummed on guitars. The atmosphere was that
of a Turkish bath. Twelve brown young *gitanas* danced to a
rhythmic clapping of hands. I confess that after half an hour
of this whirling, stamping, and clapping I had had enough. It
seems to me that Spanish dancing lacks variety. I have seen the
best, for in New York the Marqués de Cuevas put down a dancing
floor in his drawing-room and, a great enthusiast, he had the
finest Spanish dancers perform. I saw Argentinita, and Antonio
and Rosario. There are no better in the world, and the greatest
of all guitarists played there, Segovia. But here we were jammed
in a low cave, with twenty fat gypsy mammas clapping their
hands, skirts swirling, dust rising, in an odour of sweating
bodies, with dark young gypsies shouting *Ole ! Ole !* and stimu-
lating passion by shaking their black hair down over their eyes.

Over and over again they whirled, stamped and clapped. These dances are straight out of Africa, or, possibly, have they travelled from the land of the whirling Dervishes ? The standard of beauty was low. Presently, in a pause, an old grandmother raised a curtain at the end of the cave and there lay a young woman in bed with a three-days' old baby at her breast. The infant stared and took in its future with dark eyes.

I am told that the greatest, the doyen of all dancers, is Lola Medina. She is now middle-aged. She married a Spanish pilot officer who had to resign his commission for having wedded a gypsy. She lives in a luxurious cave, as caves go, with good furniture, a small patio, and even a telephone. She is a great figure on the Albaicín and was a friend of the Spanish poet Garcia Lorca, who wrote a poem in her cave. To-morrow evening I am to be taken to see her. She has made history in another way. A great Spanish lady, a member of one of the first aristo-cratic families in Spain, a daughter of the Master of the Horse to King Alfonso, she has turned her back on society and, despite wealth and position, has gone to live with Lola Medina. From Court to cave in quest of the simple life.

April 13.

This evening I was taken to call on Lola. Leaving our car, we climbed up to the cave of the famous Flamenca dancer, sur-rounded by a swarm of gypsy children, all begging. We arrived at a white mound with an outer gate, unlike any of the other earth-dwellings, and rang a bell. We were then ushered into an outer cave room. Low, cut out of the chalky hillside, it was spotlessly white and very well furnished. The chief wall ornaments were highly-polished copper pans. Lola Medina received me with great dignity, a middle-aged, black-haired gypsy with fine hands and eyes. It was a five-roomed cave and like all these places whose chimneys consist of a pipe pushed up through the soil, it had electric light. Behind the sitting-room was a bedroom with a large French bed. I was astonished to see at the bedside a white telephone. I learned there was a safe in which the resi-dent Donna Tola, as she is called, keeps her jewels. The gypsies of the Albaicín are now quite accustomed to this aristocratic lady arriving and departing in a chauffeured limousine. On the wall of the sitting-room there was an inset tile. On it was the simple inscription " Here Garcia Lorca wrote a poem." He was in this cave only a few days before he was taken and shot by the Falangists, as he was held to have Red associations, being brother-in-law of the Socialist Mayor of Granada. They slaughtered all the Socialists of Granada in those terrible days of 1936. Later, when the death of the poet raised world-wide indignation, and created special feeling in Argentina, prejudicing a commercial treaty then being negotiated, the Falangists tried to put the murder at the door of the Clericals, with whom they were then on bad terms. The truth of the affair is still debated.

My hostess produced a bottle of sherry and we drank. During a pleasant conversation my eye fell on a photograph on the table. It was of Donna Tola, said my hostess. I looked at it more closely and could scarcely suppress a cry. Some twenty-three years ago, in October 1927, I had gone with my friend Count Armand de La Rochefoucauld to visit his parents, the Duke and Duchess de Doudeauville, at their beautiful Château de Bonnétable, in the Sarthe. There was then present, with her infant daughter, a very beautiful Spanish girl, the Vicomtesse de La Rochefoucauld, wife of Sosthène, the Duke's elder son. There had been a splendid ceremony in the private chapel of the great Saavedra palace in Madrid when the young Condesa de Torre Hermosa, as she then was, daughter of the Marqués de Viana, had united by her marriage with Sosthène, two great Spanish and French houses. One glance at the photograph on the table revealed who Donna Tola was, though twenty-three years had elapsed since we had met at Bonnétable. Lola Medina confirmed my recognition. Unhappily she is away in Seville, so we shall not meet.

When I left, my hostess gave me one of the little copper pans for a souvenir, as an ash-tray, and asked me for an autographed copy of one of my novels. She had read some of them. No hostess of a French château could have played the role better.

April 14.

I lunched to-day with the British Consul, Mr. Davenhill, a figure in Granada. Don Guillermo, as he is called, has been Consul here, an honorary post, from time immemorial, certainly for the last forty years, and his father held the post before him. He lives with two sisters and brothers in a house that once had a wonderful view. Behind it rises the wooded Alhambra Hill ; eastwards is the snow-covered range of the Sierra Nevada, and far below lies the great valley, or *vega*, where the Cross and the Crescent came into such bloody conflict. Alas, there is now no view of the *vega* for the great Alhambra Palace Hôtel has robbed the villa of its panorama.

Once upon a time this villa was a casino, devoted to gambling and Flamenca dances. Here Edward VII came as a young man. Years later, in 1906, Queen Alexandra visited it, not to gamble but to honour the British Consul living there. Everyone of note who passes through Granada calls on the Davenhills, whose hospitality has no limit. I found in the Visitors' Book, a signature that struck a note of sadness. It was that of the Duke of Wellington. It was not the Iron Duke's, but that of the young sixth Duke, a soldier destined at thirty to die in battle in Sicily within a short time of inscribing his name. He had been visiting the Spanish estate given to his ancestor with the dukedom of Ciudad Rodrigo. " Should not I have signed Ciudad Rodrigo and Wellington ? " he asked the Consul, shyly, as he blotted his name.

Before lunch we went sightseeing. The cathedral is very fine and the monument of Ferdinand and Isabella in the Royal Chapel is one of the most impressive things I have ever seen. A wonderful grille, like lace in its delicacy, separates the burial chapel from the high altar. In the vault underneath the monument, " too small for so much greatness," said the Emperor Charles V, lies his mother, Joanna the Mad, her husband Philip II, a son, and her father and mother, Ferdinand and Isabella. The carved altar-piece shows Boabdil, the last of the Moorish kings, surrendering the keys of Granada to Ferdinand.

Just beyond the Davenhill villa is the house in which Manuel de Falla once lived. It is now inhabited by the Duchess de Lecera. It has a long terrace-garden overlooking the great plain and the snowy Sierra Nevada. It contains a memorial statue bust. I learned that the composer who gave to the world the music of *The Three-Cornered Hat*, made famous by the Diaghileff Ballet in 1919, and many other compositions of world-wide renown, such as *The Fire Dance*, never dined before 2 a.m. and never went to bed, for he always slept in a chair ! He would have died in his beloved Granada retreat but he was driven to desperation by a neighbour who played gramophone records. Thus music drove out music and he died in Argentina in 1946.

After lunch I walked for the third time through the courts of the Alhambra and saw the rooms occupied by Washington Irving.

He found it almost in ruins and through his famous book made Spain conscious of its great possession. Its beauty is beyond words, the views from its windows and walls looking on to ravine, snow-capped mountains and vast plain, constitute one of the sights of the world.

I am in all the bookshops here and yesterday evening I had an experience both comic and pathetic. Entering a shop I bought three books and proceeded to autograph them before having them despatched. A young assistant served me. When he saw the name I had inscribed, he gave me one frightened look and then collapsed to the ground. Two other assistants carried the poor youth into a back room. I like to think it was because I was the first author he had ever seen in the flesh and not because I look as terrible as all that!

MADRID

April 15.

Back in Madrid. At Granada, my New York friend, Lucrezia Bori, gave a farewell tea-party. After many years of triumph as an opera singer at the Metropolitan Opera House, New York, she firmly retired while in good voice. Here in Spain she is on her native soil. It is strange to reflect that she carries the blood of the Borgias in her veins, for Borgia is an Italian corruption of Borja. The notorious Italian house was an offshoot of the distinguished Spanish line, and when Cesare Borgia's father became Pope he made his elder illegitimate son Archbishop of Valencia at sixteen and cardinal at seventeen. He also bore the title of Duke of Valentinois. The younger brother, murdered by Cesare, was created Duke of Gandia in Valencia. The Duke's descendant, Francis, was Master of the Horse to Charles V, but he renounced his offices and all his estates to take holy orders, became General of the Jesuits in Spain, and after his death in 1562 was canonised as St. Francis Borgia.

April 16.

Last evening our Chargé d'Affaires, R. M. Hankey, gave a cocktail party at the British Embassy for ex-King Peter of Yugoslavia. I have a particular interest in ex-King Peter, but I was quite unaware that he knew it. " I've wanted to meet you for

a long time," he said when I was introduced, " I'm your Prince
Sixpenny in *Victoria Four-Thirty*, aren't I ? " I had written one
chapter in that novel around the assassination of Peter's father
and the taking of the little Crown Prince from his preparatory
school in England back to Yugoslavia, to ascend the throne.
I had nicknamed my character Prince Sixpenny because the little
boy when asked by his schoolfellows how much pocket-money he
had, replied, " Please, I am allowed sixpence a week."

I confessed to the indictment now made. " Well, you made me
a much nicer little boy than I ever was," said ex-King Peter.
" But that's not why I shall always be indebted to you. You
know, you were the cause of my marrying my wife ! "

I was struck dumb with astonishment and before I could ask
for an explanation our host brought up other guests and I lost
my chance. All night the query has been in my mind. We are
both staying in the same hotel and this morning I called up
ex-King Peter's room, to learn that he had left early. And now I
may never know how I came to play the marriage-broker. As
the phrase goes, I am dying with curiosity.

April 17.

Little by little I am learning something of the political set-up.
The savagery of the Civil War was appalling and reveals the fierce
fanaticism that underlies the Spanish character. They slaughtered one another by the thousand, with a bestiality beyond
belief. There is now something of a truce between the Repub-
licans and the Falangists for no one wants another fratricidal war.
Now that passions are cooled both parties are somewhat ashamed
and horrified. One hears much of the poverty and corruption
of Franco Spain. The poverty seems greatest in the countryside where many of the farm labourers are little better than serfs.
Poverty has always been a feature of Spain and it is borne with
much dignity and, oddly enough, equality of spirit. Even the
beggar is a *caballero*. " Good morning, your Excellency," says
one tattered creature to another, bowing. The persistency of
the beggars here is marked by their faultless manners, for everyone must carry himself like an *hidalgo*. The chivalry of Don
Quixote is a common cloak. When the Spanish aristocrat took
on the veneer of French culture the common man carried on
the old formal Spanish courtesy. He wore the cloak, he went
into the bullring, he kept the formal speech of the ancient régime,

C*

he was, in short, the new Don Quixote sprung from Sancho Panza.

To-day I walked through the meaner streets of the city, for it has no slums. I sat and talked, through my companion-interpreter, with the seedy citizens who haunt the dilapidated Plaza Mayor. Once it saw the vivid pageantry of Spain in the height of its glory. Now washing, " the short and simple flannels of the poor," to corrupt Gray, decorates the balconies once brilliant with the heraldry of Spain. It was from these balconies surrounding the great Plaza Mayor that our Charles I when Prince of Wales, and his companion the Duke of Buckingham, witnessed a great tournament given in his honour by Philip IV, for whose sister's hand the Prince had come to woo. Now the Plaza has a squalid air. The poor infest its once regal apartments, and lounge in the dust and sunshine. Mean shops carry on a fly-blown commerce in decaying arcades. Yet it is here one meets the Spanish people, not in the Ritz Hotel lounge or the Prado Gallery, or the popular nightclubs down the great avenues.

Beyond the Royal Palace and the Cathedral, there is a public playground filled with children and their attendant mothers. They are from the poorest classes but not one of them is dirty, or in actual rags or shows signs of malnutrition. In the villages one sees much dire poverty. The despair of the utterly beaten down is in their sallow faces and lack-lustre eyes. It is a look unseen in England, France, Holland, Germany, Austria and Italy. The anaemia of Spanish life comes from a deep unmitigated poverty and is not the product of one régime. It is foolish to accuse Franco, who is struggling with both tradition and Europe's hostility. The cure of this poverty will take a long time. The public conscience is awake in a few industrialists and large landowners ; the Franco régime has made some bold strides in housing, hospitals, education and social welfare, but, like the railways, some of the human ' rolling stock ' is worn out, finance is missing and vast areas of Spain cannot support their population. The mind, too, has to be conditioned. The mental corruption of the long and ghastly reign of the Inquisition with its spying, its dungeons, sham trials, and burnings cannot be eradicated in a generation. The Spanish people are long-suffering and when they do revolt they flare into insensate violence, more often directed against the Church and their own inexorable fate, than against any political opponent. Like much of the country, arid, lonely, burnt-up, the people take a hardness from nature, and they are merciless taskmasters to themselves. How seldom one sees the children smiling and making a joyous noise as in Italy ! The poverty of a once-affluent nation is always more debilitating than the poverty of one that has never known afflu- ence and, unlike Spain, has no memories of the days when she dominated the world. The bitterness of Spain's downfall is in her blood. The Spaniards preserve magnificent qualities of en- durance and they have a fierce touchy independence, but they have no innate gaiety of spirit, common to France and Italy, their great Mediterranean neighbours. They live in cities whose fading splendour of churches and palaces seems hostile to their basic needs. Their great cities seem to suck the life out of the country instead of vitalising it. Barcelona is a notable exception with its prosperous textile factories that clothe most of Spain.

Against all this a courageous enlightened few are waging a desperate battle. Europe has most unworthily stood aside pre- ferring to diagnose the illness rather than contribute to the cure with an economic tonic. Do we want Spain to die because she will not mumble the topical democratic *credo* ? Her people, hardworking, independent, deserve a different fate. I have come to Spain with no political bias and few prejudices. I am well aware of the frightful scenes that have been enacted in Spanish gaols in times of passion. I was long told in England that the Franco régime was oppressive, that freedom was dead, hunger rampant, misery walked the streets. For almost forty years I have earned my living as a trained observer. From what I have seen here I do not hesitate to say that many of the Repub- licans and Communists conducting propaganda against Franco Spain are either out of date, ill-informed, or wilfully perverse. Their English supporters, most of whom have never set foot in Spain, know nothing of its history and care little for its fate, are fanatical doctrinaires. Have we so much freedom in England to-day, bureaucrat ridden, with a payroll of seven thousand official spies on our domestic life, and strangled by Orders in Council doubtfully legitimate, that we can be so patronising ?

April 18.

This morning in the Academy of San Fernando I made another astonishing discovery. The Academy compares with our Royal Academy and elects distinguished artists to membership. It is housed in a somewhat gloomy palace and is famed for its collection of Goyas and Zurbarans. Here is Goya's little masterpiece, the curiously named *Burial of the Sardine*, a wild carnival scene. Zurbaran, long less-known, is now coming into wider fame and there are some who claim that he is the equal of Velasquez, which seems to me preposterous. He was a friend of Velasquez, who got him nominated Painter to the King in 1638. A peasant's son, he won early recognition and at thirty-one Seville gave him a house and appointed him 'town painter.' It was a disastrous acknowledgement for Zurbaran since all the rival artists in Seville ostracised him and prevented him from getting commissions.

After visiting the Academy's main gallery, I turned into a dark communicating room. Owing to the shortage of electricity there are certain days when the smaller rooms are not illuminated. This gallery was one of them but I chanced to discern in a corner a portrait that made me stop in my tracks. Here was Charles Roberts by Pompeo Batoni again ! The portrait is almost identical with the Prado one, and painted at the same time, but this is a three-quarter close-up study. The stance has been altered as also some details of the background. Again I wondered how, like its companion in the Prado, it had found its way from Rome to Madrid. The title was slightly altered. Instead of *Un caballero en Roma* this portrait was entitled *Caballero Ingles*. There was no available printed catalogue and apparently no record of how the portrait came into the Academy collection. I had a photograph of it taken.

April 19.

Lucienne and Juan de Cardenas came to lunch. He told me the story of his last interview with President Roosevelt when he was about to leave Washington, where he had been the doyen of ambassadors. At that farewell there were no speeches on either side.

ROOSEVELT. If I may say so, Mr. Ambassador, our two countries have had a similar experience of civil war, ending with no bitterness.

CARDENAS. If I may say so, Mr. President, your civil war was between men of high principles on either side. Ours was fought between men of honour and criminals.

ROOSEVELT. It all depends who you call criminals. In our country men who steal are criminals.

CARDENAS. In our country men who commit murders and atrocities are criminals. My secretary here saw his father and brother murdered.

The President was annoyed. No report of the leave-taking conversation was released, but six months later what the President had said was released, and not anything said by the ambassador.

I happened to remark at lunch that I had a commission from my American friend, Dorothy Quick, to buy a Spanish Madonna. Lucienne had seen one that morning in the shop of the leading antique dealer. It seemed just what I wanted. So after lunch we walked over to the shop and there I saw a Madonna, of the school of Alonso Cano, and fell in love with Her. She wore a silver crown, stood on a crescent moon, and carried an Infant of ineffable grace. I bought Her and had a great struggle not to buy for myself an alluring statue of St. Anthony of Padua. He carried, on a flat Bible, the sauciest of Holy Infants who dangled His chubby legs.

April 20.

Every day I cross from my hotel to walk for an hour or so in the Prado Gallery. What a superb collection of Velasquez, Titian and Rubens, but what a pity, the main gallery apart, that so many of the rooms are dark and unsuited for a picture gallery. When writing my book on Rome I became absorbed in the story of little Federico Gonzaga of Mantua, whom Pope Julius II took as a hostage at the age of ten. Such was the personality of the little boy, he ended by making the old man his slave. On the death of the Pope he was released and the cardinals kissed him, and all Rome cheered him, as he rode off home, Prince Charming. His later history was not charming for as the Duke of Mantua he had his mistress's husband assassinated. Here he is, as Titian saw him, robust, with a big black beard and a poodle. But he was not so robust for he died at the age of forty.

In the evening Don Antonio Pastor gave a dinner for me, about twenty guests, with a table of beautiful plate, and walls covered with excellent paintings including a delightful Goya. My hostess is herself a very fine landscape painter. There was a beautiful ' View of Madrid ' from her brush, as seen from Goya's vanished house, out of which Baron d'Erlanger took the Goya wall paintings

now in the Prado.   The whole scene at table looked like a picture
by Tintoretto.

April 22.

   Yesterday, except for a visit to the Prado, now a daily habit,
I had to stay in all day to answer letters, twenty-four in all.   What
a burden they can become !   After an active life in many parts
of the world one knows too many people.   I groan now when
Mr. A says " Oh, you must meet Mrs. Blank.   She's the sister of
Mr. Case who—— " or " Mrs. Gravestone wants to meet you,
so I promised her that I—— "   There are the thousands who
have heard me speak somewhere across two continents, a few
millions who have read my books in one language or another,
all, doubtless, admirable people and delightful to know, but
it simply is not possible to belong to everyone ; life is all too
short.   Then there are the people who are grieved because you
do not write letters to them when you are away.   These are
always the people who, having few resources of their own, are
bad correspondents and want entertainment.   The last thing
an author wants to do is to write letters.   Few have any idea
of the amount of business letters authorship entails: on agreements,
royalty accounts, agents, translators, publishers, book designers,
illustrators, multiple income-tax returns in various countries,
autograph-hunters, readers' letters, etc., etc.   Letters of this
nature comprise ten times the total of the creative writing I have
done.   My average mail is about fifteen letters a day of which
three-quarters must be answered.   I calculate that I write about
three thousand letters a year.   The cost of postage has become
quite formidable, for foreign rates are now prohibitive.   Nevertheless the pile of letters on my table each morning arouses
in me a pleasant curiosity.   If only one could be ruthless and
not answer them !

April 23.

   Dined last night with Moorsom, Ley and Pardo de Santayana
in the University Hostel where one of them lives.   It is a kind of
international house with students from all over the world.   I
learned that most of them pursued their studies at a cost of about
seven dollars a week for living ; plain living and confused thinking for the most part.   Yet what a delectable thing to be young,
poor, healthy and ambitious !   I was once all of these.   The

zest for everything is there, and Time has not given them a stock of invidious comparisons in a deteriorating world, or the fear of losing what they have laboriously saved, or of seeing the reputation they have built up crumble away.

April 28.

I was taken to-day to see an old gentleman of about ninety, the Marqués de Casa Torres. I began to wish I could meet a few more plain señors. The *titulos* fill in the foreground, in the background is a dense wood of *hidalgos*. In the eighteenth century there were 50,000 of them, and since then they have bred more marquéses, condes and condesas. It all adds to the gaiety of the scene.

To-day's Marqués was a charming old gentleman of ninety, very much alive. In his long life he had exercised a flair for pictures and here he now sat in his own gallery with several hundreds of them. He claimed to possess twenty-four Goyas, three hundred Michelangelo drawings, and five Velasquezs, including the reputed contemporaneous portrait of Cervantes. He told me that when he was fifteen his father gave him some money to buy a horse but that on his way to the auction ring he turned into an art dealer's gallery and bought a painting, to the disgust of his father. When I told him that I was much interested in an old Madrid house, called the House of the Seven Chimneys, where the British Ambassador lived when the Prince of Wales and the Duke of Buckingham arrived secretly in Madrid on their mission to win the hand of the Infanta, the Marqués informed me that Velasquez made a sketch of the Prince of Wales and the Duke visiting the House of the Seven Chimneys. He told me it existed and he would find out. I fear it does not. Velasquez painted a head of the Prince of Wales (Charles I) but it is believed to have perished in a palace fire. What would we not give for it !

My host conducted me around his gallery, where the pictures hang in five tiers, and then took me in to tea, maintaining a lively conversation with half a dozen of us. Later I went on to Count Mora's. He lives in almost the last of the great Madrid houses kept up in style. There are a magnificent ceremonial staircase, a ballroom with a painted ceiling, some fine Mignards, a giant Tiepolo canvas and a striking Madrazo portrait. There must have been a couple of hundred persons at the cocktail party, still in

full swing at nine o'clock.   The Countess took me to the library
and showed me six of my novels ;   moreover I found she *had* read
them.   Seldom have I been better housed.

My next visit that evening was to the very opposite extreme,
to squalor, and yet I was on a mission that was equally entertaining.   A few days ago, satisfying my incessant curiosity, I
went to the Museum of Reproductions behind the Ritz Hôtel.   It
is a great gloomy place filled with indifferent copies of famous
classical plaster casts.   It is used by young artists studiously
copying the sculpture.   One of these arrested my attention.   He
seemed to be not more than fourteen, a tiny pale-faced boy who
had to stand on a box before his easel.   On a large sheet he had
made a charcoal sketch of the back view of a winged Hermes.
The power and sweep of the sketch were arresting.   Through
my companion I engaged the boy in conversation.   Very shy,
we extracted his story.   Young Garcia lived in a little village
about one hundred and fifty miles south of Madrid.   The people
of his village, seeing his talent, thought it would benefit him to
visit the galleries in Madrid and to work in the Museum of
Reproductions.   They sent round the hat and raised enough to
pay his fare and to sustain him for a month in the capital.   Who
knows, perhaps they had found another Zurbaran or Velasquez !

I was so impressed by the boy's sketch that I asked if he would
like to sell it to me.   This stunned him.   It was the first offer
of the kind he had ever received.   When he had recovered breath
he said he would like to, but that it was not yet finished.   It
would be ready in three more days.   He gave me the address of
his lodging.   Thus it was that this evening, with my companion,
I went from the palace of Count Mora to the lodging of young
Garcia.   I found he had a tiny room on the third floor of a poor
lodging-house in the noisy Calle Cruz.   It had a small balcony
overlooking the street.   When we arrived it obviously was an
event in his life.   Three of his friends were in the room.   It was
so overcrowded by our arrival that the three friends went out on
to the balcony to make room for us.   Most of the space was taken
up by a large bed in which three of the boys slept.   The sketch
was pinned up on the wall over the bed.   In the faint light of
a dim electric bulb it seemed more powerful than ever.   I paid
him for the the sketch, and discovering that it had not been
' fixed ' I asked him to do this and bring it to my hotel on Sunday
morning next at eleven.

April 29.

Some Brazilian friends staying in this hotel took me by car to Avila to lunch with their host, the Marqués de Piedras Albas y Benavides. His home, the Palacio de Benavides, was for some years the home of Saint Teresa. One wing of the palace is filled with her library, and manuscripts relating to her, which the State has bought. Alas, having catalogued it, they have now left it in the damp, unheated rooms until they have the funds to proceed. It is to be hoped they will not delay too long or these precious manuscripts may fall into decay. We lunched in the garden, in the shadow of the grim stone tower of the palace. The leafy patio was dominated by a crude stone pig. It transpired that King Ferdinand had erected in Avila statues to Queen Isabella's two brothers who were not popular locally. The statues were defiled and the angry king gave orders that, having behaved like pigs, the local nobility should each keep a stone pig in his house.

The upper floor of my host's palace is devoted to a large collection of medieval armour and domestic ironwork. I should have enjoyed it more and have lingered longer if the cold had not been so intense. What an inner fire these saints must have had to sustain such cold !

When I was last in Avila I was so much impressed by the beautiful white marble tomb of Prince Juan, in the Dominican convent of Santo Tomás that I asked to visit it again. Prince Juan, the only son of Ferdinand and Isabella died in 1497, aged nineteen. He was a youth of infinite promise and the death of their only son was a terrible blow. The tomb, an exquisite thing, is the work of a Florentine artist. Near the Prince lies the beautiful tomb of his attendants, Juan de Avila and Juana Velasquez, also by the Florentine. Thus in death as in life the Prince is attended.

April 30.

A sad little comedy. Young Garcia was late. After waiting for some time I went down to the hotel desk to ask if anyone had called for me. Outside the door, beyond the big porter, stood a small boy, a roll under his arm, in company with a strange man. I went out to them and discovered that they had been trying to summon enough courage to go into the hotel. I took them up to my room. The sketch was proudly displayed by the man who said he was Garcia's teacher. He was overjoyed by my discernment and encouragement. Placing the small artist in front of the sketch which I pinned on my walls, I took his photograph. On departure, with much bowing, handshaking and *gracias* I gave the boy a copy of the Spanish edition of one of my novels. Their eyes opened wide. They had seen me in the bookshops and on the kiosks in Madrid ! *

This is my last day in Madrid. We lunched in hot sunshine on the terrace of the hotel, with rose trees in full bloom and the fountain and orchestra playing. I am sorry to go. To-night I leave for Barcelona en route for Paris. The odd and blessed thing is that throughout all this hospitality the old enemy has not stirred once, for which I am deeply thankful. I took a risk when I left Monte Carlo, and I am rewarded.

May 14.

It is drizzling in Paris—gone are the roses, the orange blossom, the golden sunshine, the dark-eyed señoritas, and the reasonable prices. " You'll find it worse in London," said an American friend. " Yes, for an Englishman," I replied, " but not for you." " How do you mean ? " " You buy your pounds at a 33 per cent discount with dollars on which you have paid about 25 per cent income tax. We change pounds devalued 33 per cent on which we have paid at a minimum 45 per cent income tax." " I'd get dizzy figuring that out," said my friend. " So do we," I answered.

---

* There was a sequel. I loaned the sketch to young Aubrey Cartwright, to hang in his rooms at Trinity College, Cambridge. It was much admired by his friends who, in the kindness of their hearts proposed raising a subscription to enable the artist to continue his studies. Alas, when I went to Spain the following year all efforts to trace Garcia failed.

England

May 24.

LONDON. The baggage survived the Cross-Channel mauling. The dear old crowded, grimy metropolis again, with the bright buses crammed with melancholy passengers. The same old smile on the faces of the two hall-porters at my club. If I could, I would arrange for them to be waiting on the other side of the Styx to welcome me on my final journey, as they have welcomed me on my journeying of thirty years. They even knew I had bought two new portmanteaux !

May 25.

Dined this evening at his club with David and his friend. David is now living in California after spells in Canada, and in Bermuda, where his people have built a villa. He is a bird of passage.

When he had taken his degree at Cambridge he went out with a cavalry regiment to India but after the orthodox life of polo-playing and bridge-playing, with officers' wives conscious of their beauty fading in the heat, and separated from their children at school in England, he became so violently anti-Poona that he resigned his commission and went off on a tour of the world. He has interests in a large jam manufacturing business. I learn that jam manufacturers are now compelled by the Government to adulterate their jams, for which they would have been heavily fined ten years ago.

The dinner at the club was surprisingly good but we could not refrain from comparisons. We had previously dined together some six months earlier at the University Club in New York, where all the dishes were too large and an air of happy prodigality reigned in the vast dining-room.

Here the dishes were sparse, a heavy late-Victorian gloom prevailed, created by large foggy mirrors, worn leather chairs, non-communicative members solemnly munching at their isolated tables, and an air of grandfather-stood-no-nonsense-from-the-servants, dispelled by the waiter's " There isn't no more of that, sir, you'll have to have Queen's Pudding." We retired to the bar and over our coffee rocked with laughter, near to tears at a reconstruction of " them was the days."

May 26.

Lunched at Claridge's Hotel with my French-American friend, Mrs. Basil Sydney, and her mother, renewing our New York and Venice associations. The dining-room was very bright and gay. The well-dressed crowd, the flowers, the food, all contrived to create a pre-war world when the pound looked the dollar in the face and no one would listen to Winston Churchill's warning of the wrath to come. My fellow-guest was Prince Alexander of Pless, a tall, handsome man who has not let harrowing experiences overwhelm him.

We naturally talked of his famous mother, the Edwardian Daisy Cornwallis West, bride of the haughty Prince von Pless who asked the family if they had ten quarterings to match the fifteen in his coat-of-arms. They produced twenty ! Her beauty and radiant personality captivated the Emperor Wilhelm. I learned that the vast Schloss Fürstenstein in Silesia had been looted and was in the possession of the Russians, and that his two young nephews were virtually prisoners in Poland. It is difficult to think of that magnificent house now a ruin. Despite its six hundred rooms they were still adding to it when I was there in 1928. It is singular to recall that Prince Alexander, or Lexel as he is called, had been born in Bruton Street only a few hundred yards from Claridge's and that at his baptism in the Chapel Royal his sponsors were Queen Alexandra, King George V (Prince of Wales), and the Crown Prince Wilhelm.

Other days and vanished kingdoms were recalled by two diners at the next table, ex-King Carol of Roumania and his wife, the former Madame Lupescu. I had last seen them when they had arrived, exiles, at Bermuda, en route for Mexico. It was a ménage not then regularised by the Church. The Governor of Bermuda was faced with an official dilemma. He could invite Carol to lunch but not the lady. I asked the Colonial Secretary how it was solved. He smiled and said—" The Governor had a good-looking young kilted officer as his attaché. We sent him down to take the lady out to lunch."

When leaving Claridge's I counted five Rolls Royces and three Bentleys, waiting outside. It costs, with depreciation allowed, at least £2,000 a year to run one of these cars. When a person in receipt of £7,000 a year is allowed to retain less than £3,000, with a steeply rising supertax on a larger income, how does he maintain a Rolls Royce? This, and apartments advertised in *The Times* at a rental of £1,500 a year, have always posed a problem for me. I sought enlightenment from the director of a motor sales agency. " A few of these cars are run out of capital. A man of means argues that when he rides in a hearse he will lose at least half of his capital in death duties, so he decides to ride during his life in a Rolls and leave nothing to the Inland Revenue harpies. Ninety per cent of Rolls Royce and Bentley owners run their cars, and pay for them, on a business expenses account."

Things Observed.

Those pre-war bands of itinerant musicians dressed in ancient frock-coats, top-hats, spats and service medals, who with a bow accosted one as " Colonel," are no longer with us but other representatives of the Ever Thirsty are still around. One accosted me in Berkeley Square to-day as " one Old Public Schoolboy to another." I asked him what Public School. " Eton," he replied promptly. I gave the beery humbug a shilling. A little later on another corner of the same Square the same Old Public Schoolboy accosted me. This time, in reply to my query, he said, " Winchester." " But half an hour ago, on the other side of the Square, you were at Eton ! You've come down in the world," I said. " So I have, sir ! " he replied cheerily, and fled. Old Wykehamists forgive me.

May 27.

Lunched with the Spanish Ambassador, the Duke of San Lucar el Mayor, at the Spanish Embassy. Since his tenure of the post he has made a reputation as the most hospitable of all the ambassadors in London. The beautiful Embassy in Belgrave Square, redesigned by the late King Alfonso and his Ambassador, the Marqués Merry del Val, once a highly popular figure in Court circles, is making history again as the scene of some of the brightest dinner parties in London. The Duke of San Lucar is a man of tireless energy, a fine linguist, and widely read as well as a gourmet of renown. My acquaintanceship illustrates the fact that one should not hesitate too much in asking a favour, as I have always done. One often has friends in unknown places. On leaving Monte Carlo for Spain this Spring I had learned of the difficulties alleged about crossing the frontier with typewriter and cameras. I wrote to the Ambassador stating my fears and my mission. He responded immediately in his own handwriting assuring me that I should encounter no difficulties, and enclosed an official letter of introduction with his own.

" I was delighted to receive your letter yesterday, and to-day, a quiet Sunday in London, when the telephone rings less often than usual and the post does not come at all, I wish to send you a line of thanks and acknowledgement. You may be happy to know that a very great friend of mine offered me a year ago, as the greatest proof of affection, a book, *So Immortal a Flower*, and because the book was such a lovely one I have always wanted to meet you since it came my way."

Now, back from my host's own country, which had given me so warm a reception, I was able to give him a personal account.

May 29.

A whole morning at my publishers, attending to publication of *And So To Rome*. I have had a happy association with them for twenty-five years. I always impress upon my colleagues, particularly the young ones, the great disadvantage of wandering from publisher to publisher in an endeavour to squeeze better terms. In the long run a publisher can only pay an author what he earns. " Advances " are illusory gains. It has long been a joke between me and my publisher that I have never drawn the advances stipulated in our contracts. An author who stays with one publisher builds up an interest, and the book trade knows where he is located for its order lists. A disastrous example of the rapacious wandering author was H. G. Wells. He went from publisher to publisher, stinging them for large advances that were seldom earned. In the end no one bid for him for he had become a bad investment. It was almost as sad an end of a great career as that of his colleague, Arnold Bennett, who, although he wrote a book, *How to Live on Twenty-four Hours a Day*, lived with such *folie des grandeurs* that, despite high earnings, he died almost bankrupt, leaving his dependants embarrassed. Yachts and fashionable cars and town houses are beyond the orbit of any author ; the time he spends enjoying them is time lost in paying for them. Writing is a one-man business and a whole-time job. You cannot float a company to produce your books.

My publishers inhabit the remaining part of a bombed building in Warwick Square, in the shadow of St. Paul's. All around them is the derelict site of streets and offices bombed out of existence. St. Paul's stands up majestically over the ruins, really visible at last. A city with any care about planning would keep the vista intact and from misfortune wring an artistic triumph. Hodder & Stoughton have made a small contribution. They have converted their ruined site into a gay rock garden whose flowers smile above the debris they spring from. There are countless stories of English tenacity in the face of disaster. Hodders stand worthily in that list. In 1933 their new building had a bad fire. In the great German raid around St. Paul's, Oct. 29, 1940, fire badly damaged their Warwick Square office and destroyed the building of their associate company nearby. In May 1941 an H.E. bomb demolished one third of their offices. The school at Bickley to which they had removed was completely destroyed by a direct hit from a V.I bomb, in June 1944. Mr. Ralph Hodder-Williams was one of four fire-watchers who crawled out, around 4 a.m., from the ruins unharmed. I was in America at the time and frequently received their business letters but there was never any mention in them of their misfortunes.

It was only when I went into the New York office of the Oxford University Press and saw the *Oxford Calendar*, 1945, that I learned that part of Hodder & Stoughton's offices had vanished. The *Calendar* had a drawing of the Oxford University Press in Warwick Square, showing a severed building adjacent, my publishers', wide open to the air, with the Hodder part vanished. I could see on the second floor, exposed to the day, the fireplace in the office where I had signed my contracts, and boisterous Mr. Percy Hodder-Williams, to whose faith in my star I owed much, had given me tea, saying, "Now, where's that new novel?"

May 30.

Motored to Princes Risborough to visit my old friend S. K. Ratcliffe. The countryside was lovely in its spring green and here one is on the foothills of the Chiltern beech woods. Of all trees the beech seems to me the grandest fellow in the forest. It has a lovely smooth trunk, clean strong branches, delicate green leaves through which the light pours in a golden flood. But its great glory is in the autumn when the forest floor is blood-red with the shedding of its leaves, and the falling sun gives an incandescent glow to a cathedral grandeur.

S.K., as we all call him, is now eighty-two and not a little like a beech tree in his sturdy evening glory. I had known of him for many years before I met him. Wherever I went on my lecture tours across the wide American continent, S.K. had been before me. We slept in the same inns, spoke from the same platforms, were met by the same committees and entertained by the same hosts. Then, one winter's day in 1927, as my train ran into snow-laden Buffalo, I passed in the Pullman-car a sturdy little man who sat clipping from newspapers. Just then a Western Union boy called " S. K. Ratcliffe ! " He stopped the boy. I then spoke to him for the first time, the apprentice to the veteran, and thus began a friendship of some twenty-three years. He knew the United States like his own back garden. He was a familiar and honoured figure on its lecture platforms. He had a gift of clear logical exposition backed by wide experience. In those days the policy of the British Raj in India was often venomously assailed in the U.S.A. Before its eventual acquisition of world responsibilities it took pleasure in applauding the liquidation of the British Empire.

India was S.K.'s particular province. He spoke from personal experience, having been editor of the Calcutta *Statesman*. He had held this chair throughout the heated Kitchener-Curzon controversy on the Indian Army. An unofficial ambassador, paying his own way, S.K. has served his country well for over thirty years. Our politicians seldom fail to receive public honours for their own well-heralded services ; in this, however opposed to each other, they find complete accord. S.K., as others of his kind, never sought and never received any official recognition. His pen, too, has never been idle. Even now, at eighty-two, he is an alert critic.

He was sad when it was borne upon him that, turned eighty, his days of transatlantic crossings and arduous train journeys over a wide continent, with one-night stands, were over. Underpaid, a journeyman in the poorly rewarded by-ways of journalism, his path was never easy or permitted relaxation. To-day a Solon, an Elder Statesman, he has no Cabinet Minister's or Civil Ser-

vant's pension to sustain an intellect as experienced and alert as
any in our midst.

I found S.K., to-day, blessed with the long companionship of a
wife whose arthritis serves only to increase his devotion, bright
and vigorous as ever in the little house on the Buckinghamshire
hillside. The political scene, personalities, and books preoccupy
him. A review for the *Observer*, *Glasgow Herald*, or *Manchester
Guardian*, is usually in hand. His fingers are on the keys of
life, and if sometimes he complains of the length of his tenure
it is only because capacity does not march with zest. I left
him after two hours of lively conversation in a garden gay with
apple-blossom. His sharp eyes twinkled as he bade me farewell
at his gate.

June 1.

In the early winter of 1926 I lived in a flat on the Promenade
des Anglais at Nice. There, at an evening party, I encountered
a singular youth of seventeen, Sir Francis Rose. It was rather
confusing since a friend of mine had a grandson, fourteen, who was
Sir Charles Rose. They were both boy-baronets and the latter,
being three years junior to Francis, was heir-presumptive to his
cousin's baronetcy ! After 1928 young Francis passed out of my
life. Last week at a cocktail party in Berkeley Square he came
into it again after twenty-two years. In that period he has found
an attractive wife and acquired some fame as an artist of the
avant-garde, with successful exhibitions in Paris, New York and
London. To-day I lunched with him and his wife in Chelsea
and we had a lively journey through the vanished years. Afterwards he took me to his studio to see his work. I should be a
hypocrite if I said I appreciated it. I was never pro-Picasso, I
am certainly not post-Picasso or pro-Moore. This limitation is
probably mine. In the air of this 'higher art' I find no oxygen.
If it is art then I do not like art. It was a jolly lunch and we
saluted each other across a gulf of murderous years.

June 3.

Down to Pilgrim Cottage to see my tenant. The old cottage
where I spent so many happy years and did so much work was as
lovely as ever. Blossom, pink-tipped, crowded the russet tree
over the well. The path to the door was a blaze of tulips, the
first roses were in bloom above the windows, and in one of the

poplars, trembling in spring leaf, a blackbird fluted. In many far places the vision of this corner of England has often come to me. And yet it is not as it was, and never again can be. The house and garden are full of ghosts, not sad ones, they are too young for that, but they crowd about me in the long backward look through twenty years—Louis Tissier, my French secretary, who loved this place so passionately, and died of consumption after four years of desperate struggle, too young to go at twenty-six ; Lucien Reid, my ward, who filled this old place with his boy's laughter, killed in North Africa at twenty-three ; beautiful Nadja Malacrida, who, leaving it after a month's dwelling here, wrote, with strange prescience, " May the ghost of my happiness haunt your garden forever," and was killed five minutes later when her car overturned, killed at thirty-six in all her charm and beauty ; zestful young Tony Allingham, grandson of the poet, who recalled with his classic beauty something of the grace of a Grecian day, smitten with a mysterious illness at twenty-nine and taken from life on a swift lapsing tide. How full and communicative was his happiness when he came over the hill to my garden, his pretty young sister Ann, seated beside him in their car. And she poor, lovely girl, doomed to a swifter and worse fate, a lieutenant in the Red Cross, murdered by bandits in Sumatra, aged twenty-five. When the ringing of the telephone breaks the quiet I recall, too, a summer's day when a mother's voice asked whether Pat had left the cottage for home. Yes, young Pat Southby had left, five hours earlier, on the short journey to his Oxford home. But that journey had ended when his motor-cycle skidded and he lay by a telegraph pole, dead at nineteen. " I love the old place. Can I come again ? " were his last words at the gate. Here, in this garden, I feel they all loved the old place, and come again.

Nor can I forget the ghost of one I never knew, Mrs. Ann Holt, an elderly American lady, who came here, saw two old cottages, bought them, and named her conversion *Pilgrim Cottage*, harking back to her adventurous English ancestors. She never returned to her homeland, she died here, and her ghost sometimes visits the garden she made and loved, and where her ashes were scattered. She left the cottage to an old English friend, a retired British Consul she had known in New York, who, in turn, lived and died here, and now lies in the country cemetery in view of its windows.

Here in the garden the verses of Gérard de Nerval come to my mind—

> *Où sont nos amoureuses ?*
> *Elles sont au tombeau !*
> *Elles sont plus heureuses*
> *Dans un séjour plus beau.*

June 6.

A very hot day. I walked this morning in St. James's Park, London's gem of gems. The fig tree by the bridge was heavy with small green figs that seem to grow simultaneously with the leaves, a lovely vision. It set me speculating on this leaf so freely employed in art galleries—it flourishes exceedingly in the Vatican's museums. Who first made it the symbol of modesty, or prudery ? It is incorrect to attribute to Adam the invention of the fig-leaf as a covering. When he and Eve, after tasting " of the Tree of the Knowledge of Good and Evil " became conscious of their nakedness (Why ? There is no proof that they had enjoyed marital relations and in any case should these be considered evil and cause a sense of nakedness ?), " they sewed fig leaves together and made themselves aprons." (Where did the first needle and thread come from ?) Though aprons are a much more adequate covering than fig leaves, the Lord God evidently thought poorly of their tailoring and Himself "made coats of skins and clothed them." (Who killed the first animals and started the oft-denounced fur industry ?)

Pondering on these problems I reached the end of the lake, where a solitary pelican stood upon a rock. He started a train of happy, sad memories. Was he the same pelican I had known thirty-one years ago ? In those exciting days I had a mother living in the Midlands while her ambitious son, who sent home thirty shillings a week, lived on forty and saved thirty, was seeking fame and fortune in London. A joke about a double chin and a liking for fish had caused him to name her Lady Pelican Pouch. The pelican in St. James's Park was created a ' cousin ' who wrote letters to Lady Pelican Pouch, describing life in London and suggesting a visit from her. The surprise of the postman delivering these letters can be imagined. " Does anyone called Lady Pelican Pouch live here ? " he asked, when the first letter arrived. My astonished mother had to admit that that was her name.

Since pelicans can live for eighty years it is quite possible that this pelican was my long-departed mother's correspondent. I have saved some of those letters. Here is one, dated May 7th, 1919.

"My dear Cousin Mary,

"I hope this finds you well and full of fish. My bill for it is enormous but, being on the staff, the Parks Committee takes care of it. I wish you would come up for a few days. There is always something doing here for one is in the very centre of things. Lloyd George went by the other morning—he lives just across the road in Downing Street—and I noticed he was duck-footed ! No wonder he shakes everything off his back !

"Yours devotedly,

PETER PELICAN.

"Duck Island, St. James's Park Lake, S.W."*

Spent an hour at Christie's and resisted a temptation to bid for an Utrillo. Lunched at the Club. At three o'clock I went to the new Italian Institute in Belgrave Square to see an exhibition of Italian book production. It was opened by the Italian Ambassador. Sir Kenneth Clark was the guest-speaker. I had last seen him in Venice where Harold Parsons had taken my friend Mrs. Murray Crane, Sir Kenneth, and myself to visit a Venetian art dealer who had a collection of Titians. No show-room could have been more historic for he inhabited the deserted Abbazia della Misericordia, old when Sansovino, Michelangelo's friend, renewed its façade. Along a cloister we came to the vast interior of the former chapel where assistants brought canvas after canvas to the easel, until we were obliged by the falling light to retreat to a small room with a better light. An astonishing exhibition closed with some works of Magnasco, now coming into vogue after long neglect.

I went from the Italian Institute to tea in the Clarges Street flat of a young friend. He is newly installed. I do not know what I coveted most, the eighteenth-century spiral staircase, with alcove, that leads up to his third-floor apartment, or the *settecento* painting of Venice, *scuola di Canaletto*, over his Regency fireplace. The little apartment had the atmosphere of a younger son come

* *The Times*, Nov. 14, 1951. The Minister of Works, replying to a question in the House of Commons asking what had happened to the pelicans that used to inhabit the lake in St. James's Park, said, " There were, until recently, two pelicans in St. James's Park, named Peter and Paul. One of the birds, aged sixty, died on October 13th. He had been blind for some time, and was kept on Duck Island. The other, a much younger bird, died on October 27th of lung disease."

up to town. His framed flower-pieces were in the mode of Jane Austen. In the evening I dined with my old friend Harry Cunningham Brodie at the Reform Club. He was avuncular to me when I was a very young man, newly come to town, and I dedicated to him my first novel *Scissors*, in 1923. Happily all three of us are in good circulation still. He gave me, as always, an excellent dinner.

June 9.

Young Aubrey Cartwright came and took me up on a former offer to play *paedagogus* to him on an Italian tour. He would like to bring with him his Eton friend, Simon Stuart. They are, at twenty, 6ft. 4in. and 6ft. 3in. tall. They have each done a year's Army service in Germany and in Malaya respectively. I fear I shall look like a desiccated clergyman between them on the Grand Tour.

I have known Aubrey since as a very young boy he crossed the Atlantic to spend Christmas with his mother in New York, after a war separation of six years in which time he had grown from a frail to a tall boy at Eton. His appearance in her Fifth Avenue drawing-room provoked, by his fair English complexion and blond hair, a dinner guest to exclaim, in the words of Pope Gregory, *Non Angli sed angeli*. His call to-day had a gracious background—to endorse his mother's invitation to her villa at Cap d'Antibes before we go on tour. So the autumn plan is made. Cap d'Antibes, Florence, Siena, Lake Garda, Zell-am-Zee, Salzburg. It is all somewhat perilous, I fear. Travel has the most disintegrating effect on the soundest friendships.

June 10.

To Sutton Place, near Guildford, the guest of the Duke and Duchess of Sutherland for a week-end party. I arrived in time for lunch. A house party of twenty guests, including the Chilean Ambassador and wife, the Persian Ambassador and wife, young Lord and Lady Duncannon, young Lord Westmorland, young Sir Edward and Lady Paston-Bedingfield, etc. ; a case of youth at the prow and a few buffers at the helm, a simile nautically wrong since buffers are always alongside.

This is one of the most beautiful Tudor mansions in England, built wholly of mellow brick, with wings at right angles to the great hall. Here one is at the very roots of English history, both tragic and splendid. Sutton Place was a manor settled by Henry VII on his mother, Margaret, Duchess of Beaufort, after the Battle of Bosworth Field in 1485. When the Duchess died she left the manor to her grandson, Henry VIII, who, eleven years later, granted it to his " noble and well-beloved Privy Councillor, Sir Richard Weston, Knight." King Henry's " trusted servant and minister " as he called him, built the present house in 1523. He was fortunate in his period and architect. It is contemporaneous with those triumphs of Tudor brickwork, Hampton Court, Trinity College, Cambridge, and Christ Church, Oxford, early examples of unfortified residences without battlements or moats. The Renaissance-Gothic proclaims itself in these buildings, with its experiment in dressing brick with terra-cotta. Sir Richard Weston in the course of his duties undoubtedly had seen the French chateaux during his appointment in 1518 to the court of Francis I. Later he had travelled with Henry VIII to the Field of the Cloth of Gold. About this time Henry's architect, Girolamo de Trevizi, had introduced terra-cotta into brick fabric. It had been used at Sutton Place not as an applied ornament but as a constructional fabric. Thus it is one of the few houses in the country where we find Italian *cinquecento* terra-cotta blended in the greatest harmony with late Tudor-Gothic, in arches, parapets, mullions and groins. The surprising thing is that it has not deteriorated in the English climate. The effect is superb. The long front of the great house, with its wavy chimney stacks and mullion windows is a blending of honey-coloured terra-cotta with russet Tudor brickwork, all tinted and enriched with the patina of centuries. The north entrance court, with its twin wings is equally beautiful, centred with the great door. Above the door, in heraldic pattern, are terra-cotta squares stamped with the rebus of the builder R.W. and the 'tun' motif from his arms.

One enters the house through a small hall, with a parlour that was formerly an armoury or guardroom, and turning left, steps into the Great Hall, used as a lounge. Its proportions, height, length and breadth, are magnificent. It is lit by tall mullion windows with rich armorial bearings. A small Tudor door, opened, provides a perspective of wonderful beauty across the wide lawn, gay with the flowers in the parallel herbaceous borders. Between them a pathway ends before a bronze copy of Cellini's Perseus, of heroic proportions, silhouetted against the sky.

Within the great hall, with its Tudor fireplace carrying the pomegranate symbol of Catherine of Aragon, what memories are evoked! This ancient house has over it the shadow of a great drama. Sir Richard Weston had an only son and heir, Francis, a young man at Court. When the doom of poor flighty Anne Boleyn was inevitable, young Francis was suddenly arrested on the suspicion of being the Queen's lover. Her execution could be more easily justified if infidelity could be added to the charges against her. Ill-starred young Francis Weston provided the required justification for her execution—how rightly or wrongly will never be known. Two days before Anne Boleyn met her fate at the block, young Weston was executed. That he was the only son of Henry VIII's "trusted friend and minister" availed him nothing. Fear of that ruthless monarch is revealed by the fact that Sir Richard remained on amicable terms with his son's slayer for the next thirty-three years. And here in his great house, even after the tragedy which had deprived him of his heir, Sir Richard entertained King Henry and kept there "a grete carpete to lay under the Kynge's fete," as the record runs.

We lunched to-day in the long dining-room in the west wing. It is a superb wainscotted room terminating in a great mullion window running from ceiling to floor. The first view of my fellow guests revealed a high standard of feminine beauty, set by my hostess. Slim, with beautiful colouring, lovely dark eyes and great vivacity of manner she struck a note of infectious gaiety. I was not yet sure who was who, but vis-à-vis, a very pretty girl in her early twenties confessed she was dying to ask me a lot of questions. I told her I was happily in the dock. "No—the witness-box, you're going to be cross-examined, not accused," said my hostess. The cross-examination began.

"When you write about people are they real people, partly real or wholly imaginary? Mrs. Silving, for instance, the old American grandmother in *The Guests Arrive*, who at seventy-five escaped from her family, and travelled all over the world—did she really exist, and did you meet her in a pension lodged in a fortress on a Venetian lagoon?"

I liked this lovely girl's eagerness and was flattered by her curiosity. "You shall have a factual answer," I said. "Mrs. Silving really existed, but she was not a grandmother, she was a spinster named Miss Waite. Her home was in Princeton, New Jersey. She had left for a month's holiday in Europe and stayed two years, travelling all alone. It was her first European trip and her relations were scared about it. She had fallen ill in an hotel in Venice and hearing of this retreat in the lagoon had come to it and recovered. She told me all this as she poured tea for us in Ottagono, an old octagonal island fort built five miles down the lagoon by the Venetian Republic as a defence against the Turks and the Genoese."

" Did you ever see her again ? Did she know she had been put into a book ? " demanded my fair examiner. " I'd love to be put in a book ! "

" You're a very great temptation. Beware ! " I replied. " No, I did not see Miss Waite again but there's a sequel. Many years later I made a broadcast in New York. Subsequently I received a letter from a lady who informed me that her aunt, Miss Waite, had heard my broadcast and was delighted. She was now ninety and nearly blind. Her niece wrote that she would never forget her aunt's delight on discovering that I had made her a character in a book, and as such the possessor of a motor-car, a chauffeur and a yacht. She gave me Miss Waite's address, so I wrote to the old lady."

" Oh what a lovely story ! " exclaimed my fair questioner.

" Thank you, but it's not ended yet. A few days later I received a letter in large characters, wandering over the page. A stroke had crippled her right hand, and it took two hands to guide her pencil. 'I am ninety and should have gone long ago but there is always some little odd and end for me to finish,' she wrote. The close of her letter was delightful. It was June when she wrote, and at the end, in printed letters, she put SORRY BUT TOO HOT, and signed her name in full, Marie Fox Waite. She died a year later."

The great lawn shimmered with heat. Some of us took refuge under a giant copper-beech tree. And then came the perfect hour—tea in an old pantiled summerhouse looking on to an azure swimming-pool made in a converted walled kitchen garden, ablaze with roses. We all gathered in the great hall before dinner. There was a cinema show in the east wing afterwards, the house staff seated on the wide staircase leading to the long library.

I noticed to-night at dinner, beyond the long table gleaming with silver and flowers—never have I seen such flowers in a house, displayed with unerring artistry—luminous under the shaded

CHARLES ROBERTS
(1753–1824)

From the painting by Pompeo Batoni
Rome, 1778

SUTTON PLACE

candles, a portrait of Henry VIII hanging on the oak-panelled wall. Its force and beauty hypnotised me and I knew I had often seen reproductions of it. When we rose from the table I discovered who was the magical artist. The oval portrait of the King, wickedly potent, was by Holbein, as vivid as on the day he painted it from the life. It had been in the collection of Horace Walpole and was acquired at the Strawberry Hill sale in 1842.

June 11.

Another radiant day. It has been almost too hot, a singular confession for a sunlover like myself, but this is June in all her full-leafed splendour. The heat shimmered over the meadows. Although this great mansion is within less than four miles of Guildford there is not a house in sight, nothing but level fields and screens of tall elms. The lawn has a tremendous length, fronting the whole façade of the house. I took my garden chair over to the far side in the shade of the copper-beech in order to absorb the utter loveliness of this mellow old home of the departed Westons. There were crazy windows out of alignment, corresponding to no floor level. Possibly they belonged to secret rooms, lost corridors. The Tudor chimneys clustering above the roof had a drunken unsteadiness. In the blazing sunlight the old house took a peach-bloom on its face. The gnarled mauve wistaria bowered the leaded windows and terra-cotta mullions. On the lawn the Duke and a guest were in keeping with the manorial scene, they were practising archery. Their arrows flew down the greensward and thudded on the ringed target. Most of the guests in long chairs were buried under Sunday newspapers, absorbing political poison that provoked spasmodic exclamations. Why should the dose be larger on Sundays than on other days, I wondered.

Towards noon I took my camera and wandered in search of colour shots. My host was now engaged with a Major from *The Times* and went off to show him the new polo ground he had laid down, on which there was to be an opening match in the afternoon. I walked down past the giant *Perseus* at the end of the herbaceous border and took a path leading to a wooded dell. There I stumbled on sheer enchantment. The slender River Wey ambles through the grounds, and, below slopes of crimson rhododendrons, it feeds a small lake patterned with water lilies. In the dead centre of the still water, overhung with a green lacework of

D

leaves, rose a solitary blood-red flower. It was the high note of a composition thrilling to a colour photographer. I shot in delight, and left nothing of beauty defiled by massacre.

There was a buffet lunch at midday, with some forty guests at the table. The newcomers were the polo team and wives who had come over from Henley-on-Thames to inaugurate the field. Soon after lunch we all went down to watch the game, the Duke captaining his team against the visitors. It was blazing hot. The new field is beautifully situated in a great meadow bordered by a coppice. The game ended, there was a large cocktail party by the swimming-pool. A golden light began to outline the tall elms. 'Now drew still evening on.' As I walked over the lawns, with the violet shadows of the old house creeping over them, I felt that here was a beauty wholly English in character, wistful, rich with the memories of far off happy-unhappy days, unequalled any-where in the world. And I was sad to think that, like the light, it was fading from the English scene, for these ancient houses and all they have sprung from and grown with are doomed. The richly patterned life of the exclusive few is giving place to the unspectacular welfare of the many. In that change, inevitably due, a focus of culture and craftsmanship is being lost.

I had been wondering all the time how my host contrived to maintain in the face of exorbitant taxation and punitive death duties this ancient grace of living. In very few of the great houses to-day is the week-end party of twenty guests a possibility. Yesterday evening in the drawing-room I discovered it was all a somewhat ingenious illusion. The house for much of the week is not the Duke's exclusive own. He has joined the noble order of turnstile-keepers, and the half-crowns of the crowds that tramp through the halls and galleries serve to postpone their demolition. The servants who attend us with an old-world solicitude are a phantom army. They are called up from old retainers scattered by drastic economy. Like the guests they are week-enders, arriving before lunch on Saturday and departing after dinner on Sunday, when the empty rooms fall back into the charge of a butler and a skeleton staff. This heroic hospitality is also based on pillage. These great houses are consuming themselves while a rapacious State batters at their doors ; the revenues that once maintained them are now diverted to officialdom, to distribution of coupons, registration forms, and all the elephantine performance of a public authority muddling a private job. And the illusion ?

Wandering through these beautiful rooms I have been overwhelmed by the magnificent family pictures. The bulk of this great collection formerly housed at Stafford House and Bridgewater House, London mansions only a few hundred yards apart, was acquired from the Duke of Orleans at the beginning of the eighteenth century. To these pictures have been added ancestral portraits, commissioned by judicious forebears. The Lawrence portraits alone are magnificent. A series of duchesses of surpassing beauty decorate the drawing-room. Two of them have vanished, on transatlantic journeys. Several dukes had several wives, all painted by the great masters of their eras, sometimes repeatedly, since you cannot have too many phases of the woman you love. This was fortunate, for, as the present duke tells one a little ironically, it is easy to sacrifice one duchess for the maintenance of the others. A much-married duke with a much-painted duchess served posterity in a manner he knew not. But I shivered for the glorious portraits still hanging in this drawing-room. Reynolds, Hoppner, Lawrence are here in all their glory.

In the Great Hall hangs Walker's superb study of Robert Devereux, 3rd Earl of Essex, son of Queen Elizabeth's lover. Romney's fascinating portrait of a handsome young man in a yellow silk jacket and lace collar, George Granville, 2nd Marquis of Stafford, and the portrait of his sister Caroline, who later became Countess of Carlisle, are alluring, and the same artist has a group of the Leveson-Gower family, a large picture dominating the end of the hall, that in sheer beauty of young womanhood bears the hallmark of this artist's genius. The tragic Earl of Strafford, another who suffered at the hands of princes, looks down at us in Stone's portrait, and Reynolds' proud Earl of Ligonier sits his charger on a large canvas. A bold soldier, he lived to the ripe age of ninety. His name recalls his nephew who fought a duel in the Green Park with young Alfieri the poet, who had got entangled with his accommodating wife. He could have slain the youth but he gallantly pinked him, whereupon the gay young poet went back to his box at the opera.

After tea I mounted the stairs and examined the library housed in the long gallery of the east wing. When I was here fifteen years ago, on a grey November day, the great room had a ghostly air and chilled my spirit. Libraries, however dignified, are usually cheerful places. To-day, even with the afternoon sunshine lighting the landscape, I felt it was not a very companionable place, an impression enhanced by two things. All the books were inaccessible, behind a wire mesh, and in a table cabinet in the centre of the room was displayed a cambric ruff that had adorned the neck of the saintly Sir Thomas More when he laid his head on the block on Tower Hill. It is stained with his blood. This ruff passed from a near relation to the Westons, a grim relic for a family whose heir was to feel the executioner's axe by order of the same monarch. The mystery of the wire mesh over the books was solved by the butler. " It's to stop the books being stolen, sir," was the answer to my question. I assumed he was alluding to sightseers and not to guests !

Down in the hall I had a chance before we went in to another cinema show to ask Lord Westmorland a question provoked by his name. When poor John Keats went to Rome to die, his faithful friend Severn, being young, handsome and vivacious, and somewhat a hero of a tragic episode, was taken up by the fashionable English colony. Foremost in this society was dashing Lady Westmorland. Spoilt, vain, imperious, she could brook no opposition of her will or suffer anything that conflicted with her selfish desires. She had for companion-slave a lovely girl, her ward, the orphan daughter of Lord Montgomery. When the arrow of Cupid pierced her and young Severn, the enraged Lady Westmorland, losing at one blow a handsome young man to dance attendance on her, and a timid dependant, banished them from her presence in fury. I asked Lord Westmorland whether in the family archives there were any papers left by his ancestress. He thought there were but they had not yet been investigated. The letters of Lady Westmorland, if they exist, might throw an interesting light on life in Rome in those early days of Keats and Severn.

Lord Westmorland evoked another romance. Sarah Child, the rich banker's daughter, defied her father and ran off to Gretna Green in 1782 with the handsome young Earl of Westmorland, who died within a few months of the marriage, leaving a daughter who married the Earl of Jersey and reigned at Osterley Park. And romance was present even now, for Lord Westmorland's fiancée was in our house party and they were married a few days later.

June 12.

I left this morning, in perfect June weather. The house had a sad muted beauty with all the life departed from it. My host and hostess were leaving for Cornwall. To-morrow the coconut matting will be laid down through the rooms on view. To see them without their occupants, without the evening fire flickering in the grates, without the long dining-table shining with silver in the candlelight, without the quiet movement of servants, the laughter of guests, the rattle of the backgammon board in the great hall, the strain of piano music in the flower-embowered drawing-room, without a friendly dog doing his round of tail-wagging—without these living assets the great house is only a museum.

At the end of the drive I stopped the car to take one last look at Sutton Place, so mellow in the morning sunshine. For the present it is owned and graced by two dispensers of great hos-pitality but with a cost and effort that cannot be long maintained. A manner of life, patterned by the centuries, will soon be no more than a legend.

June 15.

> I have seen beauty beyond belief,
> An English lane in summer leaf,
> And walked in sleepy country towns,
> And met the west wind on the downs :
> Oh, I have travelled the whole world round
> To find the home place holy ground !

June 19.

My old enemy is on the rampage again—three days in bed and the old dismal diet dominated by the milk bottle. I review possible sins provoking this visitation. Perhaps I have worked too hard. Twenty thousand words in seven days at my time of life is probably excessive but it is hard to slow up when one has generated speed. I recall, a young man, one night in 1917 during a bombing in the Euston Road, how my host at dinner, Joseph Conrad, told me that he considered three hundred words a day good going. Three hundred words only ! In those days I was capable of five thousand and the day was not long enough. But what a three hundred his were ! Like a well-tempered coil the spring is still in them. Looking back, I wonder how many million words I have written. I published my first article at fourteen, that is forty-four years ago. Now with some thirty books behind me, the invention is slower—or have I become more fastidious ?   I wrote *Spears Against Us* in four weeks, *Victoria Four-Thirty* in six.   They have both of them passed into twenty-five impressions and are still going strong after some eighteen years. Now I take three or four years to complete a novel, rejecting and rejecting the theme before I begin.   ' The first fine careless rapture ' belongs to Spring and the lyricism of youth.

June 21.

I have been greatly saddened by the belated news of the death of an old friend of my early youth.   On my return from U.S.A. in 1946, he welcomed me with great affection after long separation. Two years ago I was distressed by a change in his manner.   He became to others as well as to myself suspicious, morose and a recluse.   There was an occasion when I was deeply hurt by his conduct but with a great effort I refused to quarrel or protest. To-day I am grateful that somehow I smothered my resentment. Poor fellow, he shut himself off from his friends and died almost secretly in hospital far away from his home.   At his funeral there were only four people ;   neither his only brother nor a single one of his relations was present.   I learn now that he died of cancer of the lung and am told that the onset of this unsuspected malady may have changed his character, unknown to himself.   How careful we should be in judgement of those whom we think we know intimately.

June 23.

Out of my bed and to Nottingham to see my only brother. When I am fractious about my health I look at him and feel chastened.   What is a happy life ?   From the age of twenty-six onwards, for some forty-four years he has been a victim of a chronic duodenal ulcer.   On many occasions I have rushed to attend his funeral but each time the ' corpse ' has risen and confounded us.   Four drastic operations have neither cured nor killed him.   He has been saved not by doctors and surgeons who have done their best but by a devoted wife.   They were boy and girl lovers, they married young, they reared a family.   Fate has ordained that they should live all their lives in simple content within a three-mile orbit—unlike their world-wandering brother. Their interests are as far removed from mine as the North Pole from the Equator, and the climate of their lives has been just as different.   I sometimes wonder if we are brothers at all.   The gap between us, with a brother and sister dead in childhood in the intervening years, has made us almost strangers, for he was married while I was at school. Untemperamental and un-adventurous, I know that he regards my life as exhaustingly ambitious and dedicated to a remorseless Muse. His grandchild, the garden, the bowling-green are the boundaries of his tranquil world. I have never heard a complaint from him although he has lived under the sword of Damocles all his life. Repeated hemorrhages have made him of such frailty that strangers look in wonder at a perambulating skeleton. Nothing daunts him and his courageous wife. There was one occasion when, after a sudden collapse in an empty house, his life was sustained by a faithful dog licking his face until the alarm brought help. I have been fortunate in that I have been able to make some contribution to two lives marked by gallantry and devotion. Last year, unhappy that after a long life they had never seen the wider world, I induced them to cross the Channel and make a Continental tour. My sister-in-law, with a Swiss father, had never seen Switzerland. It was a tremendous adventure but, alas, at Cortina, Fate struck, and the journey onwards to Venice was made lying in the back of the Pullman-autobus. I was in Venice when they arrived and at one glance I feared what was impending. In the *scirocco*-smitten September afternoon, believing that some air might help my brother, we ventured out in a gondola. In the middle of the Grand Canal he began to pump out his life's blood. I remember, while endeavouring to cope with this hemorrhage, seeing out of the corner of my eye the guests departing from Countess Volpi's palazzo, after a luncheon party to which I had been invited. How little they knew what was taking place in mid-Canal as their gondolas took them away !

In panic we got back to the hotel—the gondolier went to pieces and wobbled down the Canal. We waited a long time for a doctor and then for the hospital ambulance. It came after two hours, an unbelievably antiquated affair, an open rowboat with a canvas cover. The stretcher was a basket chair. The journey by canal took three-quarters of an hour. At the hospital bureau-cracy demanded a passport and wanted a large form filled in while the patient, sitting on a chair, vomited blood into a waste-paper basket. Later an insensible figure was carried up three floors and through two wards of an adapted monastery. Not a single medical officer or nurse spoke anything but Italian. My own, for medical contingencies, was inadequate. I insisted on a bed in the public ward afraid of what might happen in a private room from neglect or inability to speak the language.

At five o'clock the next morning my sister-in-law and I were awakened and told to hurry to a deathbed. We walked in the dawn through the labyrinthine streets of a Venice with which I am fortunately familiar. We were taken to the 'dying man' with a screen round his bed. " He will live," said his wife, knowing every shade of his face. The doctors said nothing, convinced the bed would soon be available. For twelve days my sister-in-law made her daily trek to the hospital. It was quicker by foot than by gondola, and somehow, without one word of Italian, after some coaching, she learned the devious route. The hospital staff now fought gallantly for the patient. The condition of ' the Inglese ' became a challenge. The whole ward adopted him. A red-bearded monk, a Maltese, boasted British nationality, without one word of English, and through ties of race was very solicitous. For two weeks the patient could not be moved. In the third week, I decided to fly my brother back to England. On the day of that decision thirty patients in the ward flapped the sleeves of their white nightgowns, crying " *Volo! Volo!* " in happy demonstration of the coming flight. At the hour of departure my brother visited the beds and shook the hands of all the patients, then, led by a beaming staff, went down to the waiting gondola. He spent the last night, in a Venice he had not seen, at the Luna Hotel. Early the next morning he flew over the Alps homewards on his maiden flight, thus ending his first continental trip. He can just recall seeing, semi-conscious from fatigue, the white cliffs of the English coast. Four months later he dug over his garden !

This evening he met me with his car and was very concerned about my condition. Later—" I should like to see Venice again," he said. When I suggested they should be my guests next autumn his wife looked up from her sewing and said quietly, " I think our travelling days are over, Daddy. We mustn't be too adventurous." There spoke the pilot of a long, happy and unadventurous life of almost seventy years rich with content.*

* While typing out this entry, Jan. 12, 1952, in Alassio, Italy, I received a letter from my brother, informing me that on Christmas Eve he was found on the floor in a pool of blood, rushed to hospital and given a transfusion in a critical condition. He wrote " The old shock-absorber is out again. Everybody wonderfully kind but what a nuisance I am ! "

June 28.

In town again to see my doctor. I lunched with Miss Bridget Keir who lives in a top-floor Chelsea studio overlooking the Thames. Two years ago in a Venetian hotel I heard a commotion on a small canal beneath my window. I looked out. I saw a large elderly lady being induced by gesticulating Italians to walk a narrow flexible plank that bridged the watery gap between the quay and a gondola. It was an unnerving task, fraught with peril, for the gondola, under the weight of the embarking lady, took a threatening list and the plank bent ominously. At last, amid great clamour, the lady crossed the plank and collapsed in the gondola seat while her sketching apparatus was handed in. At the moment of achievement, watching from my balcony, I shouted " Bravissimo ! " and led the applause. The plank-walker looked up and bowed with a Victorian grace. Then she set forth on her day's sketching. We were great friends from that time on. And now we have had a reunion in Chelsea.

Alas, the splendid lunch set for me was all in vain. At three o'clock I rang a bell in Harley Street and was promptly ordered to bed for a month, on my prison diet again. I promised to obey. I did not inform His Vigilance, an admired and trusted friend, that I must delay twenty-four hours as I had a speech to make on the morrow. Fergusson Hannay understands well my difficult and temperamental calling for he married Doris Leslie, the novelist. But I knew, notwithstanding, he would brook no delay.

June 29.

Twenty years ago a slip of a young woman, Christina Foyle, started on behalf of her father's great bookshop a monthly luncheon at which she invited celebrities to address the guests in the dining-room of one of London's largest hotels. The Foyle Luncheons are now almost a national institution. There can be few of the leading personalities of Great Britain who have not been Christina Foyle's guest speakers. They cover politics, law, literature, art, drama, music and the Church. An audience of eight hundred guests is often achieved. I was one of Miss Foyle's earliest speakers, making my first appearance on March 17, 1932. The chief speaker on that occasion was the gifted and picturesque Miss Radclyffe Hall, whose fame had sprung, in those susceptible

D*

days when readers were avidly following the trail of D. H. Lawrence through his sexual earthly paradise, from a frank and skilfully written story of homosexuality. Although this became almost a fashionable subject at ' intellectual ' dinner parties, where the ignorant and the informed archly skirmished, it was still an unbelievable abnormality that sent the Recorder of London, Sir Ernest Wild, into paroxysms of rage in which he browbeat his victims, professing he could not believe his ears, though these had been hearing, *ad nauseam*, the same evidence for twenty years. Perhaps his name added heat to his horror. Miss Radclyffe Hall's book *The Well of Loneliness* had quite overshadowed her greater achievement *Adam's Breed*, following a trial for indecency before a judge who, if he was as shocked and astonished as he professed to be, should not have been a judge at all, being incredibly ignorant of human nature.

At the Foyle luncheon at Grosvenor House, Miss Radclyffe Hall was introduced by Sir Arbuthnot Lane. I proposed the toast of ' Literature,' and Miss Sheila Kaye-Smith responded. Naturally on this occasion Miss Radclyffe Hall drew many kindred spirits, and on rising to speak, confronted by close-cropped feminine heads, some stiff collars and monocles, I began somewhat naughtily by saying that I rose from a deep well of loneliness in so foreign a landscape. As usual, it was a highly entertaining luncheon.*

It is one of the great merits of Miss Foyle's direction that she casts her net wide and provides the most comprehensive public platform of the day. The occasion of to-day's lunch at the Grosvenor House Hotel, at which I was the guest speaker, was the publication of the report of the Gower Committee on the Preservation of Historic Houses. It had been appointed by the

---

* Miss Christina Foyle, asked for a confirmation of date, has supplied me with a verbatim report of that lunch of twenty years ago. Sir Arbuthnot Lane, introducing the guest, said, "She has drawn here one of the most remarkable collections of men and women . . . she must feel very strongly that the heart of the public is beating in unison with hers, in spite of what has been said against her." Proposing the toast of Literature, I said, ". . . I did not think I should live to see the day when Miss Radclyffe Hall, who has thrice been prosecuted in British police courts, would be brought here, a medical chairman on one side, and a woman police inspector on the other. I think it shows, once you give birth to an idea pregnant with courage, enterprise and insight, that courage will eventually, despite all obstacles brought against it, triumph, no matter what power has attacked it ; and I want to say here what I said in print at the time, that I consider these proceedings were a disgrace to the English system of law. I am very glad that my opportunity of speaking should coincide with the presence of a lady who has not only distinguished our literature, but has stood fearlessly for freedom of thought and expression."

Labour Chancellor of the Exchequer, Sir Stafford Cripps, to enquire into the ways and means of preserving the stately and historic houses of Britain from falling into the bankruptcy and ruin induced by punitive death duties and exorbitant taxation. My chairman on this occasion was Sir John Anderson, distinguished by many years of public service, a notable Chancellor of the Exchequer. At the high table we were supported by a representative company, including Viscount Esher, the Earl of Warwick, Lord de Lisle and Dudley, Lady Utica Beecham, Sir Cuthbert de Hoghton, etc., embarrassed owners of historic houses. They had been gathered by our indefatigable convener as relics of a glorious past or as examples of a class obstinately living in great mansions, doomed to decay.

My chairman astonished me by embarking on a glowing eulogy of the Labour Chancellor for his prescience and public spirit in appointing the Gowers Committee. The Committee, which included Sir John Anderson's wife, has certainly done a thorough job in its report, but it is deeply depressing with its recital of the ruin overtaking our historic mansions and their treasures. It makes recommendations, such as relief from strangling taxes, and the financial assistance of owners faced with heavy repair and maintenance costs. Unlike Sir John, I cannot take a rosy view of Sir Stafford Cripps' benevolence towards these doomed houses. He is the foremost member of a Government whose policy is the abolition of the aristocracy, the suppression of personal wealth, and the reduction by taxation of everyone to a low level of equality. In view of his own and his party's avowed antagonism to all the owners of these great houses, and the class they represent, and the perfervid belief that their extinction is long overdue, Sir Stafford's solicitude for the survival of our great mansions strikes me as being illogical if not eccentric. For though Sir Stafford has receded from an earlier ambition to abolish the British monarchy and unite with the Communists, the party of which he is the foremost brains and ornament has shown a vindictive pleasure in encompassing the ruin of these great houses by taxation amounting to virtual confiscation. To this it has often added the demagoguery of the guttersnipe—calling its opponents ' vermin,' etc. Sir Stafford, himself, is the author of a capital levy on investments, since normal taxation would not support the profligacy of his party's policy, and to this he has added a 33 per cent capital levy on the British public by his devaluation of sterling—although it is not yet aware of it, deluded by the belief that American imports will carry the levy.*

Sir Stafford nine times vehemently denied any possibility of the devaluation of the £, and then devalued it within a fortnight of his last denial. When Mr. Churchill made caustic comments on this ninefold somersault Sir Stafford was deeply offended. Despite my chairman's glowing tribute to the creator of the Gowers Committee, and his faith in the adoption of its findings, I share none of his optimism. I see it only as a piece of political legerdemain designed to end in pious professions and no action. Time will show how right or wrong I am.†

I therefore expressed my dissent from Sir John Anderson's eulogy of his fellow Chancellor of the Exchequer. Surely it is a question of principle ? If you plan for the liquidation of a capitalist or aristocratic form of society you cannot believe in the preservation of houses that embody and draw their glory from such a society. They are now to have a posthumous existence, decaying birdcages with moulting birds inside them, the wool stuffing gaping through the damask, the carpets showing threadbare, the gardens running to seed and the roofs riddled with dry rot, as is the story all over Britain to-day. This ruin cannot be evaded by noble owners collecting half-crowns from the motor-bus crowds that tramp through their halls. As museums these historic buildings are depressing and superfluous. They were beautiful because of the life that created them and flowed through them. This country is now cluttered with great houses, empty, servantless, unheated, settling into dust. If we no longer believe in tradition, if we must hold that the creators of these houses are reprobates, degenerates, constituting the ' vermin ' of a scurrilous Cabinet Minister, then the Socialised State should demolish these houses, examples of past wickedness. For Sir Stafford Cripps, the bearleader of the iconoclasts, the arch-apostle of austerity, the High Executioner of the capitalist, to profess solicitude for the haunts of the wicked, even on grounds of aesthetic value or public entertainment, seems to me a perverse and confused performance.

---

* It knows now. " The devaluation of the £ contributed nothing to a solution of the dollar problem. By the end of 1950 England's imports rose by 43 per cent in one year, while her exports rose only 20 per cent. The difference has been carried by the public in increased prices."—*The Times*, Sept. 25, 1951.

† When the Labour Party lost office in October 1951, nothing whatever had been done to implement any of the findings of the Gowers Report, eighteen months after its publication.

Having spoken to this effect, I sat down.   Lord Warwick, alone, owner of the historic Warwick Castle, was hopeful something would be done and gave the public an excellent character regarding its behaviour in his castle.   I do not doubt the good behaviour of the public in most instances but why, on payment of half a crown to a desperate owner, should they feel a prescriptive right to walk through another man's private house ? *

June 30.

I am in bed to-day, in a state of collapse.   I went without food for eighteen hours in order to fulfil my engagement at the Foyle luncheon.   I had to hold on to the microphone-stand to get through my speech—the first time I have ever willingly used that abominable instrument, the promoter of slovenly diction.   I pray that my doctor may not read this morning of yesterday's disobedience.

July 14.

Still in bed on the same monotonous diet.   I wonder if I shall be fit to leave for Cap d'Antibes next week.   To-day I was visited by my friend Seddon Cripps (Lord Parmoor).   A greater con-trast to his ascetic brother could not be imagined.   Robust, hearty, with a rollicking sense of humour, a deep love of the land and of horses, he is to me the embodiment of an eighteenth-century squire.   I regret two things : that he sold the Parmoor estate, which robbed him of a natural background, and that he resigned the Bursarship of Queen's College, Oxford.   He had beautiful rooms there, most tastefully furnished, in the first court, where he entertained delightfully.   One Christmas Day I was his guest at the famous college dinner when the great Boar's Head is brought into the candle-lit dining-hall.

This feast commemorates the scholar of Queen's who while walking on Shotover Hill was charged by a wild boar.   He thrust the Aristotle he was reading down the boar's throat, choked it, cut off its head, and brought it home for supper—the victory of intellect over brute force !   This deed is celebrated in a Canticle sung every Christmas night in College Hall, when the butler brings in the boar's head.

* One week after this lunch the Duke of Marlborough announced that owing to the destructive behaviour of the public he might have to refuse any further admittance to Blenheim Palace, or the loan of his premises for any public purpose.   Hundreds of pounds worth of damage had been done to the grounds and premises.

"The boar's head in hand bear I,
Bedecked with bays and rosemary.
And I pray you, my masters, merry be ye,
Quot estis in convivio."

I regret that Seddon never asked me to the New Year's Day
dinner when, after the blowing of a trumpet, the Bursar enters and
presents every guest with a needle threaded with silk, saying—
" Take this and be thrifty."

July 16.

A long inward debate whether to risk the journey to Cap
d'Antibes to stay with Mrs. Aubrey Cartwright.   I have progressed from bismuth and milk to fish and mush.   I tried to
persuade myself that the sunshine and beauty of the Riviera coast
will work their exterior magic on my inner chaos.   In my heart
of hearts I know this is nonsense but a little nonsense is often a good
tonic.   I must be on my guard against the temptations of my
hostess's chef.   Mastering my irresolution, I picked up the telephone and ordered a berth on the Blue Train.   Then I began to
pack, by instalments.   My everlasting problem on setting forth is
not clothes but the books and manuscripts I must drag around with
me in order to pursue my vagrant calling.   Items : a typewriter
(not for composition but to enable correspondents to read my
letters) ; dictionaries—English, French, German, Italian, Latin,
in pocket editions ; the typescript of a new novel and its printed
proofs ; four manuscript books of this diary to-date ; three pens
and an unspillable inkpot, well-tested, since the tragedy in which
I lost two suits, five shirts, a dressing-gown and miscellaneous
articles—how much an ounce of ink can destroy! ; a letter-file,
springback binders, a lightweight writing-board for work in bed,
three Guida d'Italia, Campbell's *Classical Rome*, Baedeker's
Austria, etc.   Such has been the lifelong burden no ingenuity can
reduce.   I should like, as Hugh Walpole did, to take with me a
miniature bedside library, and a small household god—mine is
a porcelain monkey with its paw to its brow, bought in Bonn, and
called by me, ' *the Bonne Idée*,' an inspirational ju-ju.

I confine all this material to one bag.   The Customs man
never believes it is as innocent as it looks.   To prove that it is all
a means to a professional end, I carry one of my own books.   This

exhibition of authorship, from inkpot to wrapper, allays all suspicion that I am smuggling typewriters, or cryptic scripts.   When
inclined to complain of all this impedimenta I recall Paderewski
who travelled not only with a concert grand piano but with a
tuner for it, and with a pantechnicon to hold it ; or the member
of an orchestra who carries around a bass fiddle, or drums,
triangle and cymbals.   An author is fortunate.   Reduced to the
minimum equipment of a pen, he can operate.   Short of paper,
I once wrote an article on the blank back of a conveniently long
(in this sense) hotel bill.

France

CAP D'ANTIBES

July 22.

A HALCYON crossing, the 'rosy-fingered' dawn breaking over grey-white Avignon in the cool Provençal morning. On the train I met Lady Norman, after fifteen years. She is going to La Garoupe, the beautiful estate near Cannes inherited from her father, Lord Aberconway. At breakfast we glided through Toulon. In the haze of mid-morning I arrived at the station of Antibes, with Aubrey, in yellow shorts and russet shirt, a six-foot-four Apollo just out of the chariot of the sun, striding down the platform. Then the imperturbable family chauffeur ; our last meeting had been when he drove me through the palm groves across the pelican-haunted St. John's River at Palm Beach to the New York-bound train one March morning. Ruminative, stork-like, he is London-bred, but now a firmly-rooted American who regards Italy as a junk shop, the Riviera as a rubbish heap, and the Old World as a rotten apple.

A short drive and then a turning into paradise. The villa clings to a rocky ledge below a garden. Pine trees perfume the air all around it. Below, from a long level terrace one reaches a cove washed by the blue Mediterranean. Nearby, the promontory of Eden Roc puts a finger seawards ; afar, the mauve mass of the Esterel stands camel-like against the horizon. The long low villa is called *Casa Estella*, but it is the house of the sun as well as the star. I have a balcony bedroom. At night the lighthouse flashes and the sea murmurs beyond the screen doors through which comes the odour of night-scented jasmine. The scent vividly recalls how overpoweringly it invaded my room at *Estella*, the Palm Beach house of my hostess.

I have been here before and know well its enchantment. We bathe, we lunch on the terrace above a sea seen through an arabesque of twisted pine trees. We take a siesta in a shady garden alcove, aromatic with hot 'spices of the South.' We dream, we talk, and then change while the falling sun burns through the black branches and burnishes the silken sea. The air is so still that the candleflames at dinner neither wink nor waver. Tree frogs croak along the terraces, the fireflies write their brief brilliant magic on the blackboard of the night.

To-day my hostess gave a cocktail party and among some fifty guests, Sir Charles Mendl, debonair, entering his eightieth year, settled a question for me. A swimming platform is tethered off the cove. We roast, and wrangle over Eliot (genius, gibberish or inspired hooey?), drown Attlee, flay Truman, deify Gide, differ over Dali, then slip into the sea, and fry again. Suddenly I sat up and said, " This is the very raft ! " Questioning eyes gleamed through wet hair. " Bernard Shaw sunbathed here," I explained. " What ? How ? " asked a sylph in a lilac costume, rubbing the sea out of her eyes. " They've just published a pictorial life of old G.B.S. One photo shows him on a raft, bathing. The line of this cove is exactly the same. I'm certain it was here ! "

They are incredulous. " But what was G.B.S. doing here thirty years ago ? Any raft looks the same." I explained that it was not only possible but probable. About thirty years ago I had met him with young Gene Tunney, then World Heavyweight Champion, in Venice. They were touring the Continent, Tunney was interested in Shakespeare and Shaw interested in Shaw. They might well have come here. This villa had belonged to Lloyd Osbourne, the step-son of Robert Louis Stevenson. My audience was not convinced. At seven o'clock this evening Sir Charles Mendl shading his eyes as he looked seawards, remarked, " I remember coming here when Lloyd Osbourne lived in the villa and Bernard Shaw bathed off that raft ! "

Trouble has begun again. A dinner that would tempt Lucullus mocked me. I ate nothing all day and was in agony from 2 a.m. to 5 a.m. The still beauty of the night was massacred. Anthime, the young French butler, who fishes in the afternoon for octopuses with a sponge on a stick, coaxed me with hot milk. I lay in the heat and cursed my folly in inflicting myself on these kind people. The tree frogs mocked me all night. Our Italian tour is becoming problematical.

August 1.

Every day at noon there is a bathing party down by the cove. Steps have been cut along the rock terrace and we have a lower nook for the men and an upper nook—actually a dressing-room— for the ladies. There is a terrace along the rocky promontory that provides a small harbour on the cove-side. On the sea-side steps go down to a ladder and diving platform. The whole setting is idyllic : a long view of the indented cove, a pine-clad coastline and an azure sea. From the platform we look back at the garden terrace that leads up to the villa, a long two-storied house with a wide terrace on the ground floor and a balcony running along the bedrooms of the first floor. Behind the house rises a garden with a garage and guest-rooms above. A long drive connects the villa with the Cannes-Antibes road. The situation is ideal. The villa is isolated but not remote. It commands a splendid view of the coast to the far Esterel that changes colour all day and in the evening builds up a great violet wall against the starry sky.

The bathing cove is very popular with my hostess's friends nearby. Every day there is a gathering on the bathing terrace. Alas ! for me the sea is a deferred pleasure. There was a large party to-day for bathing and lunch. I sat at the long table and toyed with a little rice. It is so difficult not to attract sympathetic attention and become tiresome, as are all sick persons at a feast. The setting of this table on the tree-shaded terrace is beautiful, with the sea below, glimpsed through pine and olive branches that make a black lacework against the brilliant bay.

At the bathing cove a beautiful middle-aged lady had engaged my attention. I am one of those wretches who never register names when introduced so I did not know who she was. I was glad to find myself beside her at the table. Half-way through the meal I discovered that she was the Duchess of Leinster, formerly Mrs. Wessel, formerly Lady Churston, formerly Denise Orme, a reigning beauty of the musical comedy stage. By her first marriage to Lord Churston she was the mother of four lovely daughters, who became the Princess Aly Khan, Lady Ebury, the Marchioness of Tavistock, and the Countess Cadogan. I did not think it tactful to tell the Duchess why she interested me, her vivacious character apart. When I sailed for New York at the end of October 1939, a friend gave me a note to a fellow-passenger, the young and beautiful Duchess of Leinster. We became great friends during the voyage but I noticed at times that she was un-happy and preoccupied. Finally she told me that she had a sad mission. She was returning to her homeland in order to get a divorce from the Duke. My last sight of her, as I then thought, was at the shipside in New York as we waited to go down to the Customs shed. When I told her I would see her in a few days she surprised me by saying, " No—I've decided to go back to England on this boat. I shall not divorce my husband." Suppressing my surprise, I said good-bye to her. But the pretty young Duchess changed her mind once more, for a short time afterwards we met again in New York. She flung herself wholeheartedly into working for Bundles for Britain and we were often together in these activities. I never knew quite what she had done with the Duke and thought it tactful not to ask. I was told by a friend that the matter was in abeyance. Now, seated beside her successor, I had the answer. Without offence to either of the ladies, I confess that had I been the Duke I should have been in a great dilemma and wished myself a Turkish Pasha. A few days earlier when I had met the young Marquis and Marchioness of Tavistock, I marvelled at the latter's delicate beauty. I had no idea then that she was the daughter of Denise Orme, a replica of her mother's famed beauty in the days when young Guardsmen went to the stage door for their brides.

As I looked at the Duke seated across the table I recalled a story my father loved to tell of how the Leinster crest got its monkey. That, and Father Prout's Sermon, were his favourite stories, dramatically delivered for the delight of a small boy. The sixth baron, Gerald Fitzgerald, was a valiant soldier who dispersed the Munster rebels in 1299 and opposed Robert the Bruce. When he was an infant, asleep in Woodstock Castle, an alarm of fire was raised. The child was forgotten in the confusion and when the servants returned to search for him they found his room in ruins. Hearing a noise in one of the towers they looked up and saw an ape, usually kept chained, carefully holding the infant which it had rescued from the fire. In gratitude for his rescue the grown-up baron adopted a monkey for his crest and two monkeys for heraldic supporters. They are on the ducal arms to this day.

Few families have had a more tragic history. The tenth earl having heard that his father was to be beheaded threw off his allegiance to the English crown. On the promise of a full pardon he eventually surrendered but Henry VIII violated his promise, and he, with his five uncles, was hanged, drawn and quartered at Tyburn, and all his family honours were attainted. He was succeeded by his half-brother, Gerald. This young man, Gerald, became Master of the Horse to Cosimo de' Medici, Duke of Florence. He was educated at Rome by his kinsman, Cardinal Reginald Pole, who came within a vote of being elected Pope. He returned to England after the death of Henry VIII, and Queen Mary restored his honours and estates.

August 2.

To-day Lady Norman invited Mrs. Cartwright and myself to a quiet lunch at La Garoupe. " Nothing that can possibly hurt you ! " she said, solicitously, over the telephone. Knowing she was no mean cook, I forced myself to go out and was well rewarded. She has retreated to the Pavilion on the estate. The large house in which Lord Aberconway lived is let to Mrs. Randolph Churchill who has a house party. We dined *al fresco* in a little covered pavilion looking on to a copse of oleander trees. It was cool, and, half-starved, I ventured to eat. We discussed old friends, vanished days, a changed world, an England faced with overwhelming internal and international difficulties. Lady Norman would not let me be pessimistic. She has a tough spirit and fights back, and any suggestion from the local French that the English are back numbers, with a slipping pound, gets up her dander. She is gallantly fighting to preserve this beautiful estate fronting the sea.

After lunch we went up to the château. No one to-day would venture to build anything so palatial, with its great hall, and long, columned terrace from which the extensive grounds slope down to the rocky shore. I came here for the first time some twenty years ago. Two things then made a lasting impression on me, more than the gardens and the great white house on its eminence commanding a view of the Mediterranean : they were old Lord Aberconway, a grand figure of a man, tall, with silver locks and a beautiful face ; and the motto he had carved over the door of the mansion where he entertained so regally. The motto was a clever adaptation and reversal of the words Dante found inscribed on the portal of Hell, *Lasciate ogni speranza, voi ch' entrate.* Lord Aberconway changed *speranza* to *dolore* (' hope ' to ' sorrow '), thus making the legend read *Abandon all sorrow ye who enter this door*—a fitting welcome from one who, with his life's partner, lived to a serene old age in this paradise.

Mrs. Randolph Churchill's house party was still lunching when we arrived so we waited on the sun-smitten terrace. Presently a little boy of about ten came out. " Oh, this is Winston Churchill," said Lady Norman, bringing him forward. I looked wonderingly at the small boy fated to carry such an historic name through life, at once a great privilege and a handicap, for how can he hope, poor lad, to surpass or even equal the greatness of the name he bears ?   He is at school in Switzerland and when his young friends pester him for inside information on the course of world politics he replies, " If you'll read the newspapers you'll know just as much as I do ! "

He left us on the terrace, engrossed in a new radio, and Mrs. Churchill, with apologies, came and collected us.   We joined the guests for coffee in the belvedere at the end of the house.   The house party included Lord Beatty, Peter Rodd and Lord Stanley of Alderley.   In the year 1916 I had first met at Rosyth Admiral Beatty, a dashing, handsome figure with a dynamic personality. I had a shock on encountering him here again, wholly unchanged after thirty-three years.   For a second I had been confounded by an apparition from the past, and then realised this facsimile before me was Lord Beatty, his son, a chip of the old capstan.

A neighbouring property, Lady Pomeroy Burton's vast Château de la Cröe, has not been taken this year by the Duke of Windsor. It seems destined to play a role in international affairs.   This year's tenant has been the Italian royal family which held a con-ference there, presided over by ex-King Umberto arranging the share-out of the three million pounds left by his father in British investments, which our Government has released and the Italian Government has been unable to seize.   Umberto has been luckier than some of his royal colleagues.   He has a life interest in an insurance policy for £1,500,000, taken out in London by his grandfather.   Although he has lost forty palaces in Italy, he now lives in some state in a twenty-roomed villa near Estoril, Spain, with the royal family portraits on the walls, equerries, and ser-vants in the Savoy liveries.

The Château de la Cröe was also the scene of the stormy and protracted negotiations between ex-King Leopold and the Belgian Government, and there was much coming and going through the massive gendarme-guarded gates.   I always wanted to ask the Duke of Windsor, who paid for those gendarmes guarding him, he or the French Government, and whether he had to have them against his will?   My own memory of the villa is slightly comic.   A somewhat early guest for lunch, I was shown on to the loggia to await my hostess.   Presently a youth in a bath-gown went past me and ran lightly down the steps towards the path leading to the bathing place.   I wondered who the young house

guest was. Later, while talking to the Duchess the youth returned
up the path. It was the Duke. The figure and backview were
eighteen !

This evening we motored to Beaulieu to dine with Mr. and Mrs.
Plesch. As a diner-out I am a cheat. I accept everything to save
explanation of my illness. I have a trick of letting the servants
fill my wine glasses, thus frustrating encores ; but what restraint
I have to practise on this coast of epicures ! The villa stands
high on terraced gardens rising from the bay. As our car drew
up, a very young butler, aware of Mrs. Cartwright's physical dis-
ability, suggested we should drive round to the terrace front in
order to save a flight of steps. He jumped on to the running-
board and was most solicitous. Some twenty dinner guests were
assembled on the balustraded terrace, flanked by palms and ornamented with fairy lanterns. We looked down a vista of illuminated flowerbeds towards a moonlit sea. I congratulated my
hostess on her considerate young butler. " Young butler ? " she
reiterated. " My butler's elderly—there ! " she said, pointing
to a portly man carrying a tray of cocktails. Baffled, I was about
to make some reply when the ' young butler ' came down the
steps from the house. " Oh," said my hostess, " let me introduce
my husband's secretary, Prince Michael of Bourbon."

After dinner I talked with young Prince Michael. He is an
ingenuous lad of twenty-four, and as we talked the wonder
grew. He had been in the American and British armies, he had
been a paratrooper and had been dropped in France, Belgium,
and Malaya. He shyly confessed he had just finished a book on
his paratroop adventures. I calculated that he had joined the
forces at seventeen. When I observed that he must have been very
brave to do so much jumping so young he laughed and said,
" Oh, no—just stupid ! " We were interrupted just when I
was wondering whether I should confess the ' young butler '
mistake. I am sure he would have enjoyed it.

So home about 2 a.m., a lovely drive along the coast with the
sea shining under a brilliant moon.

August 7.

Despite my restraint I have been up three nights in succession
with my wretched old ulcer. I live in a paradise poisoned with
pain. To-day Aubrey motored me into Cannes to see the family
doctor. I have had a frightful week and have been a burden to

the whole household which is unwearyingly kind.   The French doctor went over me ;   the usual tappings and questions.   On these occasions I always feel like a broken-down gas-geyser—" You never know what may happen " says the plumber, investigating, " the whole thing may blow up."   The doctor wrote a prescription, some form of a drug to allay the pain.   What else can he do ? My concern now is whether I should attempt the motor trip with my two young friends or fly back to England.   I do not wish to spoil their holiday.

It is very hot to-night.   The tree-frogs croak incessantly. I stay out on the balcony not knowing what to do with myself. And all around lies the silent beauty of this sub-tropical night.

August 8.

We have settled our course.   Aubrey is willing to take the risk of having to dump me on the way.   I have packed.   We leave by car to-morrow at 6 a.m. for Florence, our first stage.

Italy

WE are in Florence. Yesterday morning in the first light of
the cool dawn we took the silent road to Antibes. We saw
a round red disc come up out of the sea. Then the whitewashed
villas caught up the level light on their silvery olive terraces. By
eight o'clock, passing empty Nice and Mentone, we had reached
the Italian frontier and customs house at Ponte San Luigi. Somewhere we had picked up a puncture. It was not too disastrous
for us, for as our baggage was examined we changed the wheel.
By ten o'clock, the coastal road still empty, we reached Alassio
and halted for coffee while we had the spare tyre repaired. So
here I was again in this lovely little town, menaced by overbuilding
as all along this coast, where through the winter of 1948-9 I had
rented a villa. I wrote part of *And so to Rome* sitting on my balcony,
framed in purple bourgainvillea and looking down on a terraced
garden filled with oranges, lemons and tangerines. My researches
were helped by the excellent English library at the foot of my
garden, relic of a large and almost vanished English colony.
The views over the town and bay were exquisite and until the
end of December we lunched on our balcony. At night the sea
was jewelled with the flares of the fishing fleet off Laiguelia, the
little village nestling under the dark mountain wall of Cap Mele.
I had a warm welcome from the café proprietor, the garage me-
chanics, and above all, the pretty *signorina* in the postcard shop.
I took Aubrey down the sandy beach, and through " The Drain "
(Via XX Settembre), the narrow shopping street whose arches
reveal gleaming vistas of the sea. There is now no smell, despite
the nickname once given the street by the English colony.

After an hour's halt we went on to Genoa. By noon we had
reached the hamlet of Ruta, 900 feet high, commanding a magnificent view of the great bay of Genoa, and of the promontory
of Portofino pushing its finger into the sea. A way-side café
proved irresistible in the sunshine and we took out our lunch
basket. My after-breakfast pain had miraculously not ensued
for once. Emboldened I ate some sandwiches with my milk.
It was altogether a new world at this elevation, the smiling

earth below us.   The sun was hot, the air fresh, the scenery enchanting.   We burst into song.   Life was very good.

After Rapallo the Bracco Pass was negotiated, over the high
range blocking the coastal road between Rapallo and Spezia.
In January 1949, motoring back with a friend from a visit to
the opera at La Scala, Milan, we had encountered ice and snow-
drifts on the road and in the darkening winter's afternoon felt
some apprehension.*   Yesterday the scene was wholly different.
We paused at the top of the pass at a jaunty little roadhouse with
a turret flying the Italian flag and, inevitably, the blazon of Coca-
Cola (*Bevete Coca-Cola*) which has surpassed Hannibal in all his
marches through Italy, for it has conquered everywhere.   Then,
threading a mountain valley with its stream we mounted again,
passed a lonely monastery crowning a mountain peak, and began
the tortuous descent through chestnut woods to Spezia and its
great bay.   Our road now, in the early afternoon free of motorists,
—the post-prandial spaghetti-stagger lays all Italians low—ran
through the coastal plain that has for a background the shining
Carrara mountains.   I thought of Michelangelo, fretting and
fuming as he selected his blocks of marble for the great tomb of
Julius II, never finished, and also of the block of white marble
that threw Cellini into such fury when it was given by the Medici
duchess to his rival.   Then came the romantic castle of Massa,
so enormous, spread along its precipice, that it looks like a town in
itself.   It is one of those castles that one resolves to go and see one
day but ever remain a place of dreams.   Soon the long pinewoods
of Viareggio and its great bathing beach were slipping by.   We
by-passed Lucca, its dome and towers visible, the birthplace of
Puccini.   I recalled how one wintry morning I had looked out
from an hotel window and saw two young men carrying a bass
fiddle across the Piazza in a downpour of rain, while the statue of
the Grand Duchess Marie Louise with her young son looked across
the Piazza Napoleone at the Palace in which she had reigned so
disastrously.   Strange what things stick in the memory !

The sun was reddening Brunelleschi's great dome as we drew into
Florence.   I have had a great welcome at the little pension I
frequent, with its windows overlooking the Arno, and the cypress-

* In order to avoid the Bracco Pass, the roads over the Apennines being very bad,
Byron, when he left Pisa in 1823, en route to Genoa, travelled by coach, with his
menagerie, to Lucca, and then to Lerici.   Here he was joined by the Leigh Hunts
and Trelawny and they went in three boats to Sestri Levante, one for Byron and
Teresa Guiccioli, one for Trelawny and one for the Leigh Hunt family.

crowned slope of San Miniato filling the skyline. My pleasure in this lovely day, miraculously free from pain, is increased by Aubrey's delight in this historic scene. Here are all the things, world famous, long heard of—the Ponte Vecchio, with a crimson sunset flooding through its arches, the great rose-hued dome of the Duomo, the sinister machicolated tower of the Palazzo Vecchio, Michelangelo's huge *David*, snowily naked, with the dark bronze of Cellini's *Perseus* for neighbour, the narrow streets and fortress-like palaces known to Giotto, Dante, Boccaccio, the Medici, young Raphael, Michelangelo, grim Savonarola and cynical Macchiavelli. There is nothing more thrilling than the translation of familiar legends into visual reality. I, long familiar with this famous city, take new pleasure in my companion's fresh enjoyment.

August 11.

A friend from Trieste joined us early yesterday. Four years there with the British Army have made him love the Italian scene. I am grateful for his presence for he can go sightseeing with Aubrey. I am out of commission, but there are compensations. The enchanting view across the Arno from my window consoles me. The dark cypresses on the hill-side opposite pierce the unfathomable blue sky. With this view I am reading again Macchiavelli's *Il Principe*. He lived over the river by the Via de' Guicciardini, some of it demolished by barbarian Germans.

To-day we came by car to Siena via San Gimignano where we halted for tea and visited the church of San Agostino to see the 15th century frescoes of Gozzoli, seventeen superb scenes portraying the life of St. Augustine. A gracious old verger of eighty-nine took us round and told us he had seen Queen Victoria when she visited Florence.

SIENA

August 12.

We walked through the Middle Ages to-day, along the Banchi di Sopra and down to the magnificent Square, or Campo as they call it, which contains surely the finest belfry in Europe. It is an arrow speeding to heaven and crowns this many-hilled city. The Campo is in the form of a shell and slopes towards the battlemented Palazzo Pubblico. Already the excitement of next

Wednesday's Palio is in the air. One hears a beating of drums, then out of a narrow street comes a squadron of youths in slashed doublets and parti-coloured hose. Two of them carry the silken banners of their *contrada* or parish. They wave them over their heads, pass them between their legs and then, following a skill centuries old, they launch their flags up into the air in a swift interchange and catch them again with the greatest deftness in their left hands. This flag ceremony is called *sbandierata*, and the particular movement is an *alzata*. The youths move in procession as if they had just come out of a Renaissance frieze, their comely bodies set off by tight, embroidered doublets and coloured hose. Thus paraded the Montagus and Capulets. The *cinquecento* lives again in a city whose houses were here when St. Catherine lived in a side street. French, Spanish and Italian blood has spilled on these pavements through the centuries.

August 13.

We noticed when in San Gimignano last Friday that there was to be a performance of *Lucia di Lammermoor* in the Piazza. This evening we motored across the Tuscan hills to attend it. A thunderstorm broke during our journey and the vine-clad hills were lit by tremendous flashes that gave the landscape a Dantesque aura, a sense of the overpowering hand of God above this riven paradise. It cleared by the time we reached San Gimignano whose high towers had seemed even more forbidding against the storm. The Piazza makes a natural amphitheatre, the gallery seats being the steps of the Cathedral. The stage was set against the ancient Palace of the Podestà (1239). It was a case of Scotland on the stage below, and a medieval palace above. Its embrasured windows, with their wrought-iron sconces for holding flares, framed figures as dramatic as those on the stage. There, under the stars, in an old piazza that through six centuries has seen rape, bloodshed, fratricidal feuds, the reception of kings, princes and dukes, where the façades of old buildings glimmered under the torches, and the great towers soared up dimly in the night, we heard Donizetti's opera. In the interval we walked into the long Piazza Cavour, with its great cistern and the twin towers of the Ardinghelli whose slit windows had looked down since the 13th century on God only knows what horrors that swept this embattled hill-town. And now only an air of Donizetti's sounded in the calm night, and alert little boys sold Coca-Cola and *gelati* to foreigners who swept in on big automobiles and buses and, after a few hours, swept out again, leaving the sombre walls to crumble in a half-dead citadel slumbering in the shadows of a violent past.

August 14.

This morning as we walked through the winding streets of Siena I noticed how on the upper stories of the great grim houses, standing above chasms of deep shadow, the vivid sunlight struck the balconies and roof gardens. Sunflowers seem to be in some favour here. They were used as a symbol by San Bernardino, the great Siena preacher. He is much in evidence this year of the *Anno Santo*, and there is a special exhibition in the oratory in which he lived.

This year the pilgrims have been on all the roads that lead to Rome. They vary in manner and means. The ill-equipped are the more interesting. The occupants of wagons-lits, of sporting automobiles and of road-hogging Pullman motor coaches, do not merit our attention. They will surely arrive, and quickly depart. The true pilgrim, unchanged in fifteen centuries, goes on foot. Alas, another true type has disappeared, the pilgrim on a mule or horse. In this category we would have encountered the figures of history. On the Tuscan highway from Florence to Siena I looked closely for a moment at a group of riders going Romewards in a lurid sunset. They had a Boccaccian air. Six hundred and fifty years earlier, in some such manner, there had journeyed to Rome for the First Jubilee of the *Anno Santo* a similar mounted group. It was a Florentine embassy comprising, Messrs. Ugolino de Corregio, mayor of Florence, Giotto the painter, Caselli the musician, Palli Strozzi the orator, and one, Dante Alighieri, the poet who was soon to return to Rome again and there learn the news of his lifelong exile, based on a trumped-up charge of corruption concerning the public funds.

My admiration for these pilgrims had been aroused, on the Bracco Pass, by a white-haired man with a tricycle on which he had mounted a portmanteau-box that proudly proclaimed his name and his pilgrimage, from Aberdeen to Rome. He travelled in faith and would arrive, I felt sure. All over Italy the pilgrims of every class spill into the churches, the museums and art galleries. They come variously equipped, many of them scarcely aware of what they see, dazed by the countless Madonnas and Bambinos, the legacy of the astonishing Renaissance. It is easy to make fun of these tourists, to laugh at their ignorance, their ill-digested absorption of a panorama they can scarcely comprehend, and to wonder what they derive from the kaleidoscopic frieze of history along which they hurry. But to understand all is not necessarily to profit, and when an incident in Santa Croce at Florence had provoked my mirth I felt a little contrite, on reflection. I think there must be few, among the riches of that great church holding the ashes of Michelangelo, Galileo, Machiavelli, etc., who turn aside into the Pazzi chapel to look at the memorial of a Queen who was never a Queen, and whose singular achievement is seen in the nave where Canova's clumsy mass of marble—he was prevented from using the better design, which may be seen in the Canova museum at his native Possagno—memorialises the poet Alfieri, the ' Queen's ' lover.

The monument in this side chapel to the Countess of Albany, wife of Bonnie Prince Charlie, is by Santarelli who, following the death of Canova, had a restricted but deserved vogue in Italy. We can forgive him the use of the British Royal Arms, since the Countess all her life had insisted on using them, a liberty Canova did not attempt on his beautiful cenotaph to the last three Stuarts in St. Peter's. Despite the bold assumption of royal honours, the memorial is beautiful and to me is worthy of regard since here ends, in some dignity at last, the sad and stormy story of the girl-wife, married to an elderly sot for whom, in his gallant and ill-starred youth, so many faithful adherents to the Stuart cause laid down their lives.

I was explaining to Aubrey the history of the ' Queen of England,' so beautifully memorialised in this chapel, when a man obtruded on us and with an unmistakable northern accent asked, " Who did you say she was ? " I repeated, with some impatience, my description and when I had finished, his brow puzzled, his mind uncomprehending, the inquirer whispered, hoarsely but solemnly, " Was she a saint ? " I saw then, by his clothes, the badge on his jacket, his hot, tired but intense air that he was a pilgrim, and, in the course of this great event in his life, he was collecting Saints, anxious to pay homage wherever he could. To his question " Was she a saint ? " I could only answer " By no means ! " and at that he went rapidly away. I was grateful that he had not asked me to elucidate, for what a story I might have unfolded !

In Florence in the year 1780, on St. Andrew's Day, in the

Palazzo Guadagni, the royal husband, Bonnie Prince Charlie, after heavy celebration of this Scottish national fête, attempted to strangle his young wife, because she had received some polite attention from young Count Alfieri, a guest at their table.   After another dreadful scene in the Palazzo, the Countess of Albany fled from Florence to Rome, and was given asylum by the Young Pretender's brother, the kindly Henry, Cardinal Duke of York.   Alfieri followed her to Rome.   Four years later, conditions of separation agreed upon, the Countess scandalised Europe by fleeing to Colmar, where Alfieri openly joined her. For twenty-nine years they boldly cohabited and when the death of Bonnie Prince Charlie freed her they continued their open liaison in a palace in Florence.   As a Queen she would not give up her position, nor did Alfieri desire it.   When he died, in 1803, Italy's great poet was buried in Santa Croce.   Nothing less than a memorial by Canova would satisfy the disconsolate relict.   The Church raised strong objections to a design in which her own name was ostentatiously incorporated, but she overbore the authorities and so, to-day, in Santa Croce, she makes to the world and posterity, an epigraphic notification of long years of adultery.   The crowning audacity was the selection of Fabre the painter, Alfieri's successor in the ' Queen's ' household, to conduct negotiations with the authorities for the memorial to his own predecessor.

A remarkable woman indeed, this Princess Stolberg-Gedern, wife of the Young Pretender.   Such being the story, I could make only one answer to that query of an earnest pilgrim," Was she a saint ? "   How differently I might have answered him had he encountered me, a few days later, before a house in a narrow street in Siena.   The little daughter born in 1347 to Jacopo Benincasa, the fuller, in this humble dwelling, which we visited to-day, grew up to be, all aspects considered, one of the most remarkable women in history.   Whatever view may be taken of St. Catherine's visions—" Cataleptic fits," said the unsympathetic Mr. Trollope—or of her stigmatisation, challenged by the Franciscans, jealous of their own saint's infringed monopoly, we are confronted by a woman whose faith moved mountains, who stood, rock-like, admonishing and defiant in an age of overwhelming evil in human affairs.   Her frail self-tortured body became an instrument of steel, facing ordeals unsurpassed even by the Countess Matilda or Jeanne d'Arc.   What thunder and

what persuasion she wielded, so that she was able to uproot the
timorous Pope Gregory in Avignon and drive him to move the
Papal throne back to Rome after its centuries of exile. " Was
she a saint ? " There could be no doubt about the answer to
that query.

Siena has much knowledge of saints. Her birthplace is now
a shrine in a small street on a hill. Unfortunately they have
spoilt the simplicity of the original house by adding to it a grandiose memorial building.

St. Catherine died in the year 1380. Another saint was given
to Siena in the year of her death, St. Bernardino, regarding whom,
in this year of the Pilgrimage, an exhibition has been arranged.
On a high hill overlooking the walls and towers of the city stands
the convent and church of Osservanza. Two years ago on visiting
it I was horrified to discover that it had been bombed and demolished by the Allies, attacking a railway station a mile away.
This had resulted in the loss of many of its Della Robbia works
for which it was famous. But things are never quite lost in Italy,
such are the ancient skills retained in Italian hands. Yesterday
we found the church splendidly restored, with many of the Della
Robbia pieces reconstructed, particularly a magnificent *Coronation
of the Virgin*. But the true title to fame of this restored church is
that the young Bernardino studied and preached here before
beginning his apostolate in Milan. Now in the oratory of his
name, founded in 1400, on the site where he preached, Siena has
organised a timely exhibition. All over Italy, particularly
throughout Tuscany and the north, we see the sign he invented
and which is displayed on so many buildings that echoed his
voice. It is the Constantinian symbol *I.H.S.* (*In hoc signo vinces*)
surrounded by twelve rays of the sun, symbolic of the twelve
apostles and the twelve Articles of the Faith. It is upon the
façade of the Palazzo Pubblico, facing the great Campo where
the saint preached to forty thousand people.

The exhibition we visited to-day brings one very near to this
lovable man, a tireless itinerant preacher. It contains a bust of
him by Lorenzo di Pietro, contemporaneous, which almost
speaks. He has a comic face, laughter playing around his thin
mouth and in the sharp eyes. Bald, with a long nose, a fringe of
white hair, one feels sure he was a good companion who loved
life and his fellow-men and found godliness was next to sociability.
There are specimens of his hand-writing, of such beauty as fills

one with wonder ; a letter to Contessa Colonna, of the 12th of November, 1433 ; his annotated Bible. Here also is his seal as vicar of the convent of Osservanza. Two other objects among many delighted me, the reliquary holding his simple brown habit, and a poem written in his honour on a strip of parchment ten yards long. That was the way to inscribe a poem ! He deserved every inch of it, one is sure. In his long life there was nothing but service and kindness to his fellow-men, from that day during the pestilence of 1400 when, a youth of twenty, he laboured fearlessly with a band of friends, until forty-four years later he fell asleep, worn out in service. An inventory of his possessions reveals how few are the needs of a saint.

I shall never again see my anxious pilgrim of Santa Croce. Elsewhere to his question, in this exhibition for instance, I could have made a more rewarding answer. It was an ill fate that caused us to meet in a side chapel in Florence before the memorial of a ' Queen ' of questionable morals instead of in Siena, famed for two great saints.

In the course of our walk this morning we came to the Due Porte, one of the city's medieval gates, with a large square outside it. There, deeply ensconced in the battlemented wall of the gate we were attracted by a blacksmith's shop. He made beautiful weather-vanes, urns, door hinges, locks, and bolts that would have suited a Medici fortress. From the black cavern within came a fine voice singing snatches from *La Traviata*. Outside in the sunshine a fountain spluttered, and some old women, maidens and boys were bringing amphora-shaped jugs to fill. As they stood by the fountain they held large fig-leaves over their heads for shade. Across the square there was a joiner's shop. The carpenter, too, had a voice and he now joined the blacksmith in a duet from the opera. Both were invisible. Their voices in perfect unison filled the sunny piazza. Presently, I peered into the gloom of the blacksmith's shop. His furnace glowed, he was busily hammering a bronze urn on the anvil, singing all the time. When he paused I spoke to him. He exuded the joy of life. I remarked on it. " *Sì, signor*, I sing because I live in the sun ! " It seemed to me that he lived and worked in Cimmerian gloom. To my surprise he broke into fluent French. Yes, he had worked as a young man in a garage in Paris but *la mia indipendenza è tutto*. Here he was, his own master. He worked at little jobs, he sang, he was happy. Truly independence is everything, as he said. He wiped a grimy

brow and smiled, with only two teeth.   Then, putting a hoof of a
hand on his big belly, he broke into an aria from *Madame Butterfly*.
Here was a joyful fellow indeed, but like the king in the story,
who set out to buy the shirt of a happy man, I was frustrated—
he was naked from the waist up !

It was a very different scene we encountered towards evening.
A procession came out of a side street, walking to the slow tapping
of a drum.   Behind the boy drummer were brethren of the Misericordia, black, ghoulish, with eye-slits in their conical hoods, and
carrying lit candles.   Then came, in due order, three pages in
orange doublets and crimson hose, two noble-looking youths
carrying the bright embroidered banner of their *contrada*, a small
company of mourners, and, last of all, chanting priests and sur-
pliced acolytes with candles around a black bier.   It was the
funeral of a member of a *contrada*, in this festive week of the Palio.

The flags borne by the *contrade*, or parishes, are sheer poetry.
Many of them date back to the first Palio in 1659 though they have
been seen in the Campo spectacles since 1482.   There were originally fifty-seven *contrade*, then twenty-three and finally seventeen,
six having been suppressed after a tumult following a horse-race in
1675.   The surviving *contrade* are the *Eagle, Silkworm, Snail, Owl,
Dragon, Giraffe, Porcupine, Unicorn, She-Wolf, Shell, Goose, Wave,
Panther, Forest, Tortoise, Tower* and *Ram*.   Of these, ten are selected
by ballot to run the race.   Each *contrada* is attached to an Oratory,
each has a flag of historical significance.   When Charles V visited
Siena in 1536 he conferred on *Eagle* the hereditary title of nobility
and granted it the right to place the imperial crown above the
double-headed eagle on the banner.   When all the flags of the
contrade are waving in the procession round the Campo it is an
intoxicating sight.   *Eagle's* banner is yellow with black and blue
bands ; *Silkworm*, yellow and green with pale blue bands ; *Snail*,
yellow and red with blue piping ; *Owl*, blue and red with white
bands ; *Dragon*, a gold-crowned dragon on pale blue, etc.

A few days before the race all these banners hung in the Duomo.
The three great naves and transept, with their black and white
striped columns, were a maze of colour, the shining banners lit
by the sunlight entering through stained glass.

August 15.

I stayed in bed this morning but in the afternoon got up and
motored to the Castle of Belcaro.   Our trio has been augmented

E

by my friend Kate Heckscher, who lives near Florence. After a
short run we arrived at the castle. It is hard to imagine anything
more romantic than its setting. It stands on a hill a thousand
feet high. We mounted a steep drive to some massive gates in
the heavily battlemented walls. After pulling a chain, used by a
medieval pilgrim, a great door swung open, admitting us to a
walled-in courtyard beyond which we saw stables and a garden.
Through a guardhouse we mounted a short stairway and emerged
on to the ramparts of the castle, built in the twelfth century.
An ambulatory enabled us to walk round three-quarters of the
ramparts, massively built, and rising sheer from the mount.
On the inner side we looked down on the courtyard and formal
garden, the villa-castle, and a chapel and casino. The walls of
the old fortress were restored and transformed in the 16th century
by Peruzzi, and an 18th century villa has been imposed. It rises
above the steep oakwoods that surround the fortress, with the
Tuscan valley far below. The position reminded me a little of
Segovia's famous castle. The rampart walk provided a magnificent panorama of the olive groves on the Tuscan hills. The
place must have been almost impregnable and I wondered what
desperate sieges it had known.

We descended to the courtyard and passed through a formal
garden, glowing in the afternoon sun, and entered the small
family chapel. It was beautifully kept, with some interesting
frescoes. Next door there was a casino whose long windows
looked on to the garden. Its salon was an astonishing contrast
to its chaste neighbour. It was the gayest, most ornate and
enchanting garden-house imaginable. In 1536 Peruzzi had
covered its ceilings and walls with *The Loves of the Gods*, and *The
Judgment of Paris*, all depicted in a happy and lascivious nudity,
so bright, so frolicsome, that one felt Cupid had been master
of the revels and had inspired the artist's brush. I have never
seen a gayer room or one so unblushingly dedicated to the frank
pleasures of the flesh.

On our return journey we were attracted by the monastery of
Lecceto. In the fourth century it was a hermitage, became an
abbey in 1100 A.D. and an Augustinian monastery in 1387. It
stood massive and lonely against the evening sky. We hammered
at the gates and awakened nothing but echoes. Finally an old
man came and doubtfully opened the gates, admitting us to a

courtyard with a ruinous cloister. His old wife, plucking a fowl, scolded him and us. Evidently she did not like visitors. The place was vast, empty, ruinous, and seemed to be degenerating into a farmhouse. We learned that in the Middle Ages a Pope had stayed there. It had two cloisters and some fading frescoes by Paolo di Neri in the hall, depicting Hell and Paradise, and Medieval Life in times of war and peace, all painted about 1370. The heavy decay of this monastery was made more sinister by the legend that one monk had murdered another in it. The monastery was suppressed in 1810 and has not been inhabited since ; during the last war it was a storehouse of precious paintings from the Siena Art Gallery. It preserves still its primitive form of a fortress-monastery.

The light had almost gone as we followed the downward track through the woods. Gaunt yet beautiful, the campanile stood silhouetted against the crimson sky. One day it will fall. The home of three hundred monks, flourishing in the days of the Medici, is fast crumbling into dust.

August 16.

To-day we have seen the Palio, the famous horse-race round the Campo. I was here to see it two years ago and I would willingly be here to see it every year. There is no other costume pageant to compare with it. In the centre of the Campo stood forty thousand people. All around the course, built up on the façades of shops and palaces, were tiers of seats, thronged with spectators. The Campo looked like a basket of flowers, so rich is the colour. The racecourse is the perimeter of the great Campo. The horses race in reverse to custom, that is, to the left, round the course. Every balcony, every window, every roof was alive with human faces. The great façade of the Podestà's palace fluttered with flags between armorial shields. High over all, from the slender campanile, the famous Mangia bell tolled dramatically, sending waves of sound across the many-hilled city. The race began when the sun had fallen low enough to throw a shadow over the Campo.

In the early afternoon we had been up to the Duomo to see the *contrade* arrive. Their horses and jockeys had been blessed in their own parochial churches. Now they came to salute the archbishop in the vast cathedral which, in 1880, had suggested to Wagner the setting for the temple of the Holy Grail in *Parsifal*.

At last all was ready for the great race. The contestants were lined up in a narrow street adjacent to the Campo. Suddenly a cheer broke from the expectant multitude. The mounted carabinieri, twelve abreast, rode round the course. There followed the six macebearers of the city, the flagbearers of the commune, on horseback with grooms and four centurions, twelve trumpeters and twelve musicians playing the Palio march. Next came the six flag-bearers of the city's estate and castles in the ancient Republic of Siena. There followed the page of the Captain of the People, bearing the State sword, the leader of the Sienese troops, on horseback, led by a groom, attended by six centurions. All these were in sixteenth century costumes. Now, one by one, the *contrade* entered the Campo whirling their great silken banners. A drummer led each *contrada* with two flag bearers. They marched forward making the traditional *sbandierata*, their banners waved, furled and launched into the air, to be interchanged and caught again. With each *contrada* came a Captain in armour, visored, with a great sword, two men-at-arms, three pages, the jockey on a parade horse with his groom and finally the racehorse. The *contrade* entered slowly, moving like chessmen, performing the traditional flag-waving, until all were spaced around the Campo. One looked across a sea of whirling flags, green, blue, crimson, mauve, gold, cerise, purple and lilac, each marking a cohort of attendants in slashed doublets and hose. It was as if the youth of the city had marched out of a sixteenth-century missal. Vivid, slender, handsome, the Romeos of the Renaissance were here as Pinturricchio shows them on his frescoes in the Piccolomini chapel up in the Duomo. Thus had the Dukes of Ferrara, Mantua and Urbino marched here with their gonfaloniers, their men-at-arms, squires and pages.

By the time all the *contrade* had entered the Campo, and had spaced the whole course, their shining banners were like a multi-coloured undulating carpet. Towards the end of this procession a dozen small pages in crimson hose carried on their shoulders a green rope of laurel leaves ; it was a panel of the Della Robbia children come to life. With them were six knights in armour, with closed visors, representing the suppressed *contrade*. Then, closing the procession, now beginning to mass itself in one phalanx of colour before the Palazzo Pubblico, came the great war chariot drawn by four milk-white yoked oxen. This was the *Carroccio*, a replica of the chariot from which the commanders directed the

troops in the battle.   On it a bell, the Martinella, tolled as the
chariot slowly progressed.   Before the battle it had summoned
the soldiers for a final benediction.   Above the *Carroccio* rose the
Palio itself, a long embroidered silken panel bearing the images
of the Madonna and Child, the symbol for which the race is run.

The evening light now touched the roofs of palaces and buildings, the great Campo was in the shade.   In the serene blue-green
of the evening sky the campanile, with its solemn bell still tolling,
rose splendidly outlined, arches and machicolated battlements
black against the vivid evening glow.   A great cheer greeted the
entry of the racehorses.   The jockeys, in coloured doublets, with
steel helmets—for they whipped each other as well as the horses—
rode bareback.   There was much pulling at the starting rope,
and frenzy seized the crowd as the starting cannon sounded.
This frenzy is the more singular because the race is utterly corrupt,
the issue having being bargained for by the contending *contrade*
who have made deals to eliminate dangerous competitors.   The
race is three times round the Campo.   There is one corner with
a steep descent sometimes fatal to horses and jockeys.   The bar-
ricades at this point are heavily padded.   Of the ten horses
to-day, two threw their jockeys, two ran afoul at the sharp corner.
The winner passed the post by a head and was immediately
surrounded by the carabinieri, for partisanship has sometimes
expressed itself in an attack on horse and jockey.   The race
finished, the crowd streamed over the sanded course.

Two years ago I had something of an inside view of the Palio.
My Sienese friend, Benvenuto R, a tall youth, with a classical
head of black curls, who might have posed for Giuliano de'
Medici, was the captain of his *contrada Drago*.   He wore the
traditional suit of armour, greaves, helmet with visor, and carried
a great sword.   Each *contrada* is a guild and has its own clubroom.
It is usually attached to a church.   In *Drago's* clubroom I watched
the young gallants, squires, flag bearers and pages put on their
skin-tight hose, their leather shoes of fancy design, their slashed
doublets and gay embroidered bonnets surmounting wigs of long
curls.   For four hundred years successive youths of the *contrada*
have worn these costumes, traditional from the days when Cesare
Borgia, the henchman of Charles V, and the Florentine enemy
had marched over the Republic's borders.   All the small boys of
Siena aspire to join the *sbandieri*.   You see them carefully practising the passes, the flourishes, the fling, with their diminutive

flags. Rounding a corner one morning, I encountered three pages about twelve years old, in scarlet hose and ermine-tipped doublets, seriously rehearsing while another small page rolled the drum.

In Benvenuto's *contrada* hang the Palios won on former years. There is the fiercest competition for this great trophy and a *contrada* rises in importance with the number of them. In 1948 my friend took me to the *Prova*, a rehearsal of the race in the Campo, and to the drawing of lots in front of the Palazzo Pubblico. Seventeen *contrade* only may enter ten horses. The names are placed in a rotating drum. Two guards in black and white hose stand by, holding wands. A fanfare of six trumpeters in heraldic costume opens the ceremony. Two small pages dip their hands in the drum and draw forth numbers for *contrade* and horses. Groans and cheers greet the results. The ten selected horses are paraded by their grooms, carefully guarded by each *contrada*.

That year *Lupa* won. Late in the evening we went into the *Lupa contrada*. Flags whirled, drums beat, traditional songs were sung, the streets were hung with the black and white banners of *Lupa* and torches flared in the sconces before the windows of the palaces. A delirium seized the crowd in the triumphant *contrada*. Round and round marched singing cohorts of costumed youths under their banners. We went to the clubroom. It adjoined the church of San Rocca, bright with candles. By the altar stood the Palio won that day. The clubroom was decorated with flowers, the ancient black and white costumes hung in cabinets. Former Palios decorated the walls ; there was free wine—this is the Chianti country—for all. By the entrance of the church a small room, with a grille, was lit up. Within, munching a great bale of hay with which he had been rewarded, stood *Lupa's* winning horse. There was a bouquet of flowers on his head and gay ribbons woven in his tail. He was gazed on admiringly in his hour of glory. In a month's time the traditional banquet of the *contrada* would be held in the main street. At a long table the jockey would sit at one end and the horse would have a manger at the other.

To-night I sent my companions out into the town. As I lay in bed the noise of revelry filled the air. The beating of drums, singing and cheering, flowed over the city, while, intermittently, fireworks flared. Siena will hold festival until dawn.

August 17.

Motored to-day to Castello Brolio, the fortress home of Baron Ricasoli. It is finely situated on a crest of the Chianti hills from whose terraced vineyards the famous Brolio chianti is drawn. The castle, surrounded by dramatic cypresses dominates a wide valley at a height of some fifteen hundred feet. It is an imposing mansion rising within the strong bastions of the old fortress and dates back to the ninth century. In A.D. 1009 the Marquis of Tuscany, father of the Countess Matilda of Canossa fame, ceded the castle to the monks of the Badia in Florence, and in 1141 it became the property of the Ricasoli family who still live in it. The Sienese took brief possession of this formidable Florentine outpost in 1434, imprisoning the family in the dungeons until, forty days later, the Florentines retook the fortress. It was besieged in 1478 by the Spanish troops under Ferdinand of Aragon, King of Naples, allied with Pope Sixtus IV and the Sienese, at war with Florence. After a siege of two months they captured it, and sacked and reduced it to its foundations. When the war ended, Florence, aware of its strong position as an outpost against Siena, reconstructed it, but again during the siege of Florence in 1529 the Sienese took the castle, drove out the Ricasoli family, and burned it down to the foundations. Once more the castle rose from its ancient bastions and the plan of the fortress has been preserved to this day. The castle was much restored in 1861 by the statesman Baron Bettino Ricasoli, when a new Sienese-Gothic front was added.

This Florentine family dates back to the eleventh century and has long controlled the hills of this Chianti country on the frontier of Florence and Siena. In the thirteenth century the Ricasoli were Ghibbeline in sympathy, allied with Siena against the Guelphs of Florence, but they changed sides before Siena's great victory at Montaperti and suffered in consequence. At first hostile to the rising Medici, they became strong allies though they retained their feudatory powers until 1777. They were the only barons in Tuscany. Other titles were conferred on them but they were more proud of being the sole barons of Tuscany than of being Counts of the Palatine.

The last great figure, Baron Bettino Ricasoli, known as the Iron Baron, played a great part in Florentine politics. He it was who handled the difficult negotiations when the kindly last Grand Duke of Tuscany, Leopold II, nicknamed Daddy, bowed to the

revolution inspired by the nationalism sweeping Italy in 1848.
A revolutionary named Guerrazzi led the demagogues.* The
Grand Duke swore to stand firm. " Never can it be said that I
surrendered to a party my Tuscany, which I have loved as a
bride." But the Guerrazzi faction was too strong. Leopold
wept, held out his hand to his minister Ricasoli, and departed.
The Baron noticed that when the Austrians entered Florence
they did as little damage as possible while he rated low the courage
of the local democrats. " All the shooting they did was from
behind windows." Thus ended the Grand Duchy of Tuscany.

Ricasoli's first love was his daughter. When offered the position of gonfalonier he frankly told the Grand Duke that he
would dedicate to his fellow citizens " any remnant of time not
absolutely necessary to the education of my daughter." Nevertheless, his whole life was devoted to the service of Florence.
His second love was his castle home and the great wine-producing
industry he built up at Brolio. As we approached this old castle
to-day I could understand his pride in it. It looks down on the
hills and the vast undulating plain, proud in its seigniory. The
man who had followed Cavour as President of the Council of
Ministers in 1861, the apostle of Tuscan agriculture, found here
in his castle and estate his master passion.

We arrived at a massive gate in the great bastion walls, sixty
feet high and almost a mile in circumference. Artillery had been
used against these massive walls for the first time in history when
the Sienese troops attacked the castle in 1390. The portal swung
back, and we drove up a curving ramp to the inner courtyard
of the castle. Our arrival was unexpected but our welcome
lacked no warmth. There was one note of surprise. A guest,
Lady Cartwright of Aynho (née Chigi of Siena), was at that very
moment departing—for Siena. It transpired that she was a
relation of Aubrey's, met for the first time ! We drank the
famous wine in the great dining-hall whose walls are decorated
with cartoons of the house of Ricasoli, and then went out on to

* When Byron arrived in Pisa, November 1821, with Teresa Guiccioli, a young
student at Pisa University, Francesco Guerrazzi, wrote: " At the time the rumour
spread in Pisa that an extraordinary man had arrived there, of whom people told a
hundred different tales, all contradictory and many absurd. They said he was of
royal blood, of very great wealth, of sanguine temperament, of fierce habits, masterly
in knightly exercises, possessing an evil genius, but more than a human intellect.
He was said to wander through the world like Job's Satan. . . . It was George Byron.
I wished to see him ; he appeared to me like the Vatican Apollo."—Guerrazzi.
Memorie.

the terrace built along the ramparts, with its stupendous view of
the Chianti country spread below us.   Lastly we went into the
family chapel, built in 1348 and decorated with modern mosaics.
It holds in the crypt the Ricasoli tombs.

On leaving we drove down through the cypress woods to the
valley where the great *cantine* housed the grapes brought in from
the surrounding vineyards.   Never again shall I open a bottle
of Brolio chianti without recalling this castle set on its mountain
and the hospitable family that rules over this domain.

August 19.

On the way to Florence to-day, some eight miles from Siena,
I again noticed, high on a mount by the roadside, a circular wall
with several square towers.   Obviously it was an old fortified
hill-town, possibly an outpost guarding the main road.   In the
morning light it showed up romantically and I persuaded Aubrey
to turn up a steep path until we came to a gateway in the great
wall.   When we went through we found the remains of a small
town.   The chief features of this old fortified place set among
the olive-clad hills, now dead and deserted, as it seemed, were
the great wall and the towers that encircled it.   The towers were
not equidistantly spaced.   In the great containing wall, which
had no battlements, there were two ancient gateways, one to the
north, the other to the south.   Within there was nothing but
dilapidation.   A deserted piazza had a church on one side,
and a few ruinous houses.   Not a living soul was to be seen at
that moment, though later a few curious heads appeared at old
windows.   The hand of desolating Time had fallen heavily on
this crumbling stronghold.   Yet from its position, its great walls
and gateways and towers, I imagined it had once been a place of
considerable strength and beauty.   My guidebook disdained to
mention it.   I could not see a person from whom we could learn
even its name.   Later, on a map, I found it was called Monteriggioni.   Silent, ruinous, it sat on the hill above the olive
groves while not five hundred yards away the motor traffic of
the twentieth century swept along the busy Siena-Florence
highway.

We left the place, saddened by its decay, aware of the brevity
of all Man's works, of the oblivion that follows his furious activities.   Doubtless it had known fierce assaults and been desperately defended, and across the loose cobbles of its dusty
E*

piazza, where now not even a cat moved, the trail of blood had run.

[Six months after this visit to the deserted citadel I discovered its history. Reading Dante's *Inferno* one day, I stumbled on an astonishing revelation. The poet, one foggy evening, while passing on the highway below had seen the towers of Monteriggioni rising mistily from its circular wall. Later when he wrote the thirty-first canto of the *Inferno*, he recalled this vision and, with a poet's imagination, he made use of it. In this canto he is travelling with Virgil towards the ninth Circle of Hell, in which Satan is placed, when he sees many lofty towers—*che mi parve veder molte alte torre*. Said Virgil, " Know they are not towers but giants and are in the well, around its rim, from the navel downwards." Dante describes the fearful sight of this pit of Hell:—

> "Però che come in su la cerchia tonda
> Montereggion di torri si corona ;
> cosi la proda che il pozzo circonda
> corregiavan di mezza la persona
> gli orribili giganti, cul minaccia
> Giove del cielo ancora, quando tuona."

For as Montereggioni on its round walls crowns itself
     with towers,
So, the horrible giants, whom Jove still threatens when
     he thunders from Heaven, with half their bodies
     turret the walls which surround the pit.

The towers are the implanted giants, and Dante identifies these denizens of Hell ; Nimrod, builder of the Tower of Babel, " whose face seemed as large as the pine-cone of St. Peter's at Rome." He hears Nimrod cry out in his rage. Then he sees Briareus, *immensus*, who, with a hundred arms and fifty heads, defied the gods of Olympus ; and Antaeus, unfettered although impious, because he held aloof from strife against the Gods, yet challenged Hercules who, learning that he lost his strength when he lost touch with the earth, lifted and crushed him. It is this unfettered giant who now lifts Virgil and Dante and gently lowers them into the bottom pit of Hell wherein are Lucifer and Judas.

The ruined citadel whose round wall suggested a well, or the pit of Hell, and the towers the doomed giants, was built in 1213 by the Sienese as an outpost against the Florentines. An inscription near one of the gates reads " Anno Domini MCCXIIJ ind II, mense martii . . . hoc castrum Montis Regionis in Dei fui fuit nomine inceptum et undique postea mura vallatum propriis Senensis populi laboribus et expensis. . . ." It was reduced in 1244, enlarged in 1260 when the twelve massive towers, one hundred feet apart, appear to have been added after their great victory over the Florentine Guelphs at Montaperti, and from 1349 to 1376 it was garrisoned because of the number of robberies and murders that took place within its walls. The Visconti held it for a time. It was defended against the Sienese allied with the Pope and the King of Naples in 1478. The Florentines bombarded it with artillery in 1526 and finally, on August 27th, 1554, it fell to the Marquis of Marignano, commanding general of the Medici troops. From that time on it slowly lapsed into a peaceful ruin, a spent volcano amid the olive groves but still holding some of the mystery and power of the Dantesque vision.]

Before noon we arrived in Florence. Still unwell, I went to bed wondering whether I could make the journey to Mantua on the morrow, as planned. My army friend departed for Trieste in the afternoon but a new recruit is here, Simon Stuart, Aubrey's friend. My two escorts are six-foot-four and six-foot-three. Each of them has done a year's military service after leaving Eton, each of them next term is going up to Trinity College, Cambridge. I find it difficult to believe that Simon, a lieutenant in the Scots Guards, has recently been standing up to the waist in the fetid swamps of Malaya, engaged in jungle warfare.

Things Observed.

Aubrey and Simon came back from the Uffizzi Gallery with a gem. In the Botticelli Room a bright young lady was reading out of her guidebook the description of a picture. " But which Botticelli ? " demanded her friend, " There are two—Sandro and Scuola."

August 20.

In bed most of yesterday, after arrival here, in preparation for to-day's journey to Mantua. Early this morning we crossed the

Apennines by the Futa Pass. Three years ago when I first made
this trip I was astonished to find at Pietramala, two-thousand-
five-hundred feet high, a large American soldiers' cemetery in
the bosom of the desolate mountains, a sad reminder of the
desperate fighting along this pass on the route to the Po valley.
Out of the mist the Stars and Stripes fitfully appeared under a
ray of sunshine which also lit three hundred neat headstones
marking the graves with geometrical precision. It was my
intention to halt and again visit this mountain cemetery but on
reaching Pietramala this clear sunny morning I was utterly baffled
for I could not see anywhere the great cemetery. I enquired,
almost certain that I knew its location. " They're all gone,
signor," replied an Italian to whom I addressed my query.
" Gone ? " I exclaimed, " Whatever do you mean ? The dead
don't walk ! "   " Oh, yes, they do, signor, if they have enough
dollars ! All the Americanos were dug up, boxed and sent
home." We went on, dumbfounded.*

The war-torn villages on this route have all been rebuilt.
New bridges and a splendid road bear witness to the energy and
genius of Italian workmen. We lunched in Bologna, still showing
her war scars, and passed on to Modena. I have not been here
before ; now I shall never forget it. The cathedral is one of the
jewels of Italy. It is a medieval basilica built in A.D. 1099 on
the site of a former basilica that had arisen in the fourth century
to commemorate the tomb of St. Geminiano. In the ninth century it collapsed from age. It is believed that the great Countess
Matilda helped in the reconstruction, Romanesque in style. It
possesses sculptured doors. At the main portal two lions support
two columns, above, there is a canopied tribune and over this
a fine rose window. The lions, the columns and the tribune are
repeated on the side entrance. On another side, by the fish-
market, a third door must cause every Englishman to wonder, for
over its arch are some twelfth century sculptured reliefs relating
the history of King Arthur. What is the legend of King Arthur
doing here ? Is it an aftermath of his reputed journey to Rome ?

---

* " The Government expense will be $700 per body returned. The programme
which is expected to go on for five years will require a total of $200,000,000. It
is estimated that 200,000 relatives will choose to have the body returned. The
reburial programme has absolutely no way of preventing the relatives from opening
the caskets. One officer's widow wrote the War Department saying she wished the
body of her husband returned because their child had never seen its father."—
Foreign Service. C. Lester Walker in Reader's Digest.

The interior with its three naves and a marble bridge that spans the choir is an amazing sight. The parapet of the bridge is decorated with five panels of figures in relief, carved, 1170-1220, depicting the Washing of the Feet, the Last Supper, the Kiss of Judas, Jesus before Pilate, and the Prodigal Son. They recall archaic Greek sculpture in their noble simplicity. The bridge is supported by four porphyry columns with carved capitals based on couchant lions. One mounts to it by a marble staircase at each end, rising from the nave, and from these one passes by a ' Bridge of Sighs ' over the street outside into a Sacristy. The campanile, beautifully called the Ghirlandina, is two hundred and fifty feet high and was built in 1319. Its bells send waves of sound over the plain at the foot of the Apennines. The loveliness of all this moved us greatly.

Meanwhile, leaving Aubrey and Simon in a trance within, I crossed the road to view the rose window from a distance and was arrested by that unpremeditated beauty which smites one in odd corners of Italy. It was created here by a fortuitous assembly of brickwork, an iron grille, an old bust, an heraldic shield and a ray of sunlight. The bishop's house, it had a wide archway with a barrel ceiling and at the end there was a double gate surmounted by a delicate iron grille. Through it I saw a pergola, the grapes hanging in heavy clusters. The sunshine made the green leaves of the vine translucent, the grapes were globes of jade. It was a vision of autumnal poetry, Keatsian in its lush beauty, that I shall long remember.

Our route now lay from Reggio to Mantua. We were in the rich alluvial plain of the Po, with its canals banked against the inundations that have always threatened this terrain. It is a land of rich vineyards, apple orchards and maize plots all seen from the raised embankments along which the roads run. In a short time we entered the little town of Guastalla. There seemed to be nothing but one long street, with children, dogs and old women sitting outside their houses on rush chairs. When I asked Aubrey to halt he was surprised, though he is now, I think, accustomed to my waywardness. " There can't be anything here ! " exclaimed Simon from the back seat. " There may be," I said. When writing about Princess Paolina Borghese in *And So to Rome*, I recalled that Napoleon, exasperated by her conduct as the wife of Prince Camillo Borghese—for like her other sisters she clamoured for higher rank and bigger income—settled

upon her in 1806 the pocket duchy of Guastalla.   It had once been
part of the Duchy of Mantua, ruled over by the Gonzagas from
1439 to 1746.   It brought her a small revenue and the title of
Princess and Duchess of Guastalla.   She went to look at it and was
outraged to discover that her domain consisted of a few thousand
acres and a half-dead town of only 3,000 inhabitants.   Soon
afterwards Napoleon made her husband Governor of an enlarged
Piedmont, and he and the Princess set up a puppet court in
Turin.   She sold her principality, titles included, for six million
francs and Guastalla knew her no more.

With this in mind I hoped to find some relic of the Gonzaga
or Napoleonic régime.   Presently we came to a piazza, of no
beauty, with a plain church.   Here we found a Gonzaga, high
on a plinth, one foot on the naked body of an enemy, one hand
grasping a spear, a bronze bearded effigy of Ferrante I of Gonzaga
(1507-1557), Lord of Guastalla.   He was dressed in a Roman
kilt, with sword and toga, looking like an emperor in the romantic
style.   This was the brother of that little Federico Gonzaga who
was taken as a hostage at the age of ten by Pope Julius II, and
who, in turn, took the Pope captive by his ingratiating ways.

And that was all we could find in Guastalla.   I was not satisfied.
Ferrante Gonzaga, the name haunted me.   Ten miles down the
road I knew why.   Ferrante was not a nonentity, I recollected.
The third son of the Marchesa of Mantua, he was fifteen when she
sent him with Baldassare Castiglione, the diplomat, to the court
of Charles V at Madrid.   He was very popular at the court of
the Emperor, who was to raise his brother Federico from Marquis
to Duke of Mantua.   When Charles de Bourbon with his Spanish
troops marched on Rome in 1527, Ferrante was with him and
took part in that terrible sack of the city, when the Pope was made
a prisoner in the castle of St. Angelo.   It happened that Ferrante's
mother was in Rome at the time.   She shut herself up in her
palace and gave refuge to 1,200 ladies and 1,000 citizens, while
the city ran with blood.   She appealed to her son, who was
powerless in restraining the merciless troops which committed
every possible atrocity, but he succeeded in preventing the Venetian Ambassador from being taken a prisoner to Spain.   In 1529
Ferrante commanded the forces at Florence, from which, on its fall,
Michelangelo, in fear of his life, fled to Venice.   He had been
responsible for the fortifications and thought the ire of the Pope
would fall upon him when the city surrendered.   Following

this, Ferrante distinguished himself at the siege of Tunis and in 1535 was made Viceroy of Sicily. He went with Charles V into Provence in 1536. Soon after he was accused of poisoning the Dauphin. Returning to Italy he married an heiress and bought himself the county and duchy of Guastalla, where he founded a line. Later, he caused the Emperor much trouble. Charles ardently desired the recall of the Council of Trent in order to reform the Church and combat Lutherism. Ferrante, who had been appointed Governor of Milan, desirous of showing his power, incited a rising at Piacenza. In its violent repression he killed Pierluigi Farnese, son of Pope Paul III. This so enraged the Pope that he dismissed the Council of Trent and joined forces with the Emperor's enemy, Henry II of France, supporter of Luther's backers. Thus Ferrante of Guastalla in his way contributed to Luther's triumph at a critical moment ; by such small men are great events sometimes changed in their courses. In 1551 he was accused of the massacre of five companies of Italian soldiers. In 1556 he was deprived of his Duchy, and died at Brussels a year later.

MANTUA AND LAKE GARDA

August 21.

Mantua. We arrived Sunday evening and had some difficulty in finding accommodation. The largest hotel offered us some dreary rooms down labyrinthine passages. One room possessed only a skylight. We might have put up with this but the sudden arrival of a motor-bus with twenty girls and a dozen youths, American students on tour, caused us to flee. Two incredible youths, their feet shod in Greek sandals, with skin-tight shorts, blond hair, loose wrists, shrilly voluble and arty, confirmed our resolution. Down a back street we saw a restaurant with a notice of rooms to let. They were Spartan but clean. The bath had not functioned for years, mosquitoes had met sudden death on my wallpaper, and the window was over the back kitchen. Trifles like these do not fuss the cheerful traveller. Aubrey and Simon occupied the bridal chamber, judging from the scalloped curtains and chandelier, etc. The food downstairs was excellent, the service ready and smiling. We accounted ourselves lucky in finding this retreat from *la vie de Bohême* which had threatened us.

Mantua requires a volume. There were four courts that dominated the Renaissance in Italy ; that of the Medici at Florence ; the Este at Ferrara ; the Gonzaga at Mantua ; and the Montefeltro at Urbino. Of these I think the Mantuan house is the most astonishing. It was allied to the great court at Ferrara, for Isabella was born a d'Este, the sister of the famous but briefly lived Beatrice who married the Duke of Milan, and of the Duke of Ferrara who married Lucrezia Borgia, and a sister-in-law of the Duke of Urbino. Under the Gonzagas Mantua rose to power and became the great centre of art and culture before Florence took pre-eminence. Ludovico Gonzaga in the fifteenth century called to his court Mantegna, who spent the greater part of his life there. Federico employed Giuliano Romano, and Vincenzo had Rubens for his art adviser. The court of Mantua had no equal in all Italy under the beautiful cultured Isabella. Ariosto sang her praises, Bembo, Machiavelli, and Baldassare Castiglione, prince of courtiers and diplomat, author of *The Courtier*, graced her castle. She scoured Italy for treasures of painting, sculpture and music. She commissioned Bellini, Raphael, Perugino and Leonardo da Vinci. Every skilled workman of fame in any part of Italy found himself pressed into her service. For fifty years, as Marchioness of Mantua, she was a dominating figure in a galaxy of genius that starred the Renaissance.

To-day we walked through the great palace by the lake-like Mincio. Except for a few precious rooms it is a great ruin, so vast that one can recall few palaces in the whole of Italy to match it. How was this fantastic place with its five hundred rooms, corridors, staircases, courts, galleries, tournament yards, music salon and Lilliput quarters for the dwarfs, maintained ? It is said that at one time, with its staff and retainers, eight thousand persons lived in it, a population one-quarter of that of the Duchy's capital. Time has done cruel things to it. In 1630 it was ruthlessly sacked by the Imperial troops, who left the whole of the 15th century part of the castle a ruin. Fortunately for the preservation of many great works of art an impoverished Duke had asked Rubens to negotiate the sale of some of the treasures. Thus Charles I came to possess many of these Italian masterpieces. The losses from the sack of the palace by the Imperial troops were immeasurable. The palace suffered even more from Napoleon's conquest of Mantua in 1797. The Great Robber shipped his loot to Paris. Thus the famous Francia portrait of

young Federico, painted to console Isabella when she surrendered
her son as a hostage to the Pope, fell into the hands of a French
cardinal. After his death it was sold and lost to sight in the
house of a Gloucestershire squire, and now it is the star of the
Altman Collection in the Metropolitan Museum at New York.

There was another portrait of young Federico, painted in 1513,
by Raphael when the boy was a hostage in Rome, which had a
singular history. It was found by Castiglione in the possession
of Cardinal Colonna who presented it to Federico in 1521. It
had for a companion in the nuptial chamber of the castle Titian's
portrait of the young duke. The latter is in the Prado at Madrid,
a purchase of the Spanish ambassador at the sale of Charles I's
paintings. It had been bought for Charles, together with
Michelangelo's ' Sleeping Cupid,' carved when he was twenty-
two. This Cupid was stolen by Cesare Borgia from the Duke of
Urbino on the sack of that city and given by him to Isabella
Gonzaga at her request, although her brother-in-law's property !
The Raphael portrait and the ' Sleeping Cupid ' were shipped from
Holland to England in 1632, after their sale by the Duke of
Mantua. They were in the catalogue of treasures at Whitehall
and St. James's Palace in 1639. Cardinal Richelieu bought
the portrait at the sale of Charles's effects. Later it returned to
England, appeared in the Lucy collection at Charlecote Park, was
sold, and has not been heard of since ! The Cupid completely
disappeared.

What fantastic things have happened in this Mantua palace !
The Hall of Tapestries was built as late as 1779, to hold a set of
the famous tapestries made from the cartoons of Raphael for the
decoration of the Sistine Chapel. (Another set is in the South
Kensington Museum, on loan from the Queen.) The tapestries
had been a gift to the palace chapel of Cardinal Ercole Gonzaga,
who died during the Council of Trent. In 1776 they were
moved into the palace. Then for two years they lay abandoned
in an attic where the wife of a ducal official found the nine
tapestries and renovated them with such amateur enthusiasm
that they were almost ruined. Later, experts were brought
from Milan who carefully restored them and hung them in the
long hall specially built for their display.

But their adventures had not finished, for the Austrians,
occupying Lombardia in 1866, carried them off to Vienna, where
they remained until 1919 when their restoration to Mantua was

part of the terms of the Peace Treaty following the World War. I wonder if their adventures have finished. They narrowly escaped transportation to Germany by the Nazis in 1945.

Despite the dilapidated state of the palace there are many rooms with their wonderful decorations intact. What memories the names of some of these rooms overlooking the lake invoke; the Loggia of Tasso, the Apartments of Apollo, the Cabinets of Paradise, the Loggia of Eleonora de Medici, the Hall of the Zodiac, the Corridors of the Moors, the Gallery of the Mirrors, etc.

The high spot of this pilgrimage came in the special apartments created for the Marquis Ludovico. The Bridal Chamber, in this suite, decorated with frescoes by Mantegna, between 1461 and 1474, is one of the great treasures of Italian art. The frescoes are in honour of the Marquis Ludovico and his wife. The family is shown listening to the reading of a papal brief raising the Marquis's second son, a bishop, to the Cardinalate. Here they are, as gloriously alive as when Mantegna put them on his dais and traced their features—the long-nosed Ludovico, the son Francesco the Cardinal, the Marchioness, Barbara of Brandenburg, on a chair beside her warrior-lord, the little female dwarf, the ladies of the court, the young children, the marshal in green and cream hose, the notary, the young knight, and the majordomo by his master's chair. Here they are, immortalised by the brush of genius, still glorious in colour over the fireplace in the bridal chamber. On either side of the door there is another fresco which shows Cardinal Francesco, now apostolic delegate to Bologna, on the occasion of the building of St. Andrea. The Marquis Ludovico, his father, has gone to meet him, accompanied by the Cardinal's brother, and his grandchildren, the eldest the future Marquis Francesco, warrior husband of Isabella d'Este. A little behind the spectators is a picture of walled Mantua, strong and proud. Mantua lies in the plain but in order that the spectator shall see its splendour Mantegna has painted it on a steep hillside. It was Cardinal Francesco, a lover of music, like all the Gonzagas, who commissioned Poliziano, Lorenzo de' Medici's court poet, to write *Orfeo*, the first musical drama in Italy, performed at the court of Mantua in 1472 in the presence of the Duke of Milan and the Renaissance nobles.

Happily the guide left us alone and we feasted. Simon found a chair and in a Rodinesque attitude, chin in hand, seemed there for the day. " Entrancing ! " murmured Aubrey. I was silent.

I tried to recall the life that had flowed in this room, above all, the day, four hundred years ago, when the young Duke Federico had reigned over a Duchy at the height of its fame and power, when the walls of this room had two portraits of him, one showing a boy by Raphael, the other a bearded man by Titian ; and I tried to hear the footfall of his mother, Isabella, entering to tell him that a new zithern which she had ordered from her agent in Venice had arrived, and that the court choir that evening would sing a new *strambotta* by Maestro Lara, the resident choirmaster.

In the afternoon we went to see the Palazzo del Te, the astonishing edifice of the Gonzagas built by Giuliano Romano. It was commissioned by Federico, originally intended for a stables, and erected on the edge of the town. Between 1525 and 1535 the stables grew into a magnificent villa. In the palazzo they had designed rooms for dwarfs. Here they covered the walls with frescoes of giants. Mindful of the grandiose creations of Bramante and Michelangelo in Rome, Giuliano set out to surpass them.

We went dizzily from one room to another until in the Salon of the Giants we felt quite overpowered by this tremendous physical gusto in paint. " But what did they do here ? " we asked, for these great halls were only a few minutes away from the other great halls in the palazzo. Megalomania had run riot here. The guide could give us no satisfactory answer. " *Egli faceva l'amore—amore molto curioso,*" he said, with a smirk. I could imagine nothing less conducive to *amore* than these great rooms with their acres of naked flesh sprawling over ceilings and walls. And the end of all this splendour ? The church of San Francesco, containing the three hundred monuments of the Gonzaga princes, was sacked by the French in 1797 after the long siege of Mantua. The frescoes were ruined, the tombs rifled and the ashes scattered. Not a thing remains to mark a once stately shrine rich in memorials and noble monuments. In its last decay the desecrated church became a barracks.*

In the late afternoon we paid a visit to the garden that had been laid out during the Fascist régime, alongside the Mincio, to honour the great Mantuan, Virgil, on his two thousandth anniversary. For this is Virgil's native soil and his verses come

---

* In February 1797, the young Napoleon captured Verona and besieged Mantua. It was a long siege. The garrison ate their horses and Mantua surrendered on Candlemas Day while the church bells were ringing. Twenty thousand Austrians, all that were left of a garrison reduced by fever and hunger, laid down their arms. Old General Würmser was allowed to march out with military honours.

to mind as one stands before the colossal statue of the poet dominating the memorial piazza—

> " To thee, O Mantua, I will bring back palms from Edom ; and a marble shrine will I raise on the green sward by the waters of Mincio's broad stream, where it wanders with laggard windings, fringing its banks with slender rushes."
> —Georgic III.*

The memorial was nobly carried out, with busts of other great Mantuans, but the Fascist megalomania expressed itself in a great design of the Fasces in the central bed. Mussolini's downfall brought about a violent reaction to this Fascist display. It is deplorable that the piazza has been allowed to fall into decay. Most of the trees have gone, the parterres are now a dusty field, and Virgil overlooks a dismal scene of neglect.

August 22.

I was in such pain all last night that I wondered whether I could continue the journey this morning, but at ten o'clock we set out for Verona and Lake Garda, motoring across the Lombardian plain, skirting the course of the Mincio as it hurries to join the Po. I never cease to marvel at the lushness of this wide plain, its great production of vines, maize, peaches and apples. Centuries of irrigation have created this rich garden. The roads are built high above the canalised fields, a safeguard against floods.

Verona drew us aside from our route. It is always irresistible with its vast arena, the Emperor Diocletian's gift to the Roman town before his retirement to Spalato. It is so well preserved that great spectacles, such as opera are still performed in it. The Piazza dell 'Erbe, with its column of the San Marco lion, marking the sovereignty of Venice, the gay awnings of the fruit stalls, and the façades of the noble palaces, is a gem scintillating with colour and movement. The Can Grande della Scala tombs, enclosed in an iron grille, lacelike in delicacy, draw one's attention as much for their splendour as for the fact that this family was the first to offer Dante hospitality in his exile. The della Scalas were the

---

* . . . Idumeas referam tibi, Mantua, palmas
et viridi in campo templum de marmore ponam
propter aquam, tardis ingens ubi flexibus errat
Mincius, et tenera praetexit harundine ripas.

earliest patrons of fourteenth century Italian culture. Petrarch found a home at their court, which welcomed poets, musicians and artists. And let us not forget that it was the home town of Romeo and Juliet, Shakespeare's Two Gentlemen, and Silvia, commended by all her swains.

We walked into the courtyard of the Scaliger Castle where on January 11, 1944, that Don Giovanni of the Fascist era, Count Ciano, was executed. I wondered just where was placed the chair on which he was bound. He was seated with his back to the firing squad and at the fatal moment contrived to wriggle round in order to avoid the ignominy of being shot in the back. This desperate effort resulted in his being wounded but not mortally, and the Chief of Police had to finish off the wretched man with a revolver. The malignity of that execution! Mussolini was too ill to attend the butchery of his son-in-law, father of his grandchildren. He therefore ordered a film of it to be made. The executions took place not at dawn but at nine a.m. when the light was good. The cinema operator was known to Ciano who remarked on his suitability. De Bono, aged eighty, was carried out on a stretcher. Ciano gave him encouragement. A close-up was taken of the revolver giving Ciano the *coup-de-grâce*.

The retreating Germans, true to their tradition of vandalism, blew up the battlemented fourteenth-century bridge that ran from the castle to the opposite bank of the Adige River, and also the lovely Roman bridge, a quite useless military operation. Fortunately only one of the three arches of the Scaliger Bridge was totally destroyed and I was glad to see that an effort was being made to restore it.

We have contracted a new habit. Around eleven o'clock we interrupt our sightseeing to look for a *latteria* in which to drink milk. Thus in Verona we repeated our custom in Florence, Mantua and Modena. The shop was in the shadow of the Scaliger tombs. Outside in the narrow street, where the Montagus and Capulets may have scuffled, if we allow Verona her Juliet, we looked on to a small Gothic-Venetian façade, with a sunlit balcony vivid with mauve and scarlet petunias. A radio broadcast of *Aïda* filtered in from somewhere. A large white cat sniffed at the basket of eggs on the counter, a little sloe-eyed urchin and his sister bought ices and solemnly licked them while listening to *bel canto*. Then a poor old woman (she may have been a rich peasant with a hoard of *lire*, whose son rode a Vespa motor-cycle and whose daughter wore nylons) came in, bought a bowl of milk, took a roll of bread out of her satchel and broke it up in a bowl. " That's what you should do," said Aubrey, jokingly, classing me with the toothless old crone. Nevertheless, at that moment in Verona I felt that life was extremely good.

After lunch on the beautiful piazza facing the Arena we went on our way to Lake Garda. The sun shone in a cloudless blue sky and all around us lay the green vineyards and the peach orchards. Nearing Peschiera, with a first glimpse of the blue expanse of Lake Garda we saw a roadside barrow piled high with luscious peaches for sale. We stopped the car and bought a basket, as much for the colour as for the deliciousness of this sun-warmed fruit. At Desenzano, the little town on the lake below the railway, covetously seen by all train passengers speeding from Milan to Venice, we saw the long thin promontory of Sirmione, with its memories of the villa of Catullus. His ghost moves here, on the lake he loved.

> " Salve, o venusta Sirmio, atque ero gaude ;
> gaudete vosque, o Lydiae lacus undae :
> ridete, quicquid est domi cachinnorum."

Welcome lovely Sirmio, and rejoice in your master, and rejoice ye, too, waters of the Lydian lake, and laugh out aloud whatever mirth dwells in your depths.

Catullus was the son of a prosperous Army contractor of Verona, friend of Julius Caesar. A Roman post, all the roads from the Brenner Pass came down to that city, the first line of defence against any invasion out of Rhaetia. Sirmione was the site of one of the largest granaries in Cisalpine Gaul. Catullus, born there in 84 B.C., spent his infancy at his father's villa and went to school in Verona, where the grammarian Valerius Cato taught poetry to the sons of rich men. It was here that Catullus met the woman for whom he ruined himself, Clodia, the Lesbia of his poems, and followed her to Rome in the spring of 61 B.C. He spent the last two years of his life at Sirmione, brooding on his brother's death, ' Frater, Ave atque Vale,' and died aged twenty-nine.

It was in Verona that his manuscripts were found, one of the strangest stories in literature. It seemed as if only two of his poems were to be saved for posterity, the second *Epithalamium*, in a ninth century MS, and the four-line epigram on *Priapus*, quoted by the grammarian Maurus. All the rest had disappeared until, early in the fourteenth century, a scholar discovered in Verona some manuscripts buried under a bushel measure. These disappeared again but not before they were known and widely read by Petrarch, Boccaccio and others. The two oldest copies of the poems are the Paris codex, the Sangermanensis, written before the death of Can Signorio at Verona in 1375, and the Oxford codex of the same date, a manuscript discovered by an American scholar, G. G. Hole, in 1896.*

My memory of the little town behind the old fortified walls and castle is more modern. There, on the terrace of her hotel, I had once sat and talked with Mrs. Pat Campbell, the actress, still amazing in her last years. She told me that she wondered each week how she would pay her hotel bill, a statement difficult to reconcile with the possession of a Rolls-Royce car—or perhaps explaining it. Later, Ivor Novello arrived, looking exactly as if Romeo had just come over from Verona, where indeed he was staying. He was a little mirthful about the pious fraud of Juliet's tomb which he had seen there.

After Desenzano we headed northwards along the shores of the lake. It scintillated below us in the peerless afternoon. Until the end of the World War our road by the lakeside had ended at Gargnano. The mountains here fall steeply to the lake and centuries of patient labour have terraced the mountain sides with groves of lemon trees for which the district is famous. I recalled my first visit to the lake. I was going by steamer to Riva at the head of the lake, our present destination. It called at Gardone and a merry boy came on board selling small branches of lemon trees with the lemons on them. A young man near me bought a branch and as the steamer proceeded up the lake he plucked off the lemons and ate them like cherries. I watched him until their acidity provoked such watering of my mouth that I had to turn away. Like tomatoes, it must be a cultivated taste.

We now came near to the Villa Vittoriale, at Cargnacco, on the lake shore, stolen by the mountebank poet Gabriele D'Annunzio, in 1920, from the widow of Professor Heinrich Thode, the German archaeologist, after it had been sequestrated on the outbreak of the Great War. D'Annunzio wrote over the portal " Let the Spirit of Victory bring peace upon this house of

* My own pocket Catullus is a lovely Aldine edition, Venice, 1502.

a brave man." He decorated the grounds with all manner of war scrap, including the prow of a ship, and kept six fierce dogs at his gate. When Frau Thode wrote to him asking for the return of her villa he invited her to come and see him. He received her with great unction, and said he would only be there for a few weeks. She waited in vain, and heard that he had sold the pictures and some of the contents of the villa. When she went again she succeeded in seeing him after much difficulty. He then said he had bought the villa from the Italian Government, whose property it had never been, and, a suave host, gave her a drink that nearly killed her. She lay in a state of collapse in the village inn, and then left. Despite a European outcry, which cost D'Annunzio the Nobel Prize, he never relinquished the villa. I was his guest there in 1923. It was like living in the property wing of a theatre. He dramatised every moment.

Military necessity caused a road to be driven through the rocks overhanging this part of the lake. It is an astonishing feat of engineering. The long galleries, broken at intervals by ' windows,' run for some fifteen miles at a height of about fifty feet above the lake. Villages that for centuries have been inaccessible except by boat are now linked up on the route to Riva. As we motored through Gargnano I thought of D. H. Lawrence who had written Sons and Lovers, his best work, at a village down by the shore. It was in early October 1912. He had walked with his mistress, from Austria down over the Brenner Pass. It was his first visit to Italy and the magic of this marvellous land put its spell upon him. At Riva they heard of a furnished apartment in the Villa Igea at Gargnano—a dining-room, two bedrooms, kitchen, and garden filled with peach trees overlooking the lake, for 66/- a month. They felt they had found a dwelling in Paradise. He was twenty-seven, at the beginning of his writing career. His first novel, The White Peacock, had just been published and had made some stir. He had burned his boats and he had only fifty pounds when he crossed the Italian frontier with Frieda, his professor's wife, who left home and children for him. It was an unofficial honeymoon. "I love Frieda so much, I don't want to talk about it. I never knew what love was before," he wrote to a friend.

The Lawrence legend has now travelled around the world, and the saga of this sexually obsessed, distraught man of genius has now become a story for case-books interminably written by friends, enemies, acquaintances and critics. It has all the ingredients that readers like—illicit love, early poverty, erratic temperament, rebellion against Society, and death in middle-age from consumption. I did not know him then, and when we met in Florence fourteen years later we wondered if we had passed each other in the streets of Nottingham in his youth. He was twenty and I thirteen when he went to University College, Nottingham, studying for his Teacher's Certificate.

During that winter at Gargnano, Lawrence worked on the novel, called at first *Paul Morel*, later *Sons and Lovers*, which sealed his fame. He was happy in Gargnano. " I don't believe England need be so grubby," he wrote to a friend, probably recalling the stark drabness of Eastwood, his home. " What does it matter if one is poor and risks one's livelihood and reputation. One *can* have the necessary things of life, and love, and clean warmth. Why is England so shabby ? The Italians here sing. They are very poor, they buy two penn'orth of butter and a penn'orth of cheese. But they are healthy and they lounge about in the little square where the boats come up and nets are mended, like kings." How many poor, eager young writers, before and after him, have written home from Italy like that ? There was an evening in January 1913, when he was the guest of honour in the village theatre to see a performance of *Hamlet* by some strolling players. He sat in Box No. 8 and was convulsed with laughter when Amletto, fat and forty, began the famous soliloquy " *Essere o non essere*," and collapse came when the gravedigger who held up a skull exclaimed, " *Ecco, Signore ! Questo cranio e quel . . .* "

I wanted to stop and see if a gaunt ghost walked in the Villa Igea down by the blue lake with its pinewoods, vines and lemon groves, but the light was waning and we wished to reach Riva through the darkening galleries. I noticed how the lemons in the last light of evening glowed like golden lamps against the dark wall of the mountain.

At Riva we found a pleasant lakeside hotel. The hotel where I had stayed thirty years ago with a large garden going down to a private harbour, once beautifully kept, was now a ruin, the garden overgrown, the terraces a wilderness of briar roses, shut in with rusty barbed wire. Decayed mansions are the saddest of spectacles, their deaths are so protracted.

Until the end of the first World War Austria held this charming little town at the head of the lake and called it Riva di Trento.

In 1027 it belonged to the Bishops of Trent. The Scaligers of
Verona, the Visconti of Milan and the Venetians, all held it in
turn until it passed back again to the bishops. Napoleon took
it, was ousted by the Austrians, and Bavaria held it later by the
Treaty of Pressburg. It went to Italy in 1810 and three years
later the Austrians again held it. It suffered terribly by bombardment, during the Great War, from the high mountains overhanging it, but here it is, smiling and lovely by its little port.
At the entrance to the South Tirol, it begins to take some of the
character of its neighbour with overhanging eves, and balconies
to its chalets.

Something happened to me here this evening I shall long
remember. We went into a corner shop full of mementoes for
tourists, particularly of woodcarvings by the Tirolers. My eyes
fell upon a small birdcage with one of those little artificial birds
that, wound up, open their beaks and shake their tails while
singing. The assistant seeing the fascination this object exerted
over me, wound up the bird. It began to sing. He could not
have known that I knew every note, every trill, every movement
of head and tail. Hypnotised by memory I stood and looked
but when he began to extol its merits the tears filled my eyes. I
rushed out of the shop lest my companions saw me. The
astonished assistant put back the bird on its shelf. I did not know
that after long years an old wound would open so readily. One
who had died too young, after a gallant fight for life, had given
me an artificial bird that looked and sang just as this one. The
bird on the counter must have come out of the same workshop,
though mine had come from Paris. As it sang I was no longer in
Riva but at Pilgrim Cottage in Oxfordshire, in the vanished
years. I still have my mechanical bird, but since that day I have
not had the heart to wind it up and let it sing again. . . .

> They told me, Heraclitus, they told me you were dead,
> They brought me bitter news to hear and bitter tears to shed,
> I wept as I remembered how often you and I
> Had tired the sun with talking and sent him down the sky.

August 23.

We left this morning, passing Torbole, with its dark cypresses
and little church on the mountain side. We followed the valley
of the Loppio whose lake shines in a wide valley set between the
mountains. At Rivereto I thought of young Goethe who, on a

September morning in 1786, young, ecstatic, crossed into Italy.
" How delighted I am that the language I have always loved
must now become living," he wrote.   The next day at Torbole
he took his first walk in an Italian village, observing how the
windows were covered with oiled paper instead of glass.   There
was surprise when he asked the waiter for the retiring-room.
" Here you can use it."   " Where ? "   " Here, anywhere as
you please ! "

Our valley grew grander and grander, with ruined castles
perched on precipitous rocks as we went north along the Adige
towards Trento.

Why do so many tourists neglect this beautiful and historic
city ? The Council of Trent dominates its local history.   It met
here in 1545, alarmed by the spread of Lutherism, but Pope Paul
III only wanted it to condemn the Protestant heresy and not to
deal with reforming the Church, as against Charles V's desire, to
strengthen it against Lutherism.   So he switched the Council to
Bologna in 1547, and on the killing of his son refused to recall it to
Trent for some time.   Its labours began again in Trent in
1551 and ended there in 1563.   It launched the Counter-
Reformation but was fifty years too late to keep the Catholic
West intact ; the worm of Lutherism was in its rotten timbers.
The Diet of Worms refused to recognise the Council.   The split
was irrevocable.   One thing the Council of Trent did establish ;
it made marriage a solemn rite of the Church whereas before it
had been a matter of contract only.

Now came Cavalese, the next town on our route, at a height of
three thousand feet, guarded by a great range of mountains.
This beyond question was Austria, though Italian territory.
We knew it by the costumes of the inhabitants, the chalets and
balconies gay with flowers, the blond heads of the children, the
white stockings, the short-sleeved bodices, frilled and embroidered
—all spoke of the South Tirol.   By the Peace Treaty of 1919 Italy
pushed her frontier up to the Brennero, its natural rampart, and
the German-speaking people found themselves under the arrogant
rule of the Fascist hotheads.   In the summer of 1934 I motored
through the valley with Philip Gibbs and we found the populace
burning with a sense of oppression.   They had been torn from
the motherland, and the new master was determined to show
his power.   But gone are those unhappy days when the Tirolers
had to Italianise their names, when they might not wear their

traditional white stockings and sing Andreas Hofer's song, when even German names were forbidden on the gravestones. It was fertile soil for Hitler who, making a deal with Mussolini, persuaded eighty thousand South Tirolers to migrate into Austria and Germany. Now a new Constitution, following the second World War, has restored the right to speak and teach German, and to share in the local government. Five years ago the Italian and Austrian Foreign Ministers came to an agreement which bids fair to satisfy both ethnical groups, and Austrian irredentism is dying out.

Certainly Cavalese, where we lunched, was prospering. It was thronged with Italian holiday makers. Every restaurant and hotel was full and the menus were all written out in Italian. The town hall, with its painted façade, the ancient palace of the Bishops of Trent, the coats of arms of the communes, and its gabled overhanging roof, might have been in Innsbruck or Salzburg. The town is the centre of a community that had governed eleven communes in the Fiemme Valley, which the town overlooks.

After lunch we did not linger in pretty Cavalese. We had the tremendous Pordoi Pass, 7,000 feet, ahead of us, also the Falzarego and the great range of the Dolomites. I know every inch of this wonderful road on to Cortina. It is the scene of my novel *Spears Against Us*, suggested nearly twenty years ago by seeing, over a stone wall by the foot of Monte Tofana, the graves of young Austrian soldiers who had fallen defending their homeland terrain, changed after their deaths into the alien soil of Italy; it seemed to me the height of tragic irony.

The sun was falling as we went through the crowded high street of Cortina. A tremendous climb followed, up over the Tre Croci Pass, winding in and out of thick fir forests while above us rose the wild serrated limestone peaks of the Dolomites, now flushed with the pink glow (*alpenrosen*) of the evening sun. Mighty Monte Cristallo rose up, a sheer wall of rose against a lemon-green sky. Then we went down by Innichen into the narrow valley of the Drau, now in the blackness of night, until, at a lonely outpost, lights proclaimed the Customs house of the Italian-Austrian frontier. There was a short delay while our passports were stamped ; somewhere in another room a zithern was being played. It seemed a fitting prelude to our entry into the Austrian Tirol.

Austria

IT was nine o'clock when we reached Lienz last evening, the most eastern town in the Tyrol, beautifully situated in a valley at the confluence of the Drau and the Isel. We found the town in a state of gala and a crowd thronged the central square. There was *platzmusik* from the town band, dressed in costume, with enormous wide-brimmed hats with ribbons, red coats, buttoned knee-breeches and white stockings. The girls and lads paraded up and down in their embroidered *dirndls*, and braces and *lederhosen*. The town was thronged with summer visitors, Italians mostly, who were dining at little candle-lit tables on hotel balconies overlooking the square. It all had a slightly musical comedy air, with Mitsi and Hänsel and Onkel everywhere in sight. The band played rumti-tumti-music lustily. This was all very well but we learned that the hotels were all crammed and our beds for the night began to be doubtful. It was then that we were seized by a lean youth who insisted that he could lead us to good lodgings. He was so insistent that we felt doubtful about their quality, and suspected he was a tout, but we took a chance. He jumped on the running-board of the car and directed us from the brightly-lit town into darkness. The way seemed long and tortuous, it went over a railway track and out towards the country. It was then that we saw some new housing blocks with apartments. Before one of these we halted and our guide led us up a staircase to the first floor. A quiet little woman of about forty opened the door and we stepped into a large kitchen. We were shown a double and a single bedroom, very clean with modern furniture. We moved in our things and then went out to dine.

This morning we had breakfast in the kitchen. The bath was the usual Austrian contrivance, a tall copper boiler, heated by a wood fire inserted at the base. There was no wash-basin but a loose bowl was filled at the boiler. The bath was quite good, with plenty of hot water. An excellent breakfast awaited us in the kitchen ; no butter shortage, no lack of eggs, etc. We now began to take stock of our surroundings in the morning light.

This was an apartment in a working-class housing settlement. There were three rooms—two bedrooms, kitchen and bathroom-lavatory. I discovered that our landlady had slept out. A little smiling girl appeared with a milk jug. In my bedroom there was a photograph of a young bridal pair taken some twenty years ago. I began to work out the family situation and later our quiet little landlady enlightened me. Here was a tragedy, such as had visited thousands of these homes. Our guide of the previous evening was her young married son, the little girl was her daughter-in-law's sister. She had slept out at her son's in order to free the single room. Yes, that was her photograph with her husband on their wedding day. She was a widow—possibly. Possibly? Yes, her husband had been sent to fight in Russia and perhaps had been taken a prisoner. Had she heard from him? No, not definitely, but a comrade had seen him. Thousands and thousands of Austrian soldiers were prisoners in Russia and no one ever heard from them. She tried not to give up hope. So here she was, alone in her little house, ekeing out a living by some dressmaking, washing, letting rooms to summer visitors, helped a little by her son. Waiting, hoping, waiting, for eight years now.

We strolled about in the town this morning. An amusing incident has raised my spirits. Perhaps I am not so conspicuously senile amid my young companions. We were walking along when two elderly ladies passed and we heard an unmistakable American voice say, " I should guess those are three very aristocratic young Englishmen." Bless her. A damn for the ' aristocratic ' but gratitude for the ' young.' I suspect I was well masked by my escorts.

This afternoon we made an excursion up a lovely valley threaded by a stream to Schloss Bruck, a fifteenth-century castle. Aubrey and Simon suddenly decided that a mountain peak, crowned with snow, must be climbed, and forgetting my years I started off with them. We passed an idyllic scene. A muscular youth with a bronzed torso, and a gay Tyroler hat with a feather stuck in it, was mowing a field that was one sheet of yellow flowers. Nearby a girl sat knitting under a tree, a red-cheeked, flaxen-pigtailed mädchen. It was like a line out of Theocritus, the virginal beauty of it all. They gave us a smiling *Grüss Gott* and watched us ascend, but a little further on, with something of a shock, I realised that I cannot go climbing mountains with young colts. I turned back. Passing young Corydon again, he smiled, pointed upwards, and shook his head. " *So weit !* " he said. I went across the stream and mounted to the courtyard of the castle. It was a very grim old place, a typical stronghold of some bold baron. The walls were eight feet thick, lit only by narrow embrasured windows. It held a display of armour and an exhibition of the works of local artists. There, surprisingly, I found two charming water-colours of Avila and Toledo, and my thoughts flew back to a day last March when I had seen those lovely towns.

The great salon, according to a little guidebook, had been used as a justice-hall, and witches had been tried and tortured there. What horrors these frightening places have known ! Their evil still seems to pervade the dark rooms. I wondered at the fate of one who had been a bride here in 1506, Paola, daughter of the Ludovico Gonzaga who had commissioned Mantegna to beautify his castle at Mantua. She had come here from that lovely palace set in the Mantuan plain, a home filled with music and gaiety. Young Federico Gonzaga, her great-nephew, was then five years old, and she may have dandled him on her knee. What a frightful change, this grim old castle shut in by mountains for that gay palace by the mirroring Mincio, the Germanic boors for the elegant Italian gallants ! I wondered what heartache poor young Paola, a chattel for barter, had known in this cold grey place.*

August 25.

We left in good time this morning, the great climb over the giant Gross-Glockner range ahead of us. When our landlady presented the bill for washing our shirts, for lodging and break-fasts, it was ludicrously small. We added a good sum. I think she had enjoyed our visit, it had brought some life into her quiet abode. We expressed a hope that the long-lost prisoner would return. I expect she will never quite surrender hope, poor soul. So once again I am motoring up to remote Heiligenblut, perched on a mountain ledge in the sky, backed by the vast snowy

---

* Later I found the answer to my queries in Julia Cartwright's *Isabella d'Este*— " Two of Ludovico's remaining daughters married German princes, one of whom, Count von Görtz (of Schloss Bruck) treated his wife Paola so badly that she came back to Mantua a year after the marriage, while the other, Barbara, became in 1474, the spouse of Count Eberhard von Würtemberg, the founder of the University of Tübingen." Strange that Aubrey's relation should provide the answer !

range of the Gross-Glockner with its great glacier.   Until recently
this village, with a church spire that pierces heaven, was one of
the lonely places of the alps, the outpost of a long narrow valley
frequented only by adventurous mountaineers and a few attempting the pass over the snowfields to the Fuscher valley.   But now
Heiligenblut is a village with a traffic problem, with cars and
motor-buses carrying hurried tourists through its single narrow
high street and up towards the snowy pass.   A great highway
has been carved out by Austrian-Italian enterprise and the
lonely peaks of Austria and the blue lakes of Italy are now linked.
Heiligenblut is a lovely place to linger in, half on earth, half
in heaven, with its double-decker fifteenth-century church in
which is stored a phial of the Holy Blood, brought from Constantinople by St. Briccius, from which the village derives its name.

But to-day we, too, are in a hurry for we are to sleep in Salzburg
over the great range.   Up and up, we climb on the marvellously
engineered road, with halting stations where the heated car
engines may cool.   The air grows ever sharper, the world more
dizzily distant below us until we reach the chief viewpoint, the
restaurant at Franz-Josefshöhe which commands a fine prospect of the great glacier, six miles long and one mile broad, the
largest in the Alps, and the immense snowfields.   Below us some
very diminutive figures, black insects on a white sheet, were
making their way across the *moraine*.   And there was the rock,
backed by the glacier on which, fifteen years ago, young Tony
Allingham, a friend and I had sat, so joyous on that gay morning.

There was fast climbing later until we came to the highest
section of the road, some 11,000 ft. up, and the long tunnel that
pierces the peak.   This time I wanted to walk through it, having
motored so often, and I observed now that half-way one passes
from the province of Carinthia into that of Salzburg.   This tunnel
seems to divide two worlds.   It emerges on the grey north side
of the alps.   Often one is greeted by a chill world, blanketed
by cold swirling mist, in contrast to the sunny southern side that
slopes down to the Mediterranean basin.   I often think of it as
the high wall that keeps our bad northern climate away from the
Mediterranean !   To-day we were favoured.   There was no
mist.   It was a clear summer afternoon and as we went downwards on the corkscrew road to the valley, the mountain-sides
were veined with the thin silver lines of waterfalls.   Ferleiten,
in the deep valley, is the end of the official Gross-Glocknerstrasse.

SIENA

S A.   TONY   C.R.

THE GROSSGLOCKNER AT FRANZ-JOSEFSHÖHE

"And there was the rock backed by the glacier on which, fifteen years ago, young
Tony Allingham, a friend, and I had sat."

It was dark when, skirting its beautiful lake, closed in at one end by the magnificent panorama of the snowy Grossvenediger, we came to pretty little Zell-am-See, long a favourite with me. There followed a search for lodgings, and eventually at a chalet in a garden full of sunflowers, zinnias and the coloured glass witch-balls on sticks beloved of Austrian gardens, we found a room. It was one room, indeed, with three beds, up a narrow wooden staircase to the second floor, in the house of a shoemaker with a wife, a little pigtailed girl of eleven and a tow-headed boy of five. Night had descended, Zell also was full, and we decided to make the best of it. Aubrey and I occupied the twin beds, Simon somehow accommodated himself in the small truckle bed. Across the garden, through some trees we looked on to the lake.

August 26.

I woke about seven this morning, the light filling the room. Aubrey on my left and Simon on my right were still asleep. I know the folly of stirring the young, so I picked up my book, Belloc's *Napoleon*, and began to read. Presently Simon woke, fished for a book in a knapsack on the floor—what did that knapsack not contain?—and opened it. It was Wordsworth's *Excursion*. Aubrey now joined the reading club, with Adam Smith's *The Wealth of Nations*. There was silence for half an hour until a comment on prosy old man Wordsworth set us all talking. Somehow the subject got to Simon's proposed trip next summer to Lapland and Ultima Thule, possibly an antidote to Malaya.*

It was time to get up. There was one wash-basin, the hot water came in a can. Taking priority, I put my head in the corridor and peered in at a door opposite. It was a kitchen-livingroom-cum-bedroom. Fritz, aged five, in pink-spotted pyjamas, was sitting up in bed (he had a cold and must stay there), tousling a battered cloth donkey. I opened a conversation with the infant, all smiles, one gap in his baby teeth. Then round a screen appeared Gretl, also all smiles and two neatly-braided flaxen pigtails. She seemed to be in charge of the kitchen and her young brother. *Heisses-wasser? Ja!* Ten minutes later,

---

* Simon made the trip. It took four days. London to Finland, and one week to the first Lap houses ; then four days trekking and rowing through a trackless region of woods and lakes in endless daylight. Signs, Finnish as a *lingua franca*, and balloons to please the children, were the means of communication. Then south to Helsinki, to work for three weeks in a dockyard, building a reparations ship for the U.S.S.R., in order to improve his Finnish.

F

Gretl, carrying a can of hot water almost as large as herself entered our bedroom. She was, for some reason, convulsed with mirth at the sight of three men in bed, all reading. After a giggly flirtation she retreated. " There's a lot to be said for the simple life," said Aubrey, reversing himself in bed in order to get more light on *The Wealth of Nations*. " I shall be the last to wash."

August 27.

We left Zell-am-See this morning. It was as lovely as ever, and as variable, for it rained three times between bursts of sunshine. I looked sadly at the Grand Hotel, where I had dined so well and gaily at its lakeside restaurant many years ago. It was now in the occupancy of the American army, gaunt, paintless, curtainless, dishevelled in the manner of all places that fall into the army's hands, on the road to ruin. We had a clear morning for our run through the mountainous country but in the car I had the worst attack from the old enemy that I can recall for a long time. We stopped the car in Hallein. I had gone an ominous colour. I insisted on my companions going into the hotel for lunch while I sat outside to get the air. After an interval we started off again ; my one hope was to reach Salzburg.

About three o'clock we were in the bustling little town. At the Hotel Münchnerhof I found my American friend, Mrs. Boehm, with whom I had a rendezvous. She gave one look at me and sent me to lie down. Well, I am here, despite all, in the place where I conclude my role of *paedagogus*. It has been well worth the risk.

August 28.

I am better this morning and got up before lunch. We went out into the town. The bridge is gay with flags, the Mozartians are all here as in former years, the cafés are crammed. The tourists go up into the grim little birthhouse of the genius who died in abject poverty and made a fortune for his native town. It is my first visit since the war and the lovely old city on the Salzach seems to have regained all its festival spirit. My companions are enchanted with it, and Mrs. Boehm, like a wizard, has produced two tickets for them to attend a performance at the Festspielhaus. They are in heaven.

SALZBURG

August 29.

Tea at the Café Barok with Mrs. Boehm and her Italian friends, Maestro Vittorio Gnecchi and his wife and son. A well-known Italian composer, Signor Gnecchi has had many of his compositions produced throughout Europe. He is seventy-five, a handsome and vivacious man of fine features, with that impress of Italian culture which is so attractive ; the *maestro*, in short. His wife at a similar age is still lovely, with beautiful eyes and skin. They are a handsome pair to look at. The married son is a portrait artist. I found them *molto simpatico* and we passed two hours in a conversation that had not a dull moment. We talked much of music, of the current madness of mankind, with the presage of a new war hovering over us, and we agreed that after the experience of the last thirty years most of us have been reduced to a numb fatalism. But we had lighter thoughts to divert us and dispel the shadow of war. Umbrellas are ever present in Salzburg. I had been caught in the morning on my way to St. Peter's Keller for lunch and was helped out by the manager who appears to retain a supply for trapped patrons. Signor Gnecchi, apropos of this, told a delightful umbrella story. On his birthday his wife, having often scolded him for losing his umbrellas, presented him with a most beautiful and expensive specimen. It had a gold mount and a pink rhinoceros horn handle in the form of a seahorse. " Now, as it comes from me, and is such a fine one, I shall expect you to take the greatest care of it," she said. For many months, a proud owner, he guarded it. But alas, on a visit to Paris it disappeared. He made no mention of his loss. Then one day, when it was raining hard and they were going out, he was obliged to say to his wife, " You go with your friends, I shall come later when I have finished my writing." After their departure he called a cab and scoured the umbrella shops in quest of an identical umbrella. The quest was a long one, and after inspection of dozens of specimens in many shops he was triumphant. An umbrella turned up that was almost the twin of the lost present. Signor Gnecchi returned with it in time for lunch in the hotel restaurant, which they very seldom frequented He left his coat and umbrella in the vestibule. On returning for it he was amazed to discover two umbrellas, identical ! The lost one had been

deposited there by him a week earlier and no one had taken it.
The cat was now out of the bag, with two splendid umbrellas
in hand, but Signora Gnecchi was so overcome with mirth that
he escaped a scolding.

I then contributed my story. Sickened by the continuous
loss of umbrellas, either mislaid or ' borrowed,' I have invented
a little device. This consists of a small ivory card on a string
inside the umbrella. When opened the card falls into sight
bearing the legend, *This is not yours. It belongs to.* . . . Young
Signor Gnecchi followed my story with an astonishing footnote.
Did I know that Italy was famous for umbrellas ? " Italy ? "
I queried, " the land of sunshine ! " I had always believed that
England took precedence in the trade, from climate and from
the fact that it was the birthplace of one, Jonas Hanway, its
alleged introducer in the eighteenth-century. No, asserted young
Gnecchi, Italy enjoyed world-wide renown for its umbrellas.
Agents came from all over the world to purchase them. It
seemed they go to Alpino, a village some two thousand feet high,
half-way up Monte Mottarone, above Stresa on Lake Maggiore.
Alpino not only makes every kind of umbrella, large ones,
dumpy ones, umbrellas for ladies, for carriages, fruit stalls, circus
clowns and bathing beaches, it also has a celebrated museum
in which the connoisseur of the art of umbrella-making can
follow its birth and development, from Giotto, as it were, to
Picasso. Well, one learns. I had ascended Monte Mottarone
by the electric railway to enjoy the view of the lake but no one
ever suggested stepping off at Alpino to look at umbrellas !

The conversation then turned, somehow, to plagiarism. Signor
Gnecchi, a lifelong victim of this charge, then told me one of
the most incredible stories I have ever heard. He began very
young to demonstrate his genius for music. At the age of nineteen he wrote an operetta called *Virtù d'Amore.* It was successfully produced before an audience of over three hundred invited
musical guests in the private theatre of his father's villa at Ver-
derio. This was in 1896, and the score was published that year
by Ricordi of Milan. This marked the beginning of a distinguished career. In the year 1905 another composition by
Gnecchi, an opera, *Cassandra,* was produced at the Communale
in Bologna, Toscanini conducting. It was an immediate success and established Gnecchi. So great was the success of this
opera that it crossed the Atlantic and in 1913 Maestro Campanini

conducted it at Philadelphia. The Philadelphia critics, having heard Strauss's *Elektra*, written in 1909, came out with a charge of plagiarism against Gnecchi. He had stolen many of the themes from Strauss's opera. There was an uproar. It was in vain that the critics were informed that not only had *Cassandra* been produced four years earlier than *Elektra*, but that a number of very important musical critics had brought against Strauss the very charge they now brought against Gnecchi. In an article called " Musical Telepathy ? " published in 1909, Signor Giovanni Telbaldini, a well-known critic, pointed out that he had discovered in the score of Strauss's *Elektra* no less than fifty themes that bore an astonishing resemblance to those in *Cassandra*. Each theme was printed opposite its counterpart in the two scores. A sensation ensued. There then followed another astonishing article written by the music critic and composer, Maestro Barbieri, director of the Zanella Musical Lyceum and professor at the Genoa *Conservatoire*. He had found in *Elektra* twenty themes that corresponded with themes in Gnecchi's *Virtù d'Amore*, the operetta performed and published thirteen years before Strauss's opera !

The charge of plagiarism was now so serious and the scandal assumed such proportions that it was felt some reply must be made by Strauss. A number of eminent critics, Romain Rolland, Raymond Marchal, Louis Laloy, Ludwig Hartmann and Julius Korngold asked Strauss for an explanation. He ignored all communications except one. To Romain Rolland he wrote that he had no intention of replying to any charge of plagiarism.

The Philadelphia critics, informed of this history, would not confess their ignorance nor retract a word of their abuse on learning the true facts. Whereas it was quite possible to believe that the obscure Gnecchi could borrow from the great Strauss, it was utterly impossible to believe that the great Strauss would borrow from the obscure Gnecchi, no matter what the evidence was. And such was the prestige attached to the great German composer, Gnecchi suffered all his life from this charge of plagiarism. With great delicacy he resigned from his membership of the musical directorate of *La Scala*. He did not feel it right that he should have any voice in the selection of its repertoire with this debate filling the air. His opera *Cassandra* was performed with success at Philadelphia despite the critics, and in Vienna and in other theatres of Germany and Italy. But in two of the greatest auditoriums *Cassandra* was never heard, in the *Scala* at Milan and at the *Augusteo* at Rome. When Gnecchi asked for its production at the *Scala*, Mingardi, the Director, replied that although aware of its great merits he could not produce it, out of regard for Strauss. To this day it has never been performed there ; as elsewhere, the great shadow of Strauss had fallen on the path of his victim.

Günther B, a tall youth of twenty-two, son of a Salzburg lawyer, called immediately on my arrival. In August 1937 I reached Salzburg to find all accommodation taken. The local tourist bureau sent me to an address where I found a room. In the season most Salzburg homes take in visitors. My host and hostess could not have been kinder, a young lawyer and his wife with three sons, aged ten, nine and seven. My hostess spoke a little English and I made her a gift of one of my books. What I most recall is one evening when, as their guest, I was taken to the Festspielhaus for a performance of *Don Giovanni*, with Ezio Pinza in the title role. I had arrived in Salzburg by autobus from Venice. By a mix-up one of my bags containing my dress clothes had been left behind. In those formal days evening dress was essential for the opera. I was fitted out in one of my host's suits and in borrowed plumes accompanied my hostess to the Festspielhaus. I sat firmly in my seat between the acts since my trousers were short, and the Austrian cut of my jacket made me feel somewhat of a cross between a waiter and an archduke.

Nine years later, after the end of the war, while in New York, I received one day a letter written in excellent English. It was from the elder son of my Salzburg hostess, Günther, now eighteen, informing me that his eldest brother, aged nineteen, a pilot in the German air force, had been missing in the last week of the war and all enquiries had been unavailing. His despairing mother had asked him to write and enquire whether I could make an investigation ; perhaps he was a prisoner in England, or wounded and in an allied hospital or—I replied to this sad letter and thus, after a break of nine years our link was renewed. A few weeks later the family received confirmation of the death of the boy. He had been shot down in one of the last battles over Cologne.

In the summer of 1946 I was the guest of Mrs. Aubrey Cartwright at Cap d'Antibes. A large luncheon party, including her neighbours, the Duke and Duchess of Windsor, was seated at a long table on the pine-tree shaded terrace, when my hostess's butler approached and whispered in my ear that a German youth was in the hall enquiring for me. Quite bewildered, I asked to be excused and went up into the house to investigate. There I found a tall youth in *lederhosen*, who bowed and asked if I was Herr Cecil Roberts. This tall, good-looking youth of twenty, whom I had last seen as a child of nine, and of whom I had no recollection, had hitch-hiked to Cap d'Antibes to see me. He had come from near Geneva where he had visited an aunt. Learning that I was staying in Cap d'Antibes, he walked to the French border, dodged the Customs and got on a lorry bound for Marseilles.

I returned to the terrace and explained to my hostess the situation. Here was a tired and hungry youth who had come many miles to see me. She immediately insisted on his being brought down to the table. His charming manners and good looks established him in favour at once. He asked permission to retire for a few minutes to clean up. A little later, a radiant young Austrian appeared, clad in white linen shorts and a picturesque Tyrolean jacket. We then heard the story of his adventure. Austria being short of food, and Günther undernourished from the war years, his parents had despatched him to an aunt, a nun in a convent near Geneva. Geneva was near the frontier line of France and the boy watched others jumping the frontier. He had read in a newspaper that I was visiting Cap d'Antibes. He wanted to see me. With practically no money, and no visa for France, it seemed an impossible task, but he had observed in a frontier village that the side streets circumnavigated the Customs barrier. A *wandervogel* gave him the tip. Bidding his bewildered aunt good-bye, he dodged the Douane, took cover in a lorry and was over the frontier. The lorry took him as far as Lyons. Here a kindly French couple, motoring to Cannes, gave him a lift, lodging and food, with a small gift of francs on parting, such is the charm of youth. In Antibes at last, without any clue except that I was " staying at a villa on the Cap d'Antibes coast with American friends," he tramped around and after a couple of hours found a clue.

There was a spare guest-room over the garage. My kind hostess asked him to stay the night. He stayed three nights, ate, bathed and motored, enjoying all the amenities of one of

the most beautiful villas on the French Riviera. " I am in
Paradise ! I see you, our family friend ! It is a dream ! " he
exclaimed, joyously.   One day a lunch guest, living thirty miles
north on his homeward trek, invited him to stay for a couple of
days.   So he departed on the first stage for Salzburg.   He carried in his rucksack a small box of water-colours and a sketching
pad.   In a couple of hours he had produced, one day, an excellent little water-colour of the villa on its rocky ledge and
presented it to his hostess.   It now hangs in the hall where he
made his advent.

The following year, learning that I was in Venice, he hitch-
hiked over the Alps to see me, staying with some monks in an
old monastery.   When the heart is young all things are possible.

Within a few hours of our arrival in Salzburg, Günther having
called, I introduced this young Austrian of 6ft. 2in. (with a
younger brother 6ft. 5in.) to my English companions, Aubrey,
6ft. 4in., and Simon, 6ft. 3in. !   No wonder people turn when
I walk out with these three giants.

A delightful concert this evening at the Mozarteum, the
Vierte Serenade, with Paumgartner conducting, an elephantine
figure but sensitive to the tip of his baton.   There was a crowded
assembly, acutely critical and appreciative, not one of those
indiscriminate audiences that flock to the B.B.C. and Promenade
Concerts and applaud everything hysterically in this new mass
movement of an England turned ' musical.'   It seems to me
we have only one conductor with any true genius, the explosive
Sir Thomas Beecham ;   the rest are meritorious journeymen.
Here in Salzburg one is immediately aware of the dedicated
spirit on the podium.   The conductor, the orchestra, the audience
and the *genius loci* coalesce in a sublimation of the spirit of music.
Over all hovers the gentle shade of Mozart, child of this Baroque
town in the Austrian mountains.

The programme this evening was Mozartian—the *Diverti-
mento in D♯*, the Bläser *Concertante Und Finale* and *Symphonie
Nr 33 in B♯*.   The first, in seven movements, was written in
June 1772, the work of a boy of sixteen.

In the interval Aubrey and I encountered our friend, Princess
Pignatelli and her pretty daughter.   She is staying in a chalet
on Lake Wolfgangsee with an archduchess who takes paying
guests.   She has invited us all to lunch to-morrow.   All over the
world to-day one meets derelict royalties.   They are pathetic

victims of Fate and often show considerable courage in maintaining a façade that conceals near penury. One little archduchess I know gives piano lessons in New York, and a royal
princeling, cooking meals in a Seventh Avenue bedsitting-room,
designs book-ends and prints table mats. Once a year he bank-
rupts himself with a large cocktail party. When I reproved
him for his extravagance he told me it gained dividends in invi-
tations to week-end and dinner parties, " on which I save, and on
which I gain if I am lucky at bridge.' Handsome and eligible, so
far he has not taken the usual *pis aller* and married an heiress.

This evening I diverted my young friends with an imaginary
portrait of the broken-down archduchess to be encountered on
the morrow—meagre, hungry, gimlet-eyed, Bourbon-chinned,
with black bodice, high lace-frilled collar, dyed hair, yellow
teeth, and a lorgnette on a thin gold chain. She would say
little and smile benignly, and be lame on her feet.

August 30.

At the doorway of the lodging where my companions are
staying I found this morning two small children playing. One
was a little boy of eight, the other his sister, seven. The boy was
silver-haired, blue-eyed, the girl had two tiny pigtails, and wore
a little frilled bodice. Both were nut-brown. I engaged them
in conversation and finally asked them, " Wieviel costet ein eis ? "
" Ein schilling," came the solemn answer from Hans. " Und
zwei eis ? " I asked, glancing at Mitsi. " Zwei schilling ! "
I produced two schillings to buy two ices. After a shower of
Danke sie there was a silence and then Hans, holding the two
schillings in his brown fist, said quietly. " Bitte, ich habe ein
bruder." The brother, I learned, was Gottfried, age four. I
produced another schilling. After more thanks Hans and Mitzi
scampered upstairs to inform Gottfried of his luck.

These Austrians are a handsome race. Their children, daintily
dressed and flaxen-faired, are enchanting. It is a joy to sit in
the beautiful gardens of the Mirabel Schloss and see these flower-
like creatures toddling amid the fountains and the flower-beds.
And we in our enlightenment will train them up to bomb someone,
since *dulce et decorum est pro patria mori.*

We motored this morning to an hotel at St. Gilgan on Wolfgangsee. Our hostess, fearing to strain the royal household, had
ordered lunch on the lake-side. We arrived first. A flower-

F*

decorated table on the terrace was obviously set for our party. Presently a small car arrived and out of it stepped our hostess and daughter, together with the archduke who was chauffeur, and the archduchess. The archduke was tall, grey-haired and middle-aged. One glance at his wife filled me with contrition for my caricature. She was young, very pretty and quietly vivacious. The archduke went home. (To get lunch for the little archdukes?) We proceeded to the table where our hostess had ordered a feast. I sat next to the archduchess. Dyed hair? No, the prettiest blonde curls. Yellow teeth? No, a gleaming smile. Gimlet-eyed? No, light-blue laughing eyes. High collar? No, a low-cut bodice. I learned she was the mother of two little boys, the elder aged five a Leopold, who, had Fate designed otherwise, would some day be Leopold, Grand Duke of Tuscany, living in the magnificence of the Pitti Palace at Florence, on a throne that had passed from the Medici to the Hapsburgs. One hundred years ago Leopold II reigned there. Here was a curious link with our visit to Baron Ricasoli at Brolio in Chianti. The boy's father, the Archduke Gottfried, was the great-great-grandson of Leopold II, last Grand Duke of Tuscany, over whose abdication in 1859 Baron Bettino Ricasoli had presided. The Archduke's wife, Dorothea, is the granddaughter of the last King of Bavaria She has Stuart blood in her veins What a vista of history stretched behind her, but of all this there was no consciousness in her easy manner. I learned later how much courage lay behind her gentleness.

Our gay lunch by the lakeside was crowned by three enormous *Salzburgerknockerels.* This delicious dish consists of eggs whipped into a foamy mountain. Visitors, taking a chance with a strange name on the menu are overwhelmed when it appears, for it looks like a serving of the Bernese Oberland. Our successive *Salzburgerknockerels* provoked the greatest interest among a group of tourists immured in a glass pavilion behind us. They craned their necks to observe the dish until at my suggestion Princess Pignatelli obligingly held up the last one for them to observe. Curiosity was satisfied. We lingered on at the table while a little lake steamer came and went, its destination the famed *White Horse Inn* at Wolfgangsee.

It was past three o'clock when the archduke returned to collect his wife. Discussing the war cloud that lay over the scene he told me that when they had been surrounded, the Russians, during the occupation, had behaved more correctly and had not molested them, which was more than could be said of the former Austrian Socialist Republic and the Nazis. Later, I learned more of their story from our hostess. They lived in a large chalet lent to them by another branch of the family, with only oil lamps and no modern amenities. In this chalet Wagner had lived and composed. It was not their property for it belonged to the large, dispossessed Hapsburg clan and some member might desire it, in turn, as a place of refuge. Their fortunes had vanished in the collapse of the old Austrian Empire. Stripped of most of their remaining assets, driven into exile, some of them had now crept back to their beloved Austria and somehow contrived to live. The little archduchess ran the house, attended to her three children, soon to be augmented by a fourth, and supplied the needs of her paying guests, all without any loss of dignity. But the sense of strain must be great, for another storm, the third, threatens, and may blow away like a cobweb this halting place on the lake-side.

We went on to Wolfgangsee. Lovely as it is, it is a place to be avoided in the high season. It was once an enchanting little lake-side village *sehr gemütlich*, that suggested the setting of *The White Horse Inn*, an enormously popular musical comedy. But now Wolfgangsee has become the comedy itself, prinked out, self-conscious. The old paddle-steamer that brought the Emperor Franz Joseph to the jetty amid the cheers of dirndled maidens and lederhosened youths, still comes chuffing in. Smart little diesel-engined packet boats now do the lake transport work but one old paddle-steamer is subsidised to preserve the musical comedy setting. Visitors dress themselves in native costumes. A youth, proudly displaying a pair of tanned thighs, shatters the illusion with native tones of Brooklyn or Wichita, and the blooming dirndled maiden reveals that Madison ' High ' and not Wolfgangsee has had charge of her education. Car parks have been scooped out of the narrow landscape ; the pretty little balconied hotels with their flower-boxes have put on monstrous annexes. The Platz, cluttered with picture postcard kiosks and carved souvenirs, hides under a façade of tourist junk. There is scarcely room to move. It is all very gay and high-spirited but it is as if one had walked on to the stage while the comedy was running. Possibly after July and August the lovely little town relapses into quietude, and mirrors itself in the unruffled lake, but in the high season it is too much taken over by tourist agencies.

This evening I went to the Stadt Theatre to see *Der Erste Walzer* by Oscar Straus, acted by a company from the Bavarian State Opera Theatre. Light, inconsequential, it was most daintily done. The set consisted of a large picture-frame with the ingenious assistance of a revolving stage that carried the sequence of the play moving before us. The story was of the usual Ruritanian nature. A bored young princeling of a small eighteenth-century State neglected his wife and sought diversion with a pretty actress. The only modern note was the unhappy young princess, whose beauty was hidden by a pair of large horn-rimmed glasses, making her look like an American schoolmarm. One knew, of course, that when they came off the prince would discover she was a ravishing beauty, but for the moment the farce proceeded merrily on the lines of Dorothy Parker's

> " Men don't make passes
> To girls who wear glasses."

Perhaps, quite unintentionally, the operetta was a skit on the paraphernalia of royalty : the obsequious household of officials, the boring official chores. Much riotous fun was made of the scene on the prince's birthday when he proceeded to make a lavish distribution of Orders—to the local chemist, baker, stationmaster, etc. Somehow three got left over. They were plucked off the royal cushion and pinned on the breast of the major-domo. It recalled the occasion when I heard the groan of a Consul-General who received a box of Orders for general distribution.

This merry performance proved to be a birthday festival. Oscar Straus, aged eighty, was present in a box. After the interval he came down and conducted the overture of the second act. The old gentleman, very sprightly, received a great ovation, with many floral tributes from the house and the company, after which the farce went merrily on its way. I thought how singular it was that I should chance to be present to see Oscar Straus conduct his own operetta on his eightieth birthday. Forty-three years earlier I had just graduated from the labour of Czerny's *Hundred and One Exercises for the Piano*, and my long suffering music mistress had promised me, as reward and refreshment, a light piece. She produced *The Waltz Dream* by Oscar Straus which had travelled triumphantly from Vienna to London.

That piece was chosen because, in the theatre at Nottingham, to which I had been taken, the leading role had been played by a beautiful actress, Effie Mann, daughter of Tom Mann, a Labour agitator of those days. I had met her at the home of a local M.P., the friend of her father, and had instantly given her my boy's heart. So here I sat in the Mozarteum, forty-three years later, flooded with memories, having discovered in the programme that Oscar Straus was the composer of *The Waltz Dream*.

August 31.

Every morning, soon after eight o'clock, I look out of the window of my room on the third floor of the *Münchnerhof*. Over the roof of the Hotel *Traube*, opposite, rises a green curtain of trees above which appears the red-tiled apse of the Kapuziner Kloster on the Kapuzinerberg. It is surmounted by a little open belfry crowned, for some reason, by a small fir tree from which festive ribbons flow in the breeze. I wondered what it betokens.

This morning the answer arrived in the form of Günther. The Kapuziner Kloster, he tells me, has a boarding-school for boys. One boy, in revolt, tried three times to set the school on fire. In American parlance, he was a 'firebug.' At the fourth attempt he succeeded. He was discovered too late, for part of the school and the whole of the wooden belfry were burned down. Workmen have just completed the new belfry. Günther says it is the custom here to decorate a new building on completion with a small fir-tree bedecked with ribbons. It remains until it is sere and the needles fall.

My glimpse of the Kloster, amid the beech-trees, rising over the roof of the Hotel *Traube*, which bears along its new façade the legend *Mein Leben Und End Stet In Gottes Hent 1949* evokes for me a sad memory. Later this morning I took the steep winding ascent that goes up behind the hotel and leads, through an arch in the old fortifications, up to the Kapuzinerberg. Until a few years ago the summerhouse in which Mozart wrote *Die Zauberflöte* was on this hill but it has now been removed to the garden of the Mozarteum. I could wish it had been left *in situ* but it seems that so few made the ascent and the summerhouse was falling into ruin. It was thought wise to remove and preserve it. Moreover, the Kapuzinerberg was not its original site, for it was formerly attached to the garden wall of Mozart's house in Vienna when, despairing, poor and ill, he wrote his last opera in it, the year before he died.

But it is not this relic of Mozart, or the superb view over Salzburg that is the cause of my interest. Half-way up, behind a small iron gate, there is a sloping garden with large beech-trees. On the summit stands a long rambling house with a small tower. It was built by a Prince-Archbishop for one of his mistresses. The Prince-Archbishops have decorated Salzburg similarly in several places, as in the beautiful Mirabel Schloss. It was this old *nid d'amour* on the Kapuzinerberg that became the retreat of Stefan Zweig after the first Great War, and here he renewed the career that had been sadly interrupted by that holocaust. The old house is built into the town wall. Its main salon is fronted by windows between three stone columns. Below, lies a small terrace, pleasantly shady with a lovely view over Salzburg towards the Mönchberg. It was here one evening that I was Zweig's guest, along with Max Reinhardt and some others. It was an enchanted evening. Zweig had collected there, in addition to his library, many historic manuscripts. His reputation had spread over the world. He had wholly re-established himself after the war. Then came the first rumblings of the Nazi storm and there followed the Anschlüss. Salzburg had become a virulent Nazi outpost of the siege. A Jew, he was in great danger. Zweig fled, leaving behind his treasures. When next I saw him he was coming out of a book-shop in Bath, in 1939, in the first month of the war. I heard his story. He was a sad man, a second war had caught him. I left for New York soon afterwards. One day in 1941 on the corner of Fifth Avenue and 42nd Street we met again. He was living in a small house outside New York City. He told me he would be going soon to Rio de Janeiro, with his wife, to work there on a book. He had friends in that city. He was deeply depressed. His English money was blocked by the British Treasury, and royalties in other countries were lost. In 1942 we were all stunned to learn that he had shot his wife and himself in a suicide pact in an hotel bedroom at Persepolis, a mountain resort near Rio de Janeiro. The previous day his wife had care-fully made a parcel of the book he had finished and sent it to his New York publisher. He left a last message. He was tired and despondent. His world had vanished, he felt he could not go on. "I salute all my friends. May it be granted them yet to see the dawn after the long night."

I stood in the pleasant garden, with the terrace where we had enjoyed good conversation and music. The leafy beech-trees shimmered in the sunshine, beautiful Salzburg lay in the valley below. If only he had held on a while he might have got back to this haunt he loved, writing successfully, for his last work showed no decline of intellectual power. And then, as I thought this, there intruded the words uttered by an Austrian in a café, a few hours earlier: "Those Russians are only three hours away and there is nothing as strong as tissue paper to bar that horde. We've a gang of local Communists ready to welcome them in. Tito has just made a speech threatening to grab Carinthia and we are asked to put our trust in a handful of green American, English and French boys one year out of school, and all homesick."

This morning on the bridge over the Salzach, I encountered an Austrian friend who was accompanied by the old gentleman of last night's celebration, Oscar Straus. I congratulated him on his appearance the previous evening, adding that he must be considered doubly blessed by Fate, to reach eighty years, and to have one of his plays in healthy circulation, like himself I told him I should consider myself fortunate indeed if I lived to be as healthy at eighty, with one of my books still in circulation. The old fellow seemed quite delighted by my compliment.

Still troubled by the old enemy, I have decided to try a cure at Bad Gastein. Last night Günther dined with me and said good-bye. In two days' time he is hitch-hiking to Paris. It is astonishing how young people thumb their way about Europe these days, defeating high prices and exchange controls. In olden times students tramped from country to country assisted by Mother Church whose far-flung monasteries assisted the poor wayfarer. Now the monasteries are mostly gone and other means must be found. Günther is in luck. He has corresponded with the French couple who gave him a lift two years ago. Recently their son came to Salzburg and Günther gave him hospitality. Now he is to stay with the French family in Paris. "I have learned something," he remarked. "I no longer go trekking looking like an unwashed tramp. I wear my smartest outfit. People are much more ready to give one a lift."

Things Observed.

Overheard in the hotel lounge, in a conversation between a fair prima-donna of fifty and her friend. " I'd give all my triumphs for a young Austrian with straight legs ! " This is certainly the town of male legs in excelsis. The leather shorts set off their muscular nether limbs to great advantage. These stalwart youths seem to have walked straight off one of Michelangelo's ceilings. Their features are fine. They have heads crowned with a mass of blond curls. But I think that men over forty should go into long trousers and cover the waist-line. The standard of feminine beauty is also high in Austria. The girls are often exquisite, with lovely complexion and eyes. Their hair is a crown of glory and they have an insouciance that gives them the air of having just walked out of an operetta. Their native costume of *dirndl*, a short-sleeved bodice, and pleated skirt, sets off their fresh beauty. How fitting that in one of the most lovely corners of the earth the inhabitants lend charm to the landscape.

Rumours of war surround us on all sides. The Americans have panicked home. I refuse to be intimidated. Having passed through two wars I am fatalistic about a third whose aftermath would be such that I should have no desire to survive it.

September 1.

After lunch Aubrey and Simon drove us through a downpour to the station. I have parted from my most agreeable companions with real regret. When I undertook to ' tutor ' them on this tour I had faint misgivings. One of them I knew, the other slightly. There would seem to be an enormous disparity between a world-travelled man of fifty-eight and two youngsters of twenty. We have survived the test triumphantly. We have motored, eaten, and sightseen together without one inharmonious incident. I leave them with affection for their consideration towards me, their good manners, cheerfulness, intelligence, and eagerness to examine the countless facets of this wonderful world. If Eton has moulded them, my admiration of that venerable institution is increased ; if they generally reflect the younger generation then our breed can grapple with the future.

It rained hard during our train journey through the mountain valley. A pleasant young conductor reported on the Occupation :

the Russians are dreaded, but are fortunately at the far end of Austria ; the Americans are liked for their open generosity and dollars but their rowdy drunkenness is deplored ; the British are scarcely observed ; the French are disliked for their severity and exactitude. This opinion of the French recalled to me their occupation of the Rhineland after the Armistice of 1918. When the Allied war correspondents, of which I was one, arrived at Aachen, the French were there already. The French Town Commandant had supplied himself with a number of German posters put up in Lille ordering all Frenchman to step into the gutter and take off their hats on encountering a German officer. With nice irony the French Commandant posted up these bills in Aachen, adding a fly-bill—" This now applies to you." I liked that. A deputation headed by the Mayor of Cologne had arrived at British Headquarters begging us to occupy Cologne at once. The excuse was that the local Socialists were out of hand, but our official opinion was that Cologne was eager to be occupied by the easy-going British and not by the dreaded French. Austrian experience of the occupying Allies seems to have crystallised into the following opinions ; the Russians are an unpredictable nightmare and systematic looters, with odd streaks of tolerance ; the Americans are expansive, erratic and easy-going ; the British are complacent, self-contained and imperturbable ; the French are punctilious, aloof and *sehr korrect.*

The friendly conductor, in a neat uniform with a leather satchel, offered to get us a porter at Bad Gastein. It had ceased raining. I asked him if many English came here. " Not so many now. Before the war there was quite a lot, regular, and such a nice class—the English were the best-dressed and best-mannered of all, in those days." It was pleasant, and sad, to hear. To-day on the Continent the British tourist does not count for much. They know he is short of money and they have never before seen the class of English that travels now.

The little town occupies a high ledge on the mountain, shaped like a horseshoe. Down through the heart of the town, in a deep chasm of rock, surges a silver waterfall until it reaches the floor of the green valley, where it flows through the long cultivated landscape to Hof Gastein, visible in the distance. Nature's other gift to Bad Gastein, as well as its superb position and splendid air, is the radium-charged water which gushes out of the rocks and supplies the curative baths in all the hotels.

In the spacious old days the cure addicts came to Bad Gastein. The Grand Dukes, Princes and Counts, with their fashionably attired ladies arrived with a cohort of valets, maids, grooms, coachmen and companions. The luxurious hotels with their renowned cuisine and armies of white-aproned waiters, the orchestras playing on the terraces, the lovely woods and promenades with a nicely placed *aussicht*, the shops representing famous establishments in Paris, Vienna, London, where an amorous gentleman bought a little trifle, a collar of diamonds or a string of pearls for a lovely lady, or ordered half a dozen pairs of shoes and silk shirts—all these gracious amenities took precedence of the doctors who 'vetted' the patients and prescribed the cure. Vichy, Aix-les-Bain, Wiesbaden, Carlsbad, Montecatini, Bad Gastein no more see the fashion that thronged them in the high season, 'made' by the appearance of the Emperor Joseph, the Kaiser Wilhelm I, or Edward VII. Two world cataclysms, in 1914 and 1939, swept away this privileged class. Penury, hunger, suicide took their toll. A few survived, recalling in poverty the golden days. A new breed of war profiteers and industrial tycoons, that somehow escapes the mesh of Socialism spread over the world, has stepped on to the ancient scene. With all their affluence these newcomers are pinchbeck actors lacking the finesse and the grand manner.

We drove through the dusk to our hotel. It is situated on the famous Kaiser Wilhelm Promenade, a level walk cut through a firwood on a high ledge on the mountain. Sheer below, is the long valley, locked in by green mountains, well wooded. My room has a loggia facing south, two arcades with a column, somewhat like the setting of a Fra Angelico *Annunciation*. It was dark as I looked out. Terrace on terrace, in the horseshoe curve of the mountain, lay Bad Gastein, jewelled with lights. The murmur of the waterfall pervaded the air.

BAD GASTEIN

September 2.

We have been into the little town. All day I have been walking in a dream, a dream that has come true. When I was eight years old my mother took me to an 'Exhibition' that visited my native city. It was one of the amazing Mr. Imre Kiralfy's

creations. It covered eight acres and was full of wonders. There
was a great bazaar of shops, a zoo, a gigantic waterchute, a garden
maze, a grotto through which one rode in flat boats, a scenic
railway, side shows and other wonders. The wise expenditure
of sixpence among so many attractions involved anxious decisions.
I suppose I should find it boring and garish to-day, but at eight
it was fairyland. From all this enchantment I carried away one
memory undimmed through the years. There was a sideshow
labelled *A Day in the Austrian Tyrol*. You sat in a dark booth
facing a large stage on which there was a model of a Tyrolean
village, gay with colour. It had steep mountain slopes, fir-clad,
with crests of snow and chalets perilously perched, with wooden
carved balconies bright with geraniums, and with steep overhanging roofs and green-shuttered little windows, exactly like
the Swiss cuckoo-clock that hung in our kitchen. Down through
the middle of the village, under a bridge that spanned the ravine,
rushed a waterfall coming from a glacier. There was a watermill with a large revolving wheel, there were peasants in native
costume, wagons drawn by paired horses, cattle with cowbells,
all the animal life of a day in the Tyrol. Then the scene grew
dark, black clouds obscured the mountains, there was a growing
rumble of thunder which drew nearer and nearer, and a sudden
terrifying fork of lightning, followed by a deafening crash of the
heavens and a torrential downpour of rain as the storm smote
the poor little village. My heart thumped. Would the village
be washed away, the inhabitants killed ? But the storm abated,
the light grew, a rainbow arched the sky, the rain ceased, the sun
came out and touched the glistening waterfall. The village
came to life again with the waterwheel turning merrily, the
wagons creaking, the cowbells tinkling, the birds singing. Then
the curtain fell and we came out into the ordinary day.

I have never forgotten that picture impressed on my child's
mind. Years later, travelling through Switzerland and Austria,
I had encountered something like it in real life but never the
exact conjunction of all the things I remember, the snowy peaks,
the chalets, the waterwheel, the waterfall crashing down through
the heart of the village and under the bridge that spanned the
chasm. Now here in Bad Gastein, fifty years later, I find the
exact replica of my Tyrolean dream village.

Through all those years Bad Gastein has grown into a town.
The fame of its curative waters has spread. Emperors and

empresses, princes, statesmen, famous musicians, composers and writers have flocked here, until the horseshoe ledge is thronged with hotels. Everywhere, flanking the balconied hotels, there are café terraces with gay awnings and little orchestras. There is a Kursaal with a concert hall, a casino, reading-rooms, and a lounge for taking the water. The true attraction here, the loveliness of the setting apart, is the baths. They are in the ground floor of every hotel so that the visitor has no early morning journey to make out of doors. He descends by the elevator from his bedroom to the baths and then returns to his bed for one hour of repose.

This radium-charged water is not to be trifled with. As a preliminary one must visit a doctor who will prescribe a course of baths. The usual course is a morning bath of some twenty minutes, over three weeks. Many of the visitors here are not sick, they come to be rejuvenated, to rest in the mountain air. Some of them take their cure quite seriously. They are called at five a.m., descend to the bath, remain immersed for the pre-scribed time and then return to bed where they sleep until ready for breakfast. After that the masseur comes. At eleven, dressed and looking well groomed, they take a slow promenade along to the Kursaal and café terraces, drink the water or take coffee, listen to the band which plays every morning for an hour and stroll back to lunch.

After lunch a deathly silence falls over Bad Gastein. The shops are shut, no one is seen on the streets. Everyone has retired for the afternoon siesta. About four o'clock the place comes to life again. The visitors take tea under the gay um-brellas on the sunny terraces, stroll out to a café in the woods, listen to the music which is to be found everywhere, from small orchestras to odd zithern players and jodellers. At seven o'clock preparations for dinner begin. At ten o'clock pairs of shoes begin to appear outside bedroom doors down the long corridors.

There are more lively phases such as mountain climbing, tennis, riding, and casino gambling by the frivolous whose ' cure ' is an excuse for idling. The number of tea-shops and cafés thronged after four o'clock proclaims gossip as the favourite pastime. Cakes of stupendous size and richness are consumed, with much misgiving and backsliding by ' slimmers ' and those doing the cure. After three weeks of this life in the high

mountain air nerves have vanished and the visitors look like
sleek tabby cats.

To my dismay my doctor forbade the baths. This is no cure
for ulcers unless rest, diet and general happiness constitute a
cure, which I feel they do. But my curiosity could not be
restrained and at 7 a.m., summoned by the *bademeister*, I descended to the baths. One entered a small white room. There
was a long sunken bath with a seat at either end. One walked
into it by four steps and, seated, was immersed up to the neck.
The water was warm, clear and odourless. Nearby was a tap
from which hung a rubber hose with a nozzle. Water of a higher
temperature came out of it with considerable force. With this,
under water, one performed a self-massage. A feeling of complete well-being pervaded one. A hot towel reposed in a cylinder,
a clock ticked so that one checked the prescribed time, and,
upstairs again, a warm bed and a sleep awaited one before
ringing for breakfast. Moreover a pleasant day in lovely surroundings lay ahead.

The morning sun, on days when it was sunny, poured on to
my loggia, ablaze with boxes of scarlet and pink geraniums.
I looked south over the town up towards a break in the high
mountains. The sun glistens on the powdery snow, a serene
cloud floats along the vivid blue sky, the sound of water rises
above the life of the town and its terraces of hotels. This morning
I was fascinated for ten minutes by what seemed to be a small
humming-bird. It was not more than an inch long, with a
rosy-pink throat, and wings that vibrated so rapidly that they were
invisible as the tiny creature hovered over each flower. Into
each stamen, with indescribable accuracy and speed, it thrust
an inch-long proboscis, scarcely thicker than a hair. Needle-
threading is a clumsy process in comparison. The little creature
never alighted on the flowers but performed this threading while
suspended in flight. I wondered that the proboscis did not
break off, and to my amazement I observed that it could curl
up like an elephant's trunk. The whole length of the flower-
boxes examined, my delightful visitor, a perfect helicopter,
vanished. I had seen a similar but much larger creature in
Florida, but that, I knew was a humming-bird. This, I learned
later, was a humming-bird moth.

On the opposite mountain side, half-way up, runs the railway
line from Vienna and Salzburg. It disappears into the Tauern

tunnel, eight miles long, that opens on the southern slope falling towards Italy. When the trains come, three or four times a day, mostly screened by mountain firs, they make a faint murmur and glide along, diminutive, as if they had come out of a child's playbox. They are part of our daily entertainment. A great many things seem part of a Lilliput world in this setting of high mountains and waterfalls. Hof Gastein, far away in the valley below, with its slender steeple, is another playbox object.

Along the Kaiser Wilhelm Promenade I am daily diverted by the squirrels. Some of them are brown, others are black with white fronts. For all their nervous movements and furtive airs they are as shameless as the beggars of Spain. Their common name is Hansi. Children adore them and they run along the wooden railing, stopping to put out their paws and take the proffered nuts. Query. How do they know, under the heavy winter snowfall, where they have buried their summer store? There is another little fellow who is widely popular, also named Hansi. He is the pageboy who works the lift. He must be the smallest pageboy in the world. The lift is an old-fashioned one that is set in motion by pulling a rope. To achieve this Hansi flings himself on the rope. I always expect it to carry him up through the roof. He is a silver-headed boy with ingratiating manners and a sunlit smile, eleven years old and the pet of all the visitors. Bad Gastein is full of brown-legged little boys in leather shorts who rush about carrying parcels, pulling small trolleys, assisting in shops. This morning a pocket Hercules passed me carrying on his shoulder what looked like a basket of snakes. Seeing my curiosity he smiled and stopped for me to examine his load. It was a basket of Frankfurter sausages on its way to an hotel kitchen. I contrasted this scene with one encountered any early morning in a French town—battalions of bare-legged boys on bicycles, balancing batons of bread!

I wonder when these cheerful hardworking youngsters get their schooling. I learn that the summer holiday lasts from mid-July to mid-September. In these months they rush to the hotels and shops to cope with the tourist traffic, squirrel-like storing up for the winter.

An excellent little string orchestra plays daily in the town. It also performs in the Kursaal concert hall every morning. Once a week it gives an ambitious concert. In the daytime it plays cheerful rumty-tumty music of the Lehar-Strauss variety. At the evening concert it is gravely classical.

Last night we were given a programme that included the Beethoven *Seventh Symphony* and the Rachmaninoff *Third Concerto* for piano and orchestra. A young Greek played. He had an admirable command of the keyboard, an easy technique and much power, but, playing on a concert grand, he was always on top of the small orchestra. For this *Concerto* I am perhaps too severe a critic. It evokes a memory of Rachmaninoff playing his own composition with the New York Symphony Orchestra in Carnegie Hall, New York, shortly before his death. Austere, commanding, it was an unforgettable virtuoso performance of great brilliance and clarity.

September 4.

This evening to a concert at the Kursaal. A programme by two sisters, Ingrid and Karin Gutberg, for two pianos. It is rarely one has an opportunity of hearing the Brahms *Sonata in F-minor*, and the Liszt *Concert Pathétique*. I arrived early and was much amused by yet another example of the happy-go-lucky Austrian character. The article you are promised for *Morgen* does not arrive. It will be ready on Wednesday, says the shop-assistant. Thursday and Friday pass. Most surely it will be ready *Morgen* says the amiable assistant. It comes at last on Monday with a flourish of *Bitte* and *Dankeschöne* and a general aura of smiles and courtesies so that you cannot be angry. No, says the young Adonis in the Verkhersbureau, he has no second-class train tickets, but two third-class tickets equal one second-class. " And do two second-class tickets equal one first class ? " " Oh, no. We have first-class tickets, but there are no first-class carriages on that train." You come out of the bureau dizzy but quite elated with life in Austria.

When I arrived at the concert hall the curtains were drawn across the auditorium. There was no one to collect tickets. It was fifteen minutes before the time of the concert. I entered the antechamber and sat down with about twenty other ticket-holders. All the time, until the curtain rose, twenty minutes late, there was the sound of a piano being tuned on the platform —another case of *Morgen*, I suppose. A few minutes before the performance was timed to begin a doorkeeper arrived, all smiles. He entered the antechamber, collected our tickets and then went back to the entrance door. The concert began twenty minutes late, the hall being half-full, and about a dozen of us in the front stalls. I passed the time speculating on the curious mentality of some people. They will be lavish where it is foolish and mean where it entails hardship. The seats for this concert were ludicrously cheap, 10, 6, and 4 schillings (3/-, 1/9d., 10d.). I bought two ten schilling seats for myself and my companion. That evening three quite wealthy persons staying at the most *de luxe* hotel and sustaining themselves with champagne cocktails before dinner, exulted over the cheapness of the seats. They had paid 1/9d. (24 cents) and greatly enjoyed the concert. " And how cheap ! " they exclaimed. To their amazement I protested. Here were two young girls who, after long training, were giving a two hours' programme. They had to meet their travelling, advertising and agent's expenses. If the hall had been filled at ten schillings a head it would not have brought in more than 5,000 schillings (200 dollars or £68). On what remained of this these two artists had to live. It was not possible for them to give more than three or four recitals a week. The hall was half-full, with three-quarters of the audience in the cheaper seats. I must have shaken the champagne-cocktail drinkers, for afterwards one lady said to me, " You are quite right. We ought to be ashamed of ourselves ! We readily pay fifteen dollars at Carnegie Hall for a recital that couldn't compare with to-night's."

Perhaps it is not intentional meanness as much as the common urge to get something cheap. People are more unimaginative than unkind. There is a class of people, alas, that is mean by forethought. It undertips waiters and porters and all who do the heavy and menial work that contributes to one's pleasure. As an author I am familiar with the lament of those who cannot afford to buy a book at ten shillings. They will unhesitatingly spend two pounds taking bad snapshots. They will pay fifteen shillings for a theatre seat for two hours' entertainment, but a book that gives them a week's pleasure, and can be passed on, is too costly ! The reason, of course, is that at some time they hope they can borrow it for nothing. When I left Bad Gastein there was a wretched scene between a sweating elderly porter who had struggled with three portmanteaux, searching up and down the corridor for two seats. He received a three schillings tip. His protest was met by peremptory rudeness. I gave him ten and the poor fellow overwhelmed me with thanks.

He removed his hat, shook my hand and bade me *Auf wiedersehen* and *Gute Reise*. It is true that the percentage system at hotels has become a racket. You pay 12 per cent or 15 per cent on the bill and then individually tip since there is no other way of showing gratitude for personal service. Nevertheless, I hold that since these things are part of the costs of travel they should be budgeted for, and if one cannot afford them one should not travel.

When the curtain rose there were two concert grand pianos on the platform. Owing to the smallness of the stage they had to be folded into each other, belly to belly, and to save a ricochetting of sound from upraised lids one had been removed. The companion to the resident grand piano had been imported for the evening and had required tuning. Hence the strumming we heard. Do audiences ever envision the anxieties that flit through the hearts of performers waiting in the wings ? If one piano had not been perfectly tuned in with the other. . . .

On to the stage came two young women, about twenty-five, presumably twins. They were blonde, highly-complexioned Scandinavian types. They were gowned exactly alike in sleeveless bodices with full skirts. They were lovely to look at. Almost shyly they seated themselves, face to face. They began to play the Brahms *Sonata*. It is not an easy composition. As they played there was an astonishing transformation before our eyes. Their technical command was unforced, they had considerable reserves for *allegro* and *rallentando* passages. Their interpretation, perfectly synchronised, was confident and delicate. We settled down to an enjoyable evening. The Brahms was followed by a first performance of a composition (*Salzburger Konzert*) by a living composer Heinrich Lernacher, and deserved its good reception. The programme closed with a finale of virtuosity and sonorous declamation, the *Concert Pathétique* of Liszt. The young pianists at the close received a deservedly enthusiastic acclamation.

Adjourning to a café (No " No-you-can't-be-served-after-eleven " nonsense here !) I reflected on the curious vocations people choose. These two sisters, like Siamese twins, were wedded to each other by grand pianos. Like a pair of trapeze acrobats they must synchronise perfectly. Each was dependent upon the other. There is not a great library of music written for two pianos and there are very few concert halls where it is not necessary to import a second piano and tune it in. If one player fell ill the concert was off, and if an attractive young man came along and fell in love with one of these sisters, and proposed marriage, what happened to the other? It was ridiculous to expect simultaneous love affairs and marriages. . . .

Homeward bound, crossing the bridge over the waterfall, we met our duettists, one carrying the bouquet of flowers that came with the fall of the curtain, not artificial, I was glad to observe, on tour with its recipient. A man behind them carried two bags. Obviously they were on their way to the station. They looked engagingly young and pretty. We greeted them, expressing our pleasure. They were not twins, we learned, there were two years between them. Nor were they Swedes, as we had surmised. They were Latvians. But Latvia had been gobbled up by Russia and so . . . Yes, it was difficult but they were artistes . . . Their mother had taught them when children. They had just completed their studies at the Mozarteum in Salzburg. Their next concert was in Cologne. We shook hands, wished them much success and they vanished into the night.

September 6.

A beautiful day, the sky a brilliant blue, the clouds lying in snowy fleeces over the mountain peaks. Bad Gastein was coming out of church as I walked this Sunday morning along the Promenade to the café for my morning *yoghourt*. " Isn't it good to be alive and listen to all the bells ringing madly to call God's attention to them," said my companion. A most engaging squirrel, black and white, scampering along the railing at the sight of a small boy, very elegant in full Tyrolean costume, pink spotted shirt, green jacket, leather braces and shorts, with embroidered half-hose over his calves. His shoes were of red leather. In his jaunty hat he had a pheasant feather. He looked as if he had stepped off an Austrian Christmas card. They tell me that when the lads of the village wear their feathers curling forwards it means they are spoiling for a fight. The dainty squirrel, " Really only a rat with a bushy tail," said my companion, has scented nuts in the little boy's fist. He sits up and begs so captivatingly that the boy teases him no longer. Half a dozen of us watch him eating, tiny paws grasping the nut, his jaws so busy that his cheeks vibrate like a humming-bird's wings. Did they ever get duodenal ulcers, I wondered. They eat so fast and are so highly strung.

On the way home we descended to a church whose tall shingled spire we often pass on our walks. It is the old village church of St. Nikolaus. It is in a shocking state of dilapidation. When at the end of the nineteenth century, Bad Gastein grew into a small town and spread along the mountain amphitheatre, a new church, of no beauty, was built, and St. Nikolaus fell into disuse. Its little graveyard once commanded a magnificent view of the valley, and the river running down to Hof Gastein, but a gaunt *badehaus* now obstructs the vista. Inside the church the groined stone roof is supported by a single column which gives great majesty to the church. A scaffolding showed that repairs had begun. There had been what looked like fifteenth century frescoes, of an interesting Giotto-character, but except for one wall these had almost vanished. Memorial tablets and carved rococo saints were lying in a corner. A superb baroque altar, carved in wood, and painted, filled the apse. The altar painting had no merit but on either side stood two superb baroque figures of bishops. They had vestments, mitres, and wore black gloves on their El Greco-like hands. Each carried a large black Bible. On one lay a fish, on the other, head erect, sat a white gander. I pestered everyone I met, anxious to know what is the significance of a gander seated on a Bible carried by a black-gloved bishop.

> Oh dear grave bishop, with Bible and gloves,
> Why do you carry a gander ?

Outside in the little churchyard I found a cluster of wooden crosses each with a chalet roof. They are memorials to local soldiers fallen in the 1939-45 war. Some carried photographs of lads of 18 to 22, all smiling in the beauty of their youth. Nearly all had fallen in Russia. I found these simple home-made memorials very moving, with their posies, shining on the sunlit mountainside. I was grateful because no one had committed the blasphemy of imposing a sword on the crucifixes, as on many war memorials in England.

September 7.

The very pretty waitress who brings my breakfast and also serves in the dining-room, comes from Salzburg. She does not want to go to America, an almost unique exception. An American lad with the U.S. Army in Salzburg has tried to entice her into marriage. He has shown her photographs of a large automobile, and told her that she will have one of her own. He made the mistake of showing her a photograph of Pittsburgh, his home, saying it was like Austria with its mountains. Alas! some other American when she asked him about Pittsburgh threw up his hands and cried, " Gosh, it's a lousy hole, all smoke and coal dunks. If you fall in the river you die of poison not drowning." The description was true and not true. Pittsburgh, like Sheffield, has lovely environs. But the informant came from California, and you will never get the truth about any other State from an American. The chief cause of the girl's refusal of marriage was " All American soldiers are so much drunk everywhere." One evening I saw her with a swain, superbly virile in his *lederhosen*. I cannot see how the representative of any other nation, drunk or sober, could compete against her blond Apollo.

I am repeatedly struck by the beauty of these Austrian girls, working in hotels, shops and offices. They are exquisitely dressed and always lovely and fresh to look at. Their allure is enhanced by the smiling *diablerie* of their blue eyes under tumbling blonde curls so that they seem as if they have stepped out of a Franz Lehar musical comedy, lovely brides who may pass into merry widows !

September 8.

Staying in my hotel there is a Lady Dunn. She is a ' character ' and enlivens the evenings with the recital of her various experiences. Some thirty years ago when she was a struggling music critic she conceived a great love for Salzburg. Since then the promotion of the musical festival has been her passion, with the results that she is *persona grata* with the Salzburg authorities. It is a triumph of personality.

The Old Enemy has been persistent. On three consecutive mornings it has broken my sleep at five a.m., its usual habit. But there are compensations for a bad night. I went out on to my balcony about six o'clock. The light was breaking over the eastern mountains. The valley lay unseen under a vast blanket of snowy mist, only the high peaks and fir-woods emerging, touched by the amber dawn. Then the great blanket began to

stir, rise from the valley, and roll up the mountain-side revealing
the town, the stream, and the pattern of fields in the valley with
their orderly stooks of hay standing to attention like a regiment.
Suddenly, a golden burst of light, and behold, Apollo in all his
glory riding in his chariot of the Dawn.   I went back to bed and
read.   Then came the tap of the *bademeister* on my door.   I put
on a dressing-gown, took the lift down to the baths and sank into
the lucid warm water.

Musing in the bath I recalled Lady D's amusing account of
her asking the Archbishop of Canterbury to pronounce a blessing
on the German nation.   She had a great affection for the Archbishop, Cosmo Gordon Lang, and always on her return from
Wagnerian trips to Germany she went to see him at Lambeth
Palace and give him an account of her work.   " I'm not a particularly religious woman, but one day I felt I would like his
blessing, so I asked the dear old man for it.   He told me to kneel
down and there and then he blessed me.   I asked him also to
bless my work in Germany and the German people, for I felt
my work for Wagner's music at Bayreuth was something of a
contribution to Anglo-German friendship.   That was in the
early days of Hitler.   He thereupon called down a blessing on
my labours and on the German people.   He was a beautiful
and saintly old man, though people often said he should have
been an actor with his wonderful face, voice and manner.   Some
years later I came back from Germany, after seeing the terrifying
things the Nazis did to the Jews, following the assassination of
a high Nazi official by a young French Jew in Paris.   I had
seen the night sky lit up by burning synagogues.   I told the
Archbishop about this.   He was appalled and said, ' Then I
shall withdraw my blessing on the German people.'   I told
him he couldn't.   He had given it and that was the end of it.
' I can and I will ! ' he persisted.   I retorted that he could
not, and reminded him that I had the authority of the Bible
behind me.   I recalled the story of Esau and Jacob, and
of how Isaac, when he discovered that Jacob had falsely
obtained his blessing, was unable to withdraw it and give it
to his brother.   The Archbishop saw my point and persisted
no longer."

In the town this morning I met Ernst Lothar, who wrote *The
Angel with the Trumpet* and also Daniele Varé, the Italian ex-
diplomat, who wrote *The Maker of Heavenly Trousers,* a fantasy

based on his life in Pekin.   In his delightful autobiographical
book, *Laughing Diplomat*, he tells how when he was a young man
he took a room in the vast Borghese villa between Anzio and
Nettuno.   It was here that for a whole year D'Annunzio had
lived with Eleonora Duse and wrote his *Città Morta*.   The villa
was now almost deserted.   Varé was young then and one summer
evening he was thrilled to see a mysterious lady arrive and
appear on the balcony above his apartment.   A silvery voice
quoted Juliet's balcony speech.   He applauded.   It was Duse
and she invited him up to her balcony.   She asked him his name.
When he told her she said, " Then you are a Venetian ! " and explained how she knew.   When she was acting at the Fenice
Theatre in Venice she used to go out into the little *campo* at the
side, which had a restaurant, to take the cool air between the
acts.   At the far end there was a house with a façade that had
Austrian cannon and cannon balls let into it.   It carried an
inscription proclaiming that Venice had resisted triumphantly
the Austrian invaders.   Under the inscription were Italian
names, beginning with Manin and ending with Varé.   " I
remember their names well because those men closed my grandfather's theatre in Venice," said Duse.   " That Varé was my
grandfather.   You are quite right.   I am Venetian," said the
young man.   This was the last time he saw Duse but he never
forgot her.

I told Varé I had a little footnote to his story.   For three
seasons I had lived in the House of the Cannon Balls, as they
called it.   I had a little terrace just over the inscription with
his grandfather's name on it.   I was driven out finally by the noise
of the diners at the Fenice restaurant, celebrated for its food,
who ate and talked till the small hours.   My apartment was
remarkable for having three separate staircases.   It seemed
designed for Casanova.

Walking along the Kaiser Wilhelm Promenade we encountered
Yehudi Menuhin.   He has taken a chalet up the valley for his
wife and children but goes to practise in Bad Gastein each day.
He must have a remarkable memory, not only for music but also
for names and faces.   I had met him only once, some years ago
at a dinner party in New York.   He remembered my name and
also the time and place.   " It was at Mrs. William Breed's
when I had just returned from Russia.   I remembered how
closely you cross-examined me ! " he said.

I have been told how he came to be called Yehudi, which is
Hebrew for Jew. Just before he was born his parents, good-
class Russian Jews, had emigrated to New York. Arrived there,
they experienced considerable difficulty in finding hotel accommodation owing to the tacit ban on Jews in high-class hotels.
This prejudice so incensed them they they made a vow never to
compromise about their race in any way. So they called their
son Yehudi. He was born in 1916 and made his first public
appearance in San Francisco at the age of seven.

September 9.

As I had expressed some curiosity about the source of the
radio-active waters the Kur Direktor, Herr von Limberg, kindly
took me to the Franz Joseph Spring, one of the chief sources.
It is in the mountain-side and to reach it we traversed a tunnel
320 ft. long. The atmosphere in the low tunnel cut through the
rock was that of a Turkish bath, steamy and dripping. In a
crevice of the rock we saw the water bubbling out at a temperature of 117° Fahr. There are fifty-five of these springs. Their
output is forty thousand gallons every twenty-four hours, more
than ample for the supply to the seventy hotels. Since the water
emerges at too great a heat for its use, it is conducted to three
reservoirs, for cooling, by which means the prescribed temperature can be blended by the *bademeister*.

Legend surrounds the ancient history of the springs and their
healing properties. A favourite story is that in A.D. 680 a
wounded stag escaped its hunters and on being tracked down
was discovered to be in the care of two hermits who were treating
the animal by bathing its wound with the magic waters. As
early as the thirteenth century the renown of these springs
was mentioned in a parchment containing a song of Nithardt.
In 1436 the Duke Frederick of Austria, later Roman Emperor,
came to Gastein to cure a thigh wound. After that the visitors
to this mountain resort were so numerous that a special refuge
had to be built. In 1562 the famous Fugger banking family
of Augsburg commissioned the celebrated Theophrastus Para-
celsus to investigate and report on the mining industry established
there. His report draws attention to the fact that long before
the springs had been heard of, Gastein had been famous for its
gold-mines. The local Celtic tribes had worked them. They
were displaced by the conquering Romans who exploited the

gold and silver deposits of the valley. As was the custom of
the Romans, they built roads traceable to-day. On the downfall
of the Empire the Slavs overran these Tauern mountains. In the
seventh century the gold-mining industry was seized by the Church
for its revenues. By the beginning of the fourteenth century
the Prince-Archbishops of Salzburg were masters of the domain.
From the great wealth derived from these mines they minted a
currency, built the magnificent fortress-palace, the Hohenfest-
nung, which to-day dominates Salzburg, and such trifles as the
Mirabel Schloss and the Monats-Schlösschen for their mistresses.
Following the Counter-Reformation the Church began to per-
secute the Protestant miners—

> Avenge, O Lord, thy slaughtered saints whose bones
> Lie scattered on the Alpine mountains cold.

Up to this period there was a rich commerce with Venice and
Germany. Families enjoying the proprietary rights in the gold-
mines grew in wealth, culture and learning. In the eighteenth
century religious disputes and the growing persecution of the
Protestants spelled the doom of the mining industry. The workers
fled, the mines fell into disuse. A subsequent endeavour to
re-establish the industry received its death-blow from the discovery of gold in Klondyke. The small amount of gold in the
Tauern rifts was no longer worth the labour.

But Bad Gastein had now another kind of gold-mine established
in its amphitheatre of mountains. From the fifteenth century
on, the fame of the waters had spread. Emperors and Kings began
to arrive, and with them the fashion. The Archduke Johann
of Austria, the Emperor Wilhelm I, with his ministers Bismarck
and Moltke, the Emperor Francis Joseph and his beautiful
Empress Elizabeth, these led the growing procession. Mozart's
mother was here in 1750, taking the baths. Franz Schubert
was a visitor. In those days they stayed in the water for many
hours, playing chess on floating tables. There is the story of a
Prince-Archbishop so determined on his rejuvenation that he
stayed in the water too long and collapsed and died. These
radium-active waters must not be played with.

It is odd to reflect that here, possibly, the doom of the great
Austrian Empire was sealed. In August 1865 Bismarck met
Count Andrassy here. Between them they drew up the Austro-
German Alliance. After that Austria was dragged at the tail

Jerome Zerbe

Queen Alexandra and Prince Alexander of Jugoslavia

AEROFILMS

KNOLE
from an aeroplane

of the aggressive Prussian policy until she committed suicide, on
German prompting, in July 1914, and changed the world for
all of us.

September 10.

Lady Dunn, receiving her mail—" I used to be excited by
letters. Now I feel nothing but apprehension. The rates go
up, or the Government threatens you with ' fine, imprisonment
or both.' And the taxes ! If the Government smells you with
a thousand pounds it rushes at you like a milch cow ! "

My own mail has caught up with me. A pageboy brought it
to my room in a laundry basket. A few are business letters,
some are from friends, most of them from readers of my books.
I groan but at the same time I am gratified. I have always
written to be read, if not to be written to. The discarded enve-
lopes are treasure-trove for stamp-collecting pageboys and
servants. For years I have striven in vain to find some method
of dealing with letters. When an author has done his writing for
the day the last thing he wishes to do is to begin letter-writing.
There is also the problem of accumulated friends. Having
travelled for many years in various parts of two continents I have
a wide acquaintance with Americans, Frenchmen, Italians,
Spaniards, Swiss, Dutchmen, Swedes, Norwegians, Danes,
Germans, Brazilians and Argentinians. There is the mail from
Australia, South Africa and New Zealand also. Some of these
letters are trivial or autograph-hunting, a few are insolent, some
are from cranks. " You might lend me Pilgrim Cottage for
my honeymoon, it seems just the place. My fiancée says she
would like it. I suppose you have electric light ? " Some from
strangers are kindly, interesting or pathetic. When I feel tempted
through sheer fatigue to let them go unanswered I reflect that
some lonely person living in a colonial outpost, away from the
amenities of civilisation, has written at length craving self-
expression and sympathy. Sometimes I get strange presents.
A reader of the chapter on worms in *Gone Rustic* sent me from
Australia a giant worm twenty-eight feet long. Happily it
was dead and looked like a piece of string.

I am a man of property, alas. I own some cottages that hang
round my neck like a millstone. In a misguided moment I
bought them to preserve the English countryside. Their rents
are fixed, they are a constant drain for repairs. I am involved

G

in an endless battle with housing authorities, Government depart-
ments, the County Council, etc., who seem determined to demolish them and build monstrous breeding-boxes, and disfigure
the landscape. In Rome I received a letter telling me peremptorily that one of my cottages had been condemned (it was condemned pre-war and bought on the understanding that I should
be allowed to restore it) and that it must come down at once.
As an instalment of their threat they tore out the doors and
windows. I flew home and went into battle. I uselessly interviewed authorities, including a Ministerial bureaucrat from
London who said the cottage had no historical or architectural
value and must come down. But it had great beauty, a period-
piece that matched my Pilgrim Cottage. After four weeks of
futile pleading and argument I got nowhere, so I resorted to
blackmail. I threatened to burn down the cottage and have
the bonfire filmed on the Fifth of November, as an example
of our " Come to Beautiful Britain " movement. I saved the
cottage. It stands now where it has stood in beauty for over
three hundred years. Very odd. Every authority involved
was paralysed by some other authority ; a sort of official
polio.

Another letter in the pile is a fourfold form in Swedish relating
to income-tax on a Swedish translation of one of my novels ;
this goes to my agent to be disentangled, but other cases are more
involved. Six years ago the British Council asked permission to
subsidise a Roumanian translation for propaganda purposes.
Although the British Government dislikes authors, taxes in the
year of publication income from a book that has taken three
years to write ; taxes, as income, the outright sale of literary
property ; seizes all foreign earnings, and behaves capriciously
with authors who have the effrontery to request a few of their
own pounds to travel with, in pursuance of their work; I agreed
to this Roumanian request. It seems there is now an
infinitesimal sum of *lei*, royalties, in dispute between the
E.S.T.R. the E.V.D.N., the U.N.E.S.C.O., and the Inland
Revenue. One of these wants my name on an affidavit. It
is in vain that I try to make them a present of the *lei*, and of the
Roumanian copyright in order to close this correspondence.
My royalties are blocked in Russia, Lithuania, Brazil, Czechoslovakia, Spain, and Hungary, so it matters little if my *lei* are
blocked or lost in Roumania ; anything to end the interminable

correspondence, for if I get the *lei* the Inland Revenue Department will take most of them.

Another letter is from a print and engraving dealer in London. It illustrates the ingenuity provoked by the thirst for dollars. The writer thinks I am an American. The letter was sent care of my New York publisher.

> " I beg to report that I can offer you a fine old engraved armorial bookplate of the same surname as yours, and bearing the correct Coat of Arms, as granted the family of your surname. This old bookplate is a good impression, well preserved and is framed. I will accept twenty dollars for it if you or any member of your family would like to have it."

Coats-of-arms on dinner services, and rings with crests, are a commonplace throughout the United States. There is a standing advertisement in *The New York Times* of a firm that specialises in signet rings. It frankly states " Crests traced or created." The method is simple. They turn up the same name in a book of armorial bearings and ' lift ' the whole family line. I used to visit a most amiable lady in New Jersey who had her family pedigree drawn on the wall of her entrance hall, twelve feet long and ten deep. It embraced the Plantagenet, Stuart, Capet, Bourbon and Hapsburg families. The daughter of a wealthy hook-and-eye manufacturer, she personally embraced nobility by marrying a Balkan prince. She was a past President of The Society of American Descendants of Royal and Princely Houses.

September 11.

A perfect day in this mountain paradise. After lunch we left for Venice. Through the Tauern tunnel we came out on the southern side of the great watershed that runs from Switzerland to the Dolomites. Below us lies the Mediterranean, mother of our civilisation, and the Italian cradle of the splendid Renaissance. This was my twentieth journey to Venice, and my heart quickened once again.

Kennst Du das Land
Wo die citronen blühen ?

The train was full of returning Italian holidaymakers. The carriages were noisy with them, *chiacchieri*, an incessant joyous chatter of metallic voices. They recalled sundown in Trafalgar

Square when the starlings have their bedtime chatter on the cornices of the National Gallery.

Our train halted at a small station. We were still in the Austrian Alps and some peaks of the Dolomitic range took the purple and rose tinge of sunset on their wild serrated peaks. On the track as we halted I watched a dozen young platelayers at work, half-naked, the tawny muscles of their shoulders rippling as they laboured. Michelangelo would have observed them rewardingly. Suddenly they stopped work to look up at our carriage. One of them, a young Apollo, with a magnificent head crowned with blond curls, powerful biceps, wide shoulders, and triangular torso running to a slim waist, was caught in the lurid sunset. He seemed to have stepped from his chariot of winged horses. He was at the peak of masculine beauty, as God had conceived it long ago in Eden. At this moment, immortality touching him, he lauds Creation. The years and a hard life of labour will break our young Apollo. Transient as a sunset he will fade into darkness and the dust. For a moment his candid young eyes rested on us, read the route-plate on our carriage—*Wien-Villach-Venezia-Roma*—places he will never see, to which we are carried in ease and luxury. For him only the sweat and labour of the railtrack, the obscure village, unless a new war carries him to die in a Russian swamp or an African desert, as many before. Inscrutable the vagaries of Fate that left him standing there, half-naked, a prince of Nature, and carried me, ageing and ailing, to my Italian playground. Briefly my mind toyed with a fantastic transposition that put me on the railroad track, in only a pair of leather shorts, and seated him in the train with my baggage, my West End suits, shirts made in Rome, underwear from New York, dressing-case from Madrid, the manuscript of a new book to be worked on, and enough prestige to open the doors of the most interesting houses in Europe and America. What would he make of it all, and how would he adapt himself? And what would I make of it, and how would I react? Well, I hope I should have fun, perhaps a nice simple girl to love, and certainly a good digestion. To each his heaven and hell. I never cease to wonder at these Atlases of the world. I imagine that, in their circumstances, I should be in a mood of sullen revolt, possibly a Communist, limited in vision by my environment ; or would custom have tamed me to acquiescence in a humble lot? After all, happiness is relative. " Ho la più grande richezza—quella

che consiste nel non desiderárla," said Duse after a reversal of
fortune—" I have the greatest wealth—which consists in not
wanting it."

The train moved on. Apollo and his crew receded into the
dusk.

We crawled through the mountains and halted again. This
time we were in a flower-filled station, Arnoldstein, depôt of
the American army. Four great automobiles and two jeeps
stood by the office, their lines proclaiming American wealth. A
corporal flirted over the gate with a pretty Austrian girl. He
had not a word of German but it seemed no handicap. She
carried a parcel. Presently he lifted her bodily over the fence,
took her to the jeep and shut her in, laughing. He climbed in
and they went off up the village road in a cloud of dust. A
companion, chewing, leaned out of the office window, grinned and
made a jocular comment to others within—the Company Don
Juan in action again. How far away they were from Fayette-
ville, Des Moines, St. Louis ! And when would they go home,
to remember, dimly, blonde *Fräuleins*, *apfelstrudel*, and *alpenrosen*
on the limestone peaks ?

On the railside there was a mound of sand. Five village
urchins, barefoot, shirtless, wearing the traditional leather shorts
were joyously jumping on the mound and sliding down. Suddenly I had an illustration of the innate courtesy of this people.
One brown urchin, about seven years, decided to take a running
leap along the crest. He wanted the way clear. *Achtung, bitte !*
he piped before action. " Look out, *please !* "

With total darkness we were in the Piave plain, approaching
Udine. There was no need of the passport-control to tell us this
was Italy. At every station such a commotion, a babble of
voices on crowded platforms, a wild scrimmage for seats, a loud
chorus of *Addios*. We might have been journeying into Eternity
but most of these effusive passengers were only going a few miles
along the line. The vendors of ices and newspapers croaked
hoarsely in those unlovely voices that somehow get transformed
into the world's best tenors and baritones. Here was Italy
again, seething, overpopulated, with two million unemployed,
emigration frustrated by land-mean nations, a soaring birthrate,
contraception forbidden by the Church, a people that adored
children like angels, loved wine, music, spaghetti, that worked
prodigiously from sunrise to sundown, that slept in the afternoon

and talked all the warm night under a vine or by moon-silvered
cypresses, or failing these, sat on little straw-bottomed chairs
along baked pavements in the cool of evening.   I have known
and loved this pulsating scene for over thirty years.   " Open
my heart and you will see graved inside of it *Italy*," wrote Browning.   It is engraved on mine.

Italy

VENICE

WE arrived in Venice shortly before midnight. It could not have been better. There was a swift transition from the unlovely station to the Grand Canal, with its waiting gondolas, arched bridge, the high-domed and columned portico of S. Simeone across the Canal, and a drift of music from a restaurant gay with lanterns on the water's edge. The gondolier does not follow the winding S of the Canal. Our destination being the Europa Hotel at the other end, he cut a chord across the city's waterways. Soon we had turned in a dim and soundless side canal. The white façades of palaces towered above us, we floated through chasms of masonry under a starlit sky. Here and there a small balustraded bridge arched our trail, a little *trattoria* threw a drugget of light across pavement and canal. We glided silently along the ancient ways past a church, a bell tower, a trellised vine, a silent *campo* with its marble wellhead and a burst of green branches over a high red-brick wall, by Byzantine-Gothic windows of a palace lit on the *piano-nobile*, with its lion-guarded balcony—how familiar and how dear it all was. A turn and we entered the wide Grand Canal, its vast palaces glimmering under the starlight. Then we glided again into the narrow darkness of a side *rio*. By day Venice is a roaring metropolis of tourists, a Coney Island of the Old World. The steamers hoot, the motor launches create a bombardment that ricochets from wall to wall, and the water in turmoil lashes the palace steps. The gondoliers struck when the penny steamboats invaded the solemn Grand Canal, and Ruskin, pronouncing anathema on the enchanted city of his labours, departed in disgust. From then onwards Venice was never the same. With Fascism and *treni popolari* came the tourists *en masse*. The petrol engine brought uproar to a city that had never heard the footfall of a horse since the Crusaders had passed that way. The hotels have become one-night caravanserais, the palaces are split up into one-floor apartments. But at midnight when the traffic has ceased and the footsore tourists are abed, the old enchantment revives and Pulcinetta, masked, trips down a moonlit alley.

In half an hour we were at the *Europa* having glided through a thousand years of history in a city that scarcely belongs to this planet.

A warm welcome from the staff. I have seen the dark-eyed little pageboys grow up into Romeos and the *commis* waiter become the captain of the floor. They have given me my old room. It looks down on to the long garden fronting the Grand Canal where we dine in the evenings. Its rectangular form is derived from its original use, for once upon a time this was not a green lawn flanked by the wings of hotel bedrooms but a *squero*, a boatbuilder's yard, where Venice launched her gondolas and other water craft. Its memory is preserved in the narrow way of the street entrance to the hotel—*Calle del Squero*.

Opposite my window, across the Canal, rises the tremendous dome of the Santa Maria della Salute, with its volutes, its great flight of steps and noble façade. It was built by Longhena following a decree of the Senate on October 12, 1630, desirous of offering thanks for the liberation of the city from the terrible plague. The figure of the Madonna crowns the dome. Last night when I arrived and looked out of my window she wore an aureole of electric lights, a Madonna shining in high heaven.

In Venice there is always something new to learn. After almost thirty years' admiration of this tremendous dome—I find it as remarkable as Brunelleschi's dome in Florence and Michelangelo's in Rome—I learned that its shell was not of stone but of wood, lead-covered.

This morning on the Piazza I ran into no less than five old friends, all of whom, like myself, have been coming to Venice at this season for almost thirty years. We adjourned to a table at Florian's, throughout two centuries a renowned gossip haunt, with the shades of Casanova, Canaletto, and Guardi, who came here to find customers for one of his rapid little Venetian sketches, listening in. The talk could not have been very different in their time ; what we did last night, the best restaurant to eat at, what is on at the theatre, how dear Venice has become, etc. One whole hour was lost and enjoyed at Florian's, and then, on my way to lunch with another friend, as I crossed the Piazzetta, I ran into the burly figure of Giovanni Martinelli, rubicund, curly-headed and, as always, cheerful. He has been the idol of the Metropolitan Opera House in New York for over twenty years. I last heard him sing at an afternoon concert at the University Club, along with his old colleague at the ' Met ', Giuseppe de Luca. Whenever I see him I recall not the parts I have heard him in, memorable though they are, but that once, long ago, when a handsome young tenor, a ' find ', thrilling New Yorkers, he was the soloist in the Mass for Eleonora Duse, one May day in 1924, when she lay in state in a church on Lexington Avenue, prior to the last voyage home to Italy.

I took tea with my friend Countess Piercy de Mignano in her slice of a house tucked away in the little Campo San Gregorio, almost in the shadow of S. Maria della Salute. As usual an amusing gathering and some old friends. I am delighted to find that Harold Parsons, the art connoisseur who has done so much for the Kansas City Art Gallery, is back in the Palazzo Moro-Lin whose windows command a bend of the Grand Canal. At his windows I watched the Regatta last year. It has beautiful frescoes, and from the back staircase a superb view of the Campanile.

Others present at the Countess's were Count Robilant, who lives in the Palazzo Mocenigo, Byron's old palace in Venice ; Princess Spiridon, a Greek lady who has bought the Abbazia San Gregorio from Prince Nicholas of Roumania ; and an engaging Harvard lad of literary ambitions, who visited me in England this summer. I liked his romantic touch ; he was preceded at the Countess's by his poem and a bouquet of flowers —quite in the spirit of Boccaccio. The house was formerly that of an archbishop and over the door his arms carry the Cross and Mitre. In a tiny yard abutting on to the ruined church of San Gregorio my hostess has skilfully camouflaged the stone flags with an artificial grass carpet which requires neither cutting nor weeding. It made me envious when I recalled the back-aching hours I have spent with a lawn-mower, digging out plantains, watering and scattering lawn sand. It was in this house that I heard a Russian virtuoso play on the Louis XV tympanum, an incredible evening I described in *Half Way*.

My hostess was very gay as usual. She reigns here for three months and spends the winter in Berne.

My American friend had never seen the Fenice Theatre in which was being held the Festival of International Contemporary

G*

Music. It is to my mind among the most beautiful theatres in the world with its five gold tiers of boxes, its wonderful ceiling, and the rows of candelabra that light it. The theatre has long and wonderful memories, from Goldoni onwards down to Duse, etc. It carried on during the Austrian occupation of Venice and when in it I always recall the memorable evening of December 2nd, 1856, when the Emperor and Empress, Franz Joseph and his beautiful young wife Elizabeth, occupied the royal box at a gala performance. On either side of the prompter's box stood two Croatian troopers, conscripts of the Austrian army. As the curtain rose one of them blew his nose between his fingers and thumb. The Emperor asked what they were doing there. " Your Majesty, sometimes the audience will not rise when our National Anthem is played." " And that's when you shoot ? " asked the Empress. " Yes, your Majesty," came the reply. That evening the Empress protested to her husband with the result that there was a complete change of policy. The repressive orders were repealed, an amnesty was declared, the gaols were opened, the political prisoners were released and the confiscations were restored. Most wonderful of all, the terrible old Marshal Radetzky was dismissed. A new era opened on December 3rd, 1856, in Venice.

Last night's programme had prepared us for something bizarre ; the works of Milhaud, Maderna and Schoenberg were to be performed. The opening work was a suite for two pianos and orchestra. It began with " Una Entrata dove i due pianoforti dialogano con l'orchestra." In that dialogue the orchestra never had a chance. Two agile young men sat at the keyboards and began to pound them ferociously. When one paused for breath the other increased the noise. I expected the wires to snap. The orchestra gave up and waited. The piece ended with " un ritmo di Giga o di tarantella." It seemed to the audience both, with boogie-woogie thrown in. By this time a spirit of revolt began to rise from the auditorium. The next composition was a setting of some lines by Kafka, for a soprano, two reciters and the orchestra. A man and a woman came before two microphones. They began to shout at each other, and another man went mad on a drum while a trombone blasted its way into the pandemonium. The audience shouted at the performers, the performers shouted back. It was difficult to know whether this was approval or disapproval. A lovely theatre had been converted into a madhouse. I looked at my companion, she looked at me. " I don't think I shall wait for the Schoenberg," she said. We got up and left. The night was beautiful outside and I thought of Duse who used to come out and walk in the little *campo* to get some air between the acts.

September 14.

The British Consul, Mr. Ronalds and his wife had a pleasant lunch party to-day. They occupy the first floor of the Palazzo Morosini overlooking the finest part of the Grand Canal. The guests were Princess Aspasia of Greece, the widow of the late King Constantine, Princess Cavalto and a friend, Count Carlo Robilant and his wife. I know another part of this famous palazzo, occupied by the beautiful octogenarian Countess Morosini, who has for so long been the *grande dame* of Venice, and was once its toast. This family has been famous down the centuries for its magnificent entertainments. Here in the sixteenth century lived Francesco Morosini, styled " Il Peloponnesiaco " on account of his victory over the Turks in Peloponnessus, when he captured 37 forts, 1,360 cannon and destroyed 200,000 Turks. In the courtyard of the palace, now a national monument, hang lamps from the Turkish galleons, and in the lower hall are the sword and armour of the warrior whose family gave a Doge to Venice.

There was much lively and amusing conversation. The singular Don Carlos Besteiguy was discussed. He has bought the Palazzo Labia and spent a fortune restoring it. He is a Mexican millionaire who has taken Spanish nationality, the owner of several palaces in Europe. He hopes to revive some of the gaiety and hospitality of Venice. He has collected Venetian furniture scattered all over the world, including a very large and rare carpet woven in Venice. He opened his palace with a large party this spring and next year plans an entertainment that will revive the memories of the *settecento* in its most prodigal splendour.* Meanwhile the Venetians are reaping a harvest. The palace was built for Zanfrancesco Labia in the seventeenth century. It is said that after one great feast there the owner threw the gold plate into the Canal, shouting, " Le abbia, o non le abbia,

---

* On Sept. 3, 1951, there was a costume ball of fifteen hundred guests, of a lavishness not seen in Venice since the days of Casanova. It was in excellent taste though severely criticised by the Press for its extravagance, but more because they were not allowed in. The arrival of the guests by gondola was as much a sight as the ball, It created considerable employment for the Venetians.

saro sempre Labia ! "—" Whether I have them or whether I have them not, I shall still be Labia." But Venetian gossip, which is always witty and subacid, whispered that he took the precaution of drawing a net across the canal to save the plate. This seems to have been a habit of the Italian magnates. The great banker Chigi, Raphael's patron, threw his plate into the Tiber after a banquet. Labia was a war profiteer who got himself ennobled in 1646. The species has not altered with time.

I happened to say that I had never seen the Byron apartments in the Palazzo Mocenigo. Count Robilant who lives there, sharing the palace with his brother, Andrea, at once offered to show me them after lunch. So off we went, later, to the Palazzo Mocenigo on the Grand Canal. Count Carlo occupies the top floor, where I had been his guest last year, his brother the *piano nobile*, which includes the suite once occupied by Byron. It has now been divided. Byron had six rooms along the front, in one of which he read to Shelley the first canto of *Don Juan*. In the centre was the balcony on which he, Shelley and Moore were seen. Count Andrea is in the film business in Rio de Janeiro but when he occupies these rooms he still uses Byron's sliding-top desk. At the back of the palace there is a long courtyard with trees, including a noble old bay-tree beneath which Byron dined on summer nights. The courtyard is flanked by a low wing in which the poet kept his private zoo, which once occasioned Shelley so much surprise. Doge Mocenigo was the admiral of the Venetian fleet under Don John of Austria at the great battle of Lepanto. His Doge's cap is kept on a stand in the salon, where there is also a painting by Tintoretto showing the Pope, the King of Spain and Doge Mocenigo being presented to the enthroned Almighty, after the battle of Lepanto. They look as if they were being congratulated on their victory over the Muslim Turks.

The Robilant family has its own claim to distinction, Mocenigo and Byron apart. They carry in their veins, through the Mecklenburg female branch, the Stuart blood and have the right to wear the Royal Stuart tartan.

After this enjoyable visit I walked to the Piazza and took tea. Following my custom through many years, I waited for the gold of sunset to fade over the shining mosaics and oriental cupolas of St. Mark's, and then at the vesper hour, heard the tolling of the great bell in the Campanile, which solemnly marks the passing of the day. It is tolled at three regular times, at noon, when the firing of the cannon flutters all the Piazza pigeons, at vespers, and at midnight, this last tolling the most solemn of all. Its great strokes are the quintessence of the magic of Venice. They mark the passing of life along a way of great beauty, the lore of centuries pulsating in the great waves of sound that go out over city and lagoon.

I am angry with the Venetians. The outrages they commit on this city ! Despite a local committee that is supposed to guard its beauty, there is a fresh horror every year. In the Fascist era they hung over the glorious façade of the Doge's Palace a revolting banner portraying the Duce's prognathous jaw. Part of the Lido has been transformed into a braying fairground. Coney Island accessories are slowly creeping up that golden strand where Byron and Shelley once rode their horses. Fascism brought in the *treni popolari*, with their crowds pasturing in the Piazza. An eczema of tawdry booths full of tourist junk broke out under the arches of the Palace facing the lagoon. Now the film industry has seized upon Venice for an annual Film Festival, discharging upon this venerable city all the vulgarity that permeates its activities.

This month the base of the noble Campanile has been desecrated by tubular scaffolding bearing a lurid advertisement of a sex film, the whole lit by neon lighting at night. I fear that one day they will utilise the nostrils of the bronze horses on St. Mark's to pour forth some vintage, *chianti* or *asti spumanti* with an advertising device. The yellow blaze of Coca-Cola is already everywhere. The wide lagoon that separates Venice from the mainland, the ancient waterway over which the learned young Doctor from Padua came to arraign Shylock, has a glowing nightsign proclaiming SHELL. A railway station and a towering garage having breached the citadel, the ruin progresses. Last year I watched with misgiving some building that went on behind a straw screen on the Riva. The beautiful Daniele Hotel was adding a wing. It is now disclosed. It is an appalling stone cube in the punched-out pattern of much modern architecture. The ground floor has windows that look like machine-gun slits in a concrete blockhouse. This abomination unites the Byzantine-Gothic façade of the fourteenth-century hotel with the sixteenth-century palace prisons. It is as appropriate as a glass eye in the face of a beautiful woman.

Near my hotel another horror greeted me. The ultra-Baroque façade of San Moisé, which aroused Ruskin's ire but is a superb example of Baroque gone to seed, has been put in the shade by the new entrance of the Hotel Bauer-Grunwald. It is difficult to describe this abomination of white marble, chromium balconies, glass panels and tapered columns. The old entrance, inoffensive and dwarfed, which once conducted you through the corridor of an old palace, now leads to a decorator's paradise of gleaming marble walls and scintillating chandeliers expressing a Home-from-Fifth-Avenue appeal.

Things Observed.

Down a little *calle* near my hotel there is a small courtyard. On the wall there is a plaque. It commemorates the fact that there, on the site of the San Moisé Theatre, on the night of November 3, 1810, an eighteen-year-old youth, Giacomo Rossini, made his debut with *The Marriage Broker*, and as the inscription delightfully expresses it, *prenda sua opera mosse felicemente il volo verso gloriosa immortalità*—by this work began a happy flight towards glorious immortality. So very few music-lovers seem aware of this place and its inscription. Goethe saw a performance here on the night of October 3rd, 1786, and it was then a well-established theatre. Now it is a dull suite of offices in a dead little *corte.*

September 15.

Wandering round the arcades of the Doges' Palace, I spent a morning reading the denunciatory plaques fastened on its walls by the Council of Ten, holding up Venetian delinquents to everlasting shame. There they are, and no one cares to-day who they were or what crimes they committed. And they have their immortality—of a kind. Yesterday I continued my investigation of the last days of Robert Browning in Venice. He lived in the splendid Palazzo Rezzonico which had been purchased by his son in 1889. The poet died there on December 12th, and his coffin lay in state in the great ballroom decorated with *trompe l'oeuil* by Tiepolo. It had a simple laurel wreath on top with a metal wreath of porcelain flowers and silk ribbons in front. Browning had expressed a wish to be buried with his wife in the English cemetery at Florence but the offer of a Westminster Abbey burial was accepted by the family. Venice,

however, was not cheated of a funeral procession in the poet's
honour. On Sunday afternoon, December 15th, at four o'clock,
the coffin was carried by eight *pompieri* (firemen) and placed in
a State barge provided by the Municipality. It was then taken
out to the island cemetery of San Michele, in the middle of the
Laguna Morta, a provisional resting-place. The Mayor was
among the mourners and the State barge was drawn by a steam
pinnace from the Italian Royal Navy. On the barge by the
coffin stood four municipal ushers, two sergeants of the Royal
Navy, and two *pompieri*, who, in the dusk of the falling December
day, carried lighted torches. All the windows of the palaces
along the Grand Canal were draped and lit with votive candles.
Such was Venice's noble tribute. Three days later the coffin
left Venice by train for London and the Abbey funeral. That
autumn Browning had stayed with his old friend Mrs. Bronson
at her villa at Asolo, of which he became very fond. His last
book, published on the day of his death was called *Asolando*.
It was written under the walls of the castle. He wanted to buy
a piece of land, and use the shell of a house adjacent to the
Castle, where, once upon a time, the famous Caterina Cornaro,
Queen of Cyprus, painted by Titian, had held a small court on
her retirement. On the day before Browning's death the
Municipality, to whom the property belonged, voted in favour
of his possessing it.

With much patience and cross-questioning of the officials
at the Palazzo Rezzonico, now a museum of the *Settecento* Venice,
I weeded legends from facts, and obtained the story of Browning's
last days there. The family lived on the *piano nobile*. When
the poet fell ill he was moved to the mezzanine floor so that he
could pass into the dining-room more easily, also its lower ceiling
gave him an impression of greater warmth. On his return from
the autumn months at Asolo his doctor was at a dinner party
where Browning was present. The poet had been walking on
the Lido and had caught a cold and from the bronchial condition of which the poet complained, the doctor feared his days
were numbered. When he could not rise he was carried into
the spacious bedroom belonging to his son's wife, with an open
fireplace and large windows that admitted all the sunshine.
There, two hours before midnight, on Thursday, December 12th,
he breathed his last.

One day in her palace in Florence the Contessa Rucellai, a

very old lady, the daughter of Mrs. Bronson, showed me two treasured albums of letters from the poet to her mother.   There was a letter from Browning's son, written from the Palazzo Rezzonico, Venice, at 10.30 p.m., which ran :—

> " Dearest Friend,
>   " Our beloved breathed his last as St. Mark's struck ten, with no pain, unconsciously.   I was able to make him happy a little before he became unconscious by a telegram from Smith Elder (his publisher), saying ' Reviews in all this day's papers most favourable.   Edition nearly exhausted.'   He just murmured, ' How gratifying.'   Those were the last intelligible words."

September 16

Yesterday I solved the mystery of how I was the cause of the marriage of ex-King Peter of Yugoslavia.   It has been puzzling me ever since he informed me in Madrid this spring that my novel *Victoria Four-Thirty* had resulted in his finding a wife. Last night I was the dinner-guest of Princess Aspasia of Greece, widow of King Alexander, at the "Garden of Eden," as it is called. This lagoon-bordered villa takes its name not from its heavenly setting and aspect but from the fact that once it was the garden retreat of a Mr. and Mrs. Eden.   I have known it for many years. Little Lucien Reid, of whom I became guardian, went there with his sister while living in Venice, to play with the Princess's little daughter, Alexandra, and the children of Lord Melchett, who sometimes passed the summer there as the Princess's house-guests. The garden has ghosts for me.   Lucien and Lord Melchett's boy, Derek Mond, were killed in the last war, both just turned twenty. They swam and rowed over the lagoon that lies around the great garden.   They could have had no lovelier place in which to spend their boyhood.   The blood-red sunset burnishes the lagoon at even and burns crimson along the low brick wall that encloses the garden where the cypresses stand black against the starlit sky, and where, in late autumn days, the grapes hang in heavy clusters along the pergolas.   Over the high wall, on one side, there is a wonderful view of the dome and the towers of the Redentore Church, conspicuous on the Giudecca, where this garden is situated.

I come back to the Garden of Eden every year.   The melancholy it induces is relieved by the hospitality of its beautiful châtelaine.   Last evening when I arrived I was the first of the

guests and a beautiful young woman came forward to greet me.
I seemed familiar to her and I found myself wondering where
we had met before.   A little later, when she mentioned that her
mother would be down soon—we sat in the dusk of the loggia—I
realised that this lovely young woman was the little Alexandra
who had played in the garden in those vanished years.   Fifteen
years make a great difference to a child of fourteen and that was
the number of years since I had last seen her.   We began to
talk of the past and then she said, " You know, I have wished
for a long time to see you.   How strange it is that you should be
the cause of my marrying Peter ! "

" Peter ? " I asked.   " Then you are married ?   To whom ? "

" I married Peter of Yugoslavia."

" Good Heavens ! " I cried in amazement, " Then you, or
all people, can answer a question that has been troubling me for
six months ! "

I told her then of my meeting with ex-King Peter in Madrid
and how he had told me that my novel, in which I had depicted
him as a small boy, Prince Sixpenny, had been the cause of his
meeting his wife.

" That's quite true," answered Alexandra.   " Mother had a
copy of your *Victoria Four-Thirty*.   I read it one day and fell in
love with Prince Sixpenny, the little boy who found himself a
king.   I wasn't happy until I had met him, and we fell in love
and I married him."

I was silent for a while rather overwhelmed by this chain of
circumstances.   I listened to the falling of the water in the fountain.   It had become quite dark.   The gondolier-waiter at the
water-gate was ushering in some other guests.   We rose.   As we
turned towards them I said to Alexandra, " There are fairy
stories we never write.   They are woven by life, and much more
wonderful.   This story has a footnote.   Last January I lived in an
apartment house in Monte Carlo.   I used to encounter on the staircase an enchanting little boy of about five who went up and down
with his English ' nannie.'   After some time I learned who he
was.   His name was Alexander and he was the son of King Peter
—and you.   Three links, in Monte Carlo, Madrid, and now
Venice.   I feel one thing is missing.   I should have been his
godfather."

" A novel godfather," she cried, with laughter, " for without
Victoria Four-Thirty he might never have existed."

We joined the guests. I felt that Venice had lived up to her fabled history.*

MONTECATINI

September 18.

Bagni di Montecatini. I arrived here two days ago in such a state of collapse that I had to go to bed. The old enemy has attacked again, I was too venturesome in Venice. The leading *Professore Doctore* was called in. I found him rather overwhelming at first sight, so handsome, so elegant, so great a gentleman that I feared for his medical qualifications. The Grand Hotel La Pace where I am now abed seems like a nest of rich hypochondriacs. Dr. Pisani is the leading physician at this celebrated spa. He made a most thorough examination, ordered me to get up only one hour a day, if I wish, and to take a course of fango (hot mud) baths. He gave me a new name for the old enemy. I have a ' psychiatric ulcer.' I could not resist asking him if he proposed to psychoanalyse it. " I shall try all sorts of things for it," he said, with a most disarming smile. He wrote out my diet. He drew a frightening design of my ulcer, and of my poor body where the hot mud is to be applied. It seems I am to be buried in it up to the neck. The mud is for the fibrositis.

I got out of bed to-day and betook myself to the elegant bathing establishment. I was stripped and put on a bench covered with a white cloth. A brawny man scooped out of a bucket handfulls of hot brown mud and plastered me with it. Fifty years ago I should have delighted in this, and thrown it back at him in a glorious game of mud pies. He then wrapped me up in a large sheet (what a waste of clean white linen !) and two blankets, looked at a clock and left me for thirty minutes. I felt like one of the victims in Dante's *Inferno*. After the time had expired, the man removed the blankets, scraped off the mud, put me in a hot bath and washed me down. Then back to the couch with more white sheets for half an hour of repose, whereupon I dressed and returned to La Pace.

---

* If *Victoria Four-Thirty* put them on the path to the altar, Winston Churchill certainly gave them a push. When Anthony Eden expressed his concern about the consequences that might follow the marriage of exiled King Peter in 1943, Churchill wrote, " Are we not fighting this war for liberty and democracy ? My advice to the King, if you wish me to see him, will be to go to the nearest Registry Office and take a chance. So what ? "

September 20.

I have been obliged to give up the baths. They fatigue me too much. I have slept for sixteen hours a day for the last three days and I am still utterly tired. I like Professor Pisani, my doctor, more and more. But how long shall I be a prisoner in this bed ? No letters, no newspapers, no writing, no conversation. I sleep and sleep and sleep. This afternoon I was up for an hour and went down into the hotel garden to look at a fountain which gives me the greatest pleasure. Above a shallow basin stands the bronze statue of a naked cherub. From the rim of the basin a squatting frog squirts a jet of water into the face of the chubby little fellow. He holds up two hands to shield his eyes from the water which falls down his gleaming fat little belly and thighs. He stands with one dimpled foot impulsively raised. The pose is almost identical with that of Verrocchio's famous fountain in the courtyard of the Palazzo Vecchio in Florence. Verrocchio's cherub grasps a dolphin that spouts water. This frog of the garden statue is perhaps more natural and the craftsmanship of the modern sculptor proclaims him to be the equal in genius of his *cinquecento* countryman.

September 21.

Out of bed again after lunch and walked for a short time in the garden. The rich September sunshine set ablaze the beds of the scarlet salvia and the tall cannas. Amid the palms and cypresses the pink oleanders and blue plumbago were in flower. I found a little pinewood with a space enclosed for children, deserted. There was a swing. I had not been on one for fifty years. For a quarter of an hour I happily swung myself. Then three hotel guests came round the corner, stared, and walked on. I expect one of them said, " Did you see that old buffer swinging himself ? Must be simple-minded ! "

Sometimes I am, and they are among the happiest hours of my life.

September 22.

I am becoming daring. Unknown to Professor Pisani I went out last night to a performance of *Rigoletto*. Camillo Tagliabue in the role of the Jester, a splendid voice and a superb actor. To-day we booked seats for an orchestral concert in celebration of the fiftieth anniversary of Verdi's death, and the twenty-fifth of

Puccini's. The latter had a house near here, it seems. My companion recognising the *basso profundo*, Carlo Righini, by his deep speaking-voice, congratulated him on his performance. He spoke fluent English. It seems that his mother was American, Ella Russell, a famous opera star of the era of Albani, de Reszke, etc. When my name was mentioned he stared hard for a moment and then impulsively shook my hand and said, " I never believed I should have this pleasure ! " He named half a dozen books of mine. We had a most pleasant gossip on the theatre steps. He is coming to lunch to-morrow. He told us that his tenor colleague in *Madame Butterfly* is an Australian settled in Italy.

This evening on entering the hotel lounge I met Elizabeth Arden's sister, the Vicomtesse de Maublanc, who had just arrived. She runs the Paris branch of the Arden business. No one looking at this slight frail woman, quiet in voice and manner, would ever guess the iron courage she showed during the German occupation of France. She aided the escape of our English airmen and for this she was interned by the Germans, first in the Fresnes prison, near Paris, for two months, and then in the notorious Ravensbrück camp for nine months, escaping its gas chambers. She never speaks of it.

September 23.

To-day as I went slowly down the stairs a young man in a light ' seersucker ' jacket went bounding by. It is refreshing to see youth in this palace of the aged. I surmised he was an American college boy. At the foot of the stairs he smiled at me. It was the young man I had mistaken for the butler at Beaulieu, Prince Michael de Bourbon. He has just arrived with the Plesches. It is odd but for some weeks past his face has kept recurring to me. To-day I know why and a mystery is solved. We began to talk and something in his voice gave me a clue. In 1941 I motored with Alexander Woollcott to lunch with the Russell Doubledays at their house on Long Island, in order to see Somerset Maugham who had just arrived in the United States from England, following his escape in a collier from his villa at Cap Ferrat. The Doubledays had other refugees, house guests, the Grand Duchess of Luxembourg and daughter, and her brother Prince René de Bourbon-Parme and his small son and daughter, Michael and Ann. In the next few years I frequently met Prince René and his wife, Princess Margaret of Denmark.

Like so many refugees from Europe, without finances, they put up a brave fight. He worked for a scent business and she worked in a fashion shop. I now discovered that their son Michael, the small shy boy of thirteen I talked to at the Doubledays, is my ' butler ' friend of twenty-four, the paratrooper ! His small sister Ann is now the wife of ex-King Michael of Rumania.

September 25.

There are a large number of dogs in this hotel but few children. The Italians have become great dog-lovers. Contrary to belief I find them kind to animals though it may not have been so always. I recall the retort of an old Italian dowager to an English lady who deplored the cruelty of Italians to animals, " If we are cruel to them at least we have no need of a Society for the Prevention of Cruelty to Children ! "

I lament the absence of children in this hotel. I like to hear their squeakings as they rush up and down corridors and round the flower-beds. I miss their elegance and fresh beauty when they are dressed and polished up by their nannies. The hotel lacks their happy noise. I am sure these sad dogs, trailed about by tired old ladies, miss them for romping company.

A perfect day. The sky cloudless, the sunshine lighting the Tuscan hills, the air still. This little town is a flower-bed. The avenues are shady with plane trees, the pavements and the drinking-fountains are all bordered with flowers. It is what a friend of mine calls " a manicured landscape." At this sort of thing the Italians are unsurpassed. I counted twenty-eight varieties of flowers I could name, and some I could not. Outside the great colonnade of the Tetuccio Spring, where the orchestra plays to the promenading crowd, glasses in hand, there was a banked flower-bed in the form of a calendar *Settembre 25 Lunedi* composed of seven shades of dwarf cacti. In walks ablaze with vivid cannas, scarlet salvia, tuberoses, grandifloria, white and red begonias, pink and white oleanders, banana-trees and the blooms of sub-tropical flowers set against topiary screens of box and bay, I marvelled at the giant dahlias, nine inches wide. High over all rose the little pink and orange town of Montecatini Alto, crowning the hill, clad with olive trees.

What crowds ! It is the same everywhere these years. The earth is becoming overpopulated. Medical science, aided by penicillin and other discoveries, has pushed back the frontier of death and added twenty years to the human span. Wars, with their impersonal mechanistic contrivances no longer decimate armies. The last war had a sixty per cent lower fatality list than the previous one, despite the bombing of civilians. Plagues and famines no longer carry off millions. The rising birthrate in India and its improved hygiene present a grave food problem. A great slaughterer of the human race to-day is street traffic. Perhaps Man, with his increasing knowledge, is providing the only solution of the problem he has created, the Atom Bomb, that will wipe out the spawning millions. But these thoughts did not overcloud the pleasure of this golden day. Freedom from pain and a feeling of health crowned the sunny hours.

Last night I heard *Madame Butterfly*, an excellent performance. Our guest at lunch, Carlo Righini, as Lo Zio Bonzo. The young Australian tenor was Pinkerton, but I found the singer cast for the role of Sharples, the American Consul, distracting because of his likeness to the late President Roosevelt. He seemed to be advocating the New Deal rather than warning his friend of an old one. But there was a sad ghost hovering over this performance. Two years ago in Rome we were entertained by Mrs. Panni, the daughter of De Luca, the famous baritone of the Metropolitan Opera House, New York. It was at the time when De Luca was being fêted on the fiftieth anniversary of his début as a singer, and his daughter in Rome had heard over the radio from U.S.A. her father's recital celebrating that occasion. In New York a few weeks later I had heard him in excellent voice singing with his colleague, Martinelli, at an afternoon concert at the University Club. It was in the role of Sharples that De Luca had sung at the première of Puccini's *Madame Butterfly* at La Scala on February 17th, 1904. He used to tell the story of how on the first night the Scala audience hissed and booed and almost stopped the performance. Toscanini, who had heard Puccini play the score over to him, was of the opinion that it would be a failure. It was too long and too unwieldy, he thought, the very foreign setting apart. He did not conduct it, having at that time a feud with the Scala directorate. After the failure Puccini cut and revised the opera. Three months later it was against produced at Brescia, and was a triumphant success.

The first act of our opera finished at eleven o'clock, the second at midnight. As usual small boys peregrinated the aisles selling

ices and candies. I marvelled at these children who should have
been in bed long ago. As always, they were spotlessly attired
in white shirts, white jackets and with their brief shorts well
pressed, their hair well combed, their socks and shoes tidy. Many
of them live in holes and corners with little more than a cold water
tap and scanty hygiene, yet they emerge with such elegance and
gaiety that one would imagine they possessed a strict governess
and came from well-to-do homes. I asked the bright-eyed little
chap who sold me an ice how old he was. Ten. Did he go to
school? Yes. At what hour? At eight-thirty every morning.
When did he sleep? I got a shy gleaming smile but no answer,
and he carried off his tray to another customer. He certainly
did not look tired this Sunday midnight. He was well nourished,
with bright eyes. I observed that on his shirt he had the initials
D.A. embroidered. I speculated on the possibility that they
stood for Dante Alighieri. In England the law would be very
positive about this boy. There would be a solemn outcry against
child slave labour. Yet here in Italy live the happiest, healthiest
and most adored children ever seen. This little chap was
obviously enjoying himself and making a few *lire*. All over
Italy one sees legions of merry bare-legged little boys scurrying
about on bicycles, carrying parcels, sweeping up, serving in
cafés, delivering huge bouquets of flowers, meat, bread, vegetables
and even furniture. Is it injurious to their health? Is it—but
the rising curtain cut short my speculation on the life of young
Italy.

September 26.

A letter from Günther B, my young Salzburg friend, who
hitch-hiked to Paris.

"Do you believe it, I did Salzburg-Paris, 115 km. in 17 hours?
Now I think I am king of the hiking tribe! . . . This Paris
is somewhat of a madhouse but anyhow if you are in it once it
is hard not to lose your head and heart. I have a nice little room
near Notre Dame, vis-à-vis St. Sévérin, with a little Gothic
church garden made of stone. There are flowers, beasts, dwarfs,
dragons, saints and devils, and all right in front of my window.
Below there is a courtyard with a Gothic cloister, where the
priests walk round and round and read their Breviary when it
rains, and in the middle there is an old tree. I also see the towers
of Notre Dame and all the roofs and chimneys of the Quartier

Latin. At night you have an imaginary red sky all over these strange buildings that makes the place like a fairy-tale city. Also the people here are strange. You know I don't mean the people out on the Boulevards, just the simple people in the Quartier Latin. Mostly poor, dreadfully poor but somehow satisfied with their lives. I saw a beggar weeping in the arms of his poor wife. It was a sad picture but the background was Notre Dame and that made everything beautiful. *Alors, c'est la vie, quelquefois la vie en rose, et quelquefois la vie en noir.* Do you know the book-sellers along the Seine with their green boxes ? I have already found twice your *Pilgrim Cottage* there. I am strolling along these places for hours and I am really happy to have these holydays." Ah to be young, and in Paris for the first time !

An amusing letter in my mail this morning. I saw in the Personal Column of *The Times* an advertisement of a small furnished apartment in Rome for the winter of 1950. I wrote enquiring if it would be available in the winter of 1951. My enquiry seems to have surprised the advertiser, a lady with a French-sounding name, Miss Carmen A.

" It is really thrilling to know that there is someone in the world who plans one year ahead, who is so optimistic as to think what he shall need for the winter 1951-2. Next year, isn't it far, far away ? To-day the flat in Rome is mine and is to let—next year will it still be there ? And will it still belong to me ? And will Rome be still in the free world ? And will you still have your mind unchanged ? *P.S.* I had to show your letter to the lady for whom I work, Mrs. E, because I could not read your surname. She told me you are a famous writer (are you ?) and one of her favourites, and she admires you very much and I think she would be delighted to meet you, and if you behave you will perhaps get also tea with Jersey cream. The lady is eighty and a wonderful speci-ment of the Victorian type, worth while to meet."

The bribe of Jersey cream is apropos of *Gone Rustic*, in which I stated that in my cottage I enjoyed Devonshire cream made by two Cornish sisters down my lane from Jersey cows on the Oxfordshire hills. Cream apart, I should like to meet an admirer of eighty who " is a wonderful speciment of the Victorian type." Miss Carmen A sounds delightful, too. Alas, life is too short! By the same mail I received a letter from my agent informing

me that my novel *Eight for Eternity* has been chosen as the Book
of the Month by the Argentine Book Club and by the Brazil
Book Club and will be translated into Spanish and Portuguese
respectively.   They enquire whether I could make visits to these
countries where I should have a warm welcome.   So there is
point in Miss A's enquiry query.   " Will you still have your
mind unchanged ? "   I would like to make these visits in the
near future but this winter I hope to be in the United States,
next spring in Spain, next summer in England, next autumn in
Austria and Italy, and the following winter in South Africa, if
not in Rome.   Increasing frequency in the loss of friends reminds
me of mortality and our all too brief existence in this wide world
of entrancing vistas.   Next year ?   A touch on the shoulder by
the Remorseless Angel and

> How will the change strike me and you
> In the house not made with hands ?

September 27.

A departing guest, a soignée French lady, left me a gift of a
novel.   " It is so good, so absorbing ! "   It is by a famous
Italian writer and in the first year of its translation it went through
three impressions.   It has 390 pages, and of these 300 are a
tedious repetition, narrated in the first person, of successive
sexual experiences, all described with great gusto.   On the first
page one meets a mother whose total ambition is to make her
daughter a successful whore ; on the last, the prostitute, still a
very young woman, pregnant, exclaims with the greatest satisfaction, " I thought how he would be a child of a murderer and
a prostitute ; but any man in the world might happen to kill
someone and any woman might sell herself for money." A
reviewer in our leading literary weekly found this story one of
the most significant novels of the age, written by one of the
greatest novelists of the century.

There is no accounting for the literary pundits.   I remember
years ago in my club hearing two venerable reviewers who wrote
for *The Times Literary Supplement* and *The New Statesman*, quoting
with admiration passages of obscenity from James Joyce's *Ulysses*,
then convulsing the literary world.   The book became subsequently, in a pirated edition, the British tourist's favourite
specimen of pornography smuggled in from Paris, until D. H.

Lawrence, annoyed at his rival's success in the 'thighroid' field of literature captured the trade with *Lady Chatterley's Lover*. This summer I found myself at a reading of James Joyce's *Finnigans Wake*. The recital was by readers who had studied the text and did it full justice. What I had always regarded as gibberish was now demonstrated for gibberish. No gift of declamation or exposition made sense of it. Now I learn from a book on Joyce that his devoted brother for years implored him not to waste his genius on such rubbish. Dr. Gogarty, who knew Joyce, called *Ulysses* "the greatest leg-pull in history." There is always a coterie for anything on the fringe of lunacy. For many years an artful old lady, Gertrude Stein, sat enthroned before her ecstatic worshippers while she produced deliberately illiterate and unintelligible oracles. Her first excursion in literature was a short novel, written normally. It was a psychological study of three young Lesbians on a holiday. The theme apart, it showed plainly the author's inadequate equipment as a literary artist.

The Kafka cult displaced Joyce and Stein for a time. Nevertheless these freaks are a proof of liberty of expression and should be allowed their eccentricities. They could not flourish in Russia where the State controls the writers.*

Is it the creeping years or a sojourn in this oasis where the hysteria of newspapers, the pernicious telephone and the braying of radios do not penetrate? This evening I packed and went round saying good-bye to my friends. "I leave to-morrow," I said. "But you said you were leaving on Friday!" "Yes," to-morrow," I repeated. "But to-day is Wednesday!"

September 29.

To-day we leave this cure place, where I have not taken the cure for I have been in bed eight days of the fourteen and have never risen before lunch. But I have done some work. I find bed is the best ally of a writer, for on my feet I always contrive to find something else that can be done, and thus I postpone the task of writing for which I have a singular dislike until I am immersed in it. Like a schoolboy having his first diving lesson, I shrink and shiver before the dreaded first plunge. I have done

---

* A specimen of Stein prose—" The care with which the rain is wrong and the green is wrong and the white is wrong, the care with which there is a chair and plenty of breathing. The care with which there is incredible justice and likeness, all this makes a magnificent asparagus, and also a fountain." A disciple has 'interpreted' this.

this for over thirty years though I know well the act, performed, gives pleasure.

Paying bills before departure, I sought out my doctor. He is a professor of medicine in Florence, as well as the ' cure ' physician. He is the *beau idéal* of a fashionable doctor, tall, handsome with a splendid head of greying hair, immaculate in his dress and has a most gracious manner. I could find no more creditable member of the noblest of professions. The word ' fashionable ' does him less than justice for he has the highest reputation. Many years ago I wrote the life of King Edward's surgeon. I had access to his private diaries but, alas, much therein could not be used. I asked Professor Pisani if he kept a diary. No, how could he ? " Reticence is our first recommendation." In his consulting-room to-day I found an autographed portrait of the Duke and Duchess of Windsor. They were in Montecatini last year. We discussed them. " *Molto simpatico e intelligente,*" he said of the Duke. Parting I asked for my bill. The Professor warmly grasped my hand. " Maestro, per i artisti niente ! " he said. Overwhelmed, I wondered in what other country this gesture would have been made. Possibly in France where *homme de lettres* is a title of honour. I shall try to discover a means by which I can express my appreciation.

I have been puzzled by the enigma of modern Italy as revealed here. Before the war Montecatini had a fashionable clientele. They arrived with maids and chauffeurs, they were smartly attired all day. In the evening had a man appeared without a dinner jacket he would not have been allowed in the dining-room. In these two weeks I have not seen a single dinner jacket. There are a few of the old nobility who somehow have survived two holocausts. The majority of the clients appear to consist of new-rich Milan and Turin business men, war profiteers (*pescecane*) with wives loaded with jewels on their fingers, throats and ears. Outside in the courtyard are ranked the most expensive and blatant automobiles, mostly American, imported at enormous cost, with a leaven of Alfa Romeos, Lancias, Fiats, and an odd Rolls Royce like an aloof dowager of the old régime. There are also the *de luxe* cars of the most privileged class left in the world —members of the Diplomatic Corps of all nations, who live in palaces, move in state, and maintain a royal precedence untouched by any rise in the cost of living, since their Governments foot the bills.

Montecatini, to-day, is crammed with other types of the new
rich. The shopkeeper and his jewelled spouse are also taking
the waters ; the peasant farmer is here in great numbers. You
can detect him by his raw hands, his open shirt, felt hat, rough
clothes, and cheap cheroot. He and his wife walk around and
stray into the cafés with the truculent air of a man in a first-class
compartment with a third-class ticket. They are enjoying themselves after many years of arduous labour, brought from near
poverty to prosperity by the whirligig of war. It is the business
class, however, that is most notable. They lack nothing. Their
wives patronise dressmakers, masseurs, hairdressers and mani-
curists. In adjacent bedrooms one hears slappings and poundings
proceeding from the slimming process. There is a ceaseless
traffic of young women with ' models,' and of boys with hat-
boxes. The candy shops are exhibitions of dazzling confections.
Someone buys these fancy packets at £2 and £3 a time. The
jewellers have baubles up to £1,000 and show no signs of bankruptcy. The living costs of many of these clients must be around
£10,000 a year. Does anyone pay taxes ? If they are living
out of capital, as so many of us these days, they are living out
of new capital made since 1946. The old rentier class, landowners excepted, was wiped out. In 1939 the £1 equalled 100
lire, in 1949 2,000 lire ; the dollar in 1939 20 lire, in 1949
600 lire, thirty times its old value. With a fantastic unrestricted
birthrate, blocked emigration and peasants seizing the land, how
long can Italy function ? The terrible conditions of life in about
one-third of the country was alarmingly revealed in Carlo Levi's
Jesus Stopped at Eboli, and earlier in D. H. Lawrence's novel *The
Lost Girl*, which was set in the Abruzzi. An Italian census
questionnaire asked how many persons were dwelling in caves.
Dolce far niente is enforced on two million workless. The climate,
too, can be savage, biting cold in the Alps, devastating torrents in
the valleys, far removed from the sunny smiling landscape known
only to the summer tourist. There are eighty-four Communist
mayors in the northern cities ; and Communists are bred of
discontent and misery. The Church is putting up a desperate
fight but many regard it, with its hoarded wealth, as responsible
for the past oppression of the people, because of its reactionary
political outlook. They support it in lieu of something worse,
of Communism. The Church was ravaged and plundered in
1873 by the Italian public. A second such onslaught might

shatter its temporal security and override the last barrier to Communism. The Government has a six-ringed circus on its hands. Even so, all over Italy there is a bustle, a cheerfulness, a willingness to work. Bridges are built, new roads are made, houses and offices go up, the crowd is well dressed, new cars are on the roads, money is freely spent in shops bulging with goods. Rome must be the most prosperous city in Europe to-day, as it is the most vivacious.

An Italian with whom I talked, an intelligent journalist of international experience, did not take my fearful view of Italy's position. On the contrary, he thought that we English were quite mad with our austerity. " It has become a form of national conceit with you. You feel terribly virtuous denying yourself everything you want. You lack food and cars. Everything you require has a fearful purchase-tax, your income-taxes paralyse your life and enterprise. And what has it accomplished for you ? Every year your position gets worse. This year the austerity in England is greater than in the year the war ended. You are working yourself to the point of exhaustion, your factory equipment is being worn out and not replaced, your National Debt mounts every day and you have no fun out of life whatsoever. And you imagine that all this makes you regarded with respect throughout the world, whereas your prestige was never lower. Every country is kicking you around, believing you are on the downgrade. Nobody wants your pound. You are worse off than us because you cannot feed yourselves and your standard of living is not justified by your income. To make matters worse, your climate does not permit you to live as we do, out of doors for nine months of the year in cheerful warmth. Don't think I am anti-British. In the past you have stood for a manner of life and conduct we have all hoped to emulate. You were born and reared in freedom. But not now. You live in the Misery Isles, and a great many would leave them if they could. I have just been visiting some friends in England. How do you stand it ? The dreariness, the awful food, the repressive regulations. You can't have this, you can't do that ! You cannot keep hens or build a coop for them without official permission. And the frightful taxes ; and the dislike of work because it isn't worth while ; your shops that want to close too early ; your restaurants that shut down when people want service, all this with the rain coming down, the damp, the fog, your dead gloomy Sundays. If you can't be prosperous in England what have you got ? When we fall into ruin, as we do every century or so, we have still something beautiful to look at. You can be very poor and very happy in Italy. But Birmingham, Liverpool, Sheffield, Glasgow, Manchester, London—in ruins, what will they be for tourists ? "

My Italian friend waved his hands and then solemnly added— " You were such a wonderful people, sane, generous, brave ; possibly you are still. No one is desperately hungry, I know the old are looked after, but I would rather live here with all its unemployment, its lower standard of living because we have a blue sky, wonderful fruit, and music in our hearts. As for misfortune—for over two thousand years we have been invaded at least twice every century and ruined, but you cannot depress us, or take away our *dolce far niente*, which is something your politicians can never understand. They love to make you miserable, and you love them for that very reason ! "

" And Mussolini ? " I interjected, as my friend paused.

" Ah, Mussolini ! Didn't you cut off King Charles's head and dig up the bones of Cromwell ? All nations go periodically mad. Politically we are epileptics but in between the seizures we have a better time. We enjoy ourselves."

I agreed with much of what he said but I pointed out some facts he had not considered. We have had a bloodless revolution and the fanatics who took control have led us into near bankruptcy. But there had been provocation and some things that had long been a reproach are now banished from our social conditions. One-third of the nation has been drastically abused, its economy depressed, but one-half of the nation now finds itself living in a paradise compared with the 1920s and 1930s. One had only to read the ' case histories ' set forth in Rowntree's *English Life and Leisure* to see how relatively well off these people now are, how they can indulge in little luxuries and distractions previously undreamt of, and how contented they are on the whole with their present lot. The statistics these writers produced regarding poverty in the town of York were evidence of an immense improvement during the past ten years or so. Not even the most hidebound Tory has proposed any return to the conditions that prevailed before. " It is now a matter of proportion and how much we can afford economically. We may have gone too far too fast, but we have avoided violence and eradicated poverty. We are, to-day, a Socialist State, achieved without bloodshed, in a manner that would teach Stalin a thing or two. Alas, for our ancient motto ' Rule Britannia ' we have substituted ' Fine, imprisonment, or both '," I said.

"And you have produced the greatest man in the world— Churchill ! I will concede you that," said my friend with a smile. "But can he arrest the march of Time ? Aren't you living at an impossible economic level ? We shall see. You are a nation full of surprises."

Things Observed.

A young husband and wife came in to the café I sometimes frequent. It was midnight. The wife carried a two-year-old baby in her arms, a *bimba* in a vivid striped jacket, eyes alert in her little face. On a shelf behind stood a telephone. The mother took down the receiver and applied it to the baby's ear. Its little hand clutched the vulcanite and listened. Then a seraphic smile spread over its face. When the instrument was put back it cried. The mother repeated the soothing process five times. Each time the baby listened to the crackling instrument in ecstasy. " *Ella è telefonista,*" explained the proud father, seeing our wonder. " This morning she heard her cousins talking in Viareggio ! " The couple departed, bearing away the telephone addict, wide awake at midnight.

Reading the delightful *Heber Letters 1782-1832,* I was overwhelmed by what the eighteenth-century stomach suffered. Being sensitive in that department, the ordeal of young Richard, aged ten, was formidable. He " continued in a weakly state for two or three weeks after he came home from school but Bark draughts with Elixir of Vitriol was of vast service to him." It would be the last service to me.

FLORENCE

September 30.

Yesterday I bade farewell to Montecatini and motored into Florence. After life *de luxe* in La Pace I am established again in my simple room on the Lungarno. The same room, the same view over the Arno to the cypress-crowned mount of San Miniato and the river down to the Ponte Vecchio. The heavy rains have transformed the trickle of the Arno into a muddy torrent that roars over the weirs, so that last night I had to shut my windows against the noise. The pothole in the river I inhabited in the blistering August of 1949, where I sat up to the neck reading *The Times*, has disappeared in the flood.

The tourists have gone. There are still *pellegrini*, flocks of weary women shepherded by perspiring priests. They get out of the charabancs by the Uffizi, gaze at the *David* and the *Perseus* and are hustled into the Palazzo Vecchio. But they have the air of the last leaves of summer and it is now a sadder atmosphere without the eager students, the tanned youths in cotton shorts, the belted Americans, the flannel-trousered English. However, in the Uffizi Gallery this morning I found I was mistaken. Five times in three years I have tried to study the paintings there only to find myself jostled and deafened by a babble of conducted tourists. " At last ! " I thought, when I found myself almost alone with Botticelli. A few minutes later my view was blotted out, the room loud with feet. Among the intruders a guide bawled out instructions in his dreadful English. " An here ladeez you see de most wonderfool pictures ov de time, de *Venus* de Botticelli. His name not Botticelli. Oh no ! Dat hees playname, ladeez—he was leetle fat man, so he was callada Botticelli, it means leetle barrel. De Venus you see, zo beautifool, de Greek callada goddess of Loff, bord of de sea. So she coma on a seashell with nodding, all naked, beautifool, an a lady she bring a gown for her, de lovely flowers on it you see, such as you like on dress, ladeez ! An now we lok at de *Primavera*—dere. (The whole company swings round.) " It means the Springtime. You see de beautifool girl in flowerry dress—she Spirit of Spring, in middle, Venus. To left, tree Graces, dancing, and Mercury, he a Greka god, he looka oop wid *bastone*, touching de trees for maka Spring. It ees beautifool allegroy, ladeez. An you see up dere, over all, a leetle Cupid ? He shoot arrows at all of dem, for his arrow bringa love—it ees Springtime, de Primavera—an in Springtime we wanta love, ladeez ! "

He wiped his brow. There was a faint simper among ladies wanting love. " An now we come to——— " The crowd shuffled on behind him.

The *Primavera* has never moved me to ecstasy. It is marvellous painting, inbred with paganism, but the girl with a spray in her mouth is too pot-bellied to my taste, despite the symbolism of the fecund earth. The technique is overwhelming. If I indulged in art jargon I should talk about its 'tactile values,' to borrow a term invented by the Great Cham of Art. Alas, the pigments have lost their glow and are lapsing into darkness. The beloved Simonetta in the *Venus* is all wistfulness and grace. She was to die young, mourned by all Florence, and when the news came to Lorenzo Il Magnifico he thought he discerned a new star in the sky. No Madonna is lovelier than this *Venus* of Botticelli's but the picture is marred for me by the pudding feet and bitten-off toe-nails. When he painted Simonetta with Mercury in *Primavera* both his models were dead. Simonetta, who had been Queen of Beauty at sixteen in the great tournament of 1474 in the Piazza Santa Croce, had died of consumption, and Giuliano, presented as Mercury, Lorenzo's brother, had been stabbed to death in the Cathedral during High Mass, in 1478.

Piero dei Medici took the young Botticelli into his house and he painted for him the *Adoration of the Magi*, hanging in this same room. It always gives me deep pleasure. Botticelli brought into it all the Medici family, dead and alive. His beloved patron, Piero, had escaped, through the swift intervention of his son Lorenzo, a murderous attempt on his life. This picture was commissioned for a thank-offering. Piero, splendid in scarlet, is in the middle, kneeling before the throne. His father, Cosimo, dead, is by the feet of the Holy Child. Piero's brother, Giovanni, dead, is also there, near the kneeling young Giuliano, while Piero's elder son, Lorenzo, stands to the left, pert and slightly truculent, holding a sword. The Medici household is lined up at the side. It is a friendly call on the Madonna and Child. The whole picture sings with colour and bold design.

But of all the Botticellis here my favourite is a smaller work to which I always return, the *Madonna of the Magnificat*. It was painted for his patroness, Lucrezia Tornabuoni, Piero's wife, a wise, gifted woman. Into it he brings her three children, Lorenzo, Giuliano, and their sister who leans over them. These may be idealised portraits but nothing could surpass the beauty of these boys' ingenuous faces. Lorenzo gazes at the Madonna and Child, as he holds the inkpot for the Madonna's plume pen. The doomed young Giuliano has hair of gold, and the curl for which he was famed falls over his brow. He looks wistfully at his brother. The chubby hand of the Holy Child rests on the

H

pomegranate. The whole execution is so delicate and rich in colour that one marvels at the genius of Sandro's brush.

I know two old ladies in Florence, both American, both turned eighty. This evening I went to dine with the younger one. She is smart in appearance and alive with spirit, but she lamented that she could not die. She has been a widow almost thirty years and dreams still of the felicity of her married life. This evening she was near to tears. A few days ago a little dog, deeply loved by her, was killed by an autobus. The tragedy had deepened her sense of loneliness. We dined alone. We agreed that Browning's lines—

> " Grow old along with me
> The best is yet to be,
> The last of life for which the first was made "

were nonsense. Browning was sticking his chest out. The best of life is youth, with the adventure of early manhood. Age has long shadows, physical limitations and loneliness. I am sure Browning did not believe his own lines. His heart was buried with Elizabeth Barrett Browning in the English cemetery here, and the lonely old poet ran around to tea parties in an effort to forget.

My other American friend was ill, so I could not see her. She too knew married felicity, but it came almost too late for she was 60 when she married the handsome old artist she adored. She was so innocent that she asked her doctor if she was in danger of having children. They lived like a pair of lovebirds in a pretty little Venetian cage. On his death she came to Florence where she now sits all day looking at her beloved's paintings which line the room.

I often wonder at the problem created by these women who have been long years away from their native land so that if they returned now they would be strangers. Alone, exiled in a foreign land, they seem like old ships without a harbour.

On my way to dinner with my octogenarian friend, I hesitated between chocolates, flowers, scent. Chocolates indicate a young stomach, flowers a decoration, but scent suggests allure. I chose a bottle of Eau-de-Cologne, resisting *Nuit d'Amour*. The pleasure on my hostess's face proved that a woman is never too old for that kind of compliment.

October 1.

It poured with rain all the morning in such torrents that the cypress-dotted hills across the Arno were blotted out, but after lunch it cleared and the sun reappeared. I walked to the Badia and, entering, found myself alone, a rare event these days of the motorbus tourists. What an exquisite thing is Filippino Lippi's painting of St. Bernard's *Vision of the Virgin.* The young monk in his white habit has such delicate hands, raised as he talks to the Virgin peering at him over his desk. He might be exclaiming as She touches his book that he knows that the candles supplied for Her altar have gone down in quality. The last shipment of wax was so poor ! She is accompanied by four boy-angels, but despite their wings and choirboy-expressions you know they are urchins on their best behaviour who, to-morrow, will be catapulting birds and teasing cats. The whole conception is so warmly human, so rich in colour and invention. A pleasant touch is the portrait of the devout Piero di Francesco del Pugliese who commissioned the artist to paint the picture for a church outside the walls, whence it was brought for safety to the Badia when Pope Clement VII's soldiers were marching on Florence. Piero got his own portrait in the picture for the same price. This old church, here before the Duomo, was the favourite burial place of the noble Florentine families during the Middle Ages. It is one of the very few buildings in Florence that were known to Dante, for in his day the Cathedral was only just rising from its foundations, and the Palazzo Vecchio and the Medici palaces did not exist. He was born and passed his early life near this old church. It had other associations with Dante. After the poet's death in exile Florence sought to honour him, for his renown had spread although his great poem was confined to manuscript in an era preceding the discovery of printing.* So the Signoria commissioned a Dante professor to give public lectures on *The Divine Comedy.* The lecturer was Giovanni Boccaccio, author of *The Decameron,* born eight years before Dante's death. He gave his lectures in this Badia.

The church contains two other gems, memorial tombs from the chisel of that superlative artist, Mino de Fiesole. His sculptures always delight the eye. There is nothing mournful in his

* All who have seen in the Vatican Library the manuscript copy of the *Divina Commedia,* illustrated by Botticelli himself, will know why noble connoisseurs, such as the Duke of Urbino, scorned to have printed works in their libraries.

memorials. He has an irrespressible gaiety as expressed in the adorable cherubs who guard the tomb of Count Ugo ; and his figures of Charity with her two babies, and the Madonna with Child are beauty and piety married in perfection. Mino died in 1484, only three years after the completion of this masterpiece which is as fresh as if it had been carved only this year. The other tomb, for a gonfalonier, is a triumph of harmonious design. The makers of beautiful memorials seldom lie in beautiful tombs themselves, as witness Michelangelo, Cellini, Leonardo da Vinci, etc., so that it is pleasant to see that Mino designed a most beautiful resting-place for himself, and lies beneath it in San Ambrogio, while an entrancing little boy makes a blessing over him.

When I was studying Count Ugo's tomb a youth came into the Badia and up to the memorial. He was about twenty, strongly built, with a powerful tawny throat and a mass of golden hair gathered in a cluster in the nape of the neck. There was something so familiar in the head and the pose of this youth with his strong face and firm full lips that I began wondering where I had seen him recently. Suddenly I found the clue. This was Michelangelo's *David*. Strip him and put him on a plinth and he would have been the most notable statue in Florence. The likeness was continued in the strength of his peasant's hands.

He noticed my interest and smiled, whereupon I asked him if his name was David. No, it was Luigi. Strangely enough although David was such a favourite subject with the Florentine sculptors—there are Donatello's *Davids* and Verrocchio's—David is a name seldom used in Italian. When I asked where he came from he said Settignano. He worked as a stonecutter. It explained his powerful shoulders and strong hands. He was surprised by a sudden exclamation I made on receiving this information, for it seemed to me extraordinary that he, the living replica of David, should come from Settignano where Michelangelo had lived as a child with his foster-mother, the wife of a stonecutter there. Was I an American, asked Luigi. No, but I knew America well, I answered. " I want to go there soon," he said, and then he made the gesture of all Italians when they indicate money, he rubbed a finger and thumb together. Like most of his countrymen he suffered from the usual dollar obsession. They believe gold lies on the pavements of all American cities.

This evening on my way to dine with a friend I passed the church of Ognissanti, its façade and towers rimmed with electric

lights. I stepped inside and found a crowd listening to an earnest
young Florentine monk preaching in front of the altar rails ;
thus, I suppose, had Savonarola preached. When one writes
' listening ' the word is incorrect for in most of these churches
the crowd comes and goes, gazes about it, and is seemingly quite
perfunctory in its attention to the service at the high altar. This
casualness shocks Protestants but no irreverence is implied, it
is the habit of the country. In Spain the congregation is solemn
and attentive. But I was shocked by four acolytes inside the
altar rail, two of them in white cottas, two of them in street
clothes. They leaned over the rail behind the monk, chatted,
and gazed at the congregation. The jaws of three of them worked
steadily, afflicted by that American blight, chewing-gum.

This church should have a special interest for Americans.
The Vespucci family had a house in the same street, the family
tomb is here, and it is believed that Amerigo, who gave his name
to their continent, lies among his ancestors.

I was just too early in the Ognissanti, for three days later, on
October 4th, I should have seen the church's proudest possession,
the robe of St. Francis, which is annually displayed on that date.
This church has much to be proud of for here lies Botticelli, and
appropriately, that most beautiful lady, Simonetta, his model.
Throughout his life Botticelli had two great loyalties, Lorenzo the
Magnificent and Savonarola. Under the latter's spell he grew
into a sad lonely old man, poor and crippled, all his gay and great
companions dead. Almost forgotten, aged seventy-eight, they
brought him to this church for burial, but such still was the fury
engendered by Savonarola's name, that he was placed under a
nameless tombstone, to save him from desecration by the monk's
enemies.

October 2.

This morning I investigated the hill opposite my window,
rising above the Arno. I found it marks the steep Costa di San
Giorgio that turns sharply just beyond the Ponte Vecchio on
the south bank. They are repairing the damage done by the
Germans who blew up the approaches on either side of this famous
bridge. They destroyed the other bridges over the Arno, and
one can only wonder, viewing their monstrous vandalism, that
they should have felt any qualms about blowing up the Ponte
Vecchio.

Over the Ponte Vecchio the Medici built a tremendous passage-way that ran from the Palazzo Vecchio and the Uffizi on the north bank, over the shops on the bridge, to their new residence, the Pitti Palace. It has its counterpart in the covered way that enabled the besieged Popes to take flight from St. Peter's and gain refuge in the Castle of St. Angelo. I once made the transit of the Medici passage, hung with a mile of indifferent portraits. The section crossing the bridge over the Arno had peepholes giving one ravishing vistas up and down stream. The passage then went over the Via de' Bardi by an arch and over the porch of the church of Santa Felicita, on to the Pitti Palace. Much of this passage was demolished when the Germans blew up the approaches to the Ponte Vecchio on both sides. To-day it is almost reconstructed. I passed under the new arch that carries it over the Via de' Bardi. It seems to me characteristic of our age that the bricks of the new construction are hollow. Within a square mile of this centre how many famous Italians were born and lived who brought immortal fame to this City State ! In the Via Guicciardini the palace in which Francesco Guicciardini was born still exists but the house opposite, in which lived and died Macchiavelli, has wholly disappeared in a heap of rubble.

A little way up the Costa San Giorgio stands the house in which Galileo was honoured by a visit of the Grand Duke of Tuscany in 1620. The Duke had only a few yards to go from the Pitti Palace to visit this man of genius. A grandiloquent tablet records the visit. *Qui abitò Galileo. Non sdegnò piegarse alla potenza del genio la maestà di Fernando II dei Medici.* What is not recorded is that when the Inquisition called Galileo to his trial in Rome, and after harrowing weeks pronounced its monstrous sentence on him, the Grand Duke never raised a finger to protect this great Florentine, and let the Church harass him until the close of his days. Galileo must often have set out from this house to go up the hill to his summer villa at Pian dei Giullari two miles away, where, in forced retirement, blind, condemned for heresy and near death, he received the young Milton.

How very few who climb the Costa San Giorgio turn aside by the church of that name into the little Via Scarpuccia. Here from a tiny piazza in front of the disused church one has a glorious view over Florence. The Arno and the Ponte Vecchio are immediately below, and across on the Lungarno I discovered the window of my room. Then, closely in line, came Giotto's Campanile, the machicolated tower of the Palazzo Signoria, Brunelleschi's great rose-hued dome of the cathedral, the romanesque campanile of the Badia, the crenellated Bargello, the long line of roof of Santa Croce, all gathered in the most picturesque proximity, with a background of the mountains, and Fiesole gleaming afar. At the top of the Costa I turned aside to look at the old brick fortress built by the Grand Duke Ferdinando I that lies like a starfish on the top of the hill. Visitors can no longer enjoy from it the famous panorama for it is again put to military use as the headquarters of a School of Guides. The old gateway, the Porta San Giorgio, that breaks the city wall, cannot have changed much since it was built in 1324. On the townside the fresco of the Madonna, between St. Leonard and St. George, is still beautiful after some five hundred years. Outside the gate one is immediately in the country, and over low walls one sees the olives and cypresses standing in the lovely gardens of the villas. The gate on this side carries a bas-relief of St. George and the Dragon. It stands in the third and last circuit of the walls of Florence, begun in 1824. They enclosed an area four times as large as that contained within the second circuit of 1078. This gate was the only one held by the nobles in the great struggle with the people in 1343, provoked by the rapacity of an adventurous Frenchman, Walter de Brienne, who made himself Count of Lucca, Duke of Athens, and, as representative of Charles d'Anjou, tyrant of Florence.

Turning left out of the gate, I followed a winding lane down by the old wall, amid olive, cypress and chestnut trees, towards the lower city. It is well named the Via di Belvedere. To the right rises the level plateau, the Piazzale carrying the great bronze replica of Michelangelo's *David* and the figures of the Medici tombs ; to the left, the old fortress-tower of San Niccolo, and, afar, the panorama of the city. I now identified the glorious view seen from my window. The city wall masked the long gardens of the Palazzo di Mozzi, whose belvedere, perched above the level terraces, took the morning sun as I breakfasted looking on its fresh green glory. And, descending this glorious hillside, I came down to the church of San Niccolò, in whose campanile a brave bellringer in 1530 gave refuge to Michelangelo, who, having helped to fortify the city, was terrified when it was taken by Ferrante Gonzaga for Charles V and Pope Clement VII, whom he had thereby offended.

So back to my room with a view. I have always found it impossible to have peace of mind so long as an alluring prospect is unexplored. Now I can look out of my window with a sense of completion.

October 3.

This morning to the Bargello to examine the *Davids*. The first in the Michelangelo room is the small stone figure of *David* for which I can feel no enthusiasm whatever, despite the genius of its creator. I find it lumpy. It has nothing characteristic of David, and cannot be compared with the larger marble master-piece in the Accademia and reproduced all over Florence and the world, the massive youth who symbolises male beauty. Up-stairs in the Donatello room sheer genius commands the scene. This young *David* in bronze, with his saucy brimmed hat, his naked insouciant pose, is not and never could be the slayer of Goliath. His leaf-fringed hat, the preposterously heavy long sword in his delicate hand, the long smooth thighs and undulant belly, the coltish legs enclosed in greaves, the lean back, the pert bottom, the long curls tumbling on his shoulders, all belong to some frolicsome lad, a pageboy on holiday romping by a swimming pool. Donatello made it for Cosimo de' Medici and it stood in the courtyard of his palace until the Florentine mob, inflamed by the ascetic Savonarola, rushed there to sack the palace. *David* obviously had rough handling ; there is a hole below the right knee, and the inside of the thigh has been broken and repaired. The right index finger is missing. But it sur-vived in all its beauty through five hundred years, the first nude statue of modern times, and the first in the round, for the early Italian sculptors took refuge from executive difficulties by con-fining themselves to reliefs, or figures for niches.

How different is Donatello's other statue of *David*, in marble, not bronze. The head is almost a replica of the gallant St. George, small, curled, proper for the ' very parfit knyght ' of the heroic legend, which Donatello made for an outside niche of the Or San Michele, where it stood for over four hundred years. This *David* again bears no possible resemblance to the Biblical hero. If the bronze figure came out of a school of pages, this young man came out of a *corps-de-ballet*. He is beautiful to behold, with curled head and delicately posed hand, his slender body encased in a laced doublet and sleeves, the cape thrown

over the shoulders and artily tied in a knot.   But what is *David*
doing with a toga draped round his slender waist, leaving a fold
to fall back revealing a shapely leg ?   A vine chaplet binds his
comely head.   He might well stand for the young Augustus.
As an afterthought, on the ground, as though to remind us of
the Biblical character, lies Goliath's head, with the catapult
near it.   We know, of course, that this *David* could neither have
walked nor run in his doublet and skirt, nor, we are certain, could
he have thrown anything.   The only explanation I can find
for this decorative young man is that one day Donatello said to
a handsome youth of his acquaintance—" Come along and
I'll ' do ' you as David," and then, in a mood of fantasy, instead
of stripping his model he dressed him up, forgetting his role.
So there he stands in the Bargello to-day, graceful but more like
a young actor in a Shakespearean drama than a shepherd boy
on the Judaean hills.

Verrocchio, too, does not bother about the historic David.
His creation is the companion of the bronze boy in the brim hat,
but this time he is leaner.   This charming boy by the pupil of
Donatello, and, in turn, the master of Leonardo da Vinci, is
nearer to our day, with his sensitive, sharp face.   He was displaced from the courtyard of the Palazzo Vecchio, where he once
stood, by another masterpiece from the same hand, the gay
cherub holding the dolphin on the fountain that plays itself into
every tourist's heart.   But this young immortal in doublet and
kilt, holding a short sword, could never have been a shepherd boy,
any more than Michelangelo's young all-in wrestler who could
have tackled Goliath as efficiently on the mat as on the mountain.
It comes to this, after contemplating all these Florentine Davids,
that neither Michelangelo's muscular youth, Donatello's two
picturesque lads, nor Verroccio's slip of a boy, bears any
resemblance to the rustic friend of Jonathan who went out and
slew the giant with a pebble.   Strangely enough, for that David
we must go to a sculptor of the decadence, to Bernini.   His *David*
in the Villa Borghese at Rome is a killer, caught in the act.   This
tense and powerful shepherd lad is shown tight-lipped and fierce,
his shot just delivered from a body that in its muscular co-ordina-
tion is a catapult itself, deadly in purpose, with a divine wrath.

Soon after lunch I left Florence for Rome.   In my compartment
there was a young woman of about thirty-five with an adorable

H*

little son of four.   They had been in the train three hours, coming from Milan, when I entered the compartment at Florence, and now had a four hours' journey to Rome.   In all that time, to the last moment, there was not a whimper from the little boy, nor for one moment did the mother's vigilance cease.   She talked with him, teased him, nursed him and suffered all his clambering about her with a Madonna-like sweetness.   Watching her, I became conscious of the infinite patience of motherhood, of the long hours, days, years of our unconscious childhood in which love has never failed us.   Towards the end of the journey she took him out and washed him.   He returned all dewy, his top curl combed.   The five elders in the compartment were all jaded.   An old gentleman succumbed to fatigue, and his eyes began to close, whereupon the little boy knelt down to observe the drooping eyelids, then, placing a hand on the old gentleman's knee, said sympathetically, " *Coraggio !* "

I would have been a very proud father meeting that train.

As I drove from the station to my hotel the silver splendour of the great fountain in the Piazza Esedra, flood-lit, with water tumbling and frothing about the great statue-spaced basin, filled me with ecstasy.   The fountains of Rome play themselves into the heart.

ROME

October 4.

This morning I opened the shutters and stepped out on to my balcony.   The whole city lay below me, a scene familiar through all the months I had worked here last summer finishing *And So To Rome.*   I have come back to my room with a balcony on the fourth floor.   It overlooks the gardens of the Villa Medici on the Pincio.   A vast panorama of Rome lies before me—the great green expanse of the Villa Borghese and its pinewoods, Mount Soracte rising on the horizon, the city in the valley below, with towers and *campanili*, the great dome of St. Peter's, the façade of the Vatican, the pine-clad skyline of the Janiculum, the wide Roman Campagna, with the Mediterranean Sea beyond and, to my left, the outline of the Alban Hills with Frascati and Rocca di Papa catching the evening sun.

October 5.

A glorious day. This afternoon, writing these notes on my balcony, after a siesta, I was driven indoors by the heat of the sun. Nothing yet has the autumnal tints. The trees and the bushes in the Villa Medici gardens below are a vivid green, and roses are blooming in profusion over the walls. This morning I went to San Pietro in Vincoli (St. Peter in Chains) to see the Michelangelo statue of *Moses*, which somehow has escaped me all these years. I was warned that Rome in the *Anno Santo* would be unbearable with its swarms of pilgrims. My worst fears have not been confirmed although the prices of all the hotels, restaurants and shops have soared. Why because the Pope has proclaimed this a Holy Year I should have to pay fifty cents more for a haircut I do not know.

As I neared San Pietro in Vincoli swarms of pilgrims bore down upon the place. Charabancs in the piazza discharged their loads. They were all alike, tired, ninety per cent females, wearing medallions of some fraternity, led by sturdy black little priests in enormous boots. The American contingents are more elegant and monied. They arrive in private limousines, four or five women at a time accompanied by a robust priest. I suspect that lucky Father O'Sullivan is a guest for the trip.

For the poorer pilgrims this is the event of their lives. They perspire, their feet ache, the language puzzles them, they feel a long way from home and the familiar cup of coffee, pernod or München beer, but they persevere in pious ecstasy. They have visited four basilicas and thereby gained enough indulgences to keep them out of purgatory on the final pilgrimage. They have gazed in silence on the bones of saints, pieces of the true Cross, on nails, on pillars to which St. Paul or St. Peter or Christ Himself was bound, and on gridirons on which saints were fried. This morning the attraction was not *Moses* but a piece of rusty chain in an illuminated coffer under the high altar. Usually it is exhibited only on the first of August, and thereby gave name to the Italian holiday of Ferragusto, but for this Holy Year it is on continuous exhibition. According to legend it was once two pieces of chain ; one piece bound St. Peter when imprisoned in Palestine ; one piece bound him in Rome. The Empress Eudosia sent the Palestine piece from Constantinople and gave it to Pope Leo I, in 1455, whereupon the two pieces of chain, making contact with each other, joyfully soldered themselves together. For some centuries it suffered so much from the filing of devout collectors that it had to be locked away, and is now visible only once a year.

A crowd obscured *Moses*. A priest with a Middle West accent explained that the horns on *Moses'* head, which were all we could see for the moment, did not mean that he was a satyr but that they symbolised the horn holding the oil with which Moses was anointed. This scholarship evoked a chorus of wonder. Later when the crowd thinned out and the mighty visitor from Sinai was visible in all his majesty, an American neighbour declared loudly, " All mah life Ah've never seen anything so bewtifool." Her friend agreed and fell silent. Then their priest, unkindly interrupting a lady with a Kodak camera, who was attempting to obtain something so much more easily and better obtainable from an adjacent postcard kiosk, hustled them along to look at St. Peter's chains.

I am aware that I sometimes distress my friends by not holding an orthodox opinion. *Moses* is one of these instances. It is customary to regard this work as the *chef d'œuvre* of Michelangelo. Generations of learned art critics have held this opinion. I find it an impressive monstrosity. The massive naked arms protruding from a baker's vest, the twin horns standing out of a ludicrously small head imposed upon a giant's body, above all the preposterously long beard, a cluster of serpents, clutched in one hand, all these destroy for me any majesty in the prophet's expression. The vast memorial tomb, with forty statues ordered by Julius II for his own glory, was never finished. He broke Michelangelo's heart with his contrariness, and it is ironical that he should now lie in St. Peter's without a stone to mark his resting place. Romain Rolland has made a great study of the drama of Michelangelo's frustration which should be read by all who visit this tremendous fragment, as also another fragment, *The Prisoner*, in the Louvre.

How hard these pilgrims work is revealed by a notice on my hotel board for the Third Order of Franciscan Pilgrims (U.S.A.).

Oct. 5.   8 p.m.   Arrive Rome.
Oct. 6.   7 a.m.   Mass at the Capucines General Curia.
          9 a.m.-3 p.m.   Sightseeing in the City.

Oct. 7. 7.30 a.m. Mass for Pilgrims at Capucines General
Curia. Father Clement of Milwaukee, General
of the Capucines Order, will meet Pilgrims after
Mass and give them his blessing.
4.30 p.m. Audience with the Holy Father. Bus
ready at 3.30 p.m.

Oct. 8. 6.15 a.m. Mass at Catacombs.
9 a.m. Visit of the Four Basilicas.
3 p.m. Special audience with Holy Father at
Castel Gondolfo.

Oct. 9. 9 a.m. Departure for Florence.

Three days of hustle, sometimes after sweltering trains and
long bus journeys in the great heat of July and August. But they
are happy and will long remember this pilgrimage.

October 6.

I visited to-day the Napoleonic Museum bequeathed to Rome
by a minor member of the Bonaparte clan. With great interest
I came upon the couch on which the flighty Princess Pauline was
sculptured in her famous nude pose by Canova. This, and the
couch on which Madame Récamier was displayed, must be the
two most famous pieces of studio furniture in the world. Canova
knew Madame Récamier too, when she came to Rome, and
David who painted the famous portrait of her on a couch was
once at the French Academy here. I feel that the couch should
be in Rome, to compete with Pauline's.

The museum is skilfully arranged in a series of rooms descending historically from Napoleon I down to Napoleon III,
the Empress Eugénie and the Prince Imperial. Looking at
all the pinchbeck kings, queens, princes and princesses of the
Napoleonic brood, all of whom lived in palaces in considerable
splendour long after the founder of the clan had died miserably
at St. Helena, one wonders at the colossal theft of public funds
and private loot that must have been perpetrated by the Corsican
upstart. What is strange is that the triumphant Allies should
have allowed him to retain it. None of them had a spark of
Bonaparte's genius. The most gifted was the son of Napoleon's
brother, Lucien, to whom the Pope, in gratitude to the Emperor
for bringing atheistic France back into the fold of the Church,
gave an estate with the entailed title of Prince of Canino. Lucien's

son, one of a brood of twelve children, becoming impoverished, sold his Roman estate to Prince Torlonia, the banker, and threw in the title for an extra five dollars. The other fact impressed upon me by the paintings of the Bonapartes was how they all, from Napoleon downwards, dressed themselves up with crowns, ermine robes, orders, jewels, feathers, batons, satin breeches and gowns, in an incredible pantomime of majesty. It must have impressed their dupes and hangers-on, but to modern eyes it is all ludicrous. My companion's remark summed up the effect of this gallery of portraits: " My, how they loved themselves ! "

We lunched at Fagiano's, the restaurant set out under the colonnades in the Piazza Colonna, with St. Peter on the great column from which he deposed Marcus Aurelius, whose victories pictorially encircle it. This has long been my favourite restaurant. The variety and quality of the food fill me with wonder. How these Italians eat ! I observed the party at the next table ; ham with melon and green figs, a plate piled high with *spaghetti al burro, costaletto milanese*—a whole veal chop nine inches long—string beans, fried potatoes, *zucchini, zuppa inglese*— very rich trifle with wine and cream ingredients—all this with a flask of Orvieto wine, coffee and liqueurs. No wonder Rome after midday falls into a stupor (*siesta*) and all life ceases for three hours. It is a myth that only Italians can eat spaghetti gracefully. No one can eat it gracefully. I have watched Italians for thirty years and with the most skilful performance, with all the fork-twirling, two-thirds is swallowed and the last third sucked in.

This evening in the dusk, after three hours' writing, I strolled out on to the Via Vittorio Veneto. The wide boulevard was thronged, all the outdoor cafés were packed, the shops ablaze with lights and full of wonderfully displayed confections and goods. In the restaurants they will be dining until 1 a.m. All the adjacent streets are lined with the latest automobiles. This must now be the richest and gayest capital in Europe. Paris has lost its pre-eminence, and has never had Rome's climate. London is a gloomy, regulation-paralysed poor relation that must go early to bed.

At eleven o'clock this evening I went out on to my balcony and looked down on a network of diamond lights. I can recall only two cities that match this shining splendour—formerly, Budapest with its bridges and plain, jewelled with lights seen from St. Gellert ; and New York, at Central Park, looking south on the cascades of light that outline her skyscrapers against the heavens.

October 8.

I attended the Beatification of a nun in St. Peter's this morning. This is my second Beatification. It followed the same pattern. I had a ticket for the Tribune, opposite the Corps Diplomatique. All the Cardinals were seated before us. Although I arrived early there was no seat and I had to fight for standing-room and found myself wedged in between some nuns and five fat Franciscan monks. These Beatifications take place at frequent intervals and the temporal as well as the spiritual domain of the Church is well indicated by the selection of those to be beatified from the various countries, Poland, France, Ireland, Canada, Brazil, etc. A few days before the ceremony there is the tremendous labour of the papal workmen, *sanpietrini*, as they are called, running around high galleries, swinging perilously over cornices, climbing immense ladders, with acrobatic ability, in the act of decorating the vast fane with crystal chandeliers, festoons of electric lights, scrolls of damask, and tapestries.

The nun to be beatified was portrayed, in the act of assumption, with attendant angels, on a great gaudy banner hung on one of the piers. It was most crudely painted and the nun was afflicted with frightful boots and eyebrows. It was the only exhibit of bad taste in the gorgeous pageantry of the ceremony. For many of the faithful this was a stirring experience ; the high altar rimmed in light, the music, the chanting, the purple and scarlet robes, the uniforms of the papal chamberlains, the soldiers, the Corps Diplomatique, and, high over all, the ascetic and majestic figure of the crowned Pope swaying in his chair between the white plumes and the halberds of the Swiss Guard. But I confess there were moments when, for me, the ceremony came near to vaudeville. To my horror, on the appearance of the Holy Father at the great doors, and during his procession down the nave to the high altar, the great assembly broke into applause, as if he were a prize-fighter climbing into the ring. Flashlight photographers, and cinema operators on retreating platforms, created the atmosphere of a Hollywood first night, and when the Pope seated himself on the throne in the Tribune to conduct the preliminary ritual, he was dogged by microphone stands. I tried to envision Jesus broadcasting the Sermon on the Mount, with flash bulbs, microphones and the Corps Diplomatique in attendance. Doubtless, at the Second Coming, the Public Relations officer will explain that such arrangements are necessary. And all this for the Beatification of a nun, a very humble little peasant woman in big boots whose life had been spent in prayer and good works. How had it all got this way from the simplicity of a Nazareth carpenter's son to this pontiff of the Vatican, flanked by ornate and intricate ceremonies? Near me a young tonsured monk was murmuring in a state of ecstasy. Lean and sallow, he might have posed for St. Francis and the Order of Poverty. I scanned the faces of the cardinals. Swarthy, robust, in some cases jowly, they were certainly neither aesthetic nor ascetic in appearance. The lean scholarly Pope, with his beautiful voice and aristocratic hands gave a physical distinction to his spiritual office.

I left before the conclusion of the long ceremony, pushing my way through a crowd whose chatter drowned the soaring choir. A young man in a black velvet doublet, with ruffle, knee-breeches, white gloves, buckled shoes and sword gave me a courtly bow as I passed. I tried to recall him—a member of the Black Aristocracy, a Papal Chamberlain, a Knight of Malta, Prince Ruspoli, Prince Rospigliosi, Signor Casavecchia? In vain I tried to recall his name. That evening in an hotel where I frequently dine the reception clerk gave me a bow as I passed his desk. It was my young friend of the ruffle and sword.

A most beautiful sunset with Rome " dyed in the blood of the martyrs." A pink and emerald sky, with the dark cypresses of the Villa Medici gardens silhouetted against the evening light ; below, in the valley, and climbing the hills, clusters of diamond lights. The swallows that made such a twittering at dusk all last summer are departed. Not even the warm October days delay their flight to Africa.

October 10.

In 1561, on the invitation of Pope Pius IV, Michelangelo converted into a church part of the great baths of Diocletian, built A.D. 306, the largest baths in antiquity, accommodating over three thousand Romans. He converted the *tepidarium* of the baths into the Church of S. Maria degli Angeli, utilising the

great arches of the ruin. Another part he converted into a
convent which to-day houses the priceless treasures of the National
Museum. Eight columns of the great nave of the church are
from pagan buildings ; and the altar, instead of being at the
east end of the nave, is in a side apse, Michelangelo having used
one of the great arches of the old baths. It is now the church
preferred for religious functions of a special character. It was
here that Eleonora Duse lay in state on her home-coming from
U.S.A. The whole city was in official mourning (*Lutto Cittadino*)
and Silvio D'Amico's invocation hung over the church's draped
portal—" Peace in the Lord to the restless soul of Eleonora Duse,
in the hour of her return from the last pilgrimage, is implored
by Rome and Mother Italy."

It was here I went at eleven o'clock to-day to attend the funeral
rites of the opera singer, De Luca, whose body had been brought
from New York. The coffin lay under a high catafalque, decorated with huge easel-wreaths made of dahlias, gladiolas and
tuberoses. There was a High Choral Mass with some superb
singing by the Sistine Chapel Choir. I felt how fitting it was
that this famous Metropolitan Opera House baritone, who had
delighted so many thousands, should receive these choral rites.
When we came out into the bright sunshine of this October day
the great fountain of the naiads in the Piazza dell Esedra was in
full play, jets of silver making rainbows over the dolphins and
seahorses. I do not wonder that an Italian, even after a life of
great success in America, should elect to be brought to his rest
in the Eternal City.

After lunch at Fagiano's I walked up the steps to Trinità dei
Monti, past the Villa Medici, to the Pincio gardens. The *lecci*
(ilex) with their picturesque branches over a fountain frame a
prospect of the dome of St. Peter's that has long been one of the
most painted and photographed in all Rome. Alas, the black
symmetry of these branches has been broken by the collapse
of one of the old trees. A new one has been planted but
it will be some fifty years before the famous dark frame is
restored. But in the life of Rome what is fifty or five hundred
years ?

The lovely *Viale Ippocastani*, or avenue of the horse-chestnuts,
is lined with busts of great Italians of the Renaissance. It ends
in a superb vista, Through the noble west gates of the Villa
Medici, down the ilex avenue, beyond an ornamental well, the

balcony of my room is glimpsed above the pine-trees. Parallel
to the chestnut avenue runs the *Viale dei Bimbi*. A tiny carriage
drawn by two miniature ponies, and little tricycles and scooters
await the entertainment of the *bimbi*. But for me, as for them,
the irresistible attraction under the trees here is the Punch and
Judy show. The curtain goes up at three o'clock, after the owner
has had his *siesta ;* then, along with a cluster of heavenly children,
I forget my years.

October 11.

To-day I visited S. Maria Maggiore, the Lateran, and the
Scala Santa. It is impossible to see these with any comfort.
They are thronged with pilgrims, cohorts from all over the world
making the visit to the four basilicas. The pilgrims are led
by the bearer of a black cross, with a candle-bearer on each side.
They chant in unison as they progress from altar to altar. On
the steps of the Porta Santa, now open for the Jubilee, they kneel
and kiss the threshold so that there is a continuous block. The
rosary and postcard kiosks do a tremendous trade, kept by perspiring monks who cope with a babel of languages.

The most remarkable sight to-day was at the Scala Santa.
The sacred stairs, comprising twenty-eight marble steps, are
alleged to have been those up which Christ walked at his trial
in the palace of Pontius Pilate. It is said they still retain the
stains of his blood. The faithful now make progress up them
on their knees. The stairs were crowded, six abreast, from bottom
to top. A side staircase accomodates those disinclined to progress on their knees. A notice in four languages instructed
the pilgrims. " One must go up the Holy Stairs on the knees,
never rising on the feet, to gain the holy indulgence. It is
sufficient to call to the mind with faith the sufferings of Our
Lord, or recite some jaculatory." At the top of the stairs,
after their slow progression, the pilgrims regain their feet and
are rewarded, through a grille, with the sight of a portrait of the
Saviour, painted by angels and mysteriously borne to Rome
by water.

Before the pilgrims flocked into the souvenir shop to be served
by black-habited monks, they passed a table where money was
accepted for masses. A young monk wrote down the donors'
names ; five hundred or a thousand *lire* seemed the favoured
response to the tariff shown.

Things Observed.

In a side chapel at S. Maria Maggiore a fat Frau sitting on the altar steps changing her stockings, and a few yards away an acolyte gently leading a blind old man into the confessional box, on whom he most reverently drew the curtain, and then whispered something to the priest behind the screen. He then stood quietly by, in attendance.

October 12.

When novelists make use of coincidences they are reproved by the critics. Two months ago a lady who had read *And So To Rome* wrote asking me if I would divulge the name of the hotel from whose balcony I had so wonderful a view. I did so reluctantly. This afternoon while looking at a new British car at the hotel door (wondering, as the English do, how the other fellow got it), the lady owning it asked if I was the author. She was my correspondent and had just that moment arrived with a friend and had obtained a room with a view. When I went indoors the concierge showed me a card from Assam, written by a lady saying she had mislaid her copy of *And So To Rome* in the hotel, and wondered if they had found it. Ten minutes later, in my room, the telephone rang. A young American who had lunched with me in England after presenting a letter of introduction, had heard I was in the hotel. He was in a room on my landing for one night, en route by air from Ankara to New York.

The room he had was the one occupied by another American friend all last summer, a retired Latin professor of Princeton University, John Basore. We each loved our balcony views, and after dinner we retired across the road to a little café lodged in the garden wall of the convent of the Trinità dei Monti. I miss the Professore, as the hotel servants called him. I am a great reader of inscriptions, with which Rome is covered. They are written often in a terrible dog Latin and we had many conferences over these which sorely tried his scholarship. Every evening towards sunset we had a rendezvous, having left our balconies as the swallows twittered over the Medici gardens, and stood for a time in the hotel entrance. Across the road in a high walled garden rose a superb eucalyptus-tree and some cypresses. They masked two wings of an ochre building on which the dying light fell with great beauty ; it gave us half an hour of sheer delight beyond any artist's imagining. The buildings were part of a Franciscan convent. From our garden roof we could see the Franciscan brothers playing tennis. The corner of their walled garden had a spectacular umbrella-pine that stood black against the evening sky. It was odd to see these young monks skipping about on a tennis court. When they jumped their brown habits ballooned out, revealing their white legs.

Things Observed.

A waggish fellow lives on the first floor of a house whose windows look on to the Campo Marzio. As I walked down it I was startled to see, looking over the window sill, a completely naked young woman, full-breasted, with tanned bosom and blonde hair, who smiled at me, while a shirtless boy standing by her smirked. In the next window another naked young woman, fatter, had behind her a naked man who was deriding her with arms raised, while a little girl peeked over the sill. I wondered where the police were—and wondered again when I discovered that these were the life-like creations of an outfitters' model-maker who took this means of advertising his wares. Round the corner was a seminary for young priests.

October 14.

What a stealer of time Rome is, and how irresistible a thief! Another day gone. I was up at seven and threw open the shutters, the sun streaming into my room. Below, in the nuns' kitchen garden over the way, there was a great clucking among the hens as their eggs were collected. I bathed and shaved, went back to bed, rang for breakfast and wrote for two hours. The air mail edition of yesterday's *Times* arrived, and fifteen letters. A Frenchman in Mexico has translated *Eight for Eternity* and wants the Mexican rights ; a lady in Edinburgh asks me to write a Prologue on the lines of the political survey in *And So To America*, " if the censorship would permit you " ; a tenant wants permission to erect an outhouse after a long and successful tussle with the authorities ; will I broadcast for a benevolent fund in December (I shall be in America), and lecture in Manchester next March (I shall be in Spain) ; a mortgage has been repaid, writes my solicitor, please sign the enclosed deed, witnessed by the British Consul ; a reader in New Zealand points out an error in *And So To Bath*, in its 21st reprint (there are many errors, I never saw proof sheets, being abroad in wartime, and have never been able to catch up with them) ; a friend suggests that I should write a book on a theme he outlines, " It would sell like hot cakes." How little he knows me ! I have never in my writing-life of forty years written a book with the idea of gaining a large sale. I have always written solely to please myself, on the subject that absorbed me at the moment. The fact that since my first novel published in 1923, now in its 25th impression, I have enjoyed a large sale is entirely fortuitous. It happens that the public likes the books I write. I am very grateful to it. I have been well re-warded for doing something nothing could have stopped me doing. The fact that I had been well paid for this has always surprised me since a great deal of good literary work never receives its just reward. Such success as my novels have gained has subsidised other works that called for considerable research. I have lived with a single purpose, absorbed in and dedicated to my writing and this has been its own reward. That it has gained me friends all over the world, a competence, independence, and some degree of fame is a happy chance, unless it be that singleness of mind and a steady determination to pursue one's calling command success. When one speaks of an author gaining financial reward let it be remembered that the most successful author never achieves any income comparable with that of thousands of anonymous business men. Ever since the success of my first novel in 1923—I had a lucky start—I have had the label ' best-seller ' tagged on to me. It is a silly term, much in use among the envious and those unsuccessful ' highbrows ' who spend so much time hailing one another's genius but desert to the ' best-seller ' rank at the first opportunity. As a result of the term, and the fact that an author's fame bears no proportion to the income it produces, there has grown up the legend that I am a rich man. I am be-cause, although I have never earned more on average than my doctor or tailor, my requirements have always been simple. When in my hard youth I became painfully aware of the fact that a man without independence can be kicked around, I made a resolution and kept it. During the next thirty years I lived on one half of my income and gave away one fifth. Because I bought the Austin Ten when I could have bought the Rolls Royce some of my acquaintance thought I was mean to myself—and to them. But I never expected authorship to sustain me or my good

fortune to continue, and I was never a façade-merchant. *Où
sont les grands d'antan ?*

Given the will my early resolution was a possible one before the
last war. In these days of confiscatory taxation such a thing is
not possible. I am now grateful for the honey stored in the
hive although it is much devalued by governments that throw
around paper money. The outlook is grim for the young author
to-day.

I rose, dressed and went down the Spanish steps towards the
Corso. The artists' models, as in the days of Dickens, no longer
lounge on these steps in character costume, seeking hire. Are
there artists' models any more, if so, where are they? In the
Piazza di Spagna I called on the British Consul. I know Consuls
all over the earth, pleasant ones, stiff ones, grouchy and embittered
ones, hard-working and conscientious ones. Poor fellows, they
are always on the move. There is a new Consul in Rome, very
charming. We chatted. I paid a fee and had my deed witnessed. After the call on the Consul I walked down the Via
Babuino (The Street of the Baboon). The sky was blue, the
sun so hot that I took the shady side, as did Prince Alessandro
Torlonia and his two little blond boys and daughter, all in jodh-
purs, whom I met leading their horses home after a morning
gallop in the Villa Borghese.

I turned into the Via Margutta. At one end it is blocked by
the derelict Hôtel de Russie once favoured by elegant tourists.
The Via Margutta holds many things besides studios. Fascinated,
I dawdled and stared. Here was a passage opening into a courtyard. Here a flight of steps, vine-clad, an old fountain and, from
the Pincio hill that overhangs it, a riot of leaves and plants,
gleaming with the green and gold of this sunlit autumn day.
The shops of picture-frame makers, canvas stretchers, cabinet
makers, woodcarvers, gilders, printers, engravers, a few garages
and antique shops—the pattern was fascinating. In the doorway
of an antique shop stood two marble busts on scagliola plinths.
They were of two robust matrons, Christina de' Medici and
Magdalena de' Medici. They wore wimples. How came the
wife of the Grand Duke Ferdinando I, Christina of Lorena, and
the wife of the Grand Duke Cosimo II, Magdalena of Austria,
to have arrived here, possibly from the Pitti Palace, their home
in Florence? I speculated on the vicissitudes of Fate that

brought these haughty Grand Duchesses of Tuscany to be on sale in a Bohemian Roman street.

I resisted turning down a side street alluringly called 'The Kitchen-garden of Naples,' and sauntered into the long leafy courtyard of a high ochre-washed palazzo. It had a great iron gate and pilasters marked *Studi di Pittura*. Inside, the courtyard suggested an antique dealer's haunt. There were Roman busts, torsos, fountains, sarcophagi, all jumbled up, with oleanders, creepers, and giant 'elephant's ears'. In the fold of the arms of a marble Bacchus a cat was washing herself in the sun. By a dealer's door, amid an assortment of marbles, there was a Roman memorial stone of about the second or third century A.D. Possibly it once had stood on the Appian Way. It pleased me and I played with the idea of buying it, but weight, Customs and the incongruity of the English climate deterred me. It had two delightful *putti* holding between them a floral swag ; above was carved *Lucius Rufo. Vixit Ann LXII. Dies XX.* Who was Lucius Rufo who died aged sixty-two years and twenty days ? Evidently he was faithful to the old gods and the new Christian creed had not captured him, for this was a pagan memorial. Was he a Roman, a lawyer, a senator ? Had he a family ? Someone mourned him, ordered this stone and set it up on a Roman highway. And that is all we shall ever know. He might have talked with Marcus Aurelius, or Septimius Severus whose body they brought back from York, England, in the cold shadowy North. In Rome the imagination never lacks food.

Outside again, in the Via I watched a boy drink out of one of the countless fountains of Rome ; leaning against it there was a large unframed painting of a Bacchanalian orgy that he was taking somewhere. The water flowed between two satyrs under a stone marked S.P.Q.R.

And so I came out into the Piazza di Spagna and it was time for lunch. The morning had been frittered away but what could I have achieved by industry as rewarding ? Lunch, a siesta, an hour with *The Times*, tea on the Vittorio Veneto, where it was still warm and light until six o'clock, and then home again, where I watched the sunset fade over Rome. When the lights twinkled in the valley I closed my shutters. It had been a perfect day, and throughout I had been free from pain. Life cannot offer one much more than beauty and tranquillity.

October 16.

This morning when I opened my shutters it was a day of singular radiance. Rome lay before me in a golden light of exceptional clarity. The twin towers of the Villa Medici, rising above a sea of green woods and gardens pointed with giant cypresses, took the first rays on its ochre towers and walls. Afar, between the two belfries of the S.S. Trinità dei Monti, rose that monarch of all domes in the city of towers and domes, St. Peter's. I could see one end of Bernini's great double colonnade, which almost encloses the vast piazza before the basilica, the Sistine Chapel and, to the right, the great building with four tiers of windows that held the private apartments of the Pope. The son of the Governor of the Vatican City having taken me over it, I knew the location of the Holy Father's apartment, sitting-room, bedroom, etc. Since I can identify, two miles away, his windows, I imaginatively follow his life. It amused me all last spring to think that as I shaved at my open window the Pope was shaving at his, until a Roman newspaper informed me that the Holy Father was far in advance, for he rises each morning at six o'clock and shaves with an electric razor. At the side of his palace another long low building houses the fabulous collection of the Vatican museums and library. All this lay out in the morning sun, dove-grey across the Tiber valley.

The splendour of the morning had a cloud after my telephone had rung. A very dear friend, the Marchesa Sommi-Picenardi had died in New York, her son-in-law informed me. My mind went back to all the happy hours we had spent together in New York. Our friendship had begun curiously. One evening in 1942 I went with a friend to the Metropolitan Opera House. The Marques de Cuevas (who had not then founded his ballet company), had given me two seats in his box. He had suddenly been sent into a nursing-home for an eye operation so could not be present. The curtain had risen and in the semi-darkness I was aware of one occupant, a lady. When the curtain fell on the first act and the lights went up, I saw a distinguished elderly woman, who, regarding us for a few moments, introduced herself. She was de Cuevas's other guest, the Marchesa Sommi-Picenardi. She had all the hallmarks of a *grande dame* that some American women of wealth, travelled, Paris-dressed, acquire so well. I found her story followed a familiar pattern. An American widow,

she had married a handsome Italian aristocrat and had made
her home in Italy for a number of years. A singularly able hostess,
with a flair for distinction and décor, she reigned in a beautiful
apartment in the Palazzo Barberini in Rome. After the death
of her husband, her daughter having married there, she remained
on until the entry of Italy into the war when she came home. She
then lived in a corner suite on the ninth floor of the Savoy Plaza
Hotel, attended by her devoted French maid, Anna, and a Russian
Figaro, an exile named Theodore. This couple treated the Marchesa, and later, myself, like children who must be carefully
guarded. Here in her sitting-room, with its fine pieces of jade,
its Italian pictures and a few other souvenirs of her Roman life,
the Marchesa received her friends. She always dressed in black
and her lovely grey hair fell in a loop over her brow. She wore
little of her great store of jewels but in her simplicity she was the
model of a well-dressed woman, *distinguée* in every line and
movement.

In summer my friend moved to Southampton on Long Island,
and here we were again much together as I spent my summer
vacation there. During the war her mind turned anxiously
towards her married daughter in Rome, the Countess Martini-
Crotti and her two grandchildren. The letters chronicling their
lives, now stormy, and involving a retreat into hiding at the Spanish
Embassy at one period, were read to me as soon as they arrived.
When a third grandchild was on the way we shared by proxy
the anxieties. The little Alessandra's birth was celebrated by us,
tête-à-tête, with a bottle of champagne.

When I left for Europe in the spring of 1947 there was a break
in our pleasant friendship, but I was delighted to meet her again
in Rome in the early summer of that year. She received at the
Excelsior Hotel all her old friends but I could not help being
aware that a change had come, not in her appearance, for she
was the same distinguished figure, but in her manner. There
was an air of resignation, a quietness in her smile and conversation,
and not one word to indicate illness, for it was her *credo* never to
mention illness. My last picture of her was of her presiding
over a little dinner she gave at the Excelsior one evening in July
last year, as perfect a hostess as ever.

I had looked forward to some happy hours this coming December in that ninth-floor sitting-room overlooking the Plaza and
the trees of Central Park, with Anna entering with her Mona Lisa

smile, bearing a glass of hot milk prior to my departure into the rigours of a winter's night. No more shall I know that sitting-room and my charming friend. Another door has closed in the corridor of Time.

October 17.

As I lay in bed working this morning the beautiful view through the french window was suddenly obstructed by a painters' cradle swinging up from nowhere. Two workmen were on it. Seeing me, they raised their paper caps and their plaster-spotted faces beamed as they said " *Buon giorno, signore !* " Their names I learned were Dante Rossi and Virgilio Pacchiarotto ; very appropriately, for they worked in distemper.* With these reminders of Dante and Browning I had an animated conversation. Then we decided we must all go back to work. So there I was, in bed again, writing, while outside, swinging in mid-air, Dante and Virgilio were plastering and singing, each with one of my cigarettes behind his ear.

At noon I walked down towards the Palazzo Venezia to see an exhibition. Halted by the traffic light on a street corner, two boys and a girl, not older than fourteen, stood chatting. I never cease to be entranced by the beauty of Italian children. These were blond, as are many Italians, contrary to general belief, two brothers and a sister, it seemed. The girl had a beautiful young figure. All three had dark eyes, sweeping eyelashes and finely-cut sensitive faces. The two boys were crowned by wavy chestnut locks. They all used their hands while talking, delicate and expressive. It is an everlasting wonder to me how some Italian parents produce such lovely children. You will see them all walking out together in the evening, for the family tie is strong here, young Dianas and Marios, linked up with bald, swarthy Bacchuses and ample Junos. Is there any exact age at which this transformation from slender beauty to rotund flaccidity takes

---

* In 1876 Robert Browning published a book of poems called *Pacchiarotto and How He Worked in Distemper*. Pacchiarotto was a Sienese painter born in 1474. He was an insignificant painter and reformer who worked with Pacchia and Sodoma in a studio in the old Oratory of San Bernardino. When Browning's book was published a lady sent him some money on behalf of Pacchiarotto, distressed that a poor dog should have to work in distemper!

Italian workmen still wear paper caps, made out of newspapers. I saw two working on the Vatican palace. Was it with malice aforethought that they made them out of the local Communist newspaper ? When Madame Récamier called on Canova in his Roman studio, " he came out immediately, holding his paper cap in his hand, and, bowing gracefully, invited me in."

place, or is there a gradual decline? At forty Diana and Mario
will have completely vanished.

I looked and listened while the three youngsters chattered in
their rapid Italian, from which I drew some sense. They were
hilarious about an aunt who always went to bed at ten, and would
powder ' *povero* Toto.' Who was poor Toto—a baby, or, perish
the thought, a small boy home from school? Curiosity conquered manners. I had to ask them. They looked at me
with lustrous eyes, surprised and serious in a moment, then
rippled with laughter. Toto was a naughty poodle (*cane Maltese*)
who escaped and got ' things ' (*degli abitanti*). I stood lost in
wonder at their beautiful young faces, their eyes and teeth and
eyelashes, speculating why a poodle should be, in Italian, a
Maltese dog, since I always thought its origin was French, and
what kind of a Zia they had, who went to bed at such an unnatural hour for an Italian, and who possessed a poodle with
abitanti.   And so it was that I missed the traffic lights ; and
winsome beauty was lost in the crowd.*

It was so hot to-day that I gave up the gallery excursion, sat at
a sidewalk café and let the morning drift away. On my way home
I saw a woman coming out of a restaurant. She was about
sixty, wretchedly poor, with limbs dreadfully swollen with dropsy.
She carried a canvas bag and was obviously begging food, as
so often here. Rome to-day is the gayest and richest capital in
Europe, oozing with vitality. With all this there is a shocking
disparity in human conditions, the flamboyant rich and the distressed poor cheek by jowl. It is not so blatant as in Spain,
but it exists. There is a district here in Rome called Hell's
Kitchen where thousands live in a state of unbelievable destitution,
in crowded hovels and insanitary tenements. They are without
work or any apparent social care, subsisting on minute State
allowances. The Italians are a kind people much given to
carita but they seem to have little organised social conscience.
The country seems indifferent to the menace to its security implied
by these breeding grounds of Communism. Centuries of Christianity have scarcely touched the evils of destitution in the
shadow of vast palaces and churches. What was this poor
creature doing, ambling around in pain, with a begging bag?

* It may be that the poodle took its name from Italy's most famous comedian,
Signor Toto who, in 1951, after a process in the courts, became His Imperial Highness
Prince Toto, having proved his descent from one of the Emperors of Byzantium.

Had she no one to look after her, were there no social services to give her food, rest, medical attention? Day after day I see such human wrecks in this centre of Christianity. She was a quiet-spoken woman, clean but with all the spirit beaten out of her. Side by side with this the industrialists are making great sums of money. At Monte Carlo last January all the high gambling in the Casino was by Turin, Milan and Genoa industrialists. They gave large dinner parties, they arrived in the latest American automobiles, women wore the costliest furs. It is known that millions of dollars poured into Italy under the Marshall Plan have been utilised for purposes not wholly useful to the depressed classes. The American representative of the Marshall Plan made a spirited protest, and although everything possible was done to make him retract his words, the truth of his charge remained. A gigantic and ostentatious new railway station in Rome has been built, costing £17,000,000, covering fifty acres, the finest in Europe, for a railway on which two-thirds of the passengers travel with concessions. Luxuriously re-conditioned hotels, fleets of new motor charabancs, and thousands of new automobiles, these and many other things make one realise why the social services are gravely inadequate. Yesterday the American representative of the Marshall Plan gave the Italian Government a second shock in a candid speech. He adversely criticised its financial policy. He accused the industrialists of gross profiteering, saying he could count on the fingers of his hands the firms who practised the principles of low cost and high production. Why was a metre of cotton or woollen material sold at five times its cost, why did a pair of shoes reach the consumer with 500 per cent added? Paying a tribute to Italian skill and pleasure in individual accomplishment, he asked the industrialists why, by failing to put their house in order, " they were letting leadership by default slip into the willing hands of Joseph Stalin ? "

October 18.

Two years ago a Florentine friend of mine gave me a letter of introduction to two members of the Torrigiani family settled in Rome. They were two sisters. One of them practised as a lawyer, the other was in a decorating business. Calling on them I found myself at once among friends for my books had preceded me. The younger sister, the pretty Princess Waltha Torrigiani

has married since that first call. Thus to-day I found myself
having tea with the newlyweds, Count and Countess Secco
Suardi. A more enchanting nest for domestic happiness I have
seldom seen. About a year ago I was in the Palazzo Altieri,
a vast seventeenth-century palace built around two courtyards,
off the Piazza di Jesú. On the grand staircase stands an astonishing piece of sculpture, a solitary thumb, four-foot high, a relic of
some god's statue. It also holds the bust of a Roman grammarian. The Altieri still inhabit part of this enormous palace.
They claim descent from a family established in Rome in the time
of Constantine. One descendant was the Pope Clement X.
When he was elected Pope, after a Conclave in 1670 that lasted
four months, he was eighty years of age and so terrified that he
burst into tears when the Cardinals came to escort him from his
cell. He begged to be allowed to die in peace. The old Pope
lived six more years. He enlarged his family palace and during
this process a fiery old lady refused to concede a small corner
building on the site. The powerful Pope had to be content with
incorporating the little house, still intact on the corner.

The Altieri always lived in great state, and early in the nineteenth-century the Romans used to see a state carriage, complete
with standing footmen in livery, come out of the courtyard for
the sole purpose of carrying the proud Princess to Mass at the
great Jesuit church not fifty yards distant across the road. There
was in the same century a Prince Altieri who was a great Lothario
and had a very large family. One day he admired a small
baby playing in one of the courtyards and asked a woman
in charge whose child it was. " Your Highness's," came the
answer.

When I was there last year, investigating its history, I saw
builders adding a new floor, high up on the skyline, and marvelled
that anyone should add to a palace that seemed to have hundreds
of rooms. To-day, when I arrived to have tea with my young
friends, I found it was they who had established themselves there,
stork-like. What a position ! Their apartment has a roof terrace that must offer one of the finest panoramas of Rome. They
are in the dead centre of the city and from their height survey
all its great monuments, St. Peter's, the Castle of St. Angelo, the
Quirinal, the Pantheon, the inevitable Victor Emmanuele
monument, the Campidoglio, the Villa Medici backed by the
Villa Borghese, the long green crest of the Janiculum, with the

great Garibaldi monument of the old redshirt on a horse, and the innumerable cupolas, belfries, towers and spires of the Roman churches. From this eyrie one looks down on the only Roman temple intact from pagan days, the Pantheon with its splendid dome, which from here is like a squat tortoise.

There was a gay company for tea, my hostess's mother, the beautiful Princess Torrigiani, an Australian by birth, the octagenarian Princess Boncompagni-Ludovisi, Austrian-born and full of zest, and a daughter of Prince Massimo. Here again I crossed some old trails. " Are you," I asked, " any relation of the young Prince Massimo who on March 28th, 1896, played the violin so marvellously ? " " Yes," she replied, surprised, " He was my father. He played on an Amati he owned. But how do you know ? " I laughed. " Well, an old English lady, Miss Lucas, kept a diary of the last half century in Rome where she lived with her sister from 1862. I have read it. One day she visited a palazzo where ' the young Prince, a pretty, gentle-looking creature, the grandson of the Duchesse de Berri,' astonished them with his playing." " My family has always been very musical," said the Princess. " Then that accounts for my curious experience," I said. " I was examining the courtyard of the Palazzo Massimo one day last year and was surprised to find a sheet of music that must have fallen from somewhere. It had the music and English words of *The Last Rose of Summer*, and *What Are The Wild Waves Saying ?* on either side. It seemed to me a very odd thing to find in a Roman courtyard ! "

The Massimo line has an even longer descent than the Altieri. It claims descent from Maximus Quintus Fabius 233 B.C., called the *Cunctator*, the Delayer. It was at first an abusive title because he steadily retreated before Hannibal, but in that way he wore down the foe, ' *unus homo nobis cunctando restituit rem*,' and saved Rome from the Carthaginian invaders. The present palace was constructed on the site of the houses of the Massimo destroyed by the Bourbon troops in the sack of Rome, 1527. Because of the columns used, taken from a Roman temple, it was called the Palazzo Massimo delle Colonne.

" Haven't you seen the interior ? " asked Princess Massimo. " No." I answered. " Then you must let me show you it. You know, we have a chapel, the room in which St. Philip Neri resurrected Paolo Massimo, aged fifteen, on March 16th, 1584.

Every year on the anniversary it is open to the public. You must come and see it." So I have another excursion in store.

I once wrote a novel about Hungary, *They Wanted to Live*, which was translated into Magyar, one of the most difficult languages in the world. My copy, published in Budapest at the beginning of the Communist régime, was brought to me by a refugee professor. I remarked on the difficulty of the language. Apropos of this, Princess Boncompagni, who has lost her estates in Hungary where she once spent much time, told me what an astonishing linguist the present Pope is. He speaks French, English, German, Spanish, Polish, Russian, Dutch, Greek, Latin and some Chinese. When a nuncio he went to preach in the cathedral at Budapest. Everyone expected he would do so in Italian or French. He astonished the congregation by addressing them in Magyar.

During a conversation with a Polish lady, who seemed to know my books better than I did and embarrassed me by questions about forgotten characters, I tried hard not to let my attention wander. Over the mantelpiece was one of the most beautiful paintings I had ever seen. I kept looking at it, puzzled. It was not one picture but a changing series, each more remarkable than the other. Now it was a crimson sunset against which the great dome of S. Andrea della Valle, and the still greater dome of St. Peter's, stood in black relief. Now the pine-trees along the crest of the Janiculum were silhouetted against the lemon horizon. Now the domes, towers and campaniles and roofs of all Rome took fire, the crimson sunset changed to rose, to purple and finally glimmered faintly in the oncoming darkness. My eyes followed this incredible portfolio of pictures, history in the crucible of the evanescent evening, while my ears strove to pay attention to the conversation. Then the mystery was solved. Into the chimney over the mantelpiece my ingenious young hostess had cut an oblong aperture, enclosing the glass in a white frame. Through this window on Rome she had provided an interior decoration that incorporated two thousand years of history and Nature's miracles of dawn, noon, sunset and night.

October 21.

Soon after nine o'clock this morning I was out walking in the Villa Borghese. The air was fresh, the sky a clear blue. I passed down 'The Avenue of Orange Trees' that led to the small lake. There was an artificial temple to Æsculapius, and a café with a classical façade, whose little tables, set out under trees, faced the terrace of a rose garden. I wondered if anywhere in the world there was a more enchanting scene ; and so, on what seemed a perfect summer's morning, I reached my destination, the British School in the Valle Giulia, a large classical building set on an eminence. Here are housed and boarded some twenty British students of sculpture, painting and architecture. What a marvellous world a lad, by gaining a scholarship, finds himself transported to ! All Rome and the riches of centuries are his playground.

I was amused how we revert to type. Ward Perkins, the Director of the British School, instead of being annoyed at my impromptu call—I wanted data for my new novel, *A Terrace in the Sun*, in which the hero goes to Rome on a British Academy scholarship—immediately invited me into his large study where he was dictating to his secretary. Within half an hour a pretty young cousin had brought in morning tea. Ten minutes later, Mrs. Ward Perkins, her husband and I, with baby and cat, might have composed a family scene anywhere in South Kensington, except for the brilliant October sunshine and the umbrella-pines and cypresses outside under a Fra Lippo Lippi sky.

A remark on Michelangelo led to a statement that almost bounced me out of my chair. Goethe, living in the Corso opposite the Palazzo Rondanini, stated that in its courtyard there was a massive Pietà carved by Michelangelo and left unfinished owing to his death. The *Guida d'Italia* (1925), my inseparable companion, confirmed this fact, but on going to the palace, now the Palazzo Sanseverino, I found it was not there, and no one knew where it was. It seemed preposterous that a Michelangelo work weighing a ton could disappear, but it had gone. And now I learned from Perkins that it is housed in the private villa of the Sanseverini family on the outskirts of Rome. He will take me to see it in a few days.

At six o'clock this evening the sunset from my balcony was so glorious that I broke off work and went up on to the roof garden. Against the western sky, changing from rose pink to deep vermilion, rose the silhouettes of the twin domes of the Trinità dei Monti, and between them, far off and immense, the dome of St. Peter's. Four cypresses in the garden below were like blots of ink on the crimson picture before me. Then, with swiftly falling darkness, and a thousand twinkling lights on the hills and in the valley, I went back to a different scene, a chapter in my novel describing the grimness of the English mining district in which I had placed my hero, with a resolution to bring the young artist somehow to Rome.

Things Observed.

In the Via Margutta I saw two cats sharing with a duck a meal of chicken bones. When the duck wanted a particular bone he bit the hind leg of one of the cats. The provider of this meal shooed off the duck, who waddled across the road, waited, and then came back again and pushed away the two cats. There is no water anywhere near. I suspect the duck lives in a studio.

October 23.

This afternoon it began to rain, the first I have seen in three weeks. At four-thirty the Pope appeared on the balcony at St. Peter's to bless the pilgrims. " *Papa porta pioggia,*" (the Pope brings rain), Romans say of these appearances, and to-day's rain bears them out. As I came out of the Palazzo Venezia, from an exhibition of works of art stolen by Hitler and Goering, I saw one of the scarlet-clad priestlings from the German seminary leading a crowd of pilgrims, stout, square-headed, across the Piazza Venezia. I vainly hoped he would turn aside and take them into this exhibition of loot recovered from the apostles of Kultur.

With my companion this morning I spent two hours full of interest in the church of the Ara Coeli on the Capitol. Group after group came tramping in, perspiring, breathless and reverently ecstatic. The German and Austrian groups always broke into choral singing before the high altar. The great attraction was the Holy Bambino, a wooden doll eighteen inches high, swathed in jewels and gold trinkets. It has legendary fame as a miracle worker and is credited with healing sick persons to whom it is carried. It is exhibited only once a year, in the Christmas Crib, when tiny children mount a public platform and declaim a set sermon piece before their proud parents.

This year all the holy relics are on view for pilgrims. We followed the crowd into a small room. The Bambino, glistening with gold and jewels, stood upright in an illuminated glass case. When the small room was full to suffocation a pallid young monk

I

turned a lever and the Bambino slid forward from its recess, with a collection plate in front on which lay a few suggestive lire. The company gazed in silent wonder on this gaudy doll. " Circulatio! Circulatio! " cried the monk. The pilgrims began to circulate, kissing the stand of the Bambino and dropping tribute on the plate. My friend and I escaped the smell of hot peasant bodies compressed into this chamber. It was not our idea of the odour of sanctity.

When we reached the foot of the flight of one hundred and twenty-four steps, built by the grateful Romans who had survived the plague of 1348, (Rienzi laid the first step), pilgrims were still toiling up them. One stout mother picked up a tired infant in either arm and marched steadily up the flight in the hot sun. I marvelled at such maternal fortitude. It occurred to me that if of necessity I had to earn a living a stall set up here with packets of foot powder would do a roaring trade.

October 24.

Yesterday evening at Prince Alessandro Torlonia's. His palace is just off the Via Condotti, in the Bocca di Leone, in the old part of Rome. It is the street in which the Brownings took an apartment, No. 33, for the winter when the poet was collecting data for *The Ring and the Book*. The Palazzo Torlonia has a beautiful interior court, with a grotto and fountain and a terraced façade in which stands a classical figure, spot-lighted at night, amid overhanging ferns ; all this to a tinkle of falling water. When I went up the grand staircase last year all the reception rooms were lit up and a great crowd of Roman society was flocking up to attend a reception in honour of pretty young Princess Margaret of England, then paying her first visit to Italy. The crush was so great that one could not see the splendid pictures and tapestries in the successive salons. This evening we were *en famille*. Oddly enough, I saw my first domestic fire in Rome. It had been raining all day and when I was shown into one of the salons there was a friendly fire blazing in the grate. Princess Torlonia (the Infanta Beatrice of Spain), is the daughter of the late King Alfonso and an English mother, the ex-Queen Victoria Ena of Battenberg. She was just over nineteen when the Spanish Royal family went into exile. When I was in the royal mortuary chapel of the kings of Spain at the Escorial last March I was shown an empty shelf and told it was reserved for King

Alfonso. He died in Rome, at the Grand Hotel, in 1941, and his body is awaiting the day when he can return and lie among his ancestors.

Prince Torlonia is tall and boyish in manner. When he heard that I had been recently in Spain he began to describe with much vivacity a visit he and his wife had made there two months ago, in August. The heat of Madrid is terrific in this month and everyone is away. They went quite unofficially, and it was the first return of the Infanta after some nineteen years of absence. " I wish I had your gift and could properly describe it," said the Prince. " It was the most wonderful and moving thing you ever saw. You see, we were there unofficially, the Government never showed a hand and we thought we were quietly getting away with it. Then, the day after we arrived, we were invited to the bull-fight. We were in a box high up in the arena. As soon as we entered it the crowd spotted my wife. God knows how they knew her for they hadn't seen her since she was a girl. They began to applaud and shout, and finally she had to stand up and wave to them. They gave her a terrific welcome—I had a lump in my throat, it was something ! Then, finally, they all sat down on their seats again, the toreadors' procession came into the ring and the first bull was released. They dedicated it to the President of the Toros, another to a Grandee. When the third bull fight came in the toreador marched up to our box and dedicated the bull to Beatrice, and, as the custom is, he took off his black hat and it was passed up to her, tier by tier."

" That paralysed me," interrupted Princess Torlonia, " for I knew I was expected to throw it down again into the arena, in acknowledgement of the dedication. The arena was a terrible way off ! "

" There was an old Grandee in the box who used to play tennis with my wife," continued the Prince, " and he remembered that she had a strong backhand stroke. " Give it a backhand ! " he said. So she threw it vigorously, backhand. It was simply marvellous. It skimmed through the air and landed on the arena right in front of the toreador. The whole place went mad. There must have been twenty thousand and they all rose to their feet and cheered and cheered. We thought the show would never go on. The next day the Golf Club gave a lunch for us. Everybody was supposed to be away but somehow everybody was there, the place was packed. It was the same everywhere. After four days the authorities got frightened and told us we must leave Spain. So we went up to Irun to cross the frontier. And that was the most moving thing of all. As our car went out of the town to the frontier the whole way was lined with people, thousands of them, waving ' Goodbye ! ' and shouting ' Come back ! ' But at the very frontier there was a dead silence, almost like a funeral, as we passed over. We'd such a lump in our throats at that tribute that we could not speak."

When he had finished the Princess looked at me and said, quietly, " To think they should remember me after all those years ! "

Perhaps one day the dead king will go back and his successor to the Spanish throne will walk in the solemn procession that takes the exiled monarch to lie with his forefathers in the cold Escorial.

October 26.

This morning I went to the church of S. Maria del Popolo, taking with me an umbrella and a binder with two hundred typed sheets of the second volume of *And So To Rome.* It is my custom to check my manuscript on the spot, before setting up in type what I have written, and to make supplementary notes or corrections. For three weeks I have been hard at work doing this. On arriving at the church, one of singular beauty and history, a wedding was in progress. The bridal party was at the altar, and in the seemingly casual manner of these ceremonies, visitors were strolling about the church. I was amused to see a black and white cat sitting near the bridal couple, in front of the altar-rails. I arrived just at the moment of the priest's solemn words of union. A few minute's later Handel's *Largo* and Schubert's *Ave Maria* preceded the Mass. I was working in the Chigi chapel when, to the strains of Mendelssohn's *Wedding March*, the young couple came down the nave. It is the custom for them to halt by the door and receive congratulations. The bride was not kissed by her male friends but the bridegroom was ! I thought again what a wonderful church this is. Here Luther had arrived in ecstasy on his first visit to Rome, had heard his first Mass and had prostrated himself crying " Hail ! Holy Rome ! sacred by the blood of the martyrs ! '' He was in a mood very different from that of his departure, when he shook its dust off his feet, anathema in his heart. I thought of another wedding here.

In the fifteenth century had come the young bride, Lucrezia Borgia. Her first husband had been Giovanni Sforza. He had been put aside by annulment, non-consummation alleged. Her second husband, by whom she had a son, had been murdered in his bed at the instigation of her brother, Cesare. Now she was marrying by proxy Alfonso d'Este, son of the Duke of Ferrara. When she came out of the church a great cavalcade led by her brother escorted her to the Castle St. Angelo where her father, the Pope, gave her a riotous banquet. She departed later, escorted by a mounted cavalcade, for the court at Ferrara where the bridegroom impatiently awaited her. She bore a certificate signed by the Pope affirming that she was a virgin ! To this church the body of her brother, the Duke of Gandia, was brought for interment. He had been murdered by his brother, Cesare Borgia, Duke of Valentinois. Now, when this morning's bridal couple emerged on to the steps of the church, there were automobiles and taxis waiting where once there had been gaily caparisoned horses and men in armour.

I have cause for remembering this modern wedding. After the spectators had gone, and before a horde of pilgrims had arrived, I went over to a side chapel to search for a memorial to Andreas Bregno, the sculptor. I left on the altar-rail an umbrella and my typed manuscript, open where I had made notes. When I returned five minutes later the umbrella and the manuscript had gone. The latter can have no possible value for a thief and I have a duplicate in England, but I have lost all my notes and corrections, three weeks' hard work in Rome, and I cannot now work on my book until I get the duplicate sent out to me. " Rome is full of thieves, they come for the Anno Santo," said the sacristan, despairingly. So they, too, are *pellegrini* !

October 27.

All is well. And how profitable is a little kindness ! Yesterday in the church I was asked a question by a young Jugoslav woman and friend, about one of the figures in the Chigi chapel. It was an opportunity to air my knowledge. They had been present when my loss was discovered and the two young women kindly joined me in a vain search. Yesterday afternoon while I took a siesta, the concierge in my hotel telephoned up to say a young lady wanted to see me. Wondering who this could be, I went down and found the young Jugoslav woman. She had been so distressed by my loss that she had gone back to the church two hours later, whereupon the sacristan informed her that the manuscript and the umbrella had been returned. One of a band of Austrian pilgrims when leaving the church had seen the articles on the altar-rail and, thinking they had been forgotten by one of her party, she had picked them up. At her hotel she was distressed to find no one owned them. She took them back at once to the church. I thanked the young woman and was touched to find that although she had been in Rome only one day and was leaving in three days, to travel to Venezuela, to which she was emigrating, she had sacrificed much of her precious time to assist me. I feel chastened for my hasty judgment.

October 28.

The mail has come in. For some time an Australian reader of my books has kindly sent me food parcels. Last June this lady came to Europe and although over seventy years of age she rode for three months all over France, Belgium and Great Britain, in motor buses. She much wished to see Pilgrim Cottage and I arranged a visit. We had tea under the apple-tree. To-day comes a letter from Australia. She lost her only son in the war and, a widow, turned her large house into a successful catering hostel.

"You might like to know of my safe arrival after a most wonderful journey. I only wish I had a few years longer to reflect on the wonders and beauty of this world. I am thankful that if I could not see it at seventeen I have been able to see a lot at seventy, on a Magic Carpet for the last nine months. Perhaps, also, you might be pleased to know that the high-light of my trip was meeting you and receiving your autograph in my copy of *And So To Rome.* . . . I am hoping to visit Europe again and I will then look forward to seeing the Italy you have described in this wonderful book. I know I, too, have seen such a lot yet so little compared with all there is to see, but better a little than none at all. I feel that when I sell my business I must give a donation to the blind as a thanksgiving for the blessing of good sight and the means of using it to such advantage. It is a very nice feeling to know we belong to England and England belongs to us. I should hate to think that that connection will ever be severed. Before saying good-bye I would like to thank you for the very sweet reception you gave me when visiting Pilgrim Cottage."

I spent three hours this morning in the Villa Borghese Gallery checking my Rome manuscript. In one room a thickset middle-aged man, seeing me reading a book in front of Bernini's *David*, asked, in German, if he could buy a German guidebook. He looked rather rough and I was a little surprised at his keen interest in some of the exhibits. " *Wunderbar! Wunderbar!* " he kept murmuring, as I informed him of their history. I learned a little about him. He was a farmer who, with his wife and three children, had escaped from the Russian zone of East Prussia. " All Germany will go up in flames again," he said. His desire is to emigrate to the New World. After much effort he has got as far as Rome where he is now in a state of despair. Canada, his first choice, will not give him a visa, the United States will not give him a visa, nor the Argentine, nor Brazil, Australia, New Zealand, South Africa. He wants to work to produce food, and the world wants food and its empty places cultivated. And here he is, his money running out, while every day the U.N.O. and the politicians pay lip service to freedom, equality, opportunity and the new world they claim to be making. I thought, as he told me his story, of a young Italian-American I had met some years ago in Mrs. Murray Crane's New York salon, who told me he was a composer of music. His name was Giancarlo Menotti. In his opera, *The Consul*, he has exposed far more poignantly than anyone else, the personal tragedy of the exile driven from place to place and refused a home by bureaucracy.

A few days ago I was stopped in the street by a respectable middle-aged woman who asked me the way, and whether I was an American. I think this was only an excuse to try to sell me some poor little medallions she had in a box. She spoke in bad English, then French, then Italian, until we found a *lingua franca* in German. When she found I had a little Magyar and had been in Budapest her face lit up. She was a refugee from Hungary, with a daughter, and was endeavouring to get to Brazil. She was frustrated by her inability to get visas. She showed me a photograph of her daughter, a beautiful girl of twenty, who was earning a few *lire* by acting as a nursemaid in an Italian family. She was the widow of a Hungarian advocate, with a brother-in-law in Sao Paulo. She looked worn, and I gave her some money, refusing her small medallions. As I walked to the Grand Hotel to dine with my friend I felt very grateful for my lot. A failure in the English sky of that ' so few,' in the Battle of Britain, and I might now be in a similar plight.

It was odd that on arriving at the Grand Hotel the first person I met in my friend's room was vivacious Mary Powers, who has had such a remarkable success in Menotti's *The Medium* in New York. It is now being filmed in Rome and she is playing her famous role.

October 29.

It has been a great pleasure to encounter in Rome my friend Professor Edgar Wind. Formerly with the Hamburg Art Gallery, then with the Courtauld Library in London, he went to U.S.A. about 1944. He gave some lectures on Raphael and Botticelli at Mrs. Murray Crane's evenings and hypnotised the whole company by his lucid interpretation and erudition. He now holds the chair of Philosophy and Art at Smith College, and at present is enjoying a Sabbatical Year here. He dined with me last week, and to-day invited me to join him and his wife at the *Tre Scalini* in the Piazza Navona. What a place to lunch in !—the vast rectangular piazza with Bernini's great fountain in the centre. In the eighteenth century they used to flood this piazza and hold water fêtes in it.

Although now the end of October, we dined outside at the tables spread over the pavement.

I never have a conversation with Edgar Wind without getting into a state of intellectual intoxication. Between us, we travel down the strangest alleys. He told me to-day there was a legend that the Ark had settled on the Janiculum. A Dominican monk in the eighteenth century had started it by claiming to have found manuscripts (*Liber Antiquitatum*) in which was propounded the theory that Noah was, in Hebrew, *Jajin*, wine-bibber. From Jajin came the Roman *Janus*, the two-faced god, which supported the legend that Noah faced both ways, looking before the Flood, and after the Flood !

During our lunch we were greatly interested by a table at which sat two very stout elderly women, of the prosperous peasant type, and by an adjoining table at which sat fourteen boys and one girl, ranging from sixteen years to four. The smallest boy fell backwards off his chair, with a frightful bang on his head. His mouth opened wide and I expected a terrific howl, but not

a sound came forth. Four other children rushed to pet him and
the incident passed in silence. It is singular that in Italy one
seldom hears a child cry ; possibly they do not attempt to compete
with the general noise of an Italian family. The mystery of these
fifteen children, black-headed, white-headed and blond, in some
manner related to the two fat matrons, was solved later. There
was a large wedding party indoors and all the children had been
seated at one table outside, with two grandmothers to watch
at a distance !

When I left the Winds I walked to the Spanish church, St.
Mary of Montserrat, where ex-King Alfonso lay, awaiting transfer
to the royal crypt in the Escorial. A Spanish priest conducted
me round the church, built by Sangallo in 1495 for the Spaniards
from Aragona and Catalonia, at a time when there was a large
Spanish colony gathered in Rome and around the Borgia Pope.
I was shown the tomb of the king. It carries a simple inscription
" Su Majesta El Rey Don Alfonso XIII. 1886-1941." Two men
were decorating the tomb with pink and white carnations. I
learned that this was the sister church of the Abbey of Montserrat
near Barcelona, which I visited earlier this year, and that a
procession of Spanish pilgrims to the Holy Year was expected
in a few minutes. Above the tomb of King Alfonso there was
another tomb with the heads in relief of Pope Callisto III and
Alessandro VI, two Borgia Popes. The sculptor had muddled
the design by placing on the coat of arms of Alessandro, the
Callisto bull and on the Callisto arms the bull of Alessandro's.
The bones of these Popes had had quite an adventure before
they were placed here, in one tomb, in 1889. They were brought
in 1610, by night from St. Peter's, to save them from the Roman
mob whom they had oppressed. They remained neglected and
unmarked for over two hundred and fifty years.

I was leaving the church when the Spanish pilgrims arrived,
with a Cardinal, accompanied by the Abbot of Montserrat,
who was astonished to find me here, our last meeting having
been in the private room of the Governor of Catalonia in Barcelona. All roads do indeed lead to Rome.

As I went homewards I found a great crowd outside the vast
church of S. Andrea della Valle. Entering, I found Spanish
pilgrims *en masse*, with boy scouts from Barcelona. A service
was being celebrated at the high altar. I got into conversation
with some Spaniards who were delighted when they heard I

I*

had been in Barcelona. After a while I told them the reason of my visit and when I gave my name there was an immediate shout. " But we know you ! We heard you on Radio Madrid ! Vicki Baum, Somset Mogum (Somerset Maugham), Cecil Roberts. We read all your books ! "

The conjunction of names is delightful. Before I could do anything about it I found myself holding a reception in a side chapel. Fearing this diversion might bring down the censure of the authorities I contrived to slip away. It is very odd to find one is living a sort of double life, inside and outside libraries and bookshops.

October 30.

I went up again to the Ara Coeli church to-day and found that they were preparing for a great ceremony to-morrow when they will carry an image of the Black Madonna, brought here, from the Lateran, to St. Peter's. I sat and watched the pilgrims, ninety per cent peasants, almost wholly women. After the Holy Child, swaddled in jewels, the next favourite sight is a ghastly model of a skelton lying in a habit, illuminated, under the altar of a side chapel. It is exposed in order to collect funds in support of the beatification of a certain missionary to China, here represented. Obtaining a beatification is not solely a matter of ' works ' but also of cash, judging from the number of collection boxes I have seen before portraits and effigies of candidates.

The tomb of St. Helena apart, I was much interested by a novel map, in coloured marble (*pietra dura*), of a part of Abyssinia and the Gulf of Aden, put up as a memorial to an Italian explorer, Prince Eugenio Ruspoli, who was killed by an infuriated elephant in 1893, aged 27. A nephew went there later and found the bones. Soon after my visit to the church I was lunching with a friend and found that a fellow guest was a Princess Ruspoli. I told her about the memorial I had seen and asked if the explorer was any relation. " Oh yes," she replied, " my late husband was the nephew who went through the forest on the border of Abyssinia and found his uncle's bones, in 1928." I then learned that he, in turn, was killed in the battle of El Alamein. His body was lost in the desert and never found.

October 31.

An amusing episode at the traffic crossroads as I went down the hill this morning. A young policeman stands on a dais directing the traffic. He waves his arms with so much energy that he looks as if he were conducting an orchestra. As I passed under this human windmill I said—" *Signore, lei è il Toscanini delle strade !* " (You are the Toscanini of the streets.) He was delighted and gave me a flashing smile and salute.

This evening at six o'clock there was a tremendous procession carrying the image of the Madonna down the steps from the Ara Coeli church, then across the Piazza Venezia and down the Corso Vittorio Emanuele towards the Ponte St. Angelo and St. Peter's. There were two cardinals in crimson with forty-foot trains held up by pages, over a hundred bishops wearing white mitres, plumed Papal knights of various orders, cowled and barefooted monks, nuns, in all a procession a mile long with lanterns and lit candles, wending its way between dense crowds in the Roman dusk. All the way down the wide Via Conciliazione, which now offers a superb view from the Castle St. Angelo to St. Peter's, there were moving lights and chanting priests, while from the high balconies of the palaces bordering the avenue hung rich damasks and flags. Above these were placed lit candles. One of the palaces, the Torlonia-Giraud, had once been Cardinal Wolsey's English Embassy, and it was in its garden that a Cardinal gave the famous dinner party at which it was alleged that the Borgia Pope had been poisoned.

November 2.

Yesterday was the great day of the *Anno Santo*. Taught by experience I declined a ticket for the ceremony inside the basilica of the Dogma of the Assumption of the Virgin Mary. One has to be in one's place at seven o'clock in the morning and wait several hours for the papal procession which passes in a few minutes. Thereafter one is a prisoner until the close of the long ceremony. I decided, therefore, to take my chance of seeing the ceremony outside St. Peter's, where the Dogma was to be pronounced by the Pope from the steps of the basilica, before proceeding to the service within. I was warned that I could not possibly get into the great piazza of St. Peter's as there would be quite half a million spectators there and dense crowds would block the approaches, unless I went about five a.m. and took up

a position for the ceremony due to begin at nine o'clock. But I
have learned to take no notice of such gloomy forecasts. I arrived
in the piazza shortly after eight o'clock. To my surprise I was
able, although the great space enclosed by Bernini's colonnade
was full, to weave my way slowly to a position near the great
obelisk in the centre of the piazza, facing the façade of St. Peter's.

The Roman crowd is very good-natured and there was at no
time, despite the immense throng, any pushing or exhibition of
ill-temper. It was the demeanour of a populace on holiday.
The weather was superb. The sky was a cloudless blue and the
risen sun shone resplendently behind us, directly upon the broad
steps and the wide front of St. Peter's. In the very middle stood
the canopied throne of the Pope.

People had been collecting since sunrise and now at eight
o'clock the vast piazza was full, as also all the vantage points on the
roofs of the basilica, the colonnades and the Vatican building.
The time of waiting was filled in by the continuous chanting of
a litany for over one hundred saints, the dirge, for such it seemed,
being pronounced through the amplifiers in the windows of St.
Peter's. Again and again this monotonous litany was chanted,
with its responses, until it seemed like a gramophone disc repeating
itself. Shortly before nine o'clock a long procession began to
wind its way up the steps, between the dense crowd, to reserved
places on either side of the scarlet throne. It was escorted by the
papal Swiss Guards in their full-dress uniform, with plumed
helmets, cuirasses and halberds, all gleaming in the sun. The
procession seemed interminable and heightened the expectant
mood of the crowd. It came out from the bronze doors of the
Vatican, the whole impressive hierarchy of the Church, arch-
bishops, bishops, abbots, cardinals, monsignores, some three
hundred of them. Then came a great cry " *Viva Papa !* " as
the chair, the *Sedia Gestatoria*, borne high, with the Pope on it,
was seen, swaying on the shoulders of his attendants. He leaned
forward making the sign of blessing with infinite grace as the long
colourful cortège passed through the cheering crowd and turned
slowly, ascending the great flight of steps to the throne. Some
three hundred bishops had gone before, now another three
hundred brought up the rear, all of them attired in white
mitres and copes, so that a great white wave seemed to launch
itself against the façade of the basilica and made shining breakers
on either side of the papal throne. The Pope, having dismounted

from the gestatorial chair, took his seat on the throne.   The Sistine
choir now sang the *Maria Assumpta* and other sacred music.   The
ceremony, in all its various phases, was announced to the crowd
in six languages and at the recital of the prayers the people made
responses from small books that had been distributed to this great
multitude of pilgrims from all nations.   There came the moment
for the promulgation of the Dogma of the Assumption, the great
event of the Holy Year, with the Pope standing, his arms uplifted
in the sunshine, while he pronounced the Latin formula.   There
followed an address, spoken with his beautiful clear diction, in
Italian, and the multitude joined him in a concluding prayer.
Cries of " *Viva il Papa ! Viva Maria !* " filled the air.   Suddenly
a flight of five hundred doves was released from the colonnades.
It wheeled shining in the sun before disappearing into the
distance.

The Pope and the great concourse of ecclesiastics now entered
St. Peter's where a pontifical mass was sung, in Latin and Greek,
which lasted three hours and was broadcast.   Meanwhile the
crowd in the piazza began to move.   The warm sun sent them
seeking the shade.   Many pilgrims, tired out after a long vigil,
emotionally and physically exhausted, relaxed on portable camp
chairs, or stretched themselves out on rugs over the stones.

It was now, while awaiting the Pope's return at one o'clock,
and his entry back into the Vatican palace, that one could study
the amazing variety of this crowd.   There were pilgrims from
every part of the world, led usually by their own priests and
heralded by youths bearing aloft boards with the names of the
towns from which they had come.   I noticed one board with
the legend *Belley*, carried by a French contingent.   I got into
conversation with one youth.   He seemed utterly astonished
because I knew a little about Belley, which I have never seen.
" You are famous for a Mayor you once had—the most renowned
gourmet in the world," I said, " Brillat-Savarin.   He wrote *La
Physiologie du Goût* and you have a statue to him in the Grande
Place."

" *Mais oui ! Mais oui !* " exclaimed an excited group around
me.   " But *monsieur*," said a young man, " You are English, and
yet you know about Brillat-Savarin.   How is that ? "

I explained that, his book apart, I had once stayed in a house
in the United States where he had lived for some time when he
fled from the French Revolution, and that one Thanksgiving

Day, after dining on turkey, to which he found Americans strangely addicted, his host's two pretty daughters had sung to him their *chanson nationale*, " Yankee Duddee " as he called it. My French audience was greatly amused at this information about their fellow townsman, and when we parted there was a solemn handshaking all round, after which their priest led them off towards St. Peter's.

A much stranger sight met me a few moments later. There could be no possible doubt who they were. By their beards, their long hair, despite their modern clothes, they were the Twelve Apostles ! I picked out St. John very easily, the youngest and fairest. He had a Leica camera and was busily taking photographs. I got into conversation with him. I was quite right in my surmise. The apostles had arrived in four motor-cars from Oberammergau. They were the Passion Play actors from that famous village in Bavaria. I asked him to identify his fellow apostles. " That's Judas Iscariot—buying postcards," he said, " and St. Peter's sitting at the wheel of the car with St. Luke beside him. That's Matthew talking to the priest, with James on the right." Two of the Apostles were missing, they had gone to get a snack at a portable bar just beyond the colonnade. I asked St. John if he was enjoying Rome. " *Ja ! Ja ! Es ist sehr wunderschön !* " It was the first time that he had ever been away from his mountain village.

At night the whole city was lit with fairy lanterns. We went after dinner back to St. Peter's to see the illuminations. The great dome, the whole fabric of the basilica, the palace and the colonnades, were rimmed with thousands of little flare-pots that outlined the Vatican City with their glimmering lights.

November 8.

Yesterday morning I went out on to my balcony to take a farewell of Rome. It was a heavenly morning with a clear pale blue sky. The woods of the Villa Borghese below me were a brilliant green in the early sunshine. I had paid my bill and had packed. After breakfast I went out to the nearest wineshop and bought a large bottle of Brolio Chianti, vintage 1941, to take with me. In grey old England this bottled sunshine will remind me of our day at Baron Ricasoli's. Perhaps Aubrey and Simon will sit at my table and we shall grow reminiscent. It was ten o'clock, I wondered when I should see

Rome again. I have not this time thrown a coin into the Fountain of Trevi, which act assures the traveller's return, for I gave my only coin, rare in these days of paper money, to a young Austrian who wished to ensure his return. For myself, entering one's fifty-ninth year all returns are problematical. The Invisible Visitor touches one, and the endless journey is begun.

This city has given me so much joy that I always leave it with regret and gratitude. When Pope Pio VII was taken a prisoner by Napoleon's emissary there is a story that at dawn, just before his enforced departure, weeping, he stood in the piazza of the Quirinal and blessed the sleeping city below. This morning, taking my farewell, I, too, bestowed a benediction on it.

Our long train drew out of the splendid new station. Nearly all the passengers were returning pilgrims bound for Paris or London. I do not dislike a long journey in a wagon-lit. I can catch up with much of my reading. So fortified, with papers and books, I set out for Paris. But until the Roman Campagna, the Mediterranean coast, Pisa, with its campanile and duomo, and the Carrara mountains with their gleaming peaks were passed, I could not concentrate on reading. In the waning light we ran along the much tunnelled Ligurian coast, with vivid glimpses of the evening sea. Between Spezia and Sestri Levante these marine villages, deep in their rocky inlets, have no coastal road and are accessible only from the road that runs over the high Bracco Pass. Levanto is one of these hidden villages, a pleasant little resort with a sandy shore. Here, in 1922, I spent a whole hot summer's month convalescing.

As I passed through now I was rewarded, in the sunset light, with a brief glimpse of a promontory black against the sky, and could just discern the castle perched on it. It is a stronghold with ten-foot thick walls built to resist the Saracen raiders in the fifteenth and sixteenth centuries. When I was in Levanto it was derelict and for sale. I toyed with the idea of buying it and converting it for habitation owing to its superb position and picturesque nature. I could have bought it then for £200 but a small thing put me off. There lived in Levanto a derelict Englishman, a Mr. Smith, of sixty years or so. It seemed he had come there almost forty years before and had never had the courage or the desire to go away. I was an ambitious young man and Mr. Smith, passing by, seemed a timely warning. So I dropped the idea. Years later someone bought the castle and made a splendid home of it. The manner in which I learned this was singular. In 1922 an American family was living in Levanto. They had two sons, one of them a medical student in his first year at Edinburgh. He returned to Levanto for his summer vacation. He was an Apollo of twenty, a splendid swimmer with the Australian crawl stroke. He swept all the Italian girls off their feet. In 1948, I spent Christmas at the villa of Mrs. Aubrey Cartwright, at Palm Beach, Florida. It had a beautiful azure swimming-pool. One day half a dozen lunch guests were swimming in it and a middle-aged man, with his particular style of swimming, evoked a memory. As he came out of the pool I asked him if he had ever been in Italy. Yes. In Levanto? Yes. Did his people have a villa there in 1922? Yes. Was he, then, a medical student at Edinburgh? Yes, he said, greatly surprised by these questions. I gave him my name which he remembered at once, and he told me his. He was the Apollo of 1922, now married, a medical colonel in the U.S. Army! It was then that I learned about the fate of the castle at Levanto.

England

A dreadful Channel crossing yesterday. A tunnel would save all this misery and delay, with its frightful scramble of porters and herded passengers. At any time from 1918 to 1939 the two million British unemployed, miserably maintained and demoralised by the dole, at a cost of £200,000,000 a year, could have been used to make this tunnel, but vested interests and political ineptitude conspired to defeat this long overdue development. The absurd argument that it is perilous to our strategic defence can no longer be maintained in an age of planes and bombs.

Slept at my club. How closely these bedrooms are associated with my comings and goings. From the age of twenty-four onwards, they have spaced my life. They resist innovations. When I left England last summer they were at last fitting electric heaters in the rooms. Arriving this evening in cold grey England after a bitter crossing, I found shilling-in-the-slot meters installed, a singular expression of British individualism by which you heat one room at your own expense. But no electric fires were available.

I have been down to Pilgrim Cottage, my former haunt, where I found my tenant ecstatic about her bird-haunted domain. A perfect day with the woods all golden in the sunshine, autumn's majestic pall of death over the Chiltern Hills ; England's very special quality is to be seen in her spring and autumn. They have a richness and a gentleness in their prolonged entrance and exit to be found nowhere else. In the United States and in Italy spring jumps on you.

I called on an old friend who lives in the boathouse that figured in my novel *One Small Candle*. She still has Regatta parties, when relations from all over England converge on her and somehow she finds beds for that festive week-end. But in the winter she sits alone overlooking the melancholy sweep of the swollen river, with only a few swans faithful to the scene. To-day, from her balcony, I looked down on the silver river towards the Hambleden woods, and up the river beyond the Leander Club and the graceful old Henley bridge—surely one of the loveliest vistas of England in its late autumnal mood. There was a flash of wings over us and scurrying on the glassy river—seagulls that had come one hundred miles up the Thames from the sea, harbingers, they say, of a cold winter.

I went to see what progress had been made with two Elizabethan cottages I saved by conversion, having fought a demolition order, and so preserved a lovely corner of the ancient Oxford road into which they have nestled for three hundred years. They make a companion piece to Pilgrim Cottage. After twelve months' work I find them still incomplete. I am employing a local craftsman, one who has inherited his skill with the Tudor brick. He is sorely handicapped by a morass of regulations and ' permits.' In Italy these cottages would have been converted in less than three months. A friend built a villa outside Florence this year in four months. England to-day is a slow-motion film. I see that the Trades Union Council is stopping any more industrial investigation parties going to study conditions in the U.S.A. Their reports make damaging comparisons of British and American output.

November 14.

Lunched in London with my friend Major Humphrey Sykes. We last spent some time together in Washington in 1946. Handsome, spare, he comes of hunting stock and is the great-grandson of Whyte Melville, the novelist and huntsman, creator of " The Honourable Crasher," who was killed by his horse rolling over him. " An end he could not quarrel with," observed Humphrey. After lunch we walked to my friend's room, tucked away behind Berkeley Square. I was glad to see him wearing a billycock hat. " From Lock's ? " I asked. " Yes," he replied. I had just been there myself to buy a hat, thereby continuing a family tradition, for my great-grandfather's name is in the order-book kept at Lock's. The ancient shop in St. James's Street is unchanged since the time when a fire roasted its shutters and when Byron lived next door but one, from 1808-1814.

His lodging here was more closely associated with his career than Newstead Abbey or the Palazzo Mocenigo at Venice, for he wrote here " English Bards and Scotch Reviewers," went hence to take his seat in the House of Lords " lacking a friend to accompany him," and published while here the first two cantos of *Childe Harold's Pilgrimage* and " woke one morning to find myself famous," as he put it. Alas, this dwelling of Lord Byron's was demolished some years ago—I went over it while it was being pulled down—but Lock's shop remains unchanged. The billy-cock hat still sold there takes its name from William Coke. He was the great-grandson of my kinsman Colonel Philip Roberts, grandfather of the great Coke of Norfolk, who was Billy's uncle. The billycock hat is the only purely indigenous British hat.

Billy Coke was a hunting squire who wanted a ' crash helmet ' for the field and consulted his hatmaker, a Mr. Bowler. It was in Lock's shop that the new creation was first tried on, taking its name from the originator and not the maker. Lock's assistants sniff if you are crude enough to ask for a bowler. All that happened just a hundred years ago and last month Lock's had a party to celebrate the centenary of the ' billycock ' as it is now termed, designed in 1850. The second wearer was Mr. Beilby Lawley, according to Lock's order-book. He paid twelve shillings for one on April 16, 1851. I paid three guineas for mine.

Since the billycock hat is in the family tradition I was delighted to see my friend Humphrey wearing his in the West End. I fear it is dying out in this age of sloppy clothes. The Americans call it a Derby, pronouncing it Durby, and when in Hollywood some years ago I discovered that the most star-haunted restaurant was called " The Brown Derby." I told the owner the origin of its name and he was so delighted that he cancelled my lunch bill.

One of the joys of shopping in London is visiting these traditional firms, but alas they are rapidly dying out, victims of mass pro-duction and chain stores. Last year my bootmaker near Jermyn Street put up his shutters. His premises were badly damaged by bombs. Struggling on, he found that his old customers, impoverished, could not pay his prices. His business of bespoke shoemaking had endured for one hundred and fifty years. I am glad to see that Burlington Arcade is still patronised by the young bloods who like very fancy waistcoats and Macclesfield silk ties. I went in a shop there and bought a tartan waistcoat, with coral buttons and lined with yellow chamois leather, for a young friend. I tried it on and told the assistant it was for a tall slim young man. " That's for a slim man, sir, it fits you perfectly," said the tactful assistant. My vanity much tickled, I was tempted to keep it for myself, but only the very young can wear such fine feathers becomingly.

Cast your bread upon the waters. . . . This afternoon while at tea two ladies called. I did not at first recognise them, muffled up, until they reminded me we had met in Rome. They were the ladies who had written to ask me the address of my hotel with the view described in *And So To Rome*, and who had subsequently come to the hotel. Now they called, bringing me a bottle of champagne and a cardboard box, an expression of thanks ' for my great kindness ' in Rome, as they put it. Overwhelmed, for I did very little for them, I politely refrained from peering into the box. They refused tea and departed, en route to their farm. An hour later there were loud joyous exclamations in the kitchen. The box, opened, contained two dozen eggs. A strange era when a bottle of champagne evokes a quiet ' thank you ' but a dozen eggs induce rhapsodies !

Dined with my old friends Sir Norman and Lady Birkett, *à trois*. We had not met since we crossed to New York on the maiden trip of the *Queen Elizabeth* in 1946, shortly after Sir Norman had returned from being one of the judges of the International Military Tribunal at Nuremberg. Hartley Shawcross and I were his dinner guests one evening in the Observation Grill of the Cunarder. It was an astonishing feast in those days of extreme austerity.

This evening my friend was full of good stories and memories. What law has gained literature has lost. At Cambridge he edited the *Cambridge Review*. One of its pages has a poem signed B (for Birkett) on one side and there is a sonnet on the other side. It begins " Breathless we flung us on a windy hill . . . " Rupert Brooke's now famous poem. The two B.s were matched in a public prize contest together at Cambridge. N.B. declaimed a poem ; R.B. declaimed a passage from Milton. " He had tramped in from the Old Vicarage at Grantchester (Stands the church clock at ten-to-three, and is there honey still for tea . . .) and stood up on the platform, his boots still caked with mud, with his magnificent head and fine diction, and swept us all away," said Sir Norman.

Lawyers specialize in law stories and N.B. told me one of the best. There had been a number of thefts from the rooms on the judges' corridors in the Royal Courts of Justice. On one of the less-frequented corridors, where one of the Lords Justices

had his room, a colleague came to tell him that his wallet had
been stolen from his coat while in court. The Lord Justice was
sceptical and suggested that his colleague must have left his wallet
at home ; but on going to his own coat he found that his wallet
was also missing. Outraged, they sent for the official responsible
for the corridor and questioned him. " Has any suspicious
character been seen here during our absence ? ' they asked.
" Yes—Lord Justice X—I thought it funny he should come
down here and without his robes on ! " came the answer.

N.B. and I are duodenal ulcer victims. The ulcerated are a
close fraternity. We compare notes. At eleven o'clock Lady
Birkett, solicitous for our good, appeared with two glasses of milk
as nightcaps. In the taxi home, I ruminated on Fate. We
had trodden widely divergent paths which at one point had con-
verged. Twenty-eight years ago I was a Liberal Parliamentary
candidate for East Nottingham. The sudden death of the sitting
member precipitated a contest which I saw I was going to win
at a time when my health would not have stood the dual strain
of membership of the House of Commons and the editorship
of a newspaper. Moreover, I began to feel that literature, not
politics, was my course. I retired. Norman Birkett hurriedly
stepped into my place and won the election. I wrote in *Half
Way* (1931)—that he " there began a Parliamentary career
that, in no reckless prophecy, seems destined to lead him to the
Woolsack." I was not far out. He was not, by nature, a House
of Commons man, but his quality has taken him near to the Woolsack, as a Lord Justice of Appeal.

What a pleasant evening, *intime*, full of good talk and exchanges
with a singularly rich mind.

November 15.

The state of democracy seems more perilous in U.S.A. than
anywhere else, judging from the hysteria at ports of entry, and
the formalities required. To-day at the American Consulate
I was finger-printed twelve times, once for each finger and thumb,
and twice for each hand. The official apologised.

As I walked back through Grosvenor Square, now called
Rooseveltplatz because of the statue of Roosevelt, the American
Embassy, and the Consulate there, I expressed a wish to my
companion to cross the square diagonally in order to look at the
statue. He said, " A lot of our American friends won't cross

this square, they hate that fellow so much." I was not surprised.
In America I encountered Roosevelt-haters every day. I wish
the sculptor had seated the President. I never saw Franklin
Roosevelt stand. He avoided standing because of the agony it
caused him. He carried seven pounds of iron braces on his legs.
A friend in Congress told me that when he stood to make his
Inaugural Address, beads of perspiration were on his face though
his voice rang out.

Going down South Audley Street I saw they were painting a
house where I onced stayed with a friend who owned it. He had
a passion for musical boxes and I remember picking my way to
bed over twenty-two of them. He sold up and went to Bermuda.
I do not know whether the musical boxes went with him to give
him tinkling music there.

Things Observed.

A captain in a Black Watch kilt, arm in arm with an Indian
woman who had a jewel in her nose and wore a light blue sari.
They entered a block of flats. No one looked at them. London
is utterly uninquisitive.

November 16.

This morning I received a letter from a London hospital. It
was from a young friend who in his last year at Oxford had a
brain tumour. After a severe operation he was left with a half-
paralysed face. He returned to his home in Australia a year
later, somewhat recovered, and then took a position in Damascus.
There one day he was stricken with paralysis from the neck down.
He was flown to England and fought a battle royal with the
immigration authorities who feared he had poliomyelitis. He
gained admittance. He has been in hospital three months. To-day
he wrote—" My progress continues at its steady slow pace—but
it is progress. I can now walk a little with the aid of callipers.
It's very hard work and will be a long time before I'm really
mobile. Also there has been some improvement of the paralysis."
He is twenty-four and quite cheerful. The blessing of being able
to rise, walk, talk and enjoy the ordinary day !

November 17.

Arrived last night in Nottingham. My incredible brother
met me with his car, a skeleton at the wheel but full of good cheer.

This morning he took me to the Clifton Colliery to check the details of a novel that I began to write two months ago to be called *A Terrace in the Sun*. It started out as a story with a Mediterranean setting. Somehow, taking the bit between its teeth, it has cantered home to England. It has now developed into the life-story of a miner's son born on a Nottingham coalfield. I have written twenty novels, nineteen of them with a foreign setting, not one of them dealing extensively with my native city. Yet here, untapped, was a deep mine of personal experience and easy verisimilitude, awaiting expression. I have come to Nottingham to check my facts, refresh my memories and to amplify my material. This morning I went to the Clifton Colliery, within a mile of which I lived for many years. I went through the dreary neighbourhood that throughout my boyhood was a forbidden territory, peopled with pariahs in the social scale. Even so, I made some surreptitious visits, fascinated and terrified by the squalor and violence. The same mean streets are there to-day but how changed they are in many respects ! The dreadful long rows of 'privies' with their insanitary tubs have been converted into water closets. The public-houses have been modernised with bright well-furnished bars. I looked inside some of the little houses, standing in grim terraces with communal backyards. There was no squalor within, as once upon a time. They had radios, pianos and eighty-pound television sets. The inhabitants were neatly dressed. It is no longer possible to send pinched boys of twelve down the mines. Their fathers no longer work ten hours a day for twenty-five shillings a week. A seven-hour day is usual. The wages are around ten pounds a week. No boy under sixteen can go down the mine, and he must have preliminary training. In the bad old days the collier was brutalised and treated as a sub-human being, with no sanitation, no facility for washing except the tin bath laboriously filled from the kitchen boiler when he got home. He washed with no privacy before the children. How was it possible for them to have a sense of decency or to conduct themselves as respectable citizens ? They passed their lives underground, walking four or five miles to the coal face, labouring almost naked in a moist heat, the threat of unemployment always hovering over them. It is a miracle that instead of sullen strikes and obstinate bargainings, conducted by leaders who were regarded as dangerous revolutionaries—one recalls the hysterical Mr. Cook versus the cool

Duke of Northumberland, symbolising Chaos v. Order—there
was not a bloody revolution. A few in the capitalist camp
recognised that things must be changed, Lord Henry Bentinck,
the local member of Parliament among them, but they were
opposed by a powerful block of diehards. I knew the coalfields
of old, though superficially; if the pendulum has swung too far
in the opposite direction it is the gross injustice of the past that
has provided its momentum. Child labour in mines and factories belongs to a disgraceful past, and adult labour also can
no longer be wrung from human misery. The process of adjustment is painful but I am glad that the experiment has been
made, however inexpertly and extravagantly conducted. " Why,
those miners get twelve pounds a week ! " exclaims a white-
collar worker getting six. It seems unequal but stand at the
pithead and look at the faces and carriage of the men going
down ; go down and watch them working contorted, in conditions that allow no lay-off for smoking or idling, in darkness,
humidity and danger. Would you earn twelve pounds a week
below rather than six above ? The constant recruiting needed
to get this labour supplies the answer. I came away from the
colliery, though modernised and improved beyond recognition,
with no doubt as to my own opinion, despite Government
posters proclaiming the attractions of a miner's life.

Lunched at the County Club with B. L. Hallward, the Vice-
Chancellor of Nottingham University. Afterwards he took me
over the buildings, very surprised that I had not seen them. In
a sense I am closely associated with the university for I saw its
site before it was built ; I saw the plans as they grew on the desk
of the architect, I was present at the opening of the swimming-
pool which was the initial step towards the whole conception,
and at the laying of the foundation stone. Unhappily I was
absent in Rome when it celebrated the granting of its charter
as a university last year. I knew the remarkable man whose
vision and money had made this university possible ; a giant
among men who, paralysed on his bed for the last thirty years
of his life, directed a great business, and gave his millions to the
welfare of his city. I last saw this grand old warrior, Jesse Boot,
six months before his death in his eighty-first year, as he lay in
a darkened room of his villa at Cannes, unable to bear the daylight, almost stone deaf, but an incurable optimist. His Christmas guests were called up one by one into his darkened room

where they had a few minutes' conversation through an ear trumpet. Few of us came out of that room without a lump in the throat ; we had seen courage incarnate. When in 1938 Boots Pure Drug Company celebrated its Jubilee, Lord Trent, his son and successor, paid me the compliment of asking me to write the story of this great organisation and its founder. And now to-day I saw his dream converted into stone, a magnificent triumph, set on a hill and dedicated to youth.

Things Observed.

While waiting for my host in the lounge of the County Club, I stood by a corner window looking out on to the street. In the year 1904, a boy of twelve, I was walking past the window with my father who told me to raise my hat as he raised his to an old gentleman sitting there. He acknowledged our salutes. " That's the Duke of Rutland and you may never see him again," said my father. The Duke died two years later, aged eighty-eight, having been born in 1818. He was the seventh duke, having succeeded his brother Cecil. He had in his veins the blood of the first Earl of Rutland, 1525, who founded Belvoir Castle, and of his son Henry, who completed the first building, was Constable of Nottingham Castle (1544) and appointed the Sheriff, a character renowned in the Robin Hood legend. As Lord John Manners he had been a member of the Cabinet in 1853 when, following criticism of the events leading to the Crimean War, he had to deal with a widespread rumour that Queen Victoria and the Prince Consort had been arrested and sent to the Tower of London. Handsome, cultured, conscientious, as a young man he published a book of poems. By tearing two lines from their context he was held up to ridicule by his political opponents, and it is ironical that his title to fame to-day is from two lines of his verses supposed to epitomise the diehard spirit :—

> Let wealth and commerce, laws and learning die,
> But leave us still our old nobility !

Such was the history of the old duke sitting in the club window.

November 25.

This morning when I rose and peered out of my window across the park, the day was blotted out in a London fog. The sun looked like a poached egg flung on a blanket of murky wool. I knew, though I could not see it, that Whitehall lay below me and the clock tower of the Houses of Parliament rose beyond. Big Ben struck nine as I breakfasted, assuring me it was still there. All over the world, such is the blessing of radio, I have heard Big Ben strike the hours, and its boom always courses through my veins as only it can through those of an Englishman.

At noon I went down to Knole, Sevenoaks, to lunch with Lord and Lady Sackville. There is only one proper way to approach this magnificent pile of buildings, a town in itself, set on a hill. One must walk through the gates and along the drive that winds up and down between a forest of beech, sycamore, elm and oak. On either side of this drive there are noble vistas of greensward, and before one, grey and massive, above its long façade with turreted gatehouses and mullioned windows, rises the pointed clock tower amid the chimneys and roofs of the inner courtyards. No other mansion in England, not even Windsor Castle, seems to me so fairly set, so essentially English, built of the warp and woof of history. Here is a home I would exchange for no château, schloss, palazzo or villa anywhere in the world. It is a vintage from the English vine planted in the shady past and coexistent with England's rise to greatness.

Sometimes when approaching the house there is that most beautiful embroidery of the sylvan scene, the drift of fallow deer, moving slender-legged, dappled in shadow and sunlight, so tame that they regard you placidly with their velvety eyes.

The sun contrived to emerge as I neared the house and touched with gold the last leaves upon the giant oaks. A wistful light pervaded the forest. When I arrive at the great postern doors and stand diminutive outside, there always echoes in my mind " Childe Roland to the dark Tower came," and I almost see, on my ringing of the bell, helmeted heads appear between the crenellations of the twin towers, and damsels peering down to look at the stranger below.

Through the outer gate and hall one passes into the lovely quadrangle with its green lawns and mullioned windows reminiscent of an Oxford college. Across this one comes to the second court at whose entrance rises an oriel window amid the gables. Through this entrance appear the arcades and columns, cloister like, of the interior Stone Court, flagged, with covered walks under a Jacobean colonnade. Even now yet another, the Water

Court, appears beyond, with the lattice windows of a long gallery running above it. We approach the centre of the older house though four other courts are unseen in what is really a medieval village.

It is no longer possible to live in all of this vast mansion. The greater part of it has become a museum open to the public, who can marvel at a building that covers four acres, has seven quadrangles, one for each day of the week, fifty-two staircases, one for each week of the year, and three hundred and sixty-five rooms, one for each day of the year. It once housed one hundred and ten persons, including a concubine and a blackamoor. In a private section my host and hostess live. It is possible to heat it, and it faces the sun. Their own domain holds the essence of the time-mellowed whole, with its flagged corridors and wainscotted rooms. The sitting-room and the dining-room look out through their tall mullion windows on to the great lawns. These terraced lawns are higher than the ground floor of the house. From them one sees a long façade of Tudor gables, with the heraldic Sackville leopards rigid on their peaks, an arcaded loggia, and the long brown-red roofs weathered by five hundred years. This great house whose origin is lost in the mist of time was owned by Henry VIII and given by Queen Elizabeth to her cousin, Thomas Sackville. He was a gallant and a poet but his role was that of Lord Treasurer to the great Queen and she bestowed this house upon him in 1586. She once commanded him not to leave it for nine months because he failed to support Leicester, her favourite, in one of his feuds. Leicester had owned it briefly and a long gallery bears his name. The house's occupants have been part of the tapestry of English history, each thread a rich contemporaneous commentary of an age. On one of the doors hangs a portrait of Catherine Sackville, born in the reign of Edward IV, reputed to be in the Tower of London when the young princes were murdered. She saw Henry VII come to the throne and at ninety broke her leg by falling off an apple tree ! The turf before these windows is very green. The whole garden is enclosed by a wall, half of it a woodland of beech and chestnut called The Wilderness, half, filled with long grassy walks, little orchards and herbaceous borders ablaze with flowers in summer.

Thomas Sackville was snatched early from literature, his real interest, into politics and court service. He was rich and yet he was poor, as the rich often are, and he was peremptorily chided by his Queen for the mean manner in which he entertained Cardinal Chatillon. He humbly explained his difficulties. He lacked plate, napery and fine linen and he had to lend his own basin and ewer to his guest. There is a strangely familiar ring in his account that, although his family consisted of two hundred persons, he " somehow kept house for forty and two years in an honorable proportion . . . a very rare example in this present age of ours, when housekeeping is so decayed." And how familiar, these days, is the statement that the house given to him by the Queen in 1566 was sublet and he could not get possession until 1603. He was confirmed in his post of Lord Treasurer by James I and, running true to form, increased the tax on tobacco four years before he died.

Thomas's grandson, Richard, third Earl of Dorset, seemed to have lived in even greater state. He married an heiress, Lady Anne Clifford, with vast estates in the North. There is a catalogue of his household at Knole, a formidable list, that included Mr. Matthew Caldicott, " my Lord's favourite," four pages and two blackamoors. Not on the list, but on the payroll, was that celebrated beauty and courtesan, Mrs. Venetia Stanley, whom the Earl kept as his concubine and had children by. He settled on her an annuity of £500 per annum which, after Sir Kenelm Digby married her, was unpaid by the Earl. Sir Kenelm sued the Earl after the marriage and recovered it. Venetia Stanley was a most beautiful and desirable creature " sanguine and tractable and of much suavity." After her marriage she redeemed her honour by strict living. Once a year the Earl of Dorset invited her and Sir Kenelm Digby to dine, where " the Earl would behold her with much passion, yet only kiss her hand." Accommodating days.

Sackville's wife Anne, was a match for him. He never ceased trying to lay hands on her great estate but she withstood him, and even James I tried to browbeat her. Vain, weak, grossly extravagant but cultured, Sackville had five children by Anne who bore " many crosses and contradictions." She was determined though comely. She writes in her Diary, April 1617— " After supper I walked in the garden and gathered cherries and talked with Josiah (the French page), who told me he thought all the men in the house loved me." She was domesticated. She made jam and used up her husband's old shirts for clouts. Sackville died at thirty-five, writing her a love-letter from his deathbed. She survived him by fifty-two years. Triumphant at long last, having worn down all opposition, a ruler of Knole by her first marriage, and of Wilton by her second, she retired to her beloved North, managed her estates superbly and died at eighty-six. " I went not out all this day," she wrote on March 22, 1676. It was the last entry in her Diary, the next day she was dead.

Two hundred and seventy-four years later I am standing in a wainscotted room, before a fire in the wide Tudor fireplace, looking out across the wintry lawns when there comes in my hostess, another Anne Sackville. The traditional longevity is wonderfully maintained in my host, Charles Sackville, who this August celebrated his eightieth birthday. Four winters ago we were fellow guests at *Estella*, at Palm Beach, Florida. It possesses a large swimming-pool with turquoise-blue water. I was amazed one January morning, breakfasting on the lawn under a coconut palm, to see a strange young man make a graceful dive off the springboard. I did not know there had been an addition overnight to the house party. I went over to the pool and there, swimming briskly, was my fellow guest Lord Sackville. Quite a lot of history nestles in that handsome white head and trim body. A soldier, he was in the Manipur Expedition in 1891, A.D.C. to General Buller in South Africa, 1899, in the European War 1914-1917 (wounded twice, C.M.G., Legion of Honour, American D.S.M., Italian Croix de Guerre), rounding off this as Military Attaché at Paris, 1920-24 and as Lieutenant-Governor of Guernsey, 1925. Since then he has waged a long campaign against the Treasury (Dep. Inland Revenue) to preserve Knole.

When we had gone into the long dining-room I looked around me at the beautiful furniture, the famous portraits of Sackvilles who had lived here through the centuries, at the great oriel window occupying one end of the room, revealing a long lawn beyond, and I reflected how fortunate this old house was to have presiding over it such a handsome pair. The frame is not always so fortunate in its picture.

In a mansion of this size, filled with uncountable treasures of art and furnishings, with Holbein, Mytens, Van Dyck, Gainsborough, Hoppner on the walls, spaced with armour of tilting suits, with tapestries in the galleries and salons, damask curtains and canopies in the Venetian Ambassador's bedroom, etc., there are endless side alleys of history down which the mind can explore. The third Duke of Dorset wrote a lurid addition to the annals of the house. He lost his head over an Italian dancer, produced her at a ball wearing the family jewels, installed her in a tower at Knole, had her painted by Gainsborough and Reynolds, and modelled in the nude. He also had his servants painted, and their portraits hang now in the Black Boy Passage. Sir Joshua Reynolds painted Hwang-a-Tung, the Chinese page boy. It was more original to have a Chinese page than a French or a black one. They had all varieties at Knole. Since the days of Lady Anne the black ones had always been called John Morocco, and the passage took its name from one of these black pages killed in a fight by a house steward. Nor have recent times neglected the bizarre. One may read in that engaging book, *Pepita*, the story of another wayward dancer who captured a Sackville, told vivaciously by Victoria Sackville-West.

" What ghosts ! You should have no difficulty about foreign exchange," I said, as we discussed the present obstacles to wintering abroad. " Can't you export one ? They would be snapped up in the United States."

" You'll be surprised to learn that Knole has never possessed a ghost," said my host.

Lord Sackville saw my look of incredulity. Knole of all places without a ghost !

" And something else," he continued. " Although Queen Elizabeth gave this place to her favourite, Leicester, and later to Sackville, she never slept here ! "

Our talk turned to the theft of some of the Duchess of Sutherland's jewels. Happily those that had formed part of Marie Antoinette's necklace had been in a safe deposit. This necklace was ordered by Cardinal Rohan for the Queen, part of the roguery for which Madame Lamotte-Valois went to gaol, as narrated in Dumas's famous novel. As we talked, it came to me that Kitty Rothschild had told me how, escaping from France in 1940, she had been enabled to purchase the Long Island house, in which I was then spending Christmas with Baron Eugene de Rothschild, by the sale of her portion of the necklace.* There had been an evening when Baroness de Rothschild, the Duchess of Sutherland and Lady Sackville, each owners of a section, had dined together in Paris, thus bringing together again the divided

* See *And So To America*, Ch. XXIII, ii.

necklace. Lady Sackville's share of it, she told me, was now part
of her peeress's coronet.

When I left my host accompanied me to the postern gate and
as we stood there, looking across the park, he astonished me by
saying, " There's my Jap ! " I was a little startled. Japanese
spies at Knole, or a Japanese page in place of a Chinese one ?

" A Jap ? " I queried, looking around.

" There ! " he said, pointing at a stag that stood not ten
yards away, watching us tamely. " That's a Japanese stag.
One of my family brought some Japanese deer over with him
after leaving a diplomatic post in Japan and they've bred here
ever since."

With that last surprise I left my hatless host, frightened lest he
would catch a cold in the wintry air, and walked down the glen
from the mansion that never had a ghost, and where, to her loss
I feel, Queen Elizabeth never slept.

November 26.

Yesterday when I arrived on a visit to the country I found
my hostess almost in tears. She apologised for no carpet in
my bedroom and for three carpets lying rolled up in the hall. For
ten days she had been awaiting the van, to take away the carpets
for beating them. After lunch I borrowed an apron and a beater,
took off my coat, hung each carpet on a line strung between two
apple trees, and went to work. It took me three hours, carpets
and underfelt, and I was happy in a glorious crowd of dust.
Then I laid them, had a bath, and sat down to tea. Going
into the kitchen for a broom I heard a hideous screech coming
from the frigidaire. I asked permission to look inside. The
noise, I was told, had gone on for over a year. I got a screwdriver
and went to work. A bush in the dynamo was worn. I took
it out, adjusted it, and there was no more screeching. To-day
my right arm is stiff from the beating, and I have not written
the new chapter I planned.

I have always loved doing things with my hands, and delight in
finding any job that will postpone the self-discipline and loneliness
that are concomitants of writing. Odd jobs of this kind must
have cost me many thousands of pounds but what happiness
they have brought ! I never understand people who are content
to own things without knowing how they work. Some years
ago a writing colleague of mine, travelling with me in Austria,

was greatly distressed by the breakdown of his typewriter. He
would have to make a journey into Vienna to have it repaired.
I asked to look at it, took out the screwdriver with which I always
travel and dismantled the typewriter. I found that a cotter in the
automatic spacer had jammed and stopped the ' carriage '
travelling. In an hour the machine was working. My friend
has never recovered from it. Whenever he introduces me to
anyone he tells the story of his typewriter.

After buying my first motor-car I longed to know what was
inside the engine. I bought a technical book and took the engine
down. All went well in setting it up again until I came to a
part that required tools I did not possess. So I fetched a garage
mechanic, and I profited by watching him. That experience
was invaluable in after years. The number of distressed people
who entrust themselves to boxes of mysteries and find themselves
stranded when the slightest adjustment will set them going !
How lovely it is to use one's hands. I have wall-papered without
getting wrapped-up in sheets of paste; painted, without streaks;
puttied windows without getting gummed up—there is an art
in rolling putty so that it does not adhere to the fingers. On
buying Pilgrim Cottage I built myself a garden-house and hung
two Venetian gates on brick piers. I never mention this now because it always provokes the retort, " Oh, you're like Winston
Churchill," as though that remarkable man were the only
bricklayer in the world.

Motoring past the old house once occupied by Lady Blessington,
in Kensington Gore, I saw they were dismantling it. I bought
two old marble baths and mantelpieces, broke them into frag-
ments and layed a tessellated pavement in my walled garden.
How many of those monstrous contraptions called cisterns have I
dealt with ! I have re-washered dozens of ball cocks on these noisy
nuisances, designed to advertise every visit to the lavatory. I
once found my host painfully crawling up through a trap-door
to carry an oil lamp to the cistern, to keep it from freezing. I
ran a flex from the nearest point, put on a fifty-watt lamp and
hung it just inside the cistern cover. I then asked if I might
bore a hole in the trap-door roof. My host looked surprised.
" So that you will know when the light's on," I explained. He
has been demonstrating this contraption for years, freezeless.
When I put radiators into my old cottage I was told that the
radiators on the ground floor must be hung a foot high to ensure

a 'return flow' to the boiler on the kitchen level. I could not convince this wizard that I had lived in one-floor apartments all over the United States in which the radiators were never skied and the boiler was on the same level. Another indestructible British shibboleth.

I took a villa in Italy. In the hall there was a noble English grandfather clock, with Westminster chimes. But it did not go. My English landlord informed me that there was a local clock repairer, a derelict Russian count, living in the town, who could be called in. I did not call him in, I postponed the day's writing and had an enjoyable four hours with the clock's 'innards.' That night Big Ben chimed in the hall again.

Once there was an electric bell, from the bedroom to the kitchen, which 'had never worked.' I went into the kitchen, took off the bell-cover and discovered that a spider had died between the contact points. For how many years had that dead spider impeded traffic?

What fun it all is! Whenever I unpack on my travels my friends are always mirthful when they see a manifold screwdriver come out of my bag. Later, they are often grateful. I would as soon think of travel without a screwdriver as without trousers.

December 1.

In my paper this morning there is a picture of a chubby little boy of five standing with his governess on the deck of a steamer coming into Weymouth from Jersey. The letterpress says that he has been on holiday for six weeks and that " his governess has denied that she stated that threats were made to kidnap the little boy." I should be very sorry to learn that he had been kidnapped, though I think that many others as well as myself would be happy to run off with such an attractive little fellow. I take a particular interest in him because without me, in a way, he might never have existed. There are wicked people in this world who would spirit the boy away and possibly kill him for political reasons, because he happens to be the heir to a Balkan throne now in abeyance, being little Prince Alexander, the son of ex-King Peter of Jugoslavia. I called his father Prince Sixpenny in *Victoria Four-Thirty*. If I now wrote about the son of Prince Sixpenny I suppose I should have to call him Prince Shilling, as pocket-money even for princelings has surely doubled with the rise in the cost of living.

K

December 2.

Sixteen years ago when I published *Gone Rustic* I spoke of my desire to possess a toucan. It provoked a letter from a neighbour who wrote saying that she had once modelled one. We corresponded and she invited me to call. She was Mrs. Lionel Bulteel, living with her husband at Yewden Manor, an Elizabethan house on the Marlow Road, opposite the Hambleden Lock, near Henley-on-Thames. It is a house with Tudor chimneys and innumerable gables and little roofs playing at hide and seek. From the big drawing-room with the long windows, into which the old butler showed me, I looked on to a very long lawn with a raised garden walk along an old wall commanding a view of the Thames, a silver weir and a white watermill. The great feature of this superb lawn was the double yew hedge, four hundred years old and a hundred yards long, that made a dark tunnel with a circle of light at each end. It ran along the opposite side of the lawn, and it launched itself like a billowing green wave against the old manor.

I rarely passed a summer in England without at least one visit to my hospitable friends. One always learned something, and at their manor or at their house in London I met very interesting characters. Their own personal history is unique. To-day when I called, I found Mr. and Mrs. Bulteel cosily ensconced in a large drawing-room gaily littered with souvenirs of their long lives. Last August Mr. Bulteel was ninety. He moves easily, is very alert and bears few of the signs of age. Mrs. Bulteel is eighty-two. " I confess I enjoy being old," she said, with her quiet little voice, and with an amused air that is characteristic. " Why should I want to be young ? What you've enjoyed once you can't enjoy as much twice."

Her family is really remarkable. She was one of fifteen children, nine boys and six girls. Four of the boys were in the Eton eleven. Their uncle was Field-Marshal Lord Grenfell. Two of my hostess's brothers made history as polo-playing twins who lived with singular grace in a circle they charmed. One of them, Francis, the elder by a few minutes, went into the Army, the younger, Riversdale, went into the City to make money to help the elder brother in his career. At Eton they were indistinguishable and inseparable. They looked alike, dressed alike and were devoted to each other. Julian Grenfell the poet, and his brother, sons of Lord Desborough, were their cousins. All four

fell in the 1914-1918 war. Francis's last words to his regimental
officer, was " Tell them I die happy, loving them all." Badly
wounded in the first month of the war during the retreat from
Mons, he was the first soldier to win the V.C. in the Great War.
The twins had joined the same regiment. Riversdale was killed
in the second month of the war, aged just thirty-four, and at
the same age his brother Francis was killed eight months later.
A fighting family, two older brothers had died in the Matabele
War and at Omdurman. John Buchan wrote a memoir of the
twins.

Mrs. Bulteel, therefore, has many memories but they have to
be extracted. To-day she told me something of her uncle,
Admiral Henry Grenfell, for there were sailors in the family also,
her grandfather being Admiral John Grenfell of the Brazilian
Navy, Lord Cochrane's second in command. Admiral Henry
was far-famed for his courage and his toughness. He was
middle-weight boxing champion of the Navy. There was an
occasion, ashore in Constantinople with brother officers, when
he went to a music-hall and heard an immense Turk offering
fifty dollars to anyone who could knock him out in five rounds.
Grenfell accepted the challenge. To deceive the fellow he put
his gloves on wrongly and took a clumsy stance. The Turk
thought he had a novice to deal with, took a chance, and found
himself knocked out. Recovering, he went to the footlights and
called out, with a Limehouse accent—" Gentlemen, the hexibition
is closed ! " Then going to Grenfell, the " Turk " whispered, as
he shook him by the hand, " You're no bloody lamb ! "

Mrs. Bulteel had another story of her redoubtable uncle. He
was sent to the Pacific to arrest a chief who had eaten a missionary.
On the way to Sydney he developed so high a respect for his
prisoner that he dumped him on a desert island and reported
that, after careful consideration, he had formed the opinion that
the missionary had been entirely to blame ! My hostess had yet
another story, of her brother Riversdale, the City twin. One day
a man in a black coat and bowler hat called at Riversdale's office
and asked for him. " What name, sir ? " asked the office boy.
" King Alfonso," replied the caller. The boy stared and then
went to his chief's room. " There's a looney at the desk asking
for you, sir, he says he's King Alfonso ! " The looney was immediately shown in. The twins and King Alfonso were close
polo cronies.

My host was not out of the picture.   He is one of thirteen
children, nine sisters and four boys.   One of his sisters was Lady-
in-Waiting at Windsor to Princess Ena of Battenberg, and went
to the historic wedding when the Princess married King Alfonso
in Madrid.   She saw the bomb thrown and the terrified girl-
bride, her wedding dress covered with blood, sobbing in the arms
of her husband.   When I mentioned that I had just visited the
ex-Queen's daughter, the Infanta Beatrice in Rome, Mrs. Bulteel
fetched from a side table a water-colour portrait of the former
Princess Ena made by Lázló at Windsor Castle in 1912.   Later,
Mrs. Bulteel made me a present of a portrait of King Alfonso,
in uniform on horseback, autographed in 1912, which had
belonged to the twins.   I think Mr. Bulteel was a little afraid
that his wife might give me the Lázló portrait of Alfonso's wife,
but I put him at ease.   I then discovered that my hostess had
some Spanish blood, hence her Christian name Juanita.   She
brought me a portrait of a beautiful woman in a mantilla, her
grandmother, a South American Spaniard.

We then adjourned to the dining-room for tea, where Mr. Bulteel
made the brew and carried the full cups to the table without a
quiver, while Mrs. Bulteel sliced a chocolate cake which we all
ate.   Finding that she read Spanish I promised on leaving to
send a Spanish edition of one of my books.   I went out from this
gay, warm, hospitable house into the dark December night feeling
rejuvenated by these two bright young people.

December 4.

Yesterday, after a long day in the country, in all the perfection
of golden woods, I went to London.   I love beechwoods more
than any other.   They retain their leaves late and when they
fall they create a carpet of burning gold in the forest.   With a
touch of sun the whole scene is lit with a glory unequalled anywhere at this time of the year.   My hostess is a great bird-lover
and at breakfast yesterday we counted eight varieties that came
to feed at the window.   The starlings have no manners.   They
gobble and push away all the other birds except the pertinacious
robin whose breast now glows with a scarlet waistcoat.   I have
an idea that the frost burnishes the feathers of his breast.   The
star-turn in the garden is a missel-thrush that brings spring
notes to the wintry landscape.   He perches at dawn and dusk
on the highest poplar-tree and sings loud and lustily about what ?

It cannot be a love song, for the mating season is long past.

I went up to London to catch the 11.40 p.m. express for Glasgow, in order to lecture at the Athenaeum in a series called ' Celebrity Lectures.' It is run by an energetic Congregational minister. There seems to be no one he has not caught in his net, except the elusive Bernard Shaw, with whom he had some lively skirmishes. He has a persistency that cannot be resisted. For five years he has begged me to visit Glasgow. Each year I have put him off, saying I would consider it next time. I could not with any grace put him off again. All yesterday I found myself wondering why I was so weak. But for this engagement I should have sailed, as formerly, on the *Vulcania* from Naples to New York, the southern route through the Mediterranean via Gibraltar, by which one avoids the storms of the North Atlantic. Now I have had to make a journey from Rome to London, and to suffer the rigours of our inadequately heated hotels. After this Glasgow trip I must embark from Southampton, probably in a fog !

December 5.

What a genius we have for discomfort ! Last night I departed from Euston Station, probably the worst of the barns that masquerade as stations in London. Liverpool Street, King's Cross, Euston, St. Pancras, what sooty and dismal holes they are ; what an impression they create on the visitors to these shores ! If instead of squandering millions on the senseless and unwanted Festival we had devoted the money to building railway stations that do not shame us, we might have made a considerable contribution to our tourist propaganda, and have something to show long after the Festival has faded away. The sleeping compartments of the Glasgow express were icy cold. I asked for an extra blanket to supplement the thin pair on my bed. There were no extra blankets. I turned on the steam-heat. There was no steam-heat. It would come on later, I was told. I undressed, and got into bed shivering. At one o'clock, unable to sleep for the cold, I got up, put on my overcoat and went to bed in it. At two o'clock, unbearably hot, I got up and took off the coat, the heating had come on. But in the morning when I went to the breakfast-car, whose windows looked on a snowbound landscape, the car was icy cold. " The heating isn't working, sir, in here," said the attendant with steamy breath. I thought longingly of the cosiness of a 'roomette' in the New York-Chicago express. How do we expect to attract American tourists? If we must cajole their dollars in order to exist, having a national economy that can only support thirty millions in a country over-crowded with fifty, then an 'old-world charm' must have a new-world heating system ; but with less and dearer coal the problem seems insuperable.

On arrival in Glasgow I found an enormous bedroom reserved for me in which to rest before the evening lecture. But curiosity would not let me rest. I had been to Glasgow only once, in 1916, when I went on an official inspection tour of the Clyde ship-building yards, a conducted visit of only a few hours. Now I had a day in Glasgow on my own. I asked the way to the Art Gallery and resisted the porter's desire to send me by taxi or tram. One must walk to get the flavour of a place. I started off in the grey gloom between blocks of granite buildings. Twice I asked the way and was unable to understand the reply. A third attempt was successful. A little elderly man kindly insisted on accompanying me to the Gallery and told me I was in Sau-chiehall Street, the pronunciation of which had always fascinated and now delighted me.

" Ye'll find they don't pronounce their worrds here. They're lazy in speech," said my Glasgow friend. " You don't get the vowels sounded like you do in Spain."

" Spain ! Have you been in Spain ? " I asked, much sur-prised.

" I lived there for more than nine years."

I informed him that I had been in Spain this spring and asked him what part of it he knew. He told me he was very familiar with the South. He knew Cadiz, Granada, Ronda, Seville and Jerez de la Frontera. At this I jumped. How came it that he knew far away Jerez de la Frontera where I had had such memorable hospitality? He had been a wine merchant, he told me, and bought wines in Spain. So here we were, walking down Sauchiehall Street, exchanging reminiscences of Spain. Somehow the name of Holland came up. Business had taken him there. " I married a Dutch girl and brought her back to Glasgow. I was in S.H.A.E.F. in the last war and was glad to be sent there. I knew The Hague and Arnhem."

Half-way down Sauchiehall Street we were in Spain again, and by the time we reached the Art Gallery we were in the bullring. He agreed with me that bull-fighting had declined. He rattled off a list of famous toreadors he had seen, now long forgotten. " And here's the Gallery," he said, raising his hat, "*Buenas tardes, señor. Lo he pasado muy bien.*" I raised my hat also with foreign courtesy, as we shook hands, bowing. We parted in Sauchiehall Street like a couple of Grandees on the Alcala.

Nothing could have been more pleasant and friendly than my audience at the Athenaeum. It was prefaced by a small dinner party given for me at the Central Hotel. I was spared any preliminary speeches, a constant habit in the U.S.A., where one has to perform before and after the main event. I once told my agent, after long suffering in this manner, that he should double my fee ' if entertained.' I found an audience of about eight hundred in a congenial hall. I was told afterwards that the audience enjoyed itself greatly, which was apparent, and I was equally happy. I now feel very contrite for my reluctant mood. What had seemed an ordeal to which I had foolishly committed myself proved a real pleasure. I have been so used to American audiences in the past twenty years that an English one, or Scotch, to be accurate, has a new flavour for a somewhat jaded palate. Writing is the loneliest job on earth. One sits in silence in a room, with no apparent bricks or mortar with which to build the structure of one's imagination. The completed work is then taken away from one and distributed to the unseen public ; and there it would seem to end. But it is not so. A fortunate author finds his books are ambassadors of friendship in thousands of homes of which he has no knowledge, but these occasions when one sees one's audience in the flesh, and encounters an almost affectionate reception, are very rewarding. My readers come, in curiosity, to look at me. With equal curiosity I look at them, with a feeling of being both humbled and heartened by the labour of a pen. How fortunate that one's life's work should be the giving of pleasure !

New York

I SAILED for New York in the *Nieu Amsterdam* from Southampton this evening. I am travelling tourist-class. For thirty years I have been crossing the Atlantic, first-class. I have become very tired of the type of passengers in this class. It never changes. The industrial knights, travelling expensively on business allowances ; the film stars with their court of sycophants who act as enlarging mirrors, moving about in an atmosphere of mink, *Nuit d'Amour*, Pekinese dogs, and beribboned candy boxes ; pompous politicians dining in private suites, with their cohorts of bureaucrats and stenographers—on one voyage the chunky Mr. Molotov was guarded at each end of his corridor by two behemoths armed with revolvers ; rich American playboys and expatriated widows ; a score or so of card-shufflers and bar barnacles. I have known this kind of transatlantic company too long. Perhaps a less affluent class might prove richer in character, and, on a foreign boat, a little more cosmopolitan, with stewards not obsessed with getting dollar tips. I find this ship clean, friendly, beautifully appointed and decorated. My cabin passes the supreme test—there is a bedside light and a large paper-basket.

Why is it that no matter how many journeys one has made one always arrives on board ship exhausted, with a litter of small packets ? But now there will be leisure and calm. Three nights ago I completed my new novel *A Terrace in the Sun*. I began it on October 9th in Rome, and finished it on December 9th in London ; this represents 120,000 words in exactly two months, despite travel and many activities. Now the mosaic work begins on the fabric, chiselling, polishing, transposing, reducing, the pedestrian part so vital to the final appearance. This is my twenty-third accouchement. Parent and child are doing well.

December 14.

A gale, the ship tossing wildly. After thirty years of misery at sea I seem seasick-proof for the first time. I have tried one of the new remedies and it works ! I shall now be able to march along the deck flamboyantly and be present at all the meals, I shall be, in short, one of those odious people, as they seemed to me in the past, who enjoy sea life. Last night there was a minor tragedy. A box containing two typed copies of my novel, eight hundred sheets in all, unnumbered as yet, slipped off my dressing-table. A grinling turned the box upside down, and the ventilating fan blew the sheets all over my cabin. It has taken me two hours to put them in order again.

December 16.

As I hoped, I find my fellow passengers interesting and varied in character, among them a Rabbi, five English nurses emigrating, a Dutch dealer in jade who lives in Sumatra, an Australian who travels the world buying horses, and who has a passion for poetry, and a tall angular youth to whom I have not spoken but who fascinates me because of his amazing resemblance to El Greco's Saint Martin. "*Jeune homme charmant qui fait la grâce de son manteau à un compagnon moins favorisé,*" I murmured in Barrès' words, yet would not make his acquaintance from fear that he might not be named Martin and spoil my little conceit of a reincarnation.

My journey has been made very pleasant by an agreeable table companion, Michael X, who has a remarkably varied history for one so young. He was born twenty-five years ago in the United States. His mother is a princess of one of the historic houses of Russia allied with the Romanoffs and Obolenskys. By her three marriages my young friend has acquired a Swedish father, and Scottish and British stepfathers. He was born on the Pacific Coast and thus an American citizen ; with his wide family connections he appears to have relations in most of the capitals of Europe. He was sent at five to a French nuns' convent school for girls in the South of France, where, to his resentment, he was dressed in a blue *tablier* and made miserable in a wholly feminine establishment. Later, he went to a pre-paratory school in Scotland, which he enjoyed, and after that to an English Public School. By this time he was trilingual, speaking Russian, French, and English. Holidays were spent in various Scottish castles belonging to his Scotch relations. He told of one visit to an old aunt that was disastrous. He thought her an ogre. He kept a diary and wrote his impressions in it. One day she entered his room during his absence and read the

K*

unflattering entry about herself. She was icy that evening and asked him to leave the next day, and cut him out of her will. By virtue of his Scotch stepfather he was dressed in a kilt of the family tartan. He has fond memories of the moors and of wonderfully gay Christmas parties in grim old castles by loch and brae. On leaving school he worked for a year in the London office of an oil company, hating it, and living in dreary mean lodgings. Ultimately he joined the American Army in England, and in an engineering corps went to France. He was in the D Day invasion of Normandy. He fought through to Belgium and the Rhine. On demobilization he obtained an Army scholarship from the American Government, returned to the Pacific Coast and entered a famous university there. Restricted in means, he took odd jobs during the vacation, as is the habit of American students. He worked, variously, as a dishwasher in an Italian restaurant in Hollywood, a gang foreman of planters of tomatoes on a Sacramento Valley farm, a carpenter in a Los Angeles turner's shop, and a cattle herdsman and cowboy on a Montana ranch. After taking his B.A. degree he returned to England and France for six months, visiting his various aunts and uncles, etc., the Vladimirs, Vanyas, Serges and Natashas that rippled off his tongue. He is now en route to New York, penniless but in no way dismayed. He proposes to get a temporary job with the U.N.O. through a Russian uncle (another is a famous doctor in Seattle) and save enough money to take the M.A. course, specialising in history at his university. He is quite English in speech, frail, good-looking and modest. No one would guess that behind his reticent manner and physical delicacy there is a sturdy spirit of adventure and independence. If twenty-five years produce so many experiences one wonders what the tally will be at fifty.

December 17.

This morning I read to Michael what I wrote about him last night, asking if he had any objection. When I finished he said, " You terrify me ! I've no objection at all, I feel rather flattered but to think that anyone could listen to my chatter and get it all down with such exact detail ! How do you do it ? " I laughed. " *C'est mon métier*, and all you told me was alive," I replied.

I stay in bed until noon working and reading, thus killing the boredom of this Atlantic. I have corrected a hundred sheets of typescript and read Burchardt's *Rubens ;* the *Discoursi de Niccolò Machiavelli*, very little known, Wedgwood's *Seventeenth Century Literature*, and *The Theology of Albert Schweitzer*, half of the eight books I brought on board. The food is excellent. We all eat too much. What is the cause of this sea tradition of enormous menus, *pour passer le temps ?*

December 19.

Early this morning, with Long Island in sight, we entered the Narrows. I consider the approach to New York one of the most thrilling sights in the world. If one is fortunate, as we were this morning, the tremendous man-made skyline of the city comes into view, with its great grey monoliths, plumed with steam, reaching up to the vivid blue sky, while sunshine and deep shadows mark the chasms of this astonishing unnatural scenery.

As we drew slowly up the River Hudson to our berth, the passengers crowded the promenade deck for their first view of the new world, and shivered in the sharp air which has a glacial edge. For some of them their future life is here. Down in the third-class there are penniless youths whose future sons, graduates of universities and presidents of businesses, will be returning with their families to Europe to visit the places where their fathers, buried in American soil, were born in poverty. The day labourer's granddaughter may become an English, French or Italian countess and revive an aristocratic line with her strong peasant blood. There are three young Englishmen on board, two of them with exceptional qualifications. They have emigrated in despair of the conditions in England, where they foresee continuously encroaching bureaucratic control, crushing taxation and apathy. Yet we can ill spare them, for these are young men who have the spirit to strike out. Every time I cross the Atlantic the ship carries away from the homeland vigorous youngsters who depart with some bitterness in their hearts. Surely they are the exports we can least spare ?

The ship noses itself into its berth on the Hoboken side of the Hudson. It is the least convenient way to enter New York, for the passengers are involved in a tiresome and expensive trip across the river. Half the charm of New York, which opens suddenly like a door when the ship docks on the Manhattan shore, is lost by this cross-river landing. In one respect England is vastly superior to the U.S.A. in its landing accommodation. At Southampton we have a new building, warm, cheerful, and with all amenities, from cafés and bookstalls to waiting-rooms, and above all, with a sane and convenient customs control. The New York Customs Department has always been chaotic and primitive. To-day, as ever, we were thrown out into a vast shed, exposed to the bitter winter air. Our baggage was dumped into this shed and amid chaos we sought out our belongings and then stood in a long queue to get a customs inspector. All this took place to-day in twelve degrees below freezing, in the grimmest surroundings, with no amenities of any kind. Most of us were two hours on the dockside, following a three hours' wait on board for the immigration formalities. The process of entry, therefore, took five hours. At Southampton and Cherbourg it takes an hour. It is a strange introduction to the land of efficiency. And God help those whose papers are not in order ! They are taken off to the Siberia of Ellis Island and all the protracted processes of American law, which functions with incredible delays.

My friend G was waiting for me, as ever. He had stood behind the barrier for nearly three hours in freezing cold. A long taxi ride followed and then we were in Fifth Avenue, jammed with Christmas traffic. It is a good sight. One feels the pulse of this dynamic continent. In Europe it is all contraction and impoverishment ; here it is all expansion and prosperity. One feels it at once in the invigorating air, the brisk conglomeration of people.

I am again the guest of Mrs. Aubrey Cartwright, whose apartment is on the twelfth floor of a Fifth Avenue block that houses also three of my American friends. The position is unsurpassed. It overlooks Central Park. From the windows we look down on the charming little Zoo, with its brick pseudo-Tudor offices which seem like an annexe of Hampton Court. Its central door has a large illuminated Christmas wreath ; around are the animal houses and pens, the open-air seal pool, and the cafeteria-terrace on which I have passed many carefree hours in spring and summer.

Dusk came soon after I arrived. On Central Park South rose the great hotels. They were all lit up and formed a vast cascade of lights falling from the dark sky, a man-made Niagara. All around the perimeter of the park towered buildings, like shining honeycombs. The hour of six is the time of maximum illumination. Men are home from business, the cocktail parties are beginning, the social world is preparing to dress and dine, all the crevices and ledges in these precipices of light are occupied, the human honeycomb hums with activity.

December 21.

I have been caught up in the Christmas maelstrom. I had a warm welcome at the University Club in Fifth Avenue, within whose hospitable doors I have spent many happy hours. It is modelled on a Florentine palace and the magnificent library, copied from the Vatican Library, is *settecento*, in its decoration. It is one of the best equipped libraries in the United States and I owe much to it. For more than five years I worked here, drawing upon its resources for my work with the British Embassy and Ministry of Information, etc.

I lunched with my old friend Mrs. Murray Crane who lives on the fourth floor of our house, and then took tea with Lady Ribblesdale who has created a charming home here with old French furniture. One cannot believe one is on the twelfth floor of a skyscraper in Park Avenue. She is as lovely as ever to look at, with her curled snow-white hair. For many years she reigned in London as a post-Edwardian beauty. I think her heart is still there. She is an avid reader and misses little that has appeared in England. It gives one a shock, in this *milieu* of Louis Seize furniture, Aubusson carpets, Sèvres vases, to find on the mantelpiece a photograph of *The Ancestor*, the picturesque Lord Ribblesdale whose famous portrait by Sargent now hangs in the Tate Gallery. How far away in time and place it all is !

I have been given a copy of Boswell's *London Diary 1762-1763*, which is having a great vogue here. The Boswellians are delighted by the astonishing discovery of a diary that has been lost for almost two hundred years. It is a little hard on Boswell that a diary he wrote with great frankness at twenty-two, when heat in the blood of youth induces licentious habits if there is no moral control, should be exposed to the public eye. His shrewd old father was horrified at his son setting down all his youthful follies in this fashion. He was right. This *Diary* exposes poor Bozzy to all the charges that Macaulay brought against him. His adventures among the prostitutes of London afford us an appalling picture of the social life of the period, but the most repellent factor in this record is Boswell's own nauseating commercialism in these sordid transactions. He is delighted by street affairs for sixpence, and still more delighted when he relieves his lust for nothing. Vice anywhere is deplorable but vice practised with parsimony towards the victim is contemptible. It is a filthy record, mostly of trivialities. Were it not by Boswell it would have been regarded as the scribblings of a dirty-minded youth and not have achieved publication. True, it records the first meeting with Dr. Johnson, but the account is poor and skimpy, lacking the detail and character of the later descriptions which made him famous. Much of the *Diary* is concerned with his futile quest of a commission in the Guards. For this purpose he haunted the salons of Northumberland House, Charing Cross, seeking the patronage of the Duchess. It is singular that, as I read this *Diary* in my hostess's library, on the opposite wall hung a fine painting of Northumberland House by S. Scott, who died in 1772. He may have painted it in the very year in which Boswell was calling there. It shows the Percy lion with the horizontal tail over the gate tower. When Northumberland House was pulled down the lion was removed and placed over the gateway of Sion House at Brentford, where it may now be seen.*

December 22.

Lunched at the University Club with my *Professore*, John Basore, my old friend in Rome. Afterwards we went to Carnegie Hall to hear the New York Symphony Orchestra. He brought me a little book that he has published in which he has reversed the usual process. It is a collection of translations he has made from English into Latin verse. They are neat and delightful. Thus Bourdillon's famous quatrain *The night has a thousand eyes*, becomes—

> Mille nox oculos habet,
> et dies habet unicum ;
> at lux candida iam perit
> mundi sole cadente.

* " The fifth Duke, a practical joker, liked to stand in the road pointing at the tail of the lion. " Look, it moves ! " he would declare. Sure of the credulity of the mob, he won his bet that he could collect a crowd of one hundred in half an hour, many of whom declared that they saw the lion's tail wag."—*And So To Bath.*

It seems to be as felicitous as the original. We lived our Roman days over again. I am to visit him at Princeton next month.

This evening my young friend Michael came to dine. There is another episode to add to his extraordinary odyssey. He is delaying his journey to the California University where he plans to take his post-graduate course in order to become a professor of history, and is staying in New York to earn a little money. He has found a job on Broadway. He is the superintendent of an ' amusement park '—a saloon opening off the street which contains a shooting gallery, automatic games, and those stereo-copic machines in which one inserts a nickel and sees photos of ladies in scanty garments. He told me some astonishing stories about the toughs who haunt these places, the incredible language they speak, a drift of the underworld of spivs, dope peddlers, bums, guileless excursionists and gutter sharks. This ' park ' and three others are owned by an illiterate Italian who makes enough from them to support a family, a town apartment, a country place and a shining Cadillac car. Michael finds the work hard but of absorbing interest. He is the guest of a friend of his mother's in an East Side mansion that has a butler and an art gallery. He goes out every morning from this luxurious home to his work in the blaring Broadway amusement park. He may delay his journey to the Pacific Coast, for an attractive possibility has loomed up. He is being ' screened ' for a post as director of an army stores in Casablanca, North Africa, where the U.S.A. army has established a depot. The salary is so good that he will be able to save enough to carry him comfortably through his post-graduate course later. So adventure looms ahead for him.

December 23.

I have seen an amusing version of *Peter Pan* at a Broadway theatre. Barrie's famous excursion in whimsy has been trans-atlanticised. The family Wendy takes under her charge in the tree-tops now includes two little nigger boys, just to demonstrate there is no race feeling in New York ! They would have been ostracised in a Southern version. The pirates are now all members of a ballet presided over by a Captain Hook who wears a full-bottomed wig and looks incredibly like Charles II. The performance seemed to lack Nell Gwynn, but the children in the audience adored the play. I should like to see a Japanese version. In Rome I saw in an Italian paper a reproduction of the Assumption of the Virgin Mary, as seen in Tokyo. The Madonna had slit eyes, and a troop of attendant cherubs looked as if they had flitted out of *Madame Butterfly*.

Dined in the evening at Mrs. Cornelius Vanderbilt's. Alas, she is now almost blind, and moves in a wheeled chair, but she has lost nothing of her zest for company ; loneliness has become her great fear. The service was as flawless and the food as excellent as ever. This new home, further up Fifth Avenue, has much of the charm and stateliness of the old mansion near Rockefeller Plaza, now pulled down, but I suppress a sigh for old familiar pleasures when I pass the site of a house that once played such a great role in American society. Little by little the best residential district, which used to be around Park Avenue and Fifth Avenue from 48th Street up, is being pushed towards Harlem. Where will the millionaires and tycoons go ? Possibly they will be abolished along with their former homes. We are all rapidly becoming numbers in concrete boxes. It is now thought cunning, though expensive, to live in a converted mews in which, on Mondays, the ashbin comes out through the drawing-room. Mrs. Vanderbilt's party was very small to-night, eight at a table where I have seen forty.

December 24.

Mrs. Murray Crane has lost none of her gifts as a salonist. To-day, Sunday, at five, I again entered the familiar long drawing-room overlooking Central Park as I have done for six consecutive years, with unfailing enjoyment. Seated beneath her Carracci, and flanked by a Moreau and Augustus John's sketch of James Joyce, with her early discovery of a Salvator Dali on an easel, bought in a Paris back street for a song twenty years ago, I found a varied circle of guests displayed before her. She is very firm with the women. " They spoil symposiums," she says, " and tend to break up and monopolise conversation." To-day only one lady, an old friend, leapt the barrier, an American-Florentine, Countess Caroline Rasponi, charming to look at and to listen to. For the rest a varied and rewarding assortment. Lewis Einstein, a former American Ambassador to Czechoslovakia, Garner Romney, a good-looking youngster who presides at the United Kingdom and Ireland ' desk ' in the State Department at Washington, Lawson Dick, the bio-

grapher of the Elizabethan gossip, Aubrey, and Salvator Dali.
I asked Romney whether the coupling of the United Kingdom's
and Ireland's affairs at one desk did not provoke protests from
the Irish, who are ever alert in emphasising complete independence of the U.K. He said it did occasionally but since all
business that arose was usually united in fact it was useless to
attempt separation in compliance with theory ; and, anyhow,
it was a matter for the State Department's internal administration. All this recalls the comment of an Irish friend of mine
who travels with two passports, British and Irish. " Sure,
like the saints, I'm taking all the advantages of the Kingdom,
and none of the disadvantages."

I had last seen Dali in Rome. He invited me to visit him at
his villa on the Costa Brava in Spain. He has just opened an
exhibition here of his latest work, including the classical-sur-
realistic painting called *The Port-Lligat Madonna*. It shook rather
than shocked the Pope when Dali showed it to him. I do not
wonder. Dali, a supreme publicity man, never fails to jump
into the limelight with his fantastic creations and the promulgation of his painting *credo*. Yet in himself he is modest to a
point of shyness. I always wonder why he bothers to make such
frantic gestures. His eccentricities apart, he remains a truly
great artist, an unsurpassed colourist, and the possessor of a
very great technique. For me he is a painter of the school of
Leonardo da Vinci, and not unworthy of that master. The
dissected kidneys, the propped eyelids, the crutches and the
Freudian stage properties detract from but do not obliterate
his magnificent technique and imaginative conception. I find
The Port-Lligat Madonna an objectionable conundrum, and his
explanation of the picture quite incomprehensible. " The open
spaces cut through the human body become Mystical and
Virginal Tabernacles. The bread, enigmatic dalinian obsession,
becomes a radiant symbol of the Eucharist. The well-known
haunting eggs magically come into harmony with the one that
the divine Piero della Francesca painted as a symbol of the Resur-
rection." All this in a mixture of Dalian French-Spanish and
English. " Mais oui ! " I said faintly, and turned the talk to
Spain, mentioning El Greco's painting of Toledo, grey, arid,
tempestuous and terrifying. " Like God, he took a handful of
dust and created not Man but Toledo," said Dali. Quiet,
precise, with his neat body and pin-moustache, dressed always

in black, he resembles a French lawyer in a provincial town. There is no clue in manner or appearance to the revolutionary artist. " Freud was the first person to discover a pre-mystical state of mind in me, when, addressing Stefan Zweig, he remarked about me, ' What a prototype Spaniard, what a fanatic ! ' " Freud had a habit of seeing many strange things.

I wanted to take Dali into the library and show him one member of the Crane family excluded from the salon. It is a troupial, a most self-willed bird of shining plumage, with a neat black head, vivid yellow beak and glittering eye, who dominates the scene. " There you are, Dali," I would have said, " if I were Apuleius that's how I should see you ; never a donkey or a monkey, but a glittering bird, wilfully bizarre, divertingly egocentric."

The troupial out of his cage has two passions. He sweeps every object off his mistress's desk and stalks the cleared deck like an irate admiral. Then, perching on Mrs. Crane's shoulder, he forcibly opens her mouth with his powerful beak and taps her teeth. " I think that in a former life he was a dentist," said Mrs. Crane, describing his performance.

The diversity of this tea-time circle is as great as ever. I counted before leaving, two Americans, an Italian, two Spaniards, one Frenchman, a Pole, a Greek, one Scot and an Englishman. On Thursday night there will be a buffet supper when Soledad Miralles will give some of her Spanish dances.

December 25.

Motored out to lunch at Greenwich with my hostess's nephew and wife, a very handsome young couple whom I remember arriving at *Casa Estella*, Cap d'Antibes, two summers ago. The boy, a six-foot-three ex-U.S. Marine officer, the bride a dark beauty, partly French and Russian, they looked like those impossibly handsome honeymooners seen on a Bermuda travel poster. We motored along the magnificent Riverside Drive, with the Washington Suspension Bridge hanging like a silver chain across the River Hudson. We had an astonishing sample of New York weather, blue skies and warm sunshine, then a grey thunderous overcast followed by a swift snow blizzard that changed the wooded Driveway to an Arctic outpost ; then, again, a steely blue sky and sharp sunshine.

The young couple's home stood on a hillock overlooking a private lake with some skaters on it. One glance indoors proclaimed the presence of children. There was a twenty-foot Christmas-tree roped with fairy-lights, a room chaotic with the litter of children's presents, of an extravagance and variety found only in American homes. My host and hostess produced their offspring, and a visiting couple added their quota of chirpers to the nest. The whole scene looked, in cheerfulness and prosperity, like a colour cover of *The Saturday Evening Post*. We sat down in a long Tudoresque dining-room overlooking the lake where a Czechoslovakian neighbour cut capers on the ice with his three children. We consumed a gigantic turkey, cooked and served by a Hungarian family. A hundred years ago in these virgin woodlands the Indians were fighting a rearguard action against the adventurous white men eating up his domain. Now television, Cadillac cars and polaroid cameras are found in this home, perturbed only by the ' heathen Chinee ' who in far away Korea challenges the might of the United States. As we talked a long distance call came in from Evanston, Illinois, and I recalled another Christmas, twenty-five years ago, when I had been taken off a train at Chicago and went straight to the table of an hospitable American family in Evanston, alas, all dead in the winnowing of Time.

We got back to New York at six o'clock. I went at once to Mrs. Vanderbilt's famous Christmas Party. This was the fifth party I had attended. It had changed little ; an orchestra playing in the ballroom, log fires blazing in the great fireplaces, a twenty-five foot Christmas-tree scraping the ceiling, and some two hundred guests all in turn greeting our hostess, seated beneath the great tapestry of Alexander and Diogenes. Gracious as ever, she is now, alas, almost blind, and one turned sadly from her head of snow-white curls to the portrait of a lovely bride holding a rope of roses, painted by Madrazo sixty years ago.

It was good to see so many old friends and I found myself unwillingly holding a small reception in one corner of the ballroom. Among them was Dr. Emile Enthoven (how he romped on the piano one evening at the Hugh Bullock's, with a mountainous background of New York illuminated in the wintry night !), the Dutch doctor of music and philosophy, last met in Rome. We made an engagement for next week.

December 26.

Poor Enthoven died of a heart attack to-day.

There has been a heavy snowfall and I look down from my eyrie on a white city. In the little zoo below the polar bears demonstrate nature's colour protection. They are almost invisible with their white fur. The pigeons huddle in wintry sunshine on the white roof of the elk's house. A Christmas crowd watches the feeding of the seals ; beyond, on the new skating-rink, there is a swirl of skaters. I wonder which is the polar bear that tore off the arm of a crazy reveller who, one summer's dawn, four years ago, went too near the animal's cage. The man with the hydrogen balloon-filling machine is doing a roaring trade and the tiny tots walking with tethered balloons make a bright pattern on the black and white diagram far below me.

December 27.

Despite the traditional gaiety of the season, and a succession of lunches, dinners and cocktail parties in which this prosperous nation indulges, these are worrying times. There is only one subject discussed, the probability of war. There are general ' jitters,' deep pessimism, and divided opinions everywhere. A severe defeat in Korea has resuscitated the Isolationists who give notice to Europe and the world that they will retreat within their own fortress and bar the gate—with England as an outpost. By day and night the American soothsayers, the omniscient gentlemen who propagate their views over the radio, and pour their wisdom into magic boxes round which bewildered Americans sit like Zulus round a witch-doctor, pursue their victims even into the bathroom. One of these wizards was invited to say a few words at a large dinner-party I attended the other evening. In half an hour he succeeded in proving that Russia, whose mind he knew with all the assurance of a psychoanalyst, could not be defeated. The long table shook like an aspen leaf. A retired professor and some elderly ladies also contributed to this balance-sheet of national bankruptcy brought about " by a piano-playing President with a concert-singing daughter." My own silence in the general lament was challenged later by our host, who ascribed it to the traditional reticence of the cunning Englishman. We enjoy in the United States a dual character ; we are backward, imperialistic, and slow-witted, but we are possessed of an unfathomable cunning and mental supremacy when pitted against American diplomacy whose representatives have not the chance of a Sunday-Schoolmarm induced to play poker with a gang of card-sharpers. I privately expressed the cause of my reluctance to contribute to the general alarm. If all I had heard was true and the Russians were so omnipotent, and the Americans so incompetent, then it seemed to me that there was only one thing to do— to go and get the best terms possible from Joe Stalin.

I do not, of course, believe the soothsayers, or these ladies and gentlemen who, behind their champagne glasses, sound the tocsin of retreat. America is tougher than that, and so I kept my mouth shut. Any opinion contrary to that jury of defeatists would have been regarded as another example of European obtuseness and cunning. After occupying public platforms for thirty years I am silent these days, and on this visit I have firmly declined to open my mouth in public, a reticence unusual in one who has made seventeen lecture tours across this continent. I broke my resolution, once, to-day, however. I spoke in the Biltmore Hotel ballroom at Emma Mills' Book and Play Luncheon, constrained by an old friendship. Exactly thirty years ago, within a few hours of my arrival in New York for the first time, I was hurried on to her platform to face an audience of eight hundred diners under an endless vista of crystal chandeliers. On countless occasions afterwards I have spoken for her. A great ring-master, I wonder how many celebrities Emma Mills has taken through her hoop. I recall on that first occasion a fellow guest, the handsome Grand Duke Alexander, six-foot-three, magnificently organ-toned, astonishing an audience, largely composed of sophisticated dowagers, by treating it to a discourse on spiritual as opposed to carnal love.

December 28.

A dinner-party at Mrs. Cornelius Vanderbilt's for the opera. Twenty guests. Despite a growing infirmity that confines her to a wheeled chair, my hostess's house is as perfectly run as ever, the food, service and general atmosphere flawless. But looking down the long table last night, with its Genoa velvet chairs, chandeliers, silver candelabra, great bowls of flowers, quiet footmen marshalled by an English butler, with the Duke of Windsor by his hostess at one end of the table and the Duchess of Windsor at the other, I had a feeling, as often before in this house, which seems at times to have been transported from the

Paris of Proust's Duchesse de Guermantes, that I was living
a posthumous life. It must be the last house in America
where the old gilt Louis Seize frame holds the portrait of a
dead era.

When the hour for departure to the opera came there was a
general defection among the males and only two departed with
the ladies. Mrs. Vanderbilt did not go. I found the Duke, as
always, an attractive conversationalist. He has an eager interest
in everything and takes great pains to keep himself well-informed
and abreast of things. His voice is very pleasant, and despite
the photographs that reveal him as wrinkled and worried, he
is astonishingly young in appearance and manner. He has a
very neat slim figure, a boyish head and much charm of manner,
with, I imagine, the famous King Edward VII touch. We
somehow got on to the subject of Bonnie Prince Charlie. I
found the Duke was under the impression that Henry, Cardinal
Duke of York, was Prince Charles's uncle and not the younger
brother who became the last of the Stuarts. I ventured to correct
him and quoted the inscription on Canova's cenotaph in St.
Peter's. I mentioned the singular fact that "James III's"
wife, Princess Clementina Sobieski, had her portrait in mosaics
opposite the Stuart memorial, high up on a pier in St. Peter's.
I remarked that there is no oil painting of any kind in St. Peter's,
everything pictorial being in mosaic, but that the portrait of the
Princess, described as " Queen of Great Britain, Ireland and
France," is so deceptive that one has to use field-glasses to convince oneself that it is not in oils. For a long time the cardinals
opposed the erection of the portrait, showing the Princess
in *décolletée*, as improper, but a later Pope sanctioned the
memorial.

" You know a great deal about the Pretenders," said the Duke,
who asked many questions. I confessed the reason. It chanced
that I had recently written about them in *And So To Rome*, and
thus was well primed. The Duke said he would read the book
at once. From Pretenders we got on to postage stamps, and
he told me that, when King, he was offered five million dollars
for his father's collection. " Even had I been tempted, it was
an heirloom and could not be sold."

We had sat so long at the table that at this stage a tactful butler
approached and informed us that Mrs. Vanderbilt was in the
drawing-room upstairs !

December 29.

The pattern of the New Year begins to shape itself for me.
I have booked to sail at the end of February for Gibraltar. From
there I shall visit Tangiers and, returning, go up into Spain,
arriving for the Feria in Seville in April, after that Madrid again,
some visits to Avila, Cordoba, Mallorca, and a leisured progress
northwards via Burgos and Pamplona to Biarritz. They are
amazed here that I should adventure into the powder-keg of
Europe. I reply that one can waste one's life in apprehension
of what to-morrow may bring. If war comes it comes. We are,
to-day, quite unable to control our destiny. I may end tramping
in a queue of hungry refugees, or die penniless in an attic. For
years one has read about Russians, Austrians, Germans and Poles
reduced from affluence to beggary. What once seemed like
fiction, concerning other human beings in another world, may
to-day become a harsh reality of one's own. I have lived to see
a lifetime's savings reduced in value to one-third, and to question
the wisdom of thrift in these unsettled times. I begin to regret
that I did not buy all the things I denied myself, and do all the
improvident things I wanted to do. For it seems to me that
Governments are becoming increasingly dishonest. They legis-
late to gain votes, they bribe with subsidies, in the name of public
service, they legalise their robberies. I am nauseated with
politicians mouthing their clichés of Freedom while they impose
on the public the very shackles of Communism which they de-
nounce. I witness a younger generation growing up that accepts
this state of bondage as natural, being born to queues, finger-
prints, registration, conscription, forced levies, 'free' public
services, restriction of movement, and disguised punitive taxation.
Their forefathers would never have shown this spiritless acquiescence in Government control. I have caused myself much discomfort by a vigorous fight against these growing menaces,
determined to preserve my freedom of thought and movement,
but it grows hourly more difficult to escape the mesh of paralysing
regulations.

> We must be free or die, who speak the tongue
> That Shakespeare spake, the faith and morals hold
> Which Milton held. In everything we are sprung
> Of Earth's first blood, have titles manifold.

A proud claim. How much of it we have lost!

Yesterday I lunched with William Macaulay in his charming apartment. A small party of five including the Duchess of Windsor. She told me that the Duke had sat up until late in the night reading my book, engrossed in the chapter on Bonnie Prince Charlie. Discussing foreign languages and the gift of tongues, she said that whereas the Duke spoke fluent German and Spanish, his French made her blush. " He calls it his funeral French," she said. " Funeral French ? " " Yes, he says the only French he ever learned was at State funerals ! "

The late-in-the-night reading evoked the following letter from the Duke to-day.

" I read the pages you recommended, and despite the exhausted condition in which the completion of my Memoirs leaves me at the end of each day, I greatly enjoyed them. From the little I have read about him I have never been able to work up much enthusiasm for Bonnie Prince Charlie. He seems to have had some good public relations men to build him up in Scotland in the years immediately before 1745. But he certainly let them and all his brave loyal Highlanders down about as badly as any self-styled leader could.

" Now my disillusionment is complete, and the fine old song, ' Bonnie Prince Charlie's gang awa, will ye no come back again', can never give me a lump in the throat ! "

December 30.

The changes in weather here are fantastic. Two days ago we were wrapped in a blizzard. Yesterday it was 18° below. To-day it has been sunny and springlike. Looking down from our eyrie I have been fascinated by watching life in the Zoo below. The cafeteria-terrace has been thronged with visitors. A crowd has watched the Arctic seals in the pool, who play to the gallery at feeding-time. Four white polar bears have been sunning themselves on a rocky mount. The elephant has been peregrinating in his enclosure ; the dromedaries, the hartbeest, the elk, the hippopotamus and the kangaroo in theirs. The doors of the birdhouse have been swinging madly and the balloon boy has done a good business. To-morrow another blizzard may smite us, the thermometer drop from 62° to 18° again. If the weather does this to the thermometer, what does it do to the human system ? I am never surprised when I learn that Mr. A, so prosperous and hospitable, suddenly jumped, the night after

I dined with him, from his window on the fifteenth floor, for no apparent reason. Violin strings, alternately slack and taut, snap when violently overwound. Perhaps the same extremes snap something in the human brain. When people remark on the panicky excitability of New Yorkers I remind them that this city is in the same latitude as Rome, with the winter climate of Archangel. If you suddenly converted an Esquimo into a Roman you would not expect the self-possession of a Scot.

December 31.

The year comes to an end and with it the task of writing this diary, which I set myself last New Year's Eve. What a year ! We are now in the throes of war hysteria, with the United States and Great Britain rapidly arming and most of Korea overrun through a disastrous setback to the United Nations forces. Communistic China is successfully on the march and Russia is holding a sword of Damocles over Europe's head. Is it Peace or War ? To-night no one knows the answer. We confront a disaster that may overwhelm our civilisation. Most people are aware of it, but the mind is numbed by crisis after crisis, and a quiet fatalism seems to be overtaking the human race. A Happy New Year ? There seldom has been a gloomier prelude. The Old Year fades out in darkened skies, with the world deeply divided and gathering its antagonistic forces. One begins to wonder whether God, disgusted with the human race, is leaving it to its own destructive instincts. Never was Faith so sorely assailed.

Last New Year's Eve, in a damp and rainy Monte Carlo, I heard wassail break forth from a hundred windows. For one change since then I have deep gratitude. Then I was a sick man. Under Providence to-night, I am alive, in good health. That is the first and greatest of all riches, and thus blessed I refuse to allow myself to be paralysed by forebodings. It has been a year of much travel, varied and rich experiences, a great deal of work, in which, despite an itinerant life, I have published *And So To Rome* and thus completed a trilogy planned with *And So To Bath*, continued with *And So To America*. It has been a great and happy labour. In addition I have written a new novel, and completed this diary. Thus I have known the supreme happiness of continuous work. And with all the tribulations that visit us I would not elect to live in any other period but this, so rich in tremendous events. In the odd surge of memories of former New Year Eves my mind goes back to a small house in a provincial town to which my widowed mother and her fifteen-year-old son retreated to face their first New Year alone. On some remark of mine regarding future ambition, she observed—" One day you may be famous and rich but it doesn't mean you will be happy." I am, at this moment, neither of the former in any great degree but I am happy, that is, as happy as any sensitive human being can be who carries his accumulation of sorrows, losses, defeats and disappointments in the incommunicable loneliness of spirit that darkens man's pilgrimage.

We are now seated in the library, on the twelfth floor of this building. Below us the city is vivid with lights. Central Park South, with all its skyscraper hotels lit up, is like a cascade of diamonds, and the perimeter of the Park is outlined with jewels whose lustre reveals the towers and high-terraced apartments of the Babylon of the New World.

The radio brings to our quiet room, where I have just finished reading my new novel to my hostess, the milling thousands in Times Square, a noisier counterpart of the celebration before St. Paul's, London. The loud hum of humanity fills the room, and the night is raucous with those stentorian-voiced radio commentators who seem unable to describe anything except as if they were on the verge of delirium. A servant brings in a bottle of champagne and we toast the New Year. Here we are, pinnacled in time and space, while the great globe turns on the orbit of our unknown fate.

THE END

Index